New Day
in Babylon

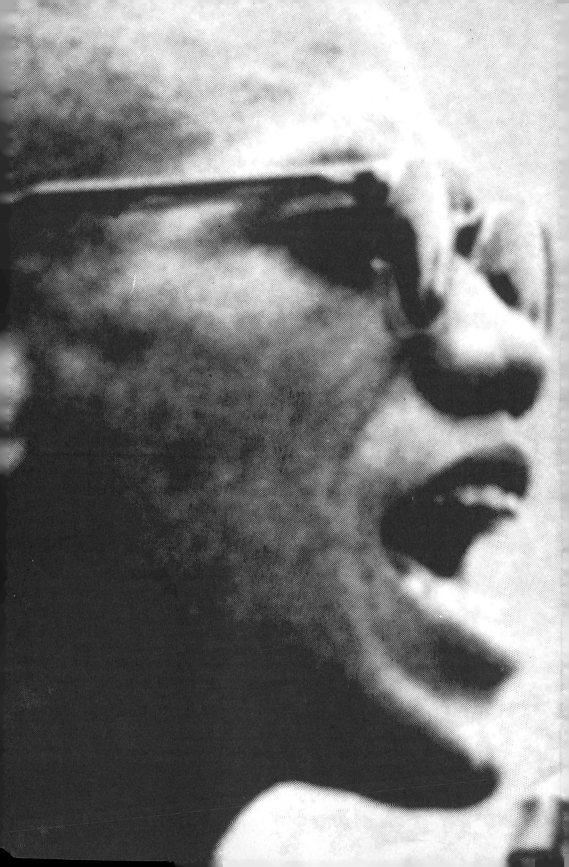

New Day in Babylon

The Black Power

Movement

and American

Culture, 1965–1975

William L. Van Deburg

The University of Chicago Press
Chicago and London

THE UNIVERSITY OF CHICAGO PRESS, 60637
THE UNIVERSITY OF CHICAGO PRESS, LTD., LONDON
© 1992 by The University of Chicago
All rights reserved. Published 1992
Paperback Edition 1993
Printed in the United States of America
09 08 07 06 05 04 03 02 01 00   4 5 6 7 8
ISBN (cloth): 0-226-84714-4
ISBN (paper): 0-226-84715-2

Library of Congress Cataloging-in-Publication Data

Van Deburg, William L.
    New day in Babylon : the Black power movement and American
culture, 1965–1975 / William L. Van Deburg.
      p. cm.
    Includes bibliographical references and index.
    1. Afro-American—Civilization. 2. Black power—United States—
History. 3. United States—Civilization—Afro-American influences.
I. Title.
E185.86.V36   1992   91-48098
973′.0496073—dc20   CIP

*If we understand ourselves to be revolutionaries,
and if we accept our historic task, then we can
move beyond the halting steps that we've been
taking. . . . Then there will be a new day in
Babylon, there will be a housecleaning in
Babylon.*

Eldridge Cleaver, 1969

To Diane
and to the memory of
Cora Ellen Van Deburg
and Tom W. Shick

Contents

Preface

At first, all I could hear were the sirens. Then I saw columns of mottled gray smoke filtering over the rooftops and trees. "Damn niggers," said one of my co-workers not quite under his breath. "Always causing trouble. Always makin' a fuss. Always demanding more, more, more. . . . Now they're burning down the whole damn north side." He paused for a moment as a fire truck screamed past the parking lot. Then, in an irritated, but unexpectedly reflective tone of voice, he asked no one in particular "Why did we bring 'em over here in the first place? What do they want anyway?"

My introduction to this particular conceptualization of the Black Power movement came as I was working my way through college by selling hardware and lawn mowers at the local Sears store. Not unlike many in my age cadre, I sought answers to my older associate's perplexing questions by taking all the "new" black history courses possible and by reading voraciously. I furiously underlined passages in my Bantam Books edition of the Kerner Commission report and devoured *The Crisis of the Negro Intellectual, White Over Black,* and Malcolm X's *Autobiography.* My education was just beginning after fourteen years of schooling.

Following the completion of a senior thesis, a dissertation, and two books on African-American slavery, I asked myself whether it might be (1) stimulating or (2) useful to apply certain of the guiding principles of modern slavery studies' dominant "culture-and-community" school to a later historical period. An article written for the *South Atlantic Quarterly,* "Black Slaves and Black Power in American Literature, 1967–80," linked past and present eras and research interests, confirming my belief that the basic conceptualization was viable. After seven years, this book is my far more developed, affirmative statement of its validity and utility. In striking fashion, the Black Power years reveal that a distinctive group culture has continued to promote resistance to oppression and to facilitate the development of positive self-worth among those who have "grown up black" within white America.

To my way of thinking, I now have addressed *both* of my old co-worker's crudely phrased questions about black history. But, as all practicing historians surely understand, only by engaging in a project such as this does one fully appreciate how much an individual removed in time, place, ethnicity, or gender *doesn't* know—and perhaps never can know—about a social movement like Black Power. Certainly, Joseph Washington, Jr., spoke for many when he noted that this topic, in particular, constitutes "a paradox surrounded by an enigma containing a mystery." Readers who feel that the work claims too much or too little for black culture (or defines it too broadly or too narrowly) are permitted to alter the claims made herein by, say, plus or minus 10 percent. No violence will be done to key findings. On the other hand, those seeking to dismiss movement participants as "violence-prone black racists" will have to pen their own, significantly different interpretive studies. So too will those seeking to make a case for the "essential Americanness" of the black cultural core by using the melting pot (rather than the salad bowl) as the most appropriate sociocultural metaphor. Such sweeping, uncritical generalizations serve only to distort the nature of a far more complex Black Power world view and to understate the uniqueness that even an "outside observer" can discover within Afro-American cultural expression.

Students of the black experience who have helped me better understand various aspects of the movement include my very talented Department of Afro-American Studies colleagues as well as Organization of American Historians and Southern Historical Association session participants Ernest Allen, John Blassingame, John Bracey, Dominic Capeci, Waldo Martin, Merline Pitre, Arvarh Strickland, and Martha Wilkerson. Greatly appreciated financial support came in the form of a sabbatical leave award, grants from the University of Wisconsin—Madison Graduate School Research Committee, and a Vilas Research Associateship in the Humanities. The contributions of these individuals and institutions have enhanced the value of this study in many ways. Unfortunately, as far as I can tell, none is willing to accept even the slightest blame for its shortcomings.

Introduction:
A Black Power
Paradigm

I never knew I was black until I read Malcolm
Denise Nicholas (actress), 1966

Slowly but purposefully the mourners moved through the maze of police barricades. Shivering in the cold evening air, they occasionally glanced up at the officers stationed on nearby rooftops and made nervous comments about the telephoned bomb threats which had begun shortly after noon. Inside the Unity Funeral Home the line continued to sprawl forward until it reached a glass-covered coffin bearing a small, oblong brass plate inscribed, "El-Hajj Malik El-Shabazz—May 19, 1925—Feb. 21, 1965." Here, overcome with emotion, some wept. Others fainted. Before the casket was closed, some twenty-two thousand people made this mini-pilgrimage in order to pay their last respects to a man *Newsweek* would call "a spiritual desperado . . . a demagogue who titillated slum Negroes and frightened whites."[1]

That postmortem estimations of Malcolm X, his character, and his belief system would sour and become more harshly critical the farther one strayed from Black America's most poverty-ridden neighborhoods is not surprising. As the most visible and vocal spokesperson for the Nation of Islam during the early 1960s, he had provoked considerable anger, apprehension, and fear. "*White America is doomed!* Death and devastating destruction hang at this very moment in the skies over America," he would thunder. "The only permanent solution to America's race problem is the complete separation of these twenty-two million ex-slaves from our white slave master."[2] Even after leaving the Nation to form the Muslim Mosque, Inc., and the Organization of Afro-

American Unity (OAAU) in the months before his assassination, his pronouncements on "the Black Revolution" were guaranteed to produce vastly different responses from Euro- and Afro-American listeners.

It was within Black America, however, that the impact of Malcolm X's thirty-nine years was most evident. While he lived, Malcolm generated fear and loathing in certain black as well as white circles. He liked to portray his ideological opponents as representatives of a "white-minded (brainwashed) minority" of Afro-Americans who were ashamed of their skin color. Having no racial pride, the black bourgeoisie were said to be involved in a continual search for ways to alter their identity by mingling, mixing, and intermarrying with whites. Their clergy-politician leadership was "hand-picked for the American Negroes by the white man himself." These integration-minded "professional beggars" were cast in the venerable Uncle Tom mold and did not represent the best interests of the black masses.[3] Such views won him few firm friends within mainstream civil rights organizations.

On the other hand, this type of impassioned rhetoric was "street smart"—it had an almost visceral appeal to a young, black, economically distressed constituency. Before his assassination, Malcolm constantly urged this constituency to question the validity of their schoolbook- and media-inspired faith in an integrated American Dream. Many responded. Following his death, Malcolm's influence expanded in dramatic, almost logarithmic, fashion. He came to be far more than a martyr for the militant, separatist faith. He became a Black Power paradigm—the archetype, reference point, and spiritual adviser in absentia for a generation of Afro-American activists. Although diverse in manner and mode of expression, it was the collective thrust of these activists toward racial pride, strength, and self-definition that came to be called the Black Power movement.

A scenario drawn from Malcolm's last days need not be cast in the tragic mode. In a sense, his demise signaled a new beginning rather than an irredeemably bleak ending. More accurately, Malcolm X was a transitional figure in the continuum of Afro-American activism. His death was a benchmark in the historical progression of black protest thought. In attempting to fathom Malcolm's world view, one necessarily grapples with the ultimate meaning of a historically significant tendency in Afro-American life and culture. To understand how he was perceived by the most sympathetic of his contemporaries is to gain valuable insight into the character of the Black Power movement during the years 1965–75.

Malcolm X

In death, Malcolm's life was not his own. According to his spiritual heirs, this was to be expected. As H. Rap Brown noted in the political autobiography *Die Nigger Die!*, "No revolutionary can claim his life for himself. The life of the revolutionary belongs to the struggle."[4] This certainly was true for Malcolm X. Following his death, spokespersons for a strikingly varied lot of political persuasions attempted to make the fallen Muslim leader into their own image. Some sought to change him into a totemic being possessed of supernatural strength and wisdom: Malcolm, the Fire Prophet, the ghetto-man in heroic proportions.[5] By facilitating this miraculous transformation from man to superman, the icon-makers hoped that their own shadows might grow longer. Others, including cultural and revolutionary nationalists, socialists, and pan-Africanists laid claim to his memory for more specific purposes.

Leaders of the Black Panther Party, for example, conceptualized their own organization as the spiritual successor to the OAAU—a living testament to Malcolm's life's work.[6] Having announced the inheritance, they proceeded to elaborate upon one component of the Muslim leader's multifaceted ideology: self-defense of the black community. As described by Eldridge Cleaver in 1968, the process of transmitting Malcolm's legacy was somewhat mystical, but to those who would listen, easily understood:

> Malcolm saw all the way to national liberation,
> and he showed us the rainbow and the golden pot
> at its end. Inside the golden pot, Malcolm told us,
> was the tool of liberation. Huey P. Newton, one
> of the millions of black people who listened to
> Malcolm, lifted the golden lid off the pot and
> blindly, trusting Malcolm, stuck his hand inside
> and grasped the tool. When he withdrew his hand
> and looked to see what he held, he saw the
> gun. . . . Malcolm prophesied the coming of the
> gun to the black liberation struggle. Huey P.
> Newton picked up the gun and pulled the trigger.[7]

Thus, as was noted by the most perceptive of his contemporaries, during the Black Power era there was a Malcolm for virtually every persuasion.[8] According to his friend and lawyer, Percy Sutton, the situation could be likened to the ancient fable of the blind man and the elephant: "One feels the ear, one feels the trunk, one feels the tail and so on, and each of them thinks he can describe the whole animal."[9] The Black Power movement was like that. Friend and foe alike claimed to have privileged information regarding its nature and ultimate purpose. Mirroring these multiple predispositions, the movement itself took on a diversity and richness of character that too often has been obscured by impassioned rhetoric and shallow historical analysis. If Malcolm X had not been available, the head of Janus could have been emblazoned on the militants' coat-of-arms.

Diversity in the treatment of Malcolm X by his legatees is wholly justifiable. He was a complex man whose interests were varied, whose pronouncements were wide-ranging. Life, he believed, was "a chronology of—*changes.*"[10] When he proclaimed Black America's right to self-defense "by any means necessary," disavowed what he termed the "disarming philosophy of non-violence," and labeled the white liberal allies of the civil rights movement deceivers and hypocrites, many Black Americans listened and agreed.[11] After he had informed his audiences that they were a colonized people, firmly linked to other black world communities by white exploitation, some began to formulate a new understanding of realpolitik. As these same people were led to believe that they could forestall the international movement toward black genocide through control of politics, businesses, educational institutions, and land, a significant number discovered a previously unrecognized approach to black solidarity. In noting that his many-hued gospel was not designed to encourage the reevaluation of whites by blacks, but rather to convince blacks of the need to reevaluate themselves, he pointed the way to psychological liberation.[12] These preachments reflect Malcolm's concern for finding solutions, however unorthodox, to the complex problems which plagued people of color during this era. The Black Power movement was like that, too. When Malcolm X spoke of the need for black unity and self-determination, for community control and the internalization of the black struggle, he foreshadowed later, more fully developed and institutionalized Black Power sentiment. As movement stalwart Stokely Carmichael would write, Malcolm knew "where he was going, before the rest of us did."[13]

Malcolm X's protest ethic contained cultural as well as political and economic components. The "Statement of Basic Aims and Objectives of the Organization of Afro-American Unity," presented at a public rally late in June 1964, made clear his belief that black culture had a central role to play in the freedom movement. He instructed those assembled at New York's Audubon Ballroom in the importance of developing pride in a common racial history, of affirming a distinctive black culture. "We must recapture our heritage and our identity if we are ever to liberate ourselves from the bonds of white supremacy," he said. "We must launch a cultural revolution to unbrainwash an entire people." In Malcolm's vision, this epic "journey to our rediscovery of ourselves" began as blacks started to rediscover the folkways and achievements of their African forebears. As this process of reeducation proceeded, they were certain to reexamine the logic of Western history. By comparing ancient glories with current poverty statistics they quite logically would conclude that New World exploiters had perpetrated gross criminal acts against the African-American people. Once the enormity of this crime was revealed, the time-honored practice of "forget and forgive" would fall into disuse. In the end, this series of progressive revelations would result in coordinated action. Infused with cultural pride and historical wisdom, oppressed blacks would, with new confidence, begin to chart their own course in world affairs. They would strive to achieve a cultural reunification of diasporan peoples and seek to generate such a renaissance of grass roots support for black creative artists that these long-suffering individuals would be freed from imprisonment in clownish Stepin Fetchit roles.[14]

For Malcolm X, Afro-American history and culture were indispensable weapons in the black quest for freedom. Here, once again, his vision was remarkably similar to that forwarded by his spiritual descendants in the Black Power movement. Some would find new use for one of his analogues which held that, just as a tree deprived of its roots withers and dies, "a people without history or cultural roots also becomes a dead people." Others would, like Malcolm, take African or Muslim names, use African proverbs in their speeches, and echo his belief that blacks in this hemisphere needed to involve themselves in a spiritual and cultural back-to-Africa movement. Still others would restate his belief that black culture was destined to emerge as the world's predominant culture—even as blacks someday would be its dominant people. Indeed, many, in various ways would employ the rhetoric of black culture as a tool of liberation. Surely, Larry Neal spoke for a good number of his fellow poets when he claimed that "behind Black doors we were all Malcolm X's."[15]

Ironically, in death, Malcolm X became enshrined in black popular culture. His message was carried to succeeding generations via his widely read, mass-marketed *Autobiography* (1965), several volumes of collected speeches, and spoken word record albums such as *Message to the Grass Roots* (1965). Posters, sweatshirts, greeting cards, and even bumper stickers bore his likeness and the inscription, "OUR SHINING BLACK PRINCE" or "ST. MALCOLM." Black college students held festivals on his birthday. Cultural nationalist groups on both coasts observed *Dhabihu*—a holiday meaning "a sacrifice" in Swahili—and participated in annual commemorative services. Overcoming his initial skepticism that Hollywood could succeed in portraying "the great jungle" of Malcolm's story, James Baldwin wrote a somewhat surreal and, at times, bawdy and soap operish screenplay based on the *Autobiography*.[16] Plans to star Billy Dee Williams in the title role came to naught, as did the entire project, but black theater audiences were treated to *Malcolm X* (1972), a Warner Brothers film biography narrated by James Earl Jones. This film and several shorter documentaries served as belated, under-budgeted, but somehow appropriate tributes to a man who, in his reefer-peddling days as "Detroit Red," screened as many as five movies per day. As the *Autobiography* revealed, Malcolm always loved "the tough guys, the action" found in films such as *Casablanca*.[17] In death he became, for many black audiences, a tough guy role model in the Bogart tradition. His big screen appearances served as case studies in the utilization of popular culture in the cause of Black Power.

Although unable any longer to add dimension to his own popular legacy, there was no shortage of literary commentators willing to elaborate on the meaning of Malcolm for the Black Power era. In plays like Norbert Davidson's *El Hajj Malik*, the fallen leader served as inspiration

Malcolm X on Black Power–era poster. Courtesy of Robin's Book Store.

and ideological yardstick for black supplicants who chanted his name, imploring the "Mr. X man" to "Reach out and touch this land"—to "Preach it man" and "tell us where to make our stand." When received, his instructions most definitely challenged what LeRoi Jones, in *The Death of Malcolm X*, labeled the "White is Right" mindset of many contemporary blacks. As interpreted by Nate, a raging, militant character in William Wellington Mackey's *Requiem for Brother X* (1966), Brother Malcolm's message to his long-suffering followers was an incendiary revelation indeed: "POWER! THAT'S THE KEY," he shouted; "POWER IN THE HANDS OF MILLIONS OF BLACK PEOPLE ALL OVER THE WORLD. . . . That's the key, you know: BLACK PEOPLE PROUD OF BEING BLACK!"[18]

Afro-American poets elaborated on the playwrights' themes. Some, like Etheridge Knight, said they barely were able to "control the burst of angry words" welling up within as they reflected on the day "Judas guns" ended Malcolm's life. Although shocked and deeply saddened by the loss, they were not devastated, because his spirit lived on. It "swirls around us/In the vital air, inspiring all," they wrote. It lived on to inspire black youth, to instruct them in the way of proper behavior, and to shame them to repentance if they found themselves backsliding from black pride. It remained alive and vital because Malcolm was the "brother of all black mankind" who virtually "became his people's anger." Born into "a long line of super-cools, doo-rag lovers & revolutionary pimps" who "tol' it lak it DAMN SHO' IS!!," Malcolm X proved that you could

> "deal death to
> Black men,
> but not to
> Black Power!"

Like slave rebels, Joseph Cinqué, Nat Turner, and Gabriel Prosser, and the militant leaders of the late sixties, he was seen as the embodiment of a timeless black rage. Like the historical movement that both preceded and followed him, his spirit lived on to influence later Afro-American cultural expression. Each had a role to play as subject matter and inspirational guide for black creative artists.[19]

Although he often made reference to black/white and Western/Third World power relationships, late in his life Malcolm X became cautious whenever called upon to detail the specifics of his black liberation philosophy. In part, this was because he had acquired a distaste for labels and factions. He urged his followers to shun them because "sometimes a label can kill you."[20] More to the point, Malcolm X was elusive in these matters because he still was journeying and searching at the time of his death. Thus, it is to his legatees that we must look to find the most fully developed meaning of Black Power for the sixties generation.

In the years since his assassination, many commentators have described Malcolm's legacy to Black America. It has been said that he instructed his people in the beauty, worth, and distinctiveness of blackness as well as in the pervasiveness and perversity of white racism. He is credited with connecting black Americans with Africa and with the African past even as he separated the black and white historical experiences. We are told that his life was a testament to the legitimacy of confronting white power with black; his death a lesson in the unmet need for Afro-American unity.[21] Few, however, have analyzed or even traced adequately the movement of these teachings as they coursed through the black American mind after 1965. Still fewer have tried to make sense of Malcolm's chief heirs, the Black Power militants, or to show how they took up the flame and exactly what they did with it. The study which follows does not attempt to answer all of the questions we need to ask about the Black Power movement, nor does it seek to record every instance in which the name of Malcolm X was invoked in support of activist goals. It does, however, explore the rise, maturation, and ultimate decline of Black Power in the context of American culture.

Why culture? As the paradigm of Malcolm X suggests, the Black Power movement was viewed and interpreted variously both within and outside the black world. Despite an observable tendency for differing factions to claim the entire movement as their own, the multifaceted nature of Black Power was one of its most significant characteristics. One important mode of Black Power expression was cultural. Playwrights, novelists, songwriters, and artists all had their chance to forward a personalized vision of the militant protest sentiment. They used cultural forms as weapons in the struggle for liberation and, in doing so, provided a much-needed structural underpinning for the movement's more widely trumpeted political and economic tendencies.

The Black Power movement was not exclusively cultural, but it was essentially cultural. It was a revolt in and of culture that was manifested in a variety of forms and intensities. In the course of this revolt, the existence of a semipermeable wall separating Euro- and Afro-American cultural expression was revealed. The distance separating the two cultural spheres mirrored significant differences in the black and white world view and situation. It was this long-standing, determinedly independent black cultural base that provided whatever cohesion the movement eventually managed to develop. Thus, this study contends that Black

Power is best understood as a broad, adaptive, cultural term serving to connect and illuminate the differing ideological orientations of the movement's supporters. Conceptualized in this manner, the Black Power movement does not appear, like it so often has, a cacophony of voices and actions resulting in only miniscule gains for black people. Viewing the movement through the window of culture allows us to see that language, folk culture, religion, and the literary and performing arts served to spread the militants' philosophy much farther than did mimeographed political broadsides. When activists entered the cultural arena—and utilized available culture-based tools of persuasion—they broadened the appeal and facilitated the acceptance of Black Power tenets. They thereby contributed importantly to making the movement a lasting influence in American culture—one whose impact could be seen long after its exclusively political agenda had disintegrated.

The chapters that follow develop these concepts more fully. Since culture can be conceptualized as an entire way of life, encompassing all aspects of a people's existence, Black Power is examined in several different contexts. Nevertheless, imaginative, intellectual, and folk expression are the major focal areas of the study. Chapter one looks at various definitions of Black Power forwarded during the 1965–75 period. Chapter two explores the historical, sociological, psychological, and ultimately cultural reasons why a Black Power movement developed during the mid-1960s. Chapter three traces the course of the movement as its adherents challenged both the structure and the modus operandi of American institutional life. Chapter four details its major ideological variants. Chapters five and six consider the broad-based cultural infrastructure of the movement, examine the nature of African-American portraiture in mainstream culture, and outline the major themes developed by Black Power activists. The concluding section explains the movement's apparent decline in the early 1970s while summarizing its contributions and reflecting upon its lasting influence.

one

What is "Black Power"?

"When I use a word," Humpty Dumpty said in a rather scornful tone, "I mean just what I choose it to mean, neither more nor less." "The question is," said Alice, "whether you can make words mean so many different things." "The question is," said Humpty Dumpty, "who is to be master." That is all. That is all. Understand that . . . the first need of a free people is to define their own terms.

Stokely Carmichael on Lewis Carroll, 1967

It was as though someone had shouted "fire!" in a dynamite factory. "We must reject calls for racism, whether they come from a throat that is white or one that is black," U.S. Vice President Hubert H. Humphrey warned fifteen hundred of the already-converted at the 1966 convention of the National Association for the Advancement of Colored People (NAACP) in Los Angeles. "It is the father of hatred and the mother of violence. It is a reverse Mississippi, a reverse Hitler, a reverse Ku Klux Klan," added executive director Roy Wilkins. Why were these normally unflappable men so upset? *Time* pinpointed the source of their unease: militant "young demagogues"—"Negro hotheads" if you will—had organized a political movement in the

South that brazenly spurned whites and seemed dangerously close to adopting a philosophy of black separatism. It was feared that their rallying cry, "Black Power," was a synonym for black Jacobinism. Catching a whiff of this juicy bone of contention, the *National Review* dug deeper. Bent on transforming the civil rights movement into a program of "confiscatory socialism, revolutionary in its essence," these upstart "preachers of black racism" were said to be blackmailing the country with threats of violence. *Newsweek* fanned the flames further by framing their commentary with a photo of black marchers carrying a poster emblazoned with a snarling panther and the words, "MOVE ON OVER OR WE'LL MOVE ON OVER YOU." During the summer of 1966, Black Power arrived on the national news scene. The initial response to this unfamiliar and somewhat foreboding concept was befuddlement and panic. Longtime civil rights activist Bayard Rustin encapsulated the spirit of the era when he noted that all revolutionary social movements experienced peaks of activity and valleys of confusion. "And we are in the valleys of confusion." Before elaboration, before analysis, before common sense, there was confusion.[1]

The birth cries of the Black Power movement reverberated throughout the popular media. Like the proverbial tried and true method of getting a mule's attention, a superabundance of sensationalized media coverage guaranteed black activists an immediate, attentive, nationwide audience for their displays of outrage and spleen. Throughout white America, evening news devotees froze, fork in mid-air, mouth agape, as a scowling Stokely Carmichael or Floyd McKissick told reporters that "the greatest hypocrisy we have is the Statue of Liberty. We ought to break the young lady's legs and point her to Mississippi."[2] More importantly, the extensive media coverage brought the militants' message home to black people. The Black Power spokespersons knew that the press would stigmatize them as part of a new and insidious criminal element, but they also recognized that this lawless, macho image had its benefits. The Black Panthers' Bobby Seale was right on target when he described how unfavorable media coverage of the Panthers unwittingly served as a recruitment device for the Party:

> A lot of people ain't gon know what's happening.
> But the brothers on the block, who the man's
> been calling thugs and hoodlums for four hundred
> years, gon say, "Them some out of sight thugs and
> hoodlums up there!" The brothers on the block
> gon say, "Who *is* these THUGS and HOODLUMS?. . .
> Well, they've been calling us niggers, thugs, and

> hoodlums for four hundred years, that ain't gon
> hurt *me*, I'm going to check out what these
> brothers is doing!"[3]

Nevertheless, once they had won the ear of the networks and news syndicates, the "brothers on the block" didn't always like what they saw or read about themselves. Calling the white press "nothing but a bunch of pigs who only lie," some complained of the media's inattention to the root causes of their disaffection. At times deeming the black press to be little better, they felt that the media stigmatized them as enemies not only of the system, but of their own people. As Floyd McKissick of the Congress of Racial Equality (CORE) complained to a national gathering of newspaper editors in 1967, reporters were focusing too narrowly on the bravado and ignoring larger issues: "All you can see, all you can hear, are two words: 'black power.' You would like us to stand in the streets and chant 'black power' for your amusement." In McKissick's opinion, the punishment for sounding rational and forwarding an in-depth critique of the black condition all too often was a total blackout of news coverage.[4]

There was much truth in these charges. Angry blacks always had made good copy. Malcolm X once complained that interviewers almost never conveyed his sentiments accurately. "If I had said 'Mary had a little lamb,'" he noted, "what probably would have appeared was 'Malcolm X Lampoons Mary.'"[5] During the investigation of the mid-sixties riots it was revealed that reporters sometimes went beyond name-calling and misquotation. They even staged disruptive events, coaxing black youths to throw rocks and interrupt traffic for the cameras.[6] Therefore, it is not surprising that throughout this period the media focused most intently on vituperative oratorical harangues and civil disturbances in progress. Relatively little attention was given to making the precise nature of the militants' grievances clear or evaluating the specific programs they developed.[7] Since the initial expression of Black Power sentiment received immediate but shallow and disjointed coverage from major news sources, popular understanding of the movement was distorted. Black Power was trivialized. Its characteristic diversity of expression was interpreted as chaos and disorganization amidst the flurry of eager reporters clamoring after the latest intemperate statement. Ideological distinctives were obscured in the glare of the camera's light. To a certain degree, blame for these developments could be shared by interviewers and respondents. The militants' outlaw image certainly wasn't created by newscasters out of whole cloth. As Malcolm X noted

Advertisement for Black Power merchandise. From *Liberator,* August 1969.

in his last days, the press always was "looking for sensationalism, for something that would sell papers, and I gave it to them."[8]

Media misperception and manipulation of the Black Power message continued throughout the decade and contributed to many long-term misunderstandings. Two key assumptions which can be placed in this category are (1) that the best—and perhaps only—way to conceptualize the movement is to treat it as part of a violent era's radicalized politics, and (2) that as an aberrant, directionless expression of rage, Black Power was incapable of making lasting contributions to black life. A more correct evaluation of the situation would be that when the long hot summers of urban rioting cooled and the media lost interest in the militants' political sloganeering, they declared the movement dead through their silence. This is not to deny that by 1975 many of the most vocal activists had been silenced, either willingly or otherwise. Neither can one explain away the fact that the movement's most effective oratory often was of an overtly political nature, was delivered in a highly volatile politicized environment, and was designed to achieve political goals. What needs to be recognized, however, is that salient facets of the Black Power experience are slighted when the media-made perspective is accepted uncritically. Neither the movement's solid foundation in black culture nor the possibility that its attraction was great enough to ensure a continuing influence in Afro-American intellectual and cultural affairs were highlighted or even given credibility by the mainstream print and electronic media. This, too, was to be expected. Throughout American history, whites have striven mightily to make proud, self-directed blacks invisible—except when they become threatening in a political sense.

The blaring news coverage did encourage Americans to ponder the difficult question, What is Black Power? To their credit, some looked beyond the evening newscast in search of answers. Social scientists and pollsters, for example, flicked off their TV sets, quickly gathered up their clipboards, and rushed to tap the public pulse. In some cases, their hurried preparation was evident. Vague and peripheral questions were asked. Commentary was published that lacked sufficient analysis. Many of the studies were far removed from any historical context. Instead of illuminating the psychological and sociological factors which spurred the new militant persuasion, survey results often revealed only the approximate number of followers a particular movement leader could count on at a particular point in time. Instead of plumbing the meaning of the Black Power slogan for the sixties generation it seemed enough to take a head count of militants. From such studies one might

 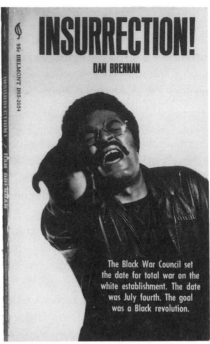

Black Power threat as portrayed in mass-market paperbacks. From Stanley Johnson, *The Presidential Plot* (1969), and Dan Brennan, *Insurrection* (1970).

learn that 25 percent of one group of respondents were very much in agreement with the statement "Rap Brown fights for what people want," or that 29 percent of another sample felt that leaders of black militant groups could be "somewhat effective" in helping blacks achieve equality, or that 14 percent "approved" and 21 percent "partly approved" of Stokely Carmichael.[9] But the country needed to know more—if only for its own good.

A quick reading of this type of data seemed to show that Black Power was scarcely more than a minority sentiment within black America. The militants seldom reached the lofty approval rate of the moderate civil rights establishment. A study of inner-city high school students might reveal that Black Panther loyalists outnumbered NAACP supporters by a slight margin, but iconoclasm in this age group was to be expected. National polls showed that only 10 percent of black Americans felt that they should operate politically as a separate group outside the two major parties and only 9 percent counted themselves as "revolutionaries." In 1970, Harris pollsters asked the question, "Do you personally want blacks to become integrated into white society, or would you rather they establish their own separate black society?" Among male respondents, three times more whites than blacks favored separation. A 1967 survey of blacks in Detroit reported that 86 percent favored integration while only 1 percent endorsed separatism. When Chicago blacks were asked who best represented their position, 57 percent chose Martin Luther King, Jr. Three percent named Stokely Carmichael. In the nation's capital, a large majority selected the most effective leader and spokesperson for blacks from among moderates such as King and Roy Wilkins while only 11 percent chose Carmichael or Rap Brown. In a 1966 national sampling of opinion on the quality of the contributions made by various individuals and groups prominent in the fight for black rights, Jackie Robinson outpolled the Black Muslims ten to one.[10]

The relish with which this news was reported suggested that at least some opinion gatherers were relieved to find that the militants had made so few converts. For example, one 1967 study found that, in Watts, 58 percent of the respondents favored the concept of Black Power while only 24 percent opposed it. Nevertheless, the authors concluded that groups such as the Black Panthers could hope for little support from the ghetto masses, that "most urban Negroes simply reject the black-power ideology." It was as if the initial burst of media coverage had stampeded analysts into passing off wishful thinking as social science gospel. So pervasive was the belief that Black Power could be conceptualized only as a political fringe movement that, in Harlem, a loose amalgam of street gangs known as the Five Percenters took their name from the notion. They reasoned that since 85 percent of black Americans were directionless and 10 percent were Uncle Toms, only the remaining 5 percent were militant enough to shape the destiny of their people.[11]

Studies that showed minimal support for the militants obscured the fact that when the various surveys are sifted more thoroughly, Black Power almost always is revealed to be more popular in its cultural aspects than it was as a political enthusiasm. Support for the movement promoting the study of African languages and culture, for example, tended to run between 40 and 60 percent of those polled.[12] Black Studies programs that would include such courses were even more popular. A 1970 Time–Louis Harris poll showed an 85 percent endorsement rate for implementation of the programs in high schools and colleges as "an important sign of black identity and pride."[13] Distinctive hair styles, clothing, cuisine, and music won endorsement from a wide range of age groups within black America. Although it was predictable that nearly 80 percent of northern blacks under the age of 30 surveyed in one poll liked the new natural hair styles, it was surprising to find that roughly half of *all* Afro-Americans agreed. Approximately four out of ten Detroit blacks questioned in 1968 approved of dashikis while some 80 percent indicated a liking for soul food and music.[14] Surveys which tested for even broader cultural concepts such as a belief that "black is beautiful" or that blacks possessed "soul" or shared a sense of collective identity solidified the notion that the cultural thrust of the Black Power movement had wide appeal.[15]

That relatively few pollsters explored the implications of this data is understandable. Most were trained in social science specialties that traditionally undervalued cultural variables. Many were just getting their feet wet in cross-cultural survey research. For some, it was a baptism with fire—and under the pressure of publication deadlines. Others were unduly influenced by what seemed at the time to be critical societal imperatives. These priorities were reflected in their surveys.[16] Did America *really* want to know the answer to the question, What is Black Power? Well, perhaps not in so many words. Of more immediate concern was the black response to questionnaire items such as, "It is true that the Negro has problems in this country but they will gradually work themselves out," "Violence serves a useful purpose in promoting the Negro's cause," or "I don't like whites." As a result, the various Black Power sentiment scales, alienation indexes, and black consciousness inventories constructed during this era proved to be rather cumbersome instruments for assaying the foundations of the movement, cultural or otherwise.[17]

More helpful were studies which allowed individual respondents to state what the Black Power slogan meant to them. Rather than merely affirming or denying a pollster's preconceived and prioritized notions, black—and white—Americans could place their personal cachet on a term that was both controversial and hard to fathom. Here, it was found that white interpretations differed from black in significant ways. For example, a 1967 survey of more than 850 Detroit residents conducted by University of Michigan researchers showed that almost 60 percent of the whites interviewed believed Black Power was synonomous with violence and destruction, racism, and black domination. Many were so frightened and bewildered by the symbolism of the militants' rallying cry that they foresaw a black takeover of the entire country or even the entire world. "The Negro wants to enslave the white man like he was enslaved 100 years ago. They want to take everything away from us— We'll all be poor," said one panic-stricken respondent. "Blacks won't be

satisfied until they get complete control of our country by force if ne-
sary," added another. "Black takeover—Take over the world because
that is what they want to do and they will," noted a third. "There's no
doubt about it. Why should they care? I'm working and supporting their
kids." Only 9 percent of the blacks interviewed held similar views.[18]
Studies such as this revealed important differences in black and white
popular opinion, but did little to uncover the underlying causes of those
differences.

Throughout the Black Power era, a variety of high-profile African-
American activists denied that they were about to initiate the apocalypse. Collectively, these denials of ill intent compose a negative definition of Black Power. What, then, was the term *not* about? Surprising
many, they claimed that Black Power was not a negative term connoting
violence. It did not speak of a vindictive desire to "get Whitey" by seizing control of the country's economic infrastructure. The ostensibly
revolutionary rhetoric forwarded by Black Power advocates was designed to rouse the slumbering black masses—not to promote riots. According to Stokely Carmichael, the initial thrust of any liberation
movement necessarily was devoted to cultivating this type of in-group
response. "The first stage is waking up our people," he noted in 1970.
"We have to wake them up to the impending danger. So we yell, Gun!
Shoot! Burn! Kill! Destroy! They're committing genocide! until the
masses of our people are awake." The Black Power vanguard was not
about to take over the country. They just wanted "to get white people off
their backs."[19]

Once aroused, the long-suffering masses might choose to engage in violent acts, but only in self-defense. Black power spokespersons felt that a
beleaguered minority could hope to survive in the violent milieu of late-
twentieth-century America only by developing the will and the ability
to retaliate against outside attacks. Black retaliatory violence was
viewed as a justifiable response to continued incidents of terrorism and
police brutality. Night-riders, assassins, and other unreconstructed
bullies had to be warned that their days of head-whipping were over.
Black people should and would fight back. As Carmichael noted, "nothing more quickly repels someone bent on destroying you than the unequivocal message: 'O.K., fool, make your move, and run the same risk I
run—of dying." Unlike the mean-spirited, aggressive violence of white
bigots, black-led retaliatory acts were viewed as being supportive of
broad human rights. They were linked to time-honored societal mores
which held that individuals were justified in fighting back in order to

preserve their person, property, or honor. They also were attached to the notion that a nation which fails to protect its citizens cannot condemn those who take up the task themselves. In sum, Black Power was seen as a force promoting, not disturbing, racial peace. The black retaliatory threat would serve to deter interracial confrontations by making whites think twice before responding to the black presence with violence.[20]

Black activists also sought to turn back charges that their slogan was the rallying cry of black racism. However valid such claims might have seemed to outsiders, movement participants held that the furor generated by Black Power was just another attempt to blame the victim—to mask white America's own racial chauvinism with ill-founded accusations about reverse discrimination. It was believed that some whites, especially those entrenched within the conservative national power structure, sought to consolidate their forces by tagging the militants with a racial supremacist label. By claiming that blacks were racists, they hoped to turn waivering voices against the movement.[21] Others, including white liberals and black moderates, were suspected of slandering Black Power supporters in order to invigorate the increasingly moribund civil rights campaign. In this scenario, the myth of black racism was designed both to isolate the upstart militants and to bolster the crumbling facade of mid-sixties interracial reform. As one commentator noted in 1966, the old-line civil rights establishment remained doggedly committed to the belief that "social revolutions could be run by 'Roberts' Rules of Order,' or by consensus."[22] Adherents of this position feared that the Afro-American component of their coalition soon would choose to go its own way. Charges of black racism were viewed as a panic-stricken response to this threatened disturbance of the status quo.

Why were the charges of racism denied so vehemently? One common response was that the threat of black racist ideology was as ahistorical as it was absurd. Much of black America's history had been occupied with the fight against racial intolerance. Why would black Americans change their strategy at this late date? How could the Black Power activists hope to end racism by perpetuating racism? Bobby Seale put the issue into perspective in a 1968 speech:

> When a man walks up and says that we are anti-
> white I scratch my head. . . . I say, "Wait a minute
> man—let's back up a little bit." That's your game,
> that's the Ku Klux Klan's game. To hate me and
> murder me because of the color of my skin. I
> wouldn't murder a person or brutalize him

because of the color of his skin. Yeah, we HATE
something alright. We hate the OPPRESSION that
we live in. . . . If you got enough energy to sit
down and hate a white person *just* because of the
color of his skin, you're wasting a lot of energy.
You'd better take some of that same energy and
put it in some motion and start dealing with
those oppressive conditions.[23]

To the militant mind, white racism had no valid black analogue. By
definition, racism involved not only exclusion on the basis of race, but
exclusion for the purpose of instituting and maintaining a system of ar-
bitrary subjugation. Throughout American history, whites, not blacks,
had been the chief supporters of this corrupt ideology. Black people had
not lynched whites, murdered their children, bombed their churches, or
manipulated the nation's laws to maintain racial hegemony. Nor would
they. To adopt the ways of the white racist as their own would be counterproductive and, for a minority group, self-destructive. What whites
called black racism was only a healthy defense reflex on the part of Afro-
Americans attempting to survive and advance in an aggressively hostile
environment.[24] In the end, wrote Eldridge Cleaver, racism would "do us
no good. It will only get us killed, and it will destroy the world."[25] Black
Power would preserve, not destroy. Its adherents vowed to fight racism
through black solidarity. They would promote color consciousness, but
in a positive way—to uplift their own group, not to tyrannize others.

Predictably, the militants of the mid sixties believed that they had
been linked to racial supremacism, black-initiated violence, and reverse
discrimination by a sensationalist, race-mongering national press
corps. While some militants deemed it presumptuous for whites even to
comment on the Black Power phenomenon, others seemed resigned to
this type of external definition. They might, for example, berate the
press for encouraging its readers to believe that the Mau Maus were
about to pillage suburbia and then become almost fatalistic over their
chances of influencing the popular media's portrayal of the movement.
As Stokely Carmichael lamented after a particularly unsatisfying appearance on the Dick Cavett Show in 1970, "they're not going to let us
on their TV show and really break down the truth to our people."[26]

Most Black Power spokespersons also believed that whites associated
their movement with violence because of an inability to cope with its
psychological implications. They spoke often of white America's deep-
rooted fear and distrust of power—especially if it was concentrated and

under black control. According to Julius Lester, a perverse concept of blackness was at the libidinal center of their misunderstanding:

> Black! That word. BLACK! And the visions came of
> alligator-infested swamps arched by primordial
> trees with moss dripping from the limbs and out
> of the depths of the swamp, the mire oozing from
> his skin, came the black monster and fathers told
> their daughters to be in by nine instead of nine-
> thirty.[27]

Lester's words undoubtedly elicited a round of nervous laughter from many white urbanites of the late sixties. Blacks, on the other hand, weren't even mildly entertained—or frightened. They were busy forwarding a far more realistic notion—the view that any manifestations of power to emerge from the nation's ghettos likely would come in only a limited range of colors.

But what about the meaning of Black Power for blacks? The truth was that the militants found it much easier to explain alleged misconceptions than to formulate succinct definitions. Evincing a characteristic bravado, some adherents boldly stated that the term easily could be defined once white America's fears were proved to be invalid. The meaning of Black Power was self-evident. Whites understood its essence because they had deprived blacks of it for centuries. Any Afro-American who claimed not to understand its basic implications was either a fool or a liar. Lexicographic confusion over Black Power was considered part of the conspiracy to discredit the movement.[28] Nevertheless, despite these confident assertions, there was considerable backpedaling when it actually came time to define the term. Some commentators found the Black Power concept complex and ambiguous. Others seemed to view it as an almost totally existential doctrine. In general, most offered both a more varied and less apocalyptic selection of possible definitions than their white counterparts.

To those most favorably inclined, Black Power was a freshly minted variant of the traditional Afro-American freedom agenda. It was "people getting together to accomplish things for the group," obtaining jobs and respect, and thereby forcing whites to realize their importance and worth. As one nineteen-year-old phrased it,

> It means mostly equality. You know, to have
> power to go up to a person, you know, no matter
> what his skin color is and be accepted on the same
> level, you know, and it doesn't necessarily have to

mean that you gotta take over everything and be a
revolutionary and all this; just as long as people
are going to respect you.[29]

Another commentator chose to express his understanding of Black
P-O-W-E-R in a more acrostic form. The P stood for persistence because
"you got to wear them down." O represented the organizational effort
needed to do so. W symbolized Whitey. He had all the power, but blacks
had to get their rightful share. The E was for effort—the sweat and heart-
aches that were invested in the movement. Finally, the R in POWER stood
for results because, simply stated, "the name of the game is win."[30] If
this was the battle plan for revolution it also was the formula for success
at Harvard Business School and in corporate boardrooms all across
America. *This* version of Black Power was grounded in pragmatism not
anarchism. It recognized that U.S. society did not function by love or
morality, but by power. As attentive students of realpolitik, the militants recognized that throughout history power more often had been
won or seized than willingly granted or shared. They also knew that
members of a minority group hoping to better its relative position in society needed to deal with their more powerful countrymen from an ever-
increasing position of strength. They needed to amass power to break
clear of the initiative-sapping stranglehold of the welfare state. They
sought the power to initiate action as well as to say "no" to public policy
proposals that ran contrary to the will and expectations of the black
community. As defined by the Black Panthers' Huey P. Newton, the militants' goals were solidly established within the American political tradition. In coining the expression "all power to the people," the Panthers
were said to have recognized that the exercise of power was a basic human need. But they also knew it was wrong to seek power over people.
What blacks sought was the power to control their own destinies. To
Newton, power was "the ability to first of all define phenomena, and
secondly the ability to make these phenomena act in a desired manner."[31] During the years 1965–75, this statement of purpose was echoed
by many other Black Power activists. Resonating most fully in the world
beyond television cameras and microphones, this passion for self-
definition better represented the views of the average black American
than did the frustrated cry "get whitey."

Conceptualizations such as these were far removed from most white
perceptions of Black Power—and even from certain of the more vivid
images forwarded through the black folk and literary expression of the
day. They suggest that the Afro-American view of Black Power was a far

more varied sentiment, different in tone and intent than perceived by whites and reported via the mainstream media. In a sense, the movement was a logical progression of the civil rights advocates' efforts to achieve dignity, equality, and freedom of choice in their adopted homeland. Certainly, Black Power differed in style and semantics from the earlier movement. The militants' spirited rallying cry emanated from a somewhat different mix of geographic, socioeconomic, and generational variables than did "One Man, One Vote," or "Freedom Now." Nevertheless, the ultimate concerns of the two movements were more compatible than contradictory. The latter would not have existed but for the former while the former was an incomplete formulation of the latter. The Black Power movement *was* radical. It sought far more than the reaffirmation of legal equality and the government's admission that it had a duty to protect the constitutional rights of its citizens. Its supporters demanded access to the basic operative force of American society: power—both actual and psychological. On occasion, it was said that this access would be gained "by any means necessary." In practice, however, a variety of more carefully defined and largely familiar methods were adapted to the task.

During the mid-sixties, the type of searching inquiries that would have revealed these complex patterns of thought seldom were entered into. Important matters went unexamined. Pollsters should have probed further. They needed to listen for hidden meanings and to do a better job of sorting braggadocio from deeply felt belief. Social scientists would have done well to consider even more complex questions, to delineate the ideological variants of Black Power, and then to see whether or not there were common denominators among them. Both sets of questioners would have benefitted from a more informed understanding of the manner in which the militants hoped to acquire power. This was especially critical because, at least at the popular level, the strategies and goals of sixties activists were difficult to separate. Often, their methodologies were perceived to *be* their goals—violence as an end in itself or disruption for disruption's sake. Finally, all who experienced the turmoil of the late sixties needed to ask whether deep-seated cultural differences between black and white had anything to do with the apparent racial gap in interpreting the Black Power concept.

Those blessed with the luxury of viewing the Black Power years through hindsight should not be too unkind to commentators who were forced to make their evaluative judgments on the spot. Honest effort must be recognized and credit given where credit is due. In their attempts to fathom the workings of the movement, social scientists of the late sixties tried to adapt the tools of their trade to the study of the era's disturbing social phenomena. Sociologists, for example, developed several useful models of collective behavior that, even today, can be utilized to study the ideological frames of reference through which Black Power supporters viewed the world. To understand the underlying ideological commitments of those who adopted the Black Power ethic is to be one step closer to gaining a clear understanding of the movement.

Students of collective behavior assert that the most important appeals of any social movement are contained in its ideology, of which there are three basic types: assimilationism, pluralism, and nationalism. Assimilationists, it is said, view the collective expression of grievances as a short-term strategy for ultimate integration into the mainstream. Not deeply concerned with altering the basic values of society or initiating fundamental institutional changes, the assimilationist merely hopes, through collective action, to win greater participation in existing societal institutions. Pluralists, on the other hand, view society as being composed of various ethnic and interest groups, all of whom are competing with one another for goods and services. This is fine, they say, as long as equal opportunities, privileges, and respect are accorded to all groups. An amicable coexistence of diverse groups would, unlike assimilation, allow each subculture to remain relatively intact. Granted equal access to power and continually strengthened and renewed through their unique cultural roots, the groups would form a multicultural society in which each component supported and enriched all others. Nationalists, by comparison, are skeptics. They are suspicious of claims that radically divergent groups long can live in peace and on a basis of equality while inhabiting the same territory or participating in the same societal institutions. Eventually, they believe, one component of the social matrix comes to dominate and oppress the others, eradicating important subgroup mores in the process. The result is assimilation by fiat and should be avoided at all costs. To avert this end, nationalists seek to strengthen in-group values while holding those promoted by the larger society at arm's length. Withdrawing from the body politic as much as practicable, they hope to win and maintain sociocultural autonomy. In sum, advocates of all three ideological camps seek the good life, which includes the exercise of choice and of power. They simply differ in their approach to obtaining it.[32]

Black Power advocates sampled all three ideologies, but found pluralism and nationalism most compatible with their sense of history, their position within contemporary society, and the nature of the task at hand. Nationalists rejected the assimilationist ethic in a somewhat more precipitous fashion than did the pluralists, but the two ideological camps were equally expressive of Black Power sentiment. It is no more valid to equate Black Power exclusively with either black nationalism or pluralism than it is to make the movement a synonym for racial violence. The black nationalist–pluralist view of the world can be encapsulated as follows: White Power, as manifested in the workings of U.S. institutional life, long had been and continues to be a major impediment to the black American's attainment of the good life. In order to challenge and ultimately to dissolve this oppressive monopoly, blacks had to mobilize, close ranks, and move toward a position of community and of group strength. This difficult process involved all aspects of black life—political, economic, psychological, and cultural. Once unity had been achieved in these areas, blacks would form a significant power bloc. They would be able to exercise true freedom of choice for the first time. Nationalists might then choose to go it alone, either in "liberated" urban enclaves, in a separate black nation-state, or simply in the realm of the psyche. Pluralists could hope to parlay their newfound racial solidarity into a representative share of both local and national decision-making power. Whatever the specific format, the new Black American would be like nothing the world ever before had seen. They would be a transformed people. And if the rest of the nation was altered in process, so much the better. "The consent of the governed" would become the watchword in national political and economic affairs. Cultural pride would replace psychological despair within black communities. The myth of the melting pot never again could be used to obscure the role of group power in ordering societal affairs.[33]

Key psychological and cultural principles undergirded the ideological formulations of both nationalists and pluralists, providing a central repository of strength for the movement as a whole. Whatever the specific power variable in their equation, whatever the strategy to obtain it, the various Black Power constituencies spoke with remarkable unity when they considered the issues of psychological liberation and cultural identity.

The concept of self-definition was central to the Black Power experience. It was an essential component of the "revolution of the mind" that militants believed was a prerequisite for the successful implementation of their plan for acquiring power.[34] Before black people could hope to become influential in the economic or political spheres, they had to define themselves. They had to win and then exercise the right to reject organizational structures, values, and methodologies that emanated from sources outside the black experience. Even political slogans and commonplace concepts such as "truth" and "beauty" had to be newly cast before they could be employed in the cause of Afro-American empowerment. No longer would whites' assumption of a unilateral power to define black as ugly, ignorant, inferior, lazy, and uncultured, depending on time, need, and circumstance remain unchallenged. Believing that a people ashamed of themselves cannot hope soon to be free, Black Power activists strived to turn a presumed deficit into a tactical advantage—to use their physical and cultural distinctives as a weapon for liberation.[35] They proclaimed that blacks were indeed beautiful. Also claimed was the right to define whites. As Huey P. Newton once declared, "we no longer define the omnipotent administrator as "the Man. . . WE define them as pigs! I think that this is a revolutionary thing in itself. . . . When black people start defining things and making it act in a desired manner, then we call this Black Power!"[36]

Both nationalists and pluralists understood that the power to define extended into the sphere of culture. Both mandated, in the words of Vincent Harding, a "turning away from assimilation and emphasizing the existence and beauty of an authentic Afro-American culture."[37] For far too long, they said, Afro-Americans had been told that they had no cultural heritage that was worthy of respect. Thus, there was a tremendous need to reclaim and preserve their group identity from what Stokely Carmichael termed "the dictatorship of definition, interpretation and consciousness."[38] Blacks needed to develop a new appreciation of their past—a rich historical pageant that had been obscured by Hollywood images of cannibalistic savages and shuffling, comic stooges. They needed to write their own histories and to create their own myths and legends. Through the process of self-discovery and self-legitimization, the Afro-American people would develop a group consciousness and pride that would serve them well in their struggle for power. This developing sense of black identity would provide a much-needed adhesive and guiding force for the Black Power movement. Here, especially, it was obvious that Black Power stood for more than the acquisition of a few additional civil rights guarantees. Black Power was a revolutionary cultural concept that demanded important changes in extant patterns of American cultural hegemony. Its advocates hoped that this revolution eventually would reach the very core of the nation's value system and serve to alter the social behavior of white Americans. But first, black Americans had to be awakened, unified, and made to see that if they were to succeed they must define and establish their own values while rejecting the cultural prescriptions of their oppressors. Without these initial victories, black self-awareness and self-confidence would remain at a low ebb. The most promising avenues of economic and political power would remain impenetrable. Indeed, blacks would continue to experience the worst kind of terrorism imaginable—cultural diffusion and cooptation without compensation or reward.[39]

In order to grasp the essence of the term, one must view Black Power in an inclusive, cultural context. Despite the media-mandated interpretation of events, the significance of Black Power could not be encapsulated in the acts of young demagogues bent on political domination and economic rapine. It was not a one-dimensional social movement sponsored by a small but vocal minority of Afro-Americans whose passion was promoting racism and violence. In truth, the movement was concerned with gaining entry into the national storehouse of influence, respect, and power. Its advocates sought the power needed to influence the affairs that most immediately affected their lives. Whether pluralists or nationalists, they hoped to become powerful by building outward and upward from a core of group values. The concept of self-definition was inextricably tied to this quest. By defining Afro-Americans as culturally distinct from the nation's white citizenry, black activists were not merely engaging in a variant of traditional majoritarian chauvinism. They were at work constructing a power base in the territory that they knew best—the very area of black life with which outsiders were the most unfamiliar. Black culture was the seedbed of the Black Power movement. Afro-American cultural expression nourished and spread its message in infancy, provided sustenance in adolescence, and preserved its spirit through the most difficult of times.

two

Precursors and Preconditions: Why Was There a Black Power Movement?

What is needed in our country is not an exchange of pathologies, but a change of the basis of society. . . . In Negro culture there is much of value for America as a whole. What is needed are Negroes to take it and create of it "the uncreated consciousness of their race." In doing so they will do far more, they'll help create a more human American.

Ralph Ellison, 1944

In the fall of 1963, John A. Williams set out in search of America. Hoping to duplicate the success of John Steinbeck's "Travels with Charley" articles, the editors of *Holiday* magazine assigned the black writer to travel about the land, taking the pulse of the country. His findings, published as *This Is My Country Too* (1965), revealed that the national character had a split personality.[1]

On the one hand, he was taken aback by the unexpected courtesy of most hotel desk clerks. Although only twenty-nine states had laws forbidding discrimination in public places, he was refused lodging only once in fifteen thousand miles of travel. He found additional hope in Atlanta's booming economy which had begun to provide equal opportunity for skilled workers, regardless of race. In Kentucky, he nearly drove his car off the road upon sighting his first all-black telephone line crew. Surprised and encouraged by many of his experiences, he wrote that people "looked you right in the eye. And I liked that."[2]

Nevertheless, it was obvious that the spirit of America continued to be troubled by the Afro-American presence. Upon entering the South, Williams was warned to "watch your step, keep your tongue inside your head, and *remember where you are*." Confederate flags on license plates, souvenir Mammy dolls, and black road gangs reinforced a message that was driven home when a New Orleans bartender would serve him only through "the Nigger Window." But the problem was nationwide. Regardless of locale, white Americans evidenced their inability to relate to dark-skinned people as individuals. Williams complained that whenever he was introduced as a writer someone invariably would rush up and exclaim, "You're James Baldwin!" before his own name could be announced. On one occasion, a Montana gas station attendant assumed that the five-foot-eight-inch writer was a member of the Harlem Globetrotters, who also were in town that day. Gaffes such as these seemed harmless, even somewhat humorous, but their cumulative effect definitely took a toll. Although he supposed it a mark of progress to be mistaken for an athlete rather than an entertainer or a musician, Williams said that both the direct and indirect insults he received during his travels angered him greatly. "I never know just how effective my words are, or even if they are understood," he wrote. "A physical attack would have been better."[3]

Williams' portrait of "the paradox that is America" ended with a paean to the beauty of the land and a warning to its people: either live up to the country's egalitarian credos or "chip them from our lives altogether." He hoped that whites would respond to the challenge. If not, the prognosis was grim. In Chicago, he had seen pickets in the Loop protesting de facto segregation and urging Christmas shoppers not to patronize white-owned stores. In Atlanta, he learned that civil rights leaders were taking "terrible psychological punishment" as they tried to keep their constituents united under the banner of nonviolence. In Detroit, a boyhood friend drove him through the black ghetto, noting that both joblessness and gun sales were on the increase. "Any kind of trouble comes as a diversion," observed Williams' host. "And if they can tie that in with striking a blow for freedom, it fits even better." In Mississippi, he was told that it was going to get worse before it got better.[4]

After gazing into this American looking glass, Williams concluded that "grim anarchy" was but one crisis away. The great majority of whites still had no intention of sharing the American dream with their Afro-American countrymen. At the same time, the black masses were becoming estranged from their traditional middle-class leaders. Their patience was wearing thin. A potentially volatile mixture was a-brewing.[5]

Williams had assayed his subject correctly. At mid-decade the United States was at the crossroads. Increasingly, black and white lives dovetailed. In many places, the two communities had begun to prove that they could coexist and work together for the common good. Racial "firsts" were becoming commonplace. The barriers were falling. Why, then, was there need for a Black Power movement?

Williams suggested one possible answer: there were too many barriers of too many different kinds and they were toppling too slowly. Black people no longer were awe-inspired every time they learned that a Gale Sayers had been named Rookie of the Year or that a Patricia Harris had been given an ambassadorship. They wanted to know the time and place of their own triumph over both institutional racism and the burden of everyday insults. In this respect, when they chanted "Black Power," they actually were saying "me power," "us power." They were seeking release from the psychological baggage they bore as a minority people. This was a broad and swelling sentiment, difficult to encapsulate and easily misinterpreted.

Most accounts of Black Power's rise have failed to plumb the depths of this group feeling or to understand its connection to the sphere of culture. As a result, our understanding of the movement has been colored by the plethora of negatives associated with its political components. Disappointment and disillusionment have been permitted to reign supreme as causative forces. From this perspective, black history is understood as one continual sorrow song. The energizing, soul-satisfying aspects of psychological and cultural liberation remain in the background, giving the impression that they were tributary, not foundational to the movement's overall thrust. Such an opinion is unfortunate, because it divests the Afro-American experience of its vigor, joy, and enthusiasm for life. To obtain a more accurate view of the Black Power movement, the focus must shift. Positive aspects of personal and group empowerment need to be stressed. The militant sentiment of the late sixties has to be placed in an appropriate historical and cultural framework.

As a political slogan, the term "Black Power" entered the vocabulary of most Americans only after 16 June 1966. On that date, in Greenwood,

Mississippi, an assembly of civil rights workers and reporters heard Stokely Carmichael declare, "The only way we gonna stop them white men from whuppin' us is to take over. We been saying freedom for six years and we ain't got nothin'. What we gonna start saying now is Black Power!" The audience responded immediately. "Black Power!" they roared, some six hundred strong. Seizing the moment, Carmichael's associate Willie Ricks, jumped to the speaker's platform. "What do you want?" he yelled. "Black Power!" the audience shouted in unison, "Black Power! Black Power! Black Power!"[6]

It was ironic, but somehow appropriate that this chant was raised in the very heartland of black powerlessness—in a state whose governor once quipped that NAACP stood for "niggers, alligators, apes, coon and possum," and in a county whose major newspaper likened Martin Luther King to Joseph Stalin.[7] The black and white participants in the "March Against Fear" were challenging both institutionalized and psychological bonds as they sought to complete the 200-mile walk from Memphis (Tennessee) to Jackson (Mississippi) begun by civil rights veteran James Meredith. The man who had integrated the University of Mississippi in 1962 had been wounded by three rounds from a shotgun on 6 June 1966, one day after beginning his trek down Highway 51. Immediately, black leaders such as Martin Luther King, Jr. of the Southern Christian Leadership Conference (SCLC), Floyd McKissick of the Congress of Racial Equality (CORE), and Carmichael of the Student Nonviolent Coordinating Committee (SNCC) rushed to the scene. They, too, were determined to show white Mississippians that black people no longer could be driven from the voting booths by white power. Through their combined efforts, Meredith hoped that blacks would come to understand that "the old order was passing, that they should stand up as men with nothing to fear."[8]

But, by mid-June, Carmichael and like-minded members of SNCC and CORE had concluded that they would stand alone, outside the traditional interracial alliance with its emphasis on love and nonviolence. After June 16, SNCC's staff was instructed that Black Power was to be their rallying cry for the rest of the march. At roadside rallies, supporters of the new ideological stance vied with champions of "freedom now," the SCLC slogan, in stirring up the crowds. By the time the column of marchers reached Yazoo City some were chanting, "Hey! Hey! Wattaya know! White people must go—must go!" Others distributed newly printed Black Power leaflets and placards. For a growing number, only Black Power could prevent outrages such as the attempted murder of

Stokely Carmichael (left) with Black Panther Party chairman Bobby Seale.
From Ruth-Marion Baruch and Pirkle Jones, *The Vanguard* (1970). By
permission of Beacon Press.

James Meredith "Power," as Carmichael told King, "is the only thing
respected in this world, and we must get it at any cost."[9]

As the marchers assembled at the state capitol in Jackson for their final rally on June 26, the winds of change, already gusting mightily, approached gale force. King resurrected his dream of the March on
Washington, affirming the notion that someday justice would become a
reality for all Mississippians. Carmichael was more impatient, more
strident. He told the eleven to fifteen thousand people in attendance
that blacks should build a power base so strong that "we will bring
[whites] to their knees every time they mess with us." Afterward, as if
throwing down a symbolic gauntlet, he approached a white SCLC staffer
and shot him between the eyes with a water pistol. The opening salvo of
the Black Power era had been fired.[10]

Although the media made it seem like a revelation, neither Carmichael's slogan nor the principles it represented were wholly new con-
structions. The twenty-five-year-old leader of SNCC claimed that he
had heard the term used in one way or another since he was a child. Indeed, less than a month before Greenwood he and other SNCC militants

had discussed Harlem congressman Adam Clayton Powell's utilization of the Black Power theme in a spring, 1966 Howard University baccalaureate address. Not long thereafter, Willie Ricks tested the effectiveness of "Black Power" at various rallies and returned with glowing accounts of the overwhelmingly positive audience response. "Ricks came back with fantastic reports," Carmichael said. "It's electrifying. The people are going wild." Persuaded that this shortened version of a phrase often used by SNCC workers in Alabama ("power for poor black people") would have great appeal, Carmichael decided to utilize the slogan himself, hoping to "give it a national forum" and force moderates to "take a stand for Black Power."[11]

Even earlier, literary and cultural figures such as Richard Wright, Lerone Bennett, Jr., and Paul Robeson had adapted the term to their own purposes.[12] Malcolm X often laced his speeches with maxims such as "You've got to get some power before you can be yourself" and "power doesn't back up in the face of a smile."[13] Young militants throughout the urban North inscribed the Black Power slogan on riot-scorched ghetto walls long before Greenwood.[14] Certainly, the seeds of Black Power were widely scattered by the time of Carmichael's speech. This is just as it should have been. The modern-day movement could have no single generative spark or individual prime mover. Its essential spirit was the product of generations of black people dealing with powerlessness—and surviving.

Black Mississippians who were well-versed in the Afro-American past could find much that was familiar in Stokely Carmichael's bold oratory. Indeed, both Black Power pluralists and nationalists had many soul mates in earlier eras. Afro-America's recognition of cultural distinctives and its peoples' desire for a greater degree of autonomy was as old as the nation itself. Expressed in various ways, the black self-definition ethic stressed group responsibility, unity, and pride—essential components of a Black Power spirit that would continue to do battle with Anglo-Saxon assumptions of intellectual and cultural superiority into modern times.

Before the Civil War, for example, black Americans worked to develop an empowering sense of group identity by distinguishing us from them—often to startling effect. As they adjusted to the reality of oppression, free blacks determined that it would be wise to "combine, and closely attend to their own particular interest." Conscious of their shared experiences and cultural traits, they formed fraternal, mutual aid, and cooperative organizations to promote black solidarity and aid in racial survival. In militant fashion, their reform conventions made it clear that black people would speak for themselves and fight their own battles, if need be, no matter what the odds. "If we act with our white friends," said one New York group, "the words we utter will be considered theirs, or their echo." While suspecting that some white reformers might prove unworthy of their trust, they nevertheless used the example of Euro-American groups (i.e. the Irish) to promote their own organizational activity. Like good pluralists, such individuals refused to countenance the notion that their "exclusive effort" necessarily separated them from the concerns of the "whole human family."[15]

Others, however, took great pleasure in trumpeting the accomplishments of heroic ancestors (who were said to include the Egyptians, Babylonians, and Phoenicians; Plato, Augustine, and Hannibal) while denigrating their white countrymen's forebears.[16] When black African civilization was "filling the world with amazement", said Henry Highland Garnet, the Anglo-Saxon "abode in caves under ground, either naked or covered with the skins of wild beasts." The most degraded creatures imaginable, these wretched beings made the nighttime "hideous" with savage shouts and darkened European skies with the smoke from their altars of human sacrifice.[17] Yes, there was a great division between us and them that was not to be accounted for by the proslavery rantings of antebellum polygenists, said the early black nationalists. Only a relatively recent loss of power occasioned by European technological advancements and slaveholding greed could account for the African-Americans' present condition as hewers of wood and drawers of water. It was believed that through individual self-affirmation and group self-determination oppressed blacks could regain their lost heritage and once again aspire to greatness as a people.

Prior to the rise of the modern movement, a separatist persuasion was evidenced in many of the alternatives blacks posed to white American exclusivism, discrimination, and violence. Certainly, Afro-America's rejection of the white-dominated antebellum colonization movement did not signal universal disapproval of the notion that black people could improve their lot by joining together to form a separate, independent state. The concept of establishing a powerful black nation outside the United States was formulated prior to the Civil War, most notably by Martin Delany and Henry Highland Garnet. It was reinvigorated during the late nineteenth century by African Methodist Episcopal (AME) Bishop Henry McNeal Turner, and flowered during the 1920s in the pages of Marcus Garvey's Negro World.[18] When Delany proclaimed that "every people should be the originators of their own designs" or Garvey trumpeted "Up you mighty Race! You can accomplish what you will!"

they reminded their people that the idea of a black-sponsored African return began with the Atlantic slave trade. This longing for a national homeland was voiced in the slave songs. It was evident in the folkloric version of black bondsmen who tolerated white oppression as long as they could and then simply rose up and flew back to Africa. In later years, the notion that a pan-African union could free blacks everywhere and for all time could be seen during the 1930s in the outpouring of support for Ethiopia in its struggles with Italy and in the *Chicago Defender*'s championing of the Mau Mau in Kenya some twenty years later. The continuum was unbroken, preserved in the Afro-American dream of a promised land where black people could achieve true nationhood. From Reverend Earl Little of Reynolds, Georgia, to his seventh child, Malcolm, to the Garvey Clubs and Hearts of Africa committees of the early 1960s, the pan-African ideal was passed on, undiminished in its attractive power. As Malcolm X's father once told him, no one knew the exact hour of Africa's redemption, but "It is in the wind. It is coming." Good Garveyites understood that "one day, like a storm, it will be here."[19]

Those of Malcolm X's spiritual heirs who envisioned a more domestic Eden also could find ample historical precedent for their views. Plans to form black colonies west of the Mississippi were drawn up long before the Civil War. A variant of this enthusiasm was seen in the late nineteenth-century resettlement movement to Kansas and Oklahoma. Benjamin Singleton's efforts to form black enclaves in the Plains States earned him the sobriquet "Pap: Moses of the colored exodus" while talk of turning Oklahoma into an all-black state was spurred by the planting of dozens of black towns—certain of which drafted restrictive (no whites) covenants. As grassroots examples of racial solidarity and self-fulfillment, these resettlement projects promoted the ethic of self-determination throughout the southern and border states. Upon visiting one such community, even Booker Washington could see that the effort represented "a dawning race consciousness, a wholesome desire to do something to make the race respected."[20] This concept of creating a black nation within a nation was carried into the twentieth century by Cyril Briggs, founder of the African Blood Brotherhood, by the Forty-Ninth State movement of Chicago lawyer Oscar Brown, and by depression era communists through their "self-determination in the Black Belt" doctrine.[21]

The spirit of modern day revolutionary nationalism also was in evidence prior to the 1960s. During the antebellum years, blacks put slaveholders on notice that Virginia's state motto, "Death to Tyrants," would be adapted to antislavery purposes if the nation's system of racial bondage was not abolished. Henry Highland Garnet's militant slogan, "RATHER DIE FREEMEN, THAN LIVE TO BE SLAVES," was printed or embroidered for framing, gracing parlor walls as far away as Monrovia. Pamphleteer David Walker was so bold as to proclaim that it was no worse to kill an oppressor than "to take a drink of water when thirsty." In their conventions, other Afro-Americans spent countless hours discussing proposals to encourage runaways and to aid slave insurrection movements. As they debated whether or not to instruct their children in "the act of war," some defended the affirmative position on the grounds that physical violence always was justified in self-defense.[22]

Those who were wedded to the notion that there was no hope of redemption without the shedding of blood elevated the insurrectionist to the rank of demigod. Nat Turner, Gabriel Prosser, Joseph Cinqué, Denmark Vesey, Madison Washington, and John Brown were revered because they dared wage unceasing war against tyranny.[23] "If the American revolutionaries had excuse for shedding one drop of blood," said the antebellum militants, "then have the American slaves for making blood to flow 'even unto the horsebridles'."[24] Slave-era revolutionaries, whether free, slave, or radical white, served as a constant reminder of black America's determination to be free, to gain and exercise power. Their actions were part of a collective struggle which became a lasting cultural symbol. Its meaning was clear to all who had experienced oppression. On the eve of the Black Power movement, their legacy was apparent in the words and deeds of Robert Williams and the Deacons for Defense. Vowing to give their all to protect civil rights workers against the attacks of white racists, they vowed to light "the torch of retribution" every time night riders attacked innocent blacks. As Deacon A. Z. Young declared, "If blood is going to be shed, we are going to let it run down Columbia Road—all kinds, both white and black. We are not going to send Negro blood down Columbia all by itself that's for sure."[25] Nat Turner couldn't have been more clear in describing what ultimately might have to be done to end black powerlessness.

Early cultural nationalists conveyed the Black Power sentiment in a somewhat more lyrical, but no less committed fashion. Employing language as a weapon of liberation, they were determined to name themselves and their organizations according to group standards. They demanded to be called "African" or "colored" rather than some slurred variant of the Portuguese os negros. Convinced that they were a black and beautiful people, they dared compare their physical characteristics with whites. It was no contest. By the time white people had been created, said commentator John S. Rock, "nature was pretty well exhausted." The lank-haired, sharp-featured Euro-American was but a pale imitation of nature's crown of creation.[26]

As opportunities for engaging in open displays of creative expression expanded, nineteenth-century Afro-Americans broadcast this spirit of group loyalty throughout black culture. With roots deep in a rich folk heritage, black poets, novelists, and dramatists fought back against those whites who would presume to "*think* for, dictate to, and *know* better what suited colored people, than they knew for themselves." They told it like it was—from a black perspective. The nation's Constitution was "a sepulchre of whited lies," its religion a seedbed of heathenism. The "clanking of chains" made "sounds of strange discord" on Liberty's plains.

> "America, it is to thee,
> Thou boasted land of liberty,"

wrote black separatist poet James M. Whitfield.

> "It is to thee I raise my song,
> Thou land of blood, and crime, and wrong."

By the end of the century, it was clear that the ever-growing variety of black-authored publications would be "a mere introduction to what will henceforth emanate from the pen of colored men and women."[27]

The black cultural output of the early twentieth century proved that Afro-Americans would continue to forward bold counterpoints to the demeaning racial caricatures so deeply embedded in white culture. Pageants celebrating the deeds of "the eldest and strongest of the races of mankind" were staged in the hope of lessening psychological burdens imposed by a theatrical marketplace that was transfixed by comedic blackface imagery.[28] As they rejected the shiftless darkey role that was so popular with white audiences, black creative artists vowed to create a national network of playwrights, actors, musicians, and dancers who could capture the essence of "what it means to be colored in America."[29] Striving for authenticity, the Harlem Renaissance generation looked to the folk tradition and to contemporary issues of black life for their subject matter. They spoke of an end to accommodation and of a new day coming when black people would wield power. Given a more open society, adequate long-term financing, and freedom from coercion, it is conceivable that these determined men and women could have changed white America's perception of black people. This was not to be. But in their spirited rejection of white formulae, their enthusiastic promotion of black cultural distinctives, and their commitment to improving black self-esteem, the Harlem Renaissance artists provided a rich, activist legacy for what would become the Black Arts movement of the sixties.[30]

The New Negro era may have been, as Alain Locke characterized it, "gawky and pimply, indiscreet and over-confident, vainglorious, and irresponsible," but its self-determination ethic was widely influential among pluralists as well as nationalists. Indeed, the DuBoisian notion that Afro-Americans were possessed of a "double-consciousness"—being both black and American at the same instant—has percolated through the years, forming a central theme of modern pluralist thought. For creative artists, double consciousness posed the vexing problem of addressing dual audiences. Like Langston Hughes, most had no desire to "run away spiritually" from their race. But, like James Weldon Johnson, they also found it impossible to "write with total disregard for nine-tenths of the people of the United States." Many hoped that someday the two audiences could be fused. Until then, black artists and writers would serve as agents of change as well as "co-worker[s] in the kingdom of culture."[31]

This heady confidence born of a positive group identity influenced lives and events far beyond the literary community. As DuBois asserted, "Negro blood has a message for the world" and that message had to be conveyed through economics and politics in order for permanent societal change to be effected.[32] Long before the protests of the Black Power era, "Don't Buy Where You Can't Work" and "Buy Black" campaigns fostered economic solidarity throughout urban black America.[33] During World War II, the March on Washington Movement (MOWM) mobilized the black masses in support of increased opportunity in the industrial workplace.[34] By the mid-sixties, Afro-America's determination to mobilize for action could be seen in the political campaigns launched by the Freedom Now party, the Mississippi Freedom Democratic party, and Alabama's Afro-American party. But even here, attempts to make a show of black power could be traced to earlier times. These efforts to educate black communities in the utilization of the established mechanisms for gaining and exercising power were foreshadowed in the work of nineteenth and early twentieth-century organizations such as the National Equal Rights League, the National Protective party of Ohio, the Niagara Movement, and the depression-era National Negro Congress.[35] Like the pluralists of more recent years, it was rare for these groups to promote a strident, inflexible, or permanent black exclusivism. Most of their adherents were not, as MOWM's

A. Philip Randolph noted, "anti-white or anti-Semitic, or anti-Catholic, or anti-foreign, or anti-labor." Instead, they promoted a positive "all Negro and pro-Negro" sentiment designed to encourage blacks to unite, fight for their citizenship rights, and thereby help make America "a moral and spiritual arsenal of democracy."[36]

While it is clear that both the nationalist and pluralist themes had antecedents in the black past, the precise relationship between these disparate outflowings of the empowerment ethic is less well established. Is it possible that certain of the early expressions of Black Power had the form, but not the substance of the latter-day movement? Some comparisons, such as those which can be made between the black student movement of the twenties and sixties, suggest that the type and degree of power sought by activists varies considerably over time, influenced greatly by blacks' acceptance of national goals as watchwords for their own group and by the extent to which they believe the majoritarian society will permit significant expansion of basic civil rights.[37]

Other modes of comparing these historical apples and oranges, such as tracing the attraction of pan-Africanist sentiment through the centuries, emphasize the predominance of continuity over change. This latter approach suggests that unchanging white attitudes of rejection and ridicule are capable of eliciting essentially the same response from Afro-Americans in different eras. Again, we must ask, "Why was there a Black Power movement in the late sixties?"[38]

Most textbook treatments of the Black Power movement have focused on disillusionment and despair as major goads to black activism. Afro-America's shift from civil rights to Black Power has been portrayed as a bleak descent into "pessimism and even cynicism." By the mid-sixties, the high hopes of earlier years had, for most, proven illusionary. It seemed that white society had determined never to concede complete equality to blacks. Their group aspirations thwarted by unemployment, poverty, and white intransigence, urban slum dwellers expressed their isolation and alienation by lashing out in the precipitous manner characteristic of frustrated but functionally powerless masses. Frustrated by the slow pace of progress, they "express[ed] their own sense of futility" by rejecting the integrationist ethic. The Black Revolution, it was said, emerged out of a "gloomy atmosphere" in which black people increasingly regarded themselves as doomed victims of modern-day neocolonialism.[39]

Certainly, historians are correct in noting the factor of despair in their accounts of Black Power's genesis. The nature of prevailing intergroup power relationships makes it imperative that black America's deep-seated frustration be included in any listing of causal factors. By the mid-sixties, many activists were at an intellectual impasse, perplexed and disillusioned. Some had begun to question whether the federal government ever could become an effective promoter and protector of civil equality. Others had lost faith in the ability of black moderates to spur renewal in the northern ghettos. Still others were becoming skeptical of the white liberals' value to the movement in the South. In black communities, both large and small, the pressure of individual and group frustration was building behind a barrier of seemingly insoluble problems. As John A. Williams recognized, both the nation and its black citizens stood at the crossroads on issues of civil rights profession, policy, and practice.

Disillusionment with the political process stemmed from the notion that the federal officials were not doing all that they could to ensure compliance with the directives included in recent civil rights and war on poverty legislation. Skeptics claimed that the Civil Rights Act of 1964 had created little more than the illusion of progress for Afro-Americans. Instances of non-compliance were highlighted by the January 1966 murder of Sammy Younge, a twenty-one-year-old college student and civil rights worker who was shot in the back of the head after demanding to use a whites-only restroom at a Tuskegee, Alabama, gas station.[40] While some activists continued to demand an increased federal commitment to ending open discrimination, others considered the legislation basically unenforceable. New and increasingly sophisticated legal evasions, meaningless tokenism, doomed, half-hearted searches for "qualified" minorities, and the ongoing problem of de facto segregation guaranteed further frustration. Moreover, the Johnson administration's growing commitment to the Southeast Asian war and the uneasiness evidenced within the white liberal camp after the Watts riot seemed to bode ill for increased funding of civil rights enforcement. Certainly, the failure of the Mississippi Freedom Democratic party to win official recognition and the state's delegate votes at the 1964 Democratic National Convention convinced many that nothing of substance could be expected from supposed political friends.[41]

Black activists also found fault with the Voting Rights Act of 1965, a landmark piece of legislation whose passage through Congress was hastened by news coverage of the violent southern response to the SCLC's Selma, Alabama, voting rights campaign.[42] Initially, however, the act was heralded as the most important political civil rights law since the Fifteenth Amendment. Black expectations were raised by the law's provisions for limiting the use of literacy tests as a suffrage qualification and for employing federal examiners and observers to register voters and monitor electoral practices. Indeed, following the law's enactment, the examiners energetically sprang into action and within a year were working in forty counties through the affected states. Southern blacks responded by packing the examiners' offices as soon as they opened each day. On the first anniversary of the law's passage, some 46 percent of adult Afro-Americans could vote in the five Deep South states to which examiners had been assigned, thereby doubling the percentage from the previous year. By 1969, approximately one million blacks had affixed their names to the registration lists. Most had been signed up by local registrars whose willingness to abide by the provisions of the law was matched only by their eagerness to avoid federal intervention in their district. In this begrudging response lay the root of a continuing problem.[43]

The presence of federal officials (or the prospect of their imminent arrival) was needed to spur action at the local level. Too often, said the critics, political considerations hindered the effective deployment of these federal regulators. Try as they might to get "an army of 2,000 federal registrars and marshals" sent to the Black Belt, the advocates of suffrage expansion soon came to understand that Washington had ultimate control of policy decisions in such matters. According to Attorney General Nicholas Katzenbach, there would be no "widespread deployment of an army of Federal examiners." Voluntary compliance was much preferred. Moreover, there was to be no massive government-sponsored effort to assist in carrying out citizenship training and voter education programs. The Justice Department's role would be limited to removing the legal, not the social or psychological obstacles to voting. After learning of these policy decisions, black activists began to wonder if southern conservatives such as Georgia's Richard Russell, chair of the Senate Armed Services Committee, and James Eastland, chair of the Senate Committee on the Judiciary and a plantation owner in Sunflower County, Mississippi, weren't running the show. After all, it seemed more than coincidental that as late as March 1966 there were thirty counties in Mississippi and twenty-nine in Georgia that had not been assigned federal registrars even though less than a quarter of their adult black residents were registered to vote.[44]

To many, passage of the Voting Rights Act was an encouraging but ultimately perplexing development in the ongoing campaign for political equality. The act bolstered black registration and, even as early as 1966, doubled the number of black elected officials throughout the South. But it also reinforced the racial conservatism of white southern politicians and produced a troublesome countermobilization. All too familiar reports circulated of sharecroppers facing eviction because they dared register. In addition, there was reason to believe that both potential voters and newly elected black officials might have cause to fear for their physical well-being. As veteran Mississippi civil rights worker Fannie Lou Hamer noted in 1967, "The only people registered now are the ones who have gone through a living hell to get registered. The first reaction of people when you ask them to register is fear, not only fear for their jobs or their home but fear of physical violence." After the passage of the Voting Rights Act, countywide at-large elections became more common and elective offices suddenly were made appointive. These actions aimed at offsetting any increase in black political power were accompanied by an unprecedented increase in white voter registration across the South which all but outstripped the widely heralded black gains. Here, certainly, was ample justification for a tempering of optimism, if not for a wholesale descent into despair.[45]

Adding to this clouding of the communal spirit was a growing dissatisfaction with the civil rights program favored by black moderates. The movement of the early sixties had spurred unprecedented federal interest in black America's quest to gain equality before the law, but, said critics, its leaders were too eager to claim success. The nonviolent direct action thrust had not purged or reconstructed the black ghetto, which, despite all efforts at reform, seemed to replenish itself with new victims daily. If black Americans celebrated the fact that southern brothers and sisters no longer were forced to take seats in the rear of the bus, they also were well aware that years of marches, speeches and petitions had failed to end de facto segregation in the North. To some, it seemed as if the civil rights establishment had achieved only a series of partial, localized victories, was too easily placated with tokenism, and spent an inordinate amount of energy pandering to the fears of paternalistic white allies. It was felt that the moderates' program could do little to improve the daily lives of the impacted black masses because it had failed to make significant inroads against two key components of black oppression—dependence and powerlessness.[46]

This litany of failures and shortcomings was accompanied by a reexamination (and eventual refutation) of the moderates' goal of societal integration. According to this long-established civil rights ideal, integration would offer blacks full and equal participation in American society. In a just social order dominant and submissive roles no longer would be assigned by race. Dissimilar peoples would banish fear and hatred, learning to accept and love one another. Such was the ideal. The reality, said critics, was that the moderates had been unable to achieve interracial community. Nevertheless, they continued to promote their threadbare ideology without acknowledging its potentially harmful implications. To a frustrated mid-sixties activist, integration appeared to be a synonym for cultural assimilation.

It was believed that a committed integrationist would barter racial identity for a nice house in the suburbs. Hoping to prove themselves to whites, they appeared anxious to part company with less upwardly mobile neighbors. Whenever they did, they solidified the impression that white society's conscienceless, materialist values were superior to their own. Finding it easier to mimic than to change white America, integrationists permitted the myth of the melting pot to obscure black America's colonial status. Certainly, said critics, their own self-hatred was less easily concealed.[47]

According to this view, the integrationists' program led not to liberation or self-determination, but to continued dependency. Barring a reciprocal (and unlikely) movement of middle-class whites to the ghetto, their exodus was certain to deprive the urban poor of talent and leadership. The whole scheme seemed a subterfuge to maintain white supremacy. As "acceptable" blacks were siphoned off into the whites' world, they were encouraged to forget their roots. In this manner, and of its own volition, the storied black vanguard consigned black cultural distinctives to history's dust bin.[48]

Activists joined this critique of integration with a denunciation of nonviolence. Here, again, their frustration stemmed from the moderates' inability to change majoritarian behavior. Although the early-sixties crusade of love and nonviolent direct action had mobilized blacks and had placed important issues before the nation, it had not put an end to white-initiated terrorism. By the middle of the decade, some Afro-Americans were willing to believe white people incapable of love. When it had been proffered by civil rights workers, racists returned hatred. All too often, nonviolent love was unrequited and unrewarded. If this pattern continued, the determinedly nonviolent approach to the expansion of black rights would have to be redirected. The assumption that one's adversaries possessed a modicum of compassion and an incipient sense of justice was an essential component of any doctrine which held that the national conscience could be moved to support federal civil rights initiatives. Increasingly, this seemed a false hope, a sign of black, middle-class naïveté, a dangerous presupposition.[49]

Among those who were searching for a fresh approach to group catharsis and empowerment, the doctrine of nonviolence became stigmatized as little more than a moral exercise. Whites, most assuredly, needed to partake of the doctrine. Blacks, however, were thought to stand in danger of being rendered psychologically impotent by it. For years, Afro-America's professions of love had been mistaken for weakness. As the decade progressed, it became clear to many that the civil rights moderates had failed to recognize this clear connection between their ideological beliefs and the movement's inability to change white behavior whenever actual power was at stake. By transforming nonviolence into a way of life, they were accused of closing the door to all other approaches and, thereby, stigmatizing their people as functionally impotent.[50]

Given the moderates' attachment to traditional views and approaches, it is scarcely surprising that they found themselves skewered by activist rhetoric. Established leaders were said to be enmeshed in a civil rights industry that was bound by middle-class values. To some, they composed a fading generation of pathetic idealists in quest of an impossible American Dream. Others saw them as calcified Uncle Toms who had to be eliminated before real social change could occur. They were modern Booker Washingtons who stood accused of failing to question the controlling values of U.S. society.[51] The NAACP's Roy Wilkins was "a white man who somehow came out the wrong color"; Black Power critic Bayard Rustin a "freak" who was "projected by the press as a leader of black people." Even the hallowed name of Martin Luther King, Jr., was dragged through the dirt. According to black critics, "Reverend Dr. Chickenwing" was more a chump than a champ. His attempt to involve the black masses in the "sham ethic" of passive resistance caused him to act like a fool—perhaps to disguise the fact that he was an informer and agent for "white Intelligence."[52] Collectively, the black civil rights establishment was characterized as an inept collection of "jive-ass leaders" who subconsciously were wedded to the notion that "niggers ain't shit." For a growing number of Afro-Americans the times were proving them to be as irrelevant as their program of integration and nonviolence.[53]

In part, dissatisfaction with black moderates stemmed from the belief that they were controlled by white liberals. To many activists, this non-black component of the civil rights coalition was more than irrelevant. White liberals were "an affliction"—an assortment of aesthetes, do-gooders, and fence-sitters who tended to confuse influence with power. Although lacking in substance and preoccupied with form and technique, they nevertheless sought always to act as power brokers— "great white fathers and mothers" who were willing to lead, but not to follow in the journey down freedom road. Motivated by guilt, they considered themselves color-blind, but this, said critics, was self-deception. Often their creed seemed to amount to little more than a mandate that one black guest be present at every important social function. Normally, they viewed Afro-Americans as victims, problems, or statistics. Seldom were people of color considered true equals—and never as creators of a distinct, viable culture. This paternalism was thought to be rooted in a guilt complex which liberals sought to alleviate by making a moral witness against overt southern bigotry. Supposedly, participation in the movement served as group therapy, making liberal whites feel guiltless and giving meaning to their sterile, middle-class suburban lives.[54]

By mid-decade, even those whites who had rejected mainstream values found it necessary to dodge the spite-filled barbs of disenchanted former allies. College students and other members of the white counterculture were said to be more concerned with fighting for the right to wear a beard and smoke marijuana than with promoting black empowerment. Hippies in particular were criticized for practicing the technique of avoidance rather than confrontation and for attempting to appropriate the cultural argot of black America. In reality, the white counterculture was composed of "suburbanite acne pickers" who held a romanticized view of the urban black lifestyle. Under their tattered, unkempt exteriors they were mirror images of the white middle class. Unlike the poor blacks whose culture they attempted to imitate, all the hippies had to do to reap the advantages of their class was to clean up, clear out their drug-fogged brains, and rejoin the ranks of the economically secure. Surely, said a growing number of black activists, no lasting coalition could be made with such people.[55]

At times it seemed as if not even the return of John Brown could rid the black activists of their suspicion of white motivation and commitment. Marxists, supporters of Students for a Democratic Society (SDS), and other left-leaning political types were accused of forwarding variants of a Eurocentric ideology that contained virtually all of the pitfalls of traditional integrationism. Blacks who adopted the "sterile, Marxist jargon" of the New Left were said to have fallen under the influence of an oversimplified, deceptively false doctrine tailored mainly for white westerners. Such "fad chasers" chanced sacrificing key Afro-American distinctives for the dubious privilege of cozying up to white radicals. For many, neither communism nor socialism spoke to the needs of modern black America. Refusing to admit that racism had become impervious to the social composition of the state, these ideological belief systems seemed incapable of "defin[ing] and giv[ing] life to Blackness." The leftists' analysis of American capitalism was said either to disregard or to distort the cultural factors of black life even as it encouraged the notion that blacks were too inept to lead their own revolution.[56]

Nowhere was the growing black alienation from the white liberal world made more evident than in the SNCC-sponsored Mississippi Summer Projects of 1964–65. Designed to dramatize and, hopefully, to ease the plight of disfranchised, illiterate, poverty-stricken southern blacks, the Freedom Summer program of voter registration, community organization, and educational enrichment was conceptualized as an interracial effort. It was felt that the active participation of large numbers of white volunteers from northern colleges would ensure media coverage, spur financial contributions, and bring new skills, energy, and idealism to the movement. SNCC leaders assumed that Mississippi officials could not easily thwart the will of such a large assemblage. Certainly, national public opinion would not tolerate physical assaults on the offspring of Middle America. Perhaps even the interest of the federal government could be piqued. As SNCC's James Forman noted, it was high time for the nation as a whole to feel the consequences of societal racism. "We could not bring all of white America to Mississippi," he later wrote. "But by bringing in some of its children as volunteer workers, a new consciousness would feed back into the homes of thousands of white Americans as they worried about their sons and daughters confronting 'the jungle of Mississippi.'"[57]

Before journeying south to face the enemy, the students were drilled in the techniques of nonviolence and given a crash course in regional taboos. SNCC staff members said that they should expect the worst—beatings, jailings, shootings. Self-defense workshops and role-playing sessions prepared the new recruits for the cruel verbal and psychological abuse that was certain to be visited upon "damn yankee agitatahs" and "Niggah lovahs." If attacked physically, they were taught to respond by dropping to the ground and assuming the fetal position—"head as close to your knees as possible. Legs together. Girls, keep your skirt pinned under your knees if you're modest." The volunteers were advised not to carry watches, pens, glasses, contact lenses, or more than ten dollars in cash. They were to avoid going out alone, especially after dark; to beware of cars without license tags and police without badges; and to become well attuned to local social etiquette. Profanity, drunkenness, irreligion, women in pants, and interracial dating were to be avoided at all costs.[58]

From all accounts, white Mississippi prepared for the Yankee invasion with equal vigor and attention to detail. Governor Paul Johnson asked for and received approval to increase the state Highway Patrol by two

hundred officers. Public order would be preserved by giving munici-
palities new powers to restrain movements of individuals through
house arrest and to pool police forces and equipment. It became a felony
crime to circulate materials encouraging economic boycotts. These legislative initiatives gave city officials throughout the state increased confidence that they could turn back the assault of these summer soldiers of
the civil rights movement. As Jackson Mayor Allen Thompson boasted
after increasing his police force to 450, stockpiling shotguns, tear gas,
gas masks, and even a 6.5-ton, steel-walled "Thompson Tank," "I think
we can take care of 25,000. They won't have a chance."[59]

The arrival of the volunteers ignited this volatile social tinder. As they
began the slow and often discouraging process of canvassing potential
voters, organizing rallies, and conducting voter registration classes, the
civil rights activists were baited, berated, and brutalized. Crank calls,
bomb threats, and an unrelenting barrage of vicious epithets ("white
nigger," "Jew," "Commie") made the students' lives difficult. They were
detained for investigation of alleged traffic violations, arrested for va-
grancy, and held in "protective custody" by local law enforcement officials. During the first two months of the 1964 Summer Project, SNCC's
communications staff recorded over three hundred arrests, more than
twenty-five bombings of churches and private residences, and dozens of
other incidents in which their workers were shot, beaten, or threatened
with bodily harm.[60]

It is only reasonable to assume that immersion in this steaming
cauldron of hate and violence could have molded the black and white
workers into a potent interracial strike force. But this was not to be. The
vision of an interdependent and mutually supportive civil rights coalition so graphically portrayed in SNCC's logo (a black hand clasping a
white hand superimposed on the map of Mississippi) eventually dis-
solved in backbiting and recrimination. According to black leaders, the
intrusive white presence had caused a number of problems. For example,
because of their skills and training, whites seemed always to gravitate
toward command positions. As leaders, they appeared overly officious—
even bossy. It was feared that these "fly-by-night freedom fighters" were
about to take over the movement. At best, they reinforced traditional
patterns of racial deference and dependence. Their presence in Mississippi was thought to detract from one of the Summer Project's original goals: to develop and strengthen a grass roots freedom movement
that would survive long after the northern visitors had returned to their
college classrooms.[61]

By the fall of 1965, there were those in SNCC who suspected that their white allies were becoming more trouble than they were worth. The students seemed prone to unnecessary risk-taking and their provocative behavior sometimes endangered both themselves and their black co-workers. Moreover, it was believed that some had ulterior motives for joining the movement. Rejected and cast out of their own society, such "misfits," "beatniks," and "leftovers" journeyed South to glorify self, to become martyrs, to act like "big wheels." Harsh feelings such as these contributed to the rise of separatist, Black Power sentiment among blacks active in the Mississippi Summer Projects. By the time of the Mississippi March Against Fear, many would echo the sentiments of SNCC's John Lewis: To be effective in its attempts to liberate black America the movement had to be "black-controlled, dominated, and led."[62]

To attribute the use of this separatist spirit within SNCC to dissatisfaction with the northern volunteers is, however, to reveal only part of the story. Certainly, the failure to create a sympathetic and lasting bond of unity between the black and white civil rights workers was significant. Nevertheless, dwelling on the negative, on this failure in interpersonal relations, obscures the cultural roots of Black Power. In truth, the empowering spirit of blackness which came to characterize the late sixties movement was evident, in embryo, in the Freedom Schools and cultural enrichment programs which operated in Mississippi during the summers of 1964 and 1965.

The Freedom Summer educational thrust was diverse and broad-based. It had to be. Black Mississippians were information-poor. For generations they had been trapped in a conspiracy of silence and avoidance that had denied them accurate information about the world around and beyond them. Their political-awareness quotient was far too low. They needed to learn how to tap available legal and medical assistance resources. Both young and old had to advance in basic literacy and computational skills. Furthermore, these improvements in the area of self-expression had to be accompanied by a quantum jump in the level of group self-awareness and esteem. It was in this latter area that the Freedom Schools were particularly important.

A Freedom School stood for everything that the state's public schools discouraged—academic freedom, intellectual curiosity, diversity of thought. Here, highly motivated black and white teachers were free to modify traditional classroom rules and to develop innovative teaching techniques. No matter what their age, students were encouraged to be creative, to express their ideas openly and without fear, to experiment. They received remedial instruction in mathematics, foreign languages, chemistry, and biology, but their learning experience was much broader than this. It was far more than informational.

For many, the schools were a sort of mental revolution—an unlocking of previously forbidden or hitherto unknown doors. They discussed the prevailing power structure of the Deep South, making direct connections between past and present. A teacher might ask, for example, "Who do you know that is like Joseph Cinqué?" and then follow up with a discussion of more contemporary black "rebels" who dared challenge southern power relationships. In exploring literacy as a means of political expression, some students wrote letters to the editors of local papers, criticizing segregation. Others engaged in role-play, pretending they were congressional supporters of civil rights legislation. Still others explored their own and their family's history, concluding: "This way of livelihood is not much different from slavery."[63]

Like the social sciences, the language and fine arts were employed in the cause of individual and group self-discovery. In the liberating atmosphere of the Freedom School, students sang "We Shall Overcome" in French. They produced mimeographed newspapers and playscripts which revealed that new birth was being given to the self-definition ethic. Like the editors of *Freedom's Journal*, America's first black weekly, the young black Mississippians maintained that for far too long "others have done our speaking for us." Galvanized by this notion, their literary and theatrical productions resonated with pride in themselves, as reflected in the lives of black culture heroes. Visiting performing artists from the Free Southern Theatre and the Mississippi Caravan of Music deepened these feelings as they presented dramatic tableaux of black history and held workshops in folk dancing and African song. For young and old, teacher and student, the Freedom School experience solidified the notion that Afro-Americans needed to appreciate their own culture rather than uncritically to adopt white cultural values. When, for example, teenage civil rights workers in Canton were greeted by a heckler who claimed that they "wouldn't even know what to do with [freedom]" if they had it, they immediately responded: "Well, we are on the road to getting it. When we do, we'll show you all what we'll do with it. Yes, we gonna eat in your restaurant, drive your police cars, vote and everything else." In the minds of many, the "everything else" had come to include, at a minimum, establishing and maintaining cultural parity. This incipient black consciousness both contributed to the rise of the tensions which eventually split black workers from white and anticipated later, more fully developed, expressions of Black Power.[64] If the Mississippi Summer Projects served as models for the organizational efforts of antiwar and women's rights activists, the Freedom Schools can be said to have served as precursors of the Black Studies thrust in education. The employment of cultural forms to invigorate and nourish black pride during the Freedom Summers foreshadowed the "political" utilization of music, art, drama, and literature during the late-sixties, early-seventies heyday of Black Power.

Ultimately it is to the cultural and psychological dimensions of Afro-American life that one must look in order to obtain a satisfactory answer to the question, Why was there a Black Power movement? Yes, frustration and disappointment with the performance of federal officials, black moderates, and white liberals could be found in most black communities at mid-decade. But it was not disillusionment alone that stoked the fires of Black Power. In large measure, the movement was fueled by a psychological antidote to despair that spread a positive, empowering sense of pride throughout black America. As with earlier manifestations of the black self-definition ethic, this liberating spirit often was forwarded through cultural forms and served to ease feelings of discouragement and personal failure.

No torrent of tears occluded the vision of Black Power advocates. They responded to the demands of their times with spirit and vigor—with an irrepressible creative force. This approach to the black condition permitted them to express negative feelings, to excoriate those individuals and institutions seen as promoters of despair. But it also allowed them to build for the future. Eventually, a positive psychological foundation was laid which contributed to a long-term rise in black self-esteem. It was this essentially positive sense of individual and group empowerment that had the greatest impact on black lives in recent years.

During the late sixties and early seventies, Black Power's psychological component most often was referred to as "black consciousness" or "the new blackness." Although defined in many different ways, its core assumptions and directives were as follows:

1. To become conscious of one's blackness was a healthy psychosocial development. It was to make a positive statement about one's worth as a person. By nurturing a "significant sense of self," an individual could hope to become self-reliant, highly motivated, and goal-oriented. For many, this change in adaptive behavior could be likened to one's first sexual encounter or to a religious conversion experience. As the entire range of human emotions was called into play, they would feel "alive for the first time." No longer in doubt as to their worth as human beings, race-conscious blacks felt comfortable in "speaking up, standing tall, and thinking big."[65]

2. This black self-actualization was accompanied by a corresponding questioning and rejection of many normative values forwarded by the majoritarian society. Such disassociative behavior was deemed necessary because assumptions of white superiority were so pervasive. Traditionally, Afro-Americans had received only negative psychological feedback from whites. Throughout American history, people of color had been treated as inferiors and dependents, forced to conform to white expectations and obliged to obey white authority. Their contributions to the nation's life and culture either had been ignored or considered little more than unthinking reactions to white stimuli. They had been denied true personhood. Rejecting this long-term contempt and sociocultural domination, those infused with the new blackness were to engage in assertive behavior. As they distanced themselves from the white world and its harmful psychosocial assumptions, they would strive to shape and master their environment rather than to submit tamely to it.[66]

3. After declaring themselves worthy of critiquing white values, champions of black consciousness were expected to work toward a reorientation of black life. Their mandate was to create new symbols and assumptions which would guide future generations. These were to be drawn largely from the black experience. Traditional color associations would be reversed: black skin color and physical features were to be considered good, not bad characteristics. Black lifestyles and distinctive cultural forms such as religious and musical expression would be affirmed, acclaimed, and elevated in status. In this respect, the new blackness encouraged Afro-Americans to seize control of their own self-image and to validate that image via a wide array of cultural productions. Empowered by black consciousness, they would construct a new, more functional value system emanating from and fully adapted to their unique African-American culture.[67]

4. A thoroughgoing response to this call to "collective manhood" was deemed essential to the acquisition of Black Power. Here, especially, the concept of blackness was shown to be far more than a hypothetical psychological construct. Certainly, it was no more mystical than any other form of therapy designed to serve as a goad to action. To become self-directed, to be assertive, to take pride in heritage was to remove the negative connotations of race which long had served as a constraining psychological and social force. Whites, of course, might still factor supposed racial limitations into their plans for continued societal domination, but black people endowed with black consciousness no longer would play by the old rules. Buoyed by their new, pragmatic philosophy, they would dare to be pro-black—to look, feel, be, and *do* black. As they

progressed in these consciousness-raising efforts, they would be encouraged to know that they were fulfilling an earlier, previously unanswered mandate. It was Malcolm X who had asserted that the basic need of black Americans was not to reevaluate whites (whom they knew all too well), but to seek a reevaluation of *self*. By changing their minds about themselves—by formulating a positive racial identity through self-definition and self-assertion—individual blacks could speed the process of acquiring material manifestations of group-based Black Power.[68]

Exactly how was this life-renewing consciousness acquired? Through what sort of process did Afro-Americans encounter blackness within themselves? Was the path to black consciousness open to all? During the Black Power era, various psychological models were formulated which attempted to trace the "Negro-to-Black conversion experience." Depending upon one's favored model, there were either three, four, or five stages to true blackness.[69]

In stage one, the pre-encounter phase of this identity transformation process, the subject was still a "Negro." Spawned during the slave era, Negroes, by definition, were infused with a thinly disguised self-hatred. Coveting their roles as token ethnics in a predominantly white world, they adopted mainstream values, disguised or disavowed their unique racial characteristics and culture when in the company of lighter-skinned "friends," and constantly sought ever more resplendent material symbols of prestige. They did so in order to relieve the deep, festering wounds their untenable social situation inflicted upon the psyche. Dependent upon external sources for their world view, Negroes referred to blues and jazz as "low-down and dirty," rejected the possibility of a noble African past, and deified white womanhood. The Negro's assumption that the assimilation-integration paradigm was the only acceptable model for race relations led to the charge that such individuals served as a white-controlled fifth column within the black community.

Stage two, the encounter phase, found Negroes questioning received interpretations of the world order. Jolted by a verbal, visual, or personal trauma (the assassination of Martin Luther King, Jr., or an assault by the police), they cautiously began to consider alternative views of the black condition. Before long, they experienced guilt for having abandoned the race in pursuit of an unattainable white acceptance. Then, they became angry. Recognizing the extent of their brainwashing, these newly awakened beings hurled themselves into an obsessive search for an authentic black identity.

As they entered the immersion stage, ex-Negroes underwent a liberation from whiteness and began a corresponding in-depth involvement

with blackness. They "rapped on whitey" to release tension. After "tes-
tifying" about their personal struggle to affirm racial personhood, they
joined cultural and social-action groups. Such contacts would help in ac-
tualizing their developing black identity. Soon, everything of value had
to be relevant to blackness. The white world was negated and shunned—
except when it became the subject of rhetorical outbursts designed to
affirm one's commitment to "the people." Eventually, under the influence of the former Negro's fast-swelling racial pride, the black world was
deified.

It was believed that some who progressed to this stage of the Negro-to-
black conversion process atrophied and went no further. They became
entrapped in a "blacker than thou" mind-set.[70] Determined to "out-
black" their peers, such individuals took great pleasure in putting down
others as Toms or mammies. Their oversimplified, either/or view of appropriate militant behavior was spurred by a desire to convince themselves that their blackness was pure and uncompromising. As a result,
they tended to romanticize and exaggerate their grass roots origins—to
talk loud and strike militant poses. The behavior of such "Super Blacks"
caused them to be charged with abandoning nuts-and-bolts program development for the opportunity to win symbolic victories through "mys-
tic militancy." Some even were suspected of adopting this exaggerated
"pseudoblack" persona for personal gain or to disguise the fact that they
actually were agents provocateurs and informers. In any case, theirs was
a potentially disruptive influence within the movement. It was feared
that the tensions generated by the presence of even a few Super Blacks
could lead to infighting among potential black allies.

In stage four, internalization, the new black militants discovered ways
to leaven rage with reason. They became more secure in their identity
and more receptive to concrete plans to improve the black community
through group effort. Increasingly less defensive in posture, their pro-
black attitudes became ever more expansive. They exhibited new compassion to those who had not yet begun the self-affirmation process.
Their commitment to blackness came to be characterized by ideological
flexibility, psychological openness, and a new self-confidence in interpersonal relationships. These developments allowed them both to re-
negotiate relationships with whites and to recognize the problems
facing other people of color throughout the world. Ex-Negroes who had
traveled this far in the conversion process became role models for all
other blacks. Having triumphed over self-hatred through self-definition,
they possessed the self-restraint necessary to fix their sights on the

larger goal of obtaining power. Since they now sought actual, not simply symbolic power, they were a force to be reckoned with.

During the Black Power era, Stokely Carmichael's belief that, "every Negro is a potential black man" was validated by these psychological conversion models. Because most Afro-Americans experienced similar psychological proscription, the Negro-to-Black conversion experience was open to all. But one had to assume that racial unity was possible. Personal definitions of blackness could not be so narrow as to exclude the possibility of unified action. The belief that this could be accomplished—that widespread identity transformation would bring black America together—buoyed the spirits of Black Power advocates. It was their hope and expectation that the revolutionary psychological process of *becoming* black would initiate a social revolution of great magnitude.[71]

In an important sense, the Negro-to-Black models were both initiator and resultant of the psychological processes they sought to describe. The black psychologists and educators who created these models actively challenged accepted notions of black self hatred and psychological deprivation. These newly articulated critiques on "the culture of poverty" secured their alliance with more overtly "political" Black Power spokespersons and highlighted the relationship of Afro-American culture to militant activism. To their minds, there existed a viable, supportive group culture which, in time of need, could be called upon and placed in the service of psychological liberation.

On the eve of the Black Power revolution, the various social science interpretations of race in American society tended to emphasize one of two dominant themes, or a combination of them.[72] The first stressed the black community's Americanness. In this view the impact of racism upon personality was considered superficial and transitory—subordinate to psychodynamic forces that were presumed to be universal. The Afro-American was, in effect, "a white man in a black skin." Evidencing the degree to which belief in significant group distinctives had fallen into disrepute since the intellectual community's brush with Nazism during World War II, academic supporters of this viewpoint minimized the importance of racial and cultural differences. "The Negro," they asserted, "is only an American, and nothing else. He has no values and culture to guard and protect." Despite occasional talk of psychological identification with Africa, black people were no more African than they were Irish, Danish, or Italian. They were Americans—as was their culture. Their vices and virtues, allegiances and destinies

were shared with other citizens. When such sociocultural variables di-
verged from the mainstream it was assumed that these "peculiarities"
either were exaggerations or distortions of common American traits. It
was held that these aberrant traits were occasioned by white proscription and black lower-class status. With the removal of societal impediments to progress, blacks would realize their highest aspirations. At last
they would be fully assimilated, becoming truly "quintessential Americans."[73]

A second view held that the Afro-American community abounded
with psychological cripples which no nation willingly would seek to
claim as its own. In this view, chronic social injustice had corroded and
damaged the black personality. From their earliest years as slaves of
white masters blacks had been trapped in a "tangle of pathology" which
had left "mutilating marks" of oppression on the Afro-American
psyche. In the harsh environment of plantation slavery, Africans were
"stripped bare . . . psychologically" and socialized to believe that they
were inferior human beings. In this dependency-breeding atmosphere,
black people had every reason to doubt their own self-worth and every
incentive to wallow in shame and self-hatred. As a result, by the time
slavery ended, black Americans had been socialized so thoroughly to
hate both themselves and each other that group cohesion was impossible to obtain.

Minority group culture was said to be of little help in forging black
unity. It was held that the Africans' "aboriginal culture" had been
destroyed by the transatlantic passage. As a substitute, African-
Americans subsisted on "borrowed ideals" and "foreign culture traits."
When joined with the ex-slaves' ever-present sense of shame, this frustrating obsession with whiteness produced an inner desolation that was
basically unchanged into modern times. Indeed, as manifested in the nation's urban ghettoes, the black American's "wretched internal life" had
become an open sore. With its high incidence of juvenile delinquency,
narcotic addiction, homicide, illegitimacy, and female-headed households the poverty-ridden central city served as a veritable social science
laboratory for the study of a variety of chronic, self-perpetuating
pathologies. To many, the black ghetto was proof positive that slavery
and racism had destroyed the Afro-American family, African cultural
forms, black self-esteem, and social cohesion. In this context, reconstruction of urban America necessarily involved the rehabilitation of
the black psyche—an undertaking that was deemed a monumental, if
not impossible task.[74]

Not content to view themselves and their people as either black Anglo-Saxons or case studies in pathology, black social scientists and other critics questioned the assumptions upon which contemporary interpretations of the black psyche were based. Was it plausible, they asked, for proponents of the "white man in a black skin" view to posit such a thoroughgoing homogenization of cultural forms? How could they so easily abstract an individual's lifestyle from the culture which molded it and through which it was expressed? On the other hand, did the clinicians' countertendency to view the Afro-American personality in terms of deficits cause them to overstate the pathological features of black life, thereby neglecting the black community's unique characteristics and strengths? Could the scholars be wrong in assuming that blacks fully and permanently had internalized the hatred whites directed toward them? To be blunt, were their academic studies actually clever attempts to bolster white self-worth by trumpeting middle class culture as the societal norm—and by implication labeling blacks as inferiors? Were the offending social scientists too quick to "blame the victim" by attributing the plight of inner-city blacks to lifestyle deficiencies? And, speaking of "deficiencies," why couldn't Afro-American divergence from the supposed white cultural norm be viewed within a framework of social adaptation rather than one of pathology? Certainly, intense stress might, on occasion, serve to distort psychological functions, but could it not also stimulate healthy coping mechanisms?[75]

It was not long before these questioning voices began to forward the belief that (1) as human beings exercising free will, Afro-Americans had the power to choose how they would view themselves; (2) most blacks hated their social condition far more than they hated themselves or other blacks; (3) there were numerous options other than self-hatred for channeling the frustration and aggression generated by such social conditions; and (4) the "culture of poverty" model had occluded the social scientists' professional vision, permitting them to "forget the cesspool in their own backyard." Indeed, white America's continuing employment of racism to maintain a sense of group unity and importance suggested that self-hate, insecurity, and low self-esteem more often were white than black psychological problems.[76]

Eventually, black social scientists developed what for them was a more satisfactory approach to understanding the Afro-American condition. Owing a great deal to the conceptualizations of Frantz Fanon, the black psychiatrist from Martinique who had joined a career as physician/scholar with that of political militant in the service of the Algerian revolution, they undertook the task of promoting a therapy of collective identity for black America.

Fanon, whose *Les damnés de la terre (The Wretched of the Earth)* was written during the last year of his life and published shortly before he died of leukemia in 1961, provided both revisionist social scientists and "political" Black Power militants with an ideological frame of reference.[77] Although not specifically formulated with regard to the condition of blacks in the United States, Fanon's sociopsychological analysis contained broad implications for "colonized" peoples everywhere. With only slight interpretive readjustment, Fanon's ideas were adapted to the American scene.

Chief among these understandings were that colonialism seldom was content merely to hold a people in its grip, "emptying the native's brain of all form and content." It had to distort, disfigure, and attempt to destroy a people's history and culture. If the colonial rulers succeeded in their unholy scheme, the colonized masses were certain to become slaves of "cultural imposition"—victims of white civilization who readily admitted the inferiority of their own national heritage. Accompanied by serious psycho-affective trauma, the dire resultant would be the creation of a nation of "individuals without an anchor, without a horizon, colorless, stateless, rootless." Fortunately, wrote Fanon, it was possible for the native to thwart the colonizer's will—to be overpowered but not tamed; treated as an inferior but not convinced of one's inferiority. It was the recurring dream of such oppressed peoples to "exchange the role of the quarry for that of the hunter." When the time was ripe, when their adversaries' guard was down, they would employ violence as a cleansing and empowering force.[78]

In a cultural context, such action involved mocking and insulting the colonizers' values—eventually "vomit[ing] them up" in an affirmation of one's own cultural integrity and psychological strength. To Fanon, culture was at the very heart of the freedom struggle. Revolution itself was a cultural undertaking with national consciousness constituting "the most elaborate form of culture." It was his belief that creators of culture had to withdraw from the temptation to mummify their art even as they shunned colonial cooptation. Instead of attaching themselves to abandoned traditions, creative artists were urged to "use the past with the intention of opening the future." They were to throw themselves body, soul, and talent into the national liberation struggle.

With this clarion call to action ringing in their ears, mid-sixties black intellectuals began to speak of Afro-America as an internal colony at war with the forces of cultural degradation and assimilation. They began to create what Fanon called "a literature of combat."[79]

Afro-American psychologists learned both from Fanon and from their immersion in the rapidly changing world in which they lived. They believed that mainstream psychology had contributed to the worldwide domination and subjugation of peoples of color. Indeed, this "scientific colonialism" which arrogantly presumed to know *all* about black self-conception was held to be the white colonizer's "single most powerful tool of oppression." Therefore, their aim was to formulate and establish new definitions, conceptual models, and standards of normative behavior that would be free from the controlling assumptions and values of the dominant culture. Viewing Afro-American distinctives as evidence of a non-pathological "uniqueness," they sought to help blacks gain self-esteem, reach their full human potential, and begin to "master [their] environment by changing it." To spur this process of self-actualization they urged their brothers and sisters to "become black," to ground themselves in the collective identity provided by their unique group history and culture.[80]

As formulated by these champions of "psychic revisionism," black psychology was not derived from the negative aspects of being black in white America, but rather from the positive features of traditional African philosophy. In this view, there existed a remarkably strong cultural connection between the peoples of the African diaspora. West African culture had *not* been totally destroyed by slavery. On the contrary, key components of the African worldview had survived the slave experience. The slaves' enforced isolation in the plantation South had allowed them to retain much of what was termed an "African philosophical orientation."[81]

Among other things, this unique world view posited the divinity (spirituality) of human beings; the essential oneness of humankind with nature and the universe; and the interdependence of Africans worldwide. In stark contrast, the Euro-American world view was said to be shaped by two central anti-humanistic principles: "control over nature" and "survival of the fittest." As a result, whites tended to elevate those aspects of personality that were logical, analytical, sequential, propositional, or cognitive and to suppress those that were emotional, intuitive, holistic, meditative, instinctual, or sensuous. This was unfortunate since these central elements of the black aesthetic were believed to have a built-in therapeutic value. According to the proponents of the new black psychology, only the African approach promoted the "elevation of the total person" and the achievement of optimal mental health.[82]

Inheritors of the diasporic tradition were said to manifest an "emotional chemistry" that was very different from white Americans. This was seen as a reflection of the many basic differences between African and European culture. In this context, traditional West African culture could be viewed as a backdrop to and predictor of Afro-American behavior. To recognize, participate in, and venerate black culture was to have one's spiritual core renewed, to receive effective psychotherapy treatment. By adhering to this culture-based African philosophical orientation, black Americans could draw upon the power of the collective in their struggle to become active agents in shaping the world.[83] For those who accepted the basic teachings of Fanon and the new black psychology, the Negro-to-Black conversion experience became an exercise in the recovery and transmission of psychologically-empowering cultural forms. True black consciousness was thought to be attainable once both the black psyche and black culture were viewed in a positive light and placed in the service of physical and mental freedom.

During the Black Power era, the notion that black culture could play a major role in the militant freedom movement was widely accepted if less than extensively footnoted. Fanon's writings, in particular, were fundamental to the development of Black Power ideology. After *The Wretched of the Earth* was translated into English and published in the United States in 1965, the black psychiatrist was canonized by Afro-American activists. Praising Fanon's analysis of the consciousness and situation of colonized peoples as well as his teaching that the oppressed had to oppose the oppressor in order to "experience themselves as men," Eldridge Cleaver termed *The Wretched of the Earth* "an historical event"—the "Bible" of the black liberation movement. Fellow Black Panther Bobby Seale claimed to have read the book six times, employing it as a guide in distinguishing "jive" cultural nationalists from those militants who correctly would utilize culture in the service of black liberation. SNCC's James Forman adjudged the dissemination and study of Fanon's ideas to be one of the five major causes for the rise of modern black nationalism while Stokely Carmichael revered Fanon as a "Patron Saint." CORE's Roy Innis agreed, lauding his promotion of black values and his willingness to speak out against the psychological aggression of the colonizers.[84]

During the late sixties the name and image of Fanon spread far beyond the leadership elite of the movement. By the end of 1970, his book had sold some 750,000 copies. As Dan Watts, editor of *Liberator* magazine noted: "Every brother on a rooftop can quote Fanon."[85] By adopting variants of his conceptualization, these young militants not only identified with the colonized of the world and affirmed the notion that violence could spur mental catharsis, they also acknowledged that something uniquely their own—their distinctive Afro-American culture—very well might turn out to be the most essential weapon in the struggle for Black Power. At their teacher's urging and in harmony with their own internal muse, they sought to rekindle the flame of black self-definition and thereby break the bonds of Euro-American psychological and cultural domination. Like earlier champions of change, this generation of black activists had grown tired of having outsiders speak for them. Heirs of an important Afro-American intellectual tradition, they found their own voice in and through an empowering group culture.

In the context of Black Power activism, broad-based acceptance of these principles suggests that the movement itself can be conceptualized as a revolt of culture—a contemporary activist manifestation of the long-standing divergence between black and white American cultures; between each group's distinctive "shared way of life." Like the American Revolution or the Civil War, the Black Power movement was as cultural as it was political. It involved both a contest for the control of institutions and a clash of divergent "national" identities. Both the Euro- and Afro-American cultures provided a symbolic basis for group cohesion as well as a stimulus to political mobilization. Since each forwarded a specific set of rules meant to guide human behavior, it can be said that the Black Power years witnessed a spirited conflict over the rules that would be employed to govern black America. Black activists, purporting to represent both themselves and the less vocal members of their constituency, pitted their shared worldview and standards of conduct against those of the colonizers. Seeking self-definition through various types and degrees of separation from white society, they hoped to complete the irrepressible quest for independence in thought and deed that had been thwarted so many times in the past.

That the modern movement burst upon America's consciousness when it did could have been predicted. Most of the preconditions for dissemination and acceptance of an insurgent group consciousness had been met by the midpoint of the sixties. During the civil rights era, black Americans had succeeded in liberating an unprecedented amount of "social space" within which the most fortunate among them could develop a sense of self-worth. As they worked to enlarge this space—to attain "me power," "us power"—they broke with established patterns and began to test various ideologies for personal "fit." Each individual hoped to find a new approach to life that would (1) reveal the origins and define the nature of their oppressed state; (2) justify both individual and group protest against the status quo; (3) provide an inspiring vision of a qualitatively better future; and (4) lead them, finally, to a state of "black consciousness."

In the end, their decision to adopt pluralism over nationalism or focus on economic as opposed to cultural or political issues mattered little. Whatever their ideology or primary area of interest, all Black Power advocates found that their newfound sense of self rested uneasily with inherited cultural definitions and stereotypes. Without fully understanding the processes involved, they were passing from "Negro" to "Black." Along the way, they would discard received definitions of themselves as second-class, inferior human beings. After receiving cultural nourishment they would be prepared to take collective action in support of a wide range of activist initiatives which would reveal the diversity and breadth of the movement.

three

Who Were the "Militants"?

In 1969, Nathan Hare discovered a most novel use for the Black Power slogan. As publisher of *Black Scholar*, he was in Algeria during the summer of that year to report on the First Pan-African Cultural Festival. Like any savvy tourist, he anticipated that the operatives of Algiers' service sector would pick his wallet clean if given half a chance. Certainly, a wayfaring stranger from the States provided a most tempting target for those who would demand large sums for small and imperfectly performed favors. Upon arrival, however, he was relieved to learn that if he greeted taxi drivers with a hearty "pouvoir noir," his anticipated problems would vanish. By proclaiming Black Power solidarity he "could avoid otherwise frequent overcharging, or even obtain a long free ride."[1]

As Hare's Algerian experience suggests, the term Black Power came to have a multitude of uses. To be an effective promoter of group empowerment the concept needed to be both flexible and utilitarian. Black Power had to be malleable enough to appeal to diverse audiences, at different times, in dissimilar contexts. To gain adherents, it had to be linked to practical programs for implementation. If programmatic measures were not developed to give life to the concept, all of the time and effort spent in defining its meaning would have little lasting effect. During the period 1965–75, Black Power advocates created numerous organizations of various sizes, of varying degrees of stability, with different and often conflicting ideological perspectives. This diversity of expression contributed to the movement's rapid expansion. A centralized Black Power bureaucracy might have aided internal communication and promoted efficiency, but it would have done little to spur organizational growth or to inspire deep personal commitment. The decentralized, segmented nature of Black Power allowed for innovation and adaptation to change, minimized the possibility of total burnout or suppression, and facilitated the penetration of the movement into a wide variety of sociocultural niches.[2]

An individual organization's notion of the correct approach to acquiring power was as much a function of time and place as it was of ideology. Whether a group was more attracted to pluralism than nationalism (or vice versa) certainly helped shape the nature of its agenda. But the activists' intended field of operation and the specific problems to be encountered therein were equally influential. Discussions of how to implement Black Power would move in different directions depending on whether they were being held at the Watts Happening Coffee Shop in Los Angeles or at an African Heritage Studies Association convention session. The blueprint for empowerment would not be the same at the Committee for Unified Newark as it was at Detroit's Shrine of the Black Madonna. To understand the Black Power movement it is necessary to know who the militants were, how they organized and expressed themselves, the ideologies and methodologies they employed, and the relationships they had with one another. The organizational structure of the Black Power movement was somewhat ungainly, but it can be fathomed. Militant sentiment was expressed vigorously during this era through groups which formed on college campuses, in factories and prisons, and within the armed forces. Hoping for an increased share of economic, educational, and political control, community groups campaigned on the platform of pluralism. Nationalists created new bodies to promote cultural, revolutionary, and separatist ends. Each formed part of a whole that was grounded in black culture.

Black Power on Campus

Black people have met with as great injustice from
American scholarship as they have from American life.
In fact, colleges and universities have long paved the

way for confusion and ignorance, arrogance and
presumptuousness, violence and bloodshed in black-
white relations.

Sterling Stuckey, 1971

I don't think that honkies should be in anything Black.
The only thing that crackers can do for us is give us the
money and other stuff that we need to do our thing.
Anything else they have, they can keep—their
sympathy, their ideas, and their damn advice.

Larry, Indiana University sophomore

The militants' cultural connection was most clearly evidenced within
the context of American higher education. Initially, however, the cultural aspects of black student activism were overshadowed by the sheer
drama of events taking place on the nation's college campuses. At San
Francisco State College, black students boycotted classes and picketed
classroom buildings. In teams of five and ten they entered lecture halls
to ask students and professors why they weren't supporting the strike.
Others joined raiding parties. Wearing stocking masks, they invaded
campus offices, smashed equipment, and cut telephone wires. Home-
made bombs and numerous small fires plagued security officers. Before
the campus was closed by its president, even salt and pepper shakers
from the cafeteria were being used against the police.[3] Down at the University of Mississippi, Afro-American students assembled in the student union grill, burned a small Confederate flag, and played records by
Nina Simone and B.B. King before marching on the chancellor's house.[4]
Further north, Wisconsin State–Oshkosh students presented their list
of demands and then ransacked the presidential suite. So many arrests
were made that police and sheriff's deputies couldn't handle the volume. Protesters had to be taken to jail in Hertz rental trucks. Eventually,
the board of regents expelled 90 of the 114 black students on campus.[5] At
Cornell, militants seized selected areas of the student union, which
then were designated "black tables." They carried hundreds of books
from library shelves to checkout stations where they abandoned them
as irrelevant. Then, during a Parents' Weekend where some two thousand visitors were scheduled to hear President James A. Perkins deliver
an address entitled "The Stability of the University," 120 black students
yelling "Fire!" routed visitors and employees from the student union.
When their two-day occupation of Willard Straight Hall ended, news
photographers were treated to an unprecedented spectacle. The students
exited the building in military fashion, brandishing rifles and shotguns
which had been smuggled in to thwart a rumored white assault on the

facility.[6] In the face of these campus rebellions, the grafitti which appeared one night on the City College of New York's campus seemed all too ominous. In bold letters, the message read: HONKIES: ATTENTION/YOUR TIME HAS COME. It is understandable that as of May 15, 1969, seventy-two college presidents had resigned their posts.[7]

Not all of the demonstrations resulted in violent confrontations. If disorders at the University of Wisconsin–Madison were of such a magnitude as to require the presence of 2,100 National Guard troops equipped with bayonet-tipped rifles, riot gas, and machine guns, there were many other less violent endings to campus demonstrations. At Vassar College, for example, a 1969 occupation of Main Hall concluded with the sit-in participants leaving behind a list of demands and two bouquets of yellow daisies.[8] This was the Age of Aquarius and the Black Power protesters scarcely could avoid being influenced by the spirit of the times. Indeed, the black activists were well attuned to their times. Their activities disturbed the serenity of college life—often in unique fashion—but, by the late sixties, university communities had become accustomed to student protests. In an important sense, the black students' expressions of rage at "the system" reflected their membership in a vital, militant youth culture that sought self-definition and power for all college-age Americans.

The beginnings of widespread campus unrest is commonly dated from confrontations over free speech at the University of California, Berkeley, in 1964. It was not long, however, before the scope of student concern expanded to include such issues as nuclear testing, problems of the poor, the arms race, university ties with the military-industrial complex, and conscription for the war in Vietnam. Several key values connected protest activities related to each of these targeted areas. Student activists of the mid sixties were decidedly anti-institutional. They distrusted and eschewed involvement with the conventional bureaucratic machinery of their highly technological society. Moreover, their generation was profoundly anti-authoritarian—possessing a strong antipathy toward centralized, unilateral, coercive decision-making. What they valued most highly were expressions of community, egalitarian populism ("power to the people"), and moral purity. Their youthful culture was centered upon the quest for self-expression ("doing your own thing"). Once the demonstrators learned that powerful institutions could be immobilized by expressive acts such as boycotts, sit-ins, and the "liberation" of administration buildings, there was no turning back. Through militant self-expression, they had discovered the secret to student power.[9]

Black collegians were not insensitive to these developments. They saw that mighty universities could be brought to their knees by relatively small cadres of well-organized, deeply dedicated activists. Bearing the imprint of the college-age youth culture, they too were questioning traditional values, testing the assumed authority of institutional elites, and seeking a personal and group identity that would square well with their developing values. Documenting the trend, an American Council on Education study found that 57 percent of all campus protests in 1968–69 involved black students. This high degree of representation is especially remarkable because, at the time, blacks contributed a growing, but still relatively small increment to college attendance statistics. A study conducted by the Urban Research Corporation, for example, found that in the first half of 1969, black students were involved in 51 percent of all protest incidents, yet accounted for less than six percent of the nation's total college enrollment. Afro-American collegians of this generation would have an impact on their institutions that was out of all proportion to their numbers.[10]

What triggered this phenomenon and made an upwardly mobile, but traditionally conservative group so willing to put down their books and join the white campus activists in picking up a bullhorn, placard, or brick? One explanation is that the urban rebellions of the mid-sixties served as a catalyst to black student protest. The long, hot summers of violence in northern ghettos promoted national debate on the nature of discrimination and on the institutional basis of racism. As young blacks entered colleges at a record pace between 1964 and 1970, they carried their generation's understandings and convictions from the streets to the classrooms. At the beginning of this period, there were 234,000 black collegians. Fifty-one percent were enrolled in black colleges. By the end of the decade, their numbers had grown to almost a half million, only 34 percent of whom attended black schools. With larger numbers, it became possible to envision institutional change amidst the ivy-covered halls. Grievances suppressed by earlier generations of students now were stated openly and in a collective fashion. As a result, the targets of the black youth culture's discontent became somewhat more localized than in earlier years. During the early sixties, for example, Afro-American college students were deeply involved in the southern sit-ins and the Freedom Ride movement. Their goals were recognition and enforcement of the constitutional guarantees provided by the fourteenth and fifteenth Amendments. Desegregation in the areas of public accommodations and transportation were special concerns. But by 1968, it was clear that the day now had passed when students would have to leave campus to stage a protest. They had drawn up a new list of priorities with the restrictive policies and discriminatory practices of their immediate environment at the very top. In 1967 and 1968, over 90 percent of sit-in demonstrations instituted by black students occurred on college campuses, not in segregated facilities in neighboring communities.[11]

During the Black Power era, administrators at white universities were charged with seeking to quell societal unrest through the recruitment of "non-traditional" students. It was said that in bringing large numbers of inner-city blacks to white campuses, they hoped to create a greater acceptance of the prevailing social system. An expanded black bourgeoisie would have an active, vested interest in its benefits and thus would serve as a stabilizing force among the urban masses.[12] If such ever was the case, these hopes most certainly were dashed as college presidents, deans, and department heads read through the lists of demands presented to them by menacing, dashiki-clad undergraduates.

The specific grievances of these members of the black youth culture were numerous and varied. They were aired in a highly charged atmosphere of confrontation and attempted intimidation. Demonstration leaders demanded that their concerns be addressed quickly, positively, and in full. As black student spokesperson Robert Henderson threatened when his group of one hundred confronted the University of Massachusetts administration in 1968, "We will expect a yes decision on all of these points by twelve o'clock Monday. If not, we will be back Tuesday with bigger and better things."[13] The protesters' vision of black student power ranged from open admissions for minority group applicants to required sensitivity training for white sorority and fraternity officers; from the hiring of black doctors for the infirmary to increasing the availability of black-oriented food and cosmetics in the student union shops. Typical of these often non-negotiable demands presented to administrators was the thirteen-item agenda compiled by students at Duke University in 1969. During a brief occupation of the campus administration building, the group of approximately thirty demonstrators called for initiation of a Black Studies program controlled by the students; a black dormitory; reinstatement of black students forced to withdraw because of academic difficulties; an increase in the black student population to equal 29 percent by 1973; a black advisor selected by the students; black students admitted solely on the basis of high school records; an end to police harassment; more black representation in the university power structure; reassurance of financial support; an end to the grading system for black students; funding of a black student union;

self-determination of working conditions by non-academic university employees; and total amnesty for those involved in the sit-in.[14] Here, as elsewhere, black students recognized the need to have a say in defining the nature of their education. If knowledge was power, then institutions of higher learning were academic jousting fields upon which key societal power relationships were decided. For the student protesters, greater control over their learning environment was vitally essential to the larger struggle for self-definition and power.

All concerned understood that the demographics of college life would play a central role in determining the outcome of this contest. Those of college age typically were engaged in the process of identity and value formation. They were, noted James Turner, a black student leader at Northwestern University, "going through a thing. We are going through a *rite de passage.*" From the activists' perspective, a basic concern was whether white or black cultural influence would triumph in the battle for the long-term allegiance of black youth. Campus militants hoped that their determined emphasis on "a positive program of blackness . . . on an in-gathering of black people — a focusing of energy, spiritual, cultural, and intellectual" would help their peers at white universities develop and maintain an identity strong enough to counteract the culturally debilitating forces present in white institutions.[15]

It was feared that the failure of the militants' program would mean the continuation of a totally unsatisfactory status quo. Instead of making post-secondary education relevant to minority group students, white universities would continue to "negate their existence and relegate it to trivia."[16] Traditional bourgeois values would be passed down to yet another generation hungering for token jobs within the white establishment. The degree would remain an end in itself, not a means for the transformation of American society. To the committed campus activist, this dire possibility meant that one justifiably might attend a white university to obtain technical training or to learn the jargon of a specific discipline as a "second language," but larger goals always had to remain uppermost in the student's mind. By attending a white university, Afro-Americans would gain a better understanding of majoritarian institutions. The knowledge then could be used in the cause of black liberation—to subvert the American institutional infrastructure and thereby lessen resistance to the broader Black Power quest.[17] By linking matters of education and power in this fashion, student protestors exhibited their belief that a society's institutions of higher learning not only reflect, but are capable of transforming a nation's basic value system.

Student demonstration at Howard University, 1967. From U.S. News & World Report Collection, Library of Congress.

Afro-American students attending black colleges also resisted co-option by bourgeois values. In this case, members of the militant black youth culture felt that the traditional ethics and world view of the black middle class should be rejected on at least two counts. The black bourgeoisie, they said, was elitist and its value system was self-demeaning. Since the black college was a veritable bastion of middle-class mores, it too received harsh criticism. Its "Negro" orientation was determined to be outmoded and in need of drastic alteration. It was a "freak factory" producing black people who sought to escape reality by pretending they were white. Such individuals longed to be accepted—at any cost—by white society. They modeled their world on white cultural norms, becoming all-American in a very perverse sense. Upon graduation, they would be content to fill roles already defined for them by white society.[18] According to student activists, this process of middle class acculturation no longer made any sense. Even white youth were rejecting the values forwarded by their educational institutions. Why should black students remain passive and unquestioning? To the discontented black collegian, the issues were clear. As one student leader bluntly noted in 1967, "Young Negroes don't want a rejected culture. They don't want a used culture any more than they want a used education, a used car or a used white woman."[19]

What they wanted was a sociocultural revolution on their campuses that would restructure the curriculum, relax restrictive student conduct rules, and increase the power of student governments at the expense of Uncle Tom administrators and white trustees. To change the image and focus of the A&M, A&I, and A&T schools—sarcastically referred to as "Athletes and Music, Ignorance, and Tomism" colleges—they defied administrative directives, hanged presidents in effigy, and held trustees hostage during lock-in demonstrations. Like black students on white campuses, they would threaten to use "BURN POWER" if they couldn't get "LEARN POWER."[20]

On both black and white campuses, the central coordinating mechanism for Black Power protests was the black student union. Greatly influenced by the writings of Malcolm X, members of these groups were devoted to both political activism and the promotion of black cultural expression. Members of organizations such as Columbia University's Black Student Congress, City College's Onyx Society, FMO (For Members Only) of Northwestern, and Dillard's Afro-Americans for Progress remembered their fallen spiritual leader by prominently displaying his picture on dormitory walls, spray painting his name on buildings, and even renaming "occupied" campus facilities in his honor. They also held cultural festivals to celebrate his birthday and made him the subject of numerous literary and historical writing projects. Like Malcolm, these students conceptualized their struggle as part of a broad Third World liberation movement. They, too, were colonized—unwillingly indoctrinated into an alien value system by their educational institutions. If one simply substituted "brain drain," "college system," and "student financial aid" for the more familiar terms "diaspora," "plantation," and "tenant farming," the nature of their plight became clear. With these thoughts uppermost in their minds, leaders of the Black Students Organization at Boston's Simmons College expressed a common concern when, in 1968, they accused their school of systematically excluding "all aspects of contemporary, as well as historical, black culture "from campus life.[21]

To counter this subtle cultural enslavement, black student unions monitored classes, initiated their own orientation and tutorial programs, and sponsored campus forums on a variety of issues. Their "Black Awareness Week" activities included "soul" dinners, art exhibits, and African fashion shows. Although their ideological attachments varied, student publications with names like *Mojo, The Faith,*

African World, and *The Colonist* spread the message that black culture was alive and well even in the most hostile of environments. It also was distinctive. "They [white students] are talking about the Beatles," said one black student, "and we are digging James Brown. They are doing dances Harlem was doing five months ago, and we are doing dances Harlem is doing now."[22] To give concrete form to these beliefs and to encourage black solidarity, they fought for separate facilities in which to conduct alternative educational and cultural activities. Black living, dining, and meeting areas were justified on the grounds that Afro-American students could pursue and develop a greater appreciation of their own culture if they were not constantly confronted with an intrusive and self-conscious white presence. According to one San Francisco State student, these independent facilities were imperative if blacks were to survive their contact with mainstream educational institutions. "We must," he asserted, "have the chance to appreciate our own kind and our own culture. And, you can't do this if, every time you turn around you are faced with a room full of 'crackers' "[23] Viewing demands for "Black houses" and Afro-American student centers as no more than reasonable, members of the black student unions denied charges of reverse racism. All they wanted, they said, was a place to get together by themselves, to form a mutually supportive peer group, and to create an environment that would provide relief from the pressures of university life.[24]

Many student activists believed that this type of atmosphere could be found only within a neighboring black community. When black student organizations coined group mottoes such as Stanford's "We are all in this thing together," they meant to include community members in their universe of action and concern. Students' lists of demands to administrators often included projects to aid off-campus residents. According to San Fernando Valley State activist Howard Johnson, this was done so that the rhetoric of black unity could be demonstrated and made relevant in "real world" situations. "We had to take our commitment from the ivy-tower world of academe to the grass roots, where it really counts," he said, "That's where we come from, and where our sisters, brothers, and mothers and fathers still are."[25]

In addition to urging that their universities take a more active role in community affairs by, for example, establishing branch campuses and expanding job opportunities for local residents, the student unions launched their own outreach programs. They took youngsters on field trips, tutored them in reading and math skills, and held classes in black history and culture. Class projects were transformed into canvasses to ascertain community health care and housing needs. Free lunch programs and food pantries were established and administered. By entering into these activities, the students hoped to avoid the experience of many college-educated forebears. They refused to turn their backs upon the black masses. As noted by Harry Edwards, coordinator for the United Black Students of San Jose State College, the time had passed when black college graduates would "flee to Baldwin Hills [a middle class section of Los Angeles] and eat pickles and hors d'oeuvres and watch the riots on color TV."[26] Instead, they sought to make a personal investment in the community, dedicating their skills and resources to its technical and cultural development. In return, black citizens presumably would lend their support to the revolution taking place on campus and throughout society. Certainly, a solid, functioning student-community alliance offered benefits to both groups. The students could help community residents purge themselves of the sociocultural misinformation that they had imbibed all of their lives. On the other hand, continual interaction with local residents would assure the students that they were not straying too far from the nurturing ethic of black community life—that they were remaining close to the very wellspring of Afro-American culture.[27]

If the college-educated were to reject what one Columbia University student flippantly referred to as "the white man's benevolent offer of a thirty-second vice niggership at General Motors," they needed to be strengthened by more than the encouragement of their peers.[28] The situation required that black students be provided with a complete course of study leading to personal and group empowerment. Since one of their chief roles in the Black Power revolution was to help transform American higher education, they had to make sure that their classroom instruction promoted institutional reform. To this end, they actively lobbied for the creation of Black Studies departments and programs. If the black student unions were the chief coordinators of Black Power protests, the academic programs for which they so vigorously campaigned were to be the movement's more formal link to the established university power structure.

Connecting the local citizenry, students, and campus administrators, Black Studies departments would be uniquely positioned to articulate the Black Power ethic. Although employed by an allegedly unenlightened and racist institution, staff members nevertheless could exercise their academic freedom by teaching students to understand and respect the cultural values specific to Afro-America. As a radical assertion of black peoplehood, Black Studies was thought to be capable of striking a telling blow at the intellectual and cultural underpinnings of American racism. The doctrine of Anglo-conformity would be invalidated. Whites no longer would control the context of black intellectual expression by defining the activities and experiences of white westerners as the universal yardstick of human experience. This mind control would end as a new frame of reference was offered to black youth. With this new orientation, blacks themselves could determine both the ends and ultimate beneficiaries of their college education. Strengthened by these initial victories, they would pursue their intellectual offensive against white mythmaking until all Americans recognized the unique contributions of black people to American society.[29]

As they began the process of selling the Black Studies concept to skeptical university administrators, supporters would have been well advised always to speak the same language as the bureaucrats, to address procedural concerns, and, above all, to have a fully developed fallback position if their arguments—or their bluster—failed to convince. But, caution was in short supply during the Black Power years. Whereas the process of implementing change in the university curriculum traditionally moved at a snail's pace, student activists demanded immediate action. Shrillness, confusion over priorities, and the militants' unbending stance muddied the relevant educational issues they raised. As a result, the implementation phase of the Black Studies revolution became a case study in the creation of academic chaos, misunderstanding, and mutual ill will.

College presidents who were concerned that the new departments would be highly politicized and doctrinaire definitely were not relieved to hear Nathan Hare declare that "a black-studies program which is not revolutionary and nationalistic is, accordingly, quite profoundly irrelevant."[30] Department heads who doubted that any such body of knowledge as "Black Studies" actually existed weren't about to change their opinion after reading that students at Cornell were hoping to gain approval of a new course, Physical Education 300C, "Theory and Practice in the Use of Small Arms and Hand-to-Hand Combat." White faculty members who feared that the new programs would coax black students away from traditional disciplines into a field of questionable validity had their worst beliefs confirmed when they scanned curriculum proposals, such as the one prepared by the Black Students' Alliance at the State University of New York at Albany in 1969. Their outline listed the following requirements:

> Mastery of ONE of the following disciplines:
> A) Basic reading knowledge of either Swahili,

Yoruba, Arabic, Spanish, Portuguese, or Chinese.
B) Sufficient mastery of either Akido, Karate,
Gung Fu, Judo, Riflery, or Stick Fighting.[31]

Even black scholars being considered for positions in the programs wondered how much they would have to, in the words of Yale's John Blassingame, "kowtow to the black students."[32]

For their part, campus militants suspected that the basic administrative response to their demands would be a patronizing tokenism—hiring a few powerless, untenured instructors and adding a title or two to the reading lists of courses in existing departments. They referred to these dead-end academic jobs as "assistant niggerships" and thought it foolhardy to expect that the establishment voluntarily would provide blacks with an in-depth education for liberation. To lessen the possibility of disappointment, they inflated their demands far beyond the academy's accustomed bounds of tolerance.[33]

The first principle that they sought to establish was that the departments should be black-controlled and autonomous. Based on past experience, white academicians couldn't be trusted. Although whites continued to pose as experts in the field, their studies seemed biased and misleading. Because of this, they were, according to historian Sterling Stuckey, "about as unpopular among black people as white policemen." Of all those available to teach in the new departments, white faculty members would be the least likely to gain a respectful hearing. In the classroom, they would be an instant anachronism, creating a situation which some likened to making a fox responsible for the safety of the chickens. Therefore, most teachers in the programs necessarily would be black.[34]

Second, although it was understood that the black experience had to be taught by those who had lived it, not even all blacks with earned doctorates would be considered for professorships. Formal educational credentials were for the moment less important than commitment to the principles of the movement. One dedicated community activist was deemed preferable to a whole roomful of toady black Ph.D.'s who spent their lives footnoting "slave-master historians" in "learned" journals.[35]

Third, it was felt that Afro-American control of the educational environment had to extend to the racial mix of the courses themselves. White students either had to be excluded from Black Studies classes or taught in separate sections. The presence of whites, even in small numbers, was said to have a stifling effect on black creativity. With white students present, black instructors would avoid introducing controversial topics. Fearing misinterpretation or misuse of the knowledge gained through classroom interchange, black class members would be inhibited from expressing themselves in an open and honest fashion. In any case, white students were thought to be either so guilt-ridden or so ill-informed about black life and culture that far too much valuable class time would be spent introducing them to subjects about which Afro-Americans already had considerable first-hand knowledge. As one black student at Antioch College wrote in 1969, "Black students have their hands full already, without assuming the extra burdens of white education!" Another complained: "They just waste too much time. Their thing is dialogue. Whites don't care if Black problems are solved or not. They dig intellectualism and discussion . . . So why waste time with honkies." A third added: "I'm tired of being asked how I do my Afro and how I dance."[36]

Finally, the programs had to be grounded in Black Power ideology. Black Studies was to be based on both pedagogical and ideological blackness. It was not to remain impartial in the educational arena. Its mission was to provide young people with a distinct ideological perspective on world affairs. This training would provide a useful counterbalance to the pervasive middle-class particularism of university life. If such training should be interpreted as "political", so be it. According to the Black Studies activists, a truthful observer would admit that American higher education never had been value-free. The modern university was fundamentally political. As a servant of the power structure, it worked to keep the oppressed in their place, to maintain the current power base of society. Its controlling assumptions fit all too comfortably into the prevailing social consensus.[37]

As the debate over Black Studies spread to campuses both large and small after 1966, it became obvious that the final products of the curriculum workshops, summer planning institutes, and dean's meetings were going to please hardly anyone. Many administrators felt that they had been forced to concede more than was proper. They suspected that student demands would continue to escalate even after the new academic programs were in place. They wondered whether *their* campus would become "another Antioch" with an Afro-American Studies Institute that excluded white students and faculty. Would *their* highly prized black faculty resign if forced to integrate class sections? Hadn't one West Coast professor already threatened to do so, claiming that "teaching crackers is like trying to kick your way through a steel door with boots of Jello"?[38] Where would it all end?

Black activists within the academy also were dissatisfied. The new

Afro-American Studies programs appeared to be weak, temporary structures. Many were under-funded. Most were inadequately staffed. As one commentator noted at the time, the first faculty members were assembled from a recruiting pool composed of "social workers, graduate students who have just embarked on their graduate careers, high school teachers, principals, and practically anyone who looks black or has mentioned Negroes in an article, book or seminar paper."[39] Could this ragged assemblage, even if esconced in independent programs and deemed politically correct on Black Power, successfully negotiate the numerous pitfalls of academic life? Would they survive in numbers sufficient to reorient American institutional life? In the end, as one serious-minded Berkeley graduate student asked in 1970, would they prove to their detractors that Black Studies was something more than a "cultural phenomenon which one relates to by parading around in the latest nationalist garb and talking bad"?[40]

The answers to these questions were not immediately forthcoming, but a dramatic solution was proposed: creation of a true Black University. Supporters of the Black University concept believed that dissatisfaction with the new Black Studies programs was inevitable. The student activists, they said, were attempting to avoid the hazards of institutionalization even as they sought greatly increased access to the decision-making powers of their institutions. Ultimately, whether on white or black campuses, they were forced to go through bureaucratic channels for their plans to have any hope to reaching fruition. Conceived and implemented in this fashion, Black Studies was destined to remain under some degree of external control. Realistically, it could not hope to serve as a catalyst for institutional reform. Affirming this belief, one West Coast student group noted: "control is the key word and that is why the Black Studies Department will not fulfill our desires and needs while it exists within a racist institution. We cannot be satisfied with only Black Studies in a white institution, because the Black Studies will not stay Black." The situation most definitely was "funky." In the Black University, things would be different.[41]

While not necessarily hostile to the concept of teaching Black Studies through programs, departments, regional centers, or separate colleges established within existing university structures, promoters of the most elaborate plans for a Black University envisioned creation of an entirely separate institution. The faculty of this new school would be composed largely of "Black Humanists and Specialists in Blackness" although the sciences also would be represented. Sensitive to both the needs and the values of the black community, they would design a curriculum that provided maximum focus on the black experience. At the Black University, black literature would be read aloud, acted out, and discussed in student-author classroom exchanges. Classes in black creative writing, film, dance, art, and drama would be taught by chaired professors such as Aretha Franklin, Ray Charles, Sidney Poitier, and Odetta. Historians, standing "body deep, soul deep" in their own culture would make courses on "Western Civilization" more accurate and far more relevant. Even the social and physical sciences faculty would contribute to this emphasis on value formation by exposing the ethnocentric assumptions which long had controlled the research agendas of their disciplines. In the Black University, Afro-America would redefine itself in its own black image.[42]

Ideally, the Black University would be tuition-free—funded initially by the federal government, a state legislature, or through private foundations. Room and board costs would be defrayed through work-study programs designed to involve students in the local black community. Centralized on-campus housing would encourage a spirit of unity among the student body and between students and faculty. Organized in this manner, the new institution was certain to become a mecca for "together" black professors who had been scattered randomly across the country. Disenchanted with their "affirmative action appointments" in white schools, they would be eager to help build a nationally recognized black institution.[43]

Hopefully, the best of the traditional black college faculty would join them. No longer trapped in an environment where education was treated as little more than a tool for economic advancement in white society, they now could help shift the focus of black education to more worthy ends such as alleviating black poverty and instilling self-love in black people. Even former A & I college administrators might benefit from the change. In the Black University, they neither would have to play Uncle Tom to the board of trustees nor become an Emperor Jones in the eyes of faculty and students. Instead, they would lead in convincing skeptics that there was no animus between higher education and black liberation. Indeed, to its supporters, the Black University was "the brain of the movement, that builds the engine, that puts the movement into motion."[44]

While the Black University was the most elaborate institutional model developed by the proponents of Black Power in the academy, the concept eventually was incorporated into at least two other formats. In urban community colleges and at Atlanta's Institute of the Black World, students, faculty, and administrators worked diligently to strengthen

Swahili class at Howard University. From U.S. News & World Report
Collection, Library of Congress.

the Black Power appeal by promoting the study of Afro-American history and culture. Although not as grand as plans to re-establish the University of Sankore in Timbuktu as the light of the African-American
intellectual world or to outfit a "black fleet of hope" to instruct Third
World peoples in black affairs, these innovative approaches to higher education were no less the products of their times.[45]

During the late sixties, urban community colleges became de facto
Black Universities. While some proponents hoped that a comprehensive
Black University would be located in one of the southern states, others
merely affirmed that it should be situated in a supportive Afro-
American community, North or South. A southern locale might be appropriate if the immediate goal was to transform a historically Negro
college such as Spelman, Fisk, or Howard into a modern instrument of
social change, but if a totally new institution was desired, factors other
than utilization of existing facilities would have to be given greater
weight. For those who believed that a Black University rightfully belonged to the people, there was no more salient notion than that it
should involve the total black community in its educational program. It
should be a "communiversity," where "the campus itself would be the

very sidewalks of the black community."[46] Dependent upon the local citizenry for standards and values, such schools would be far more responsive to local needs than traditional institutions. Grass roots supporters would be repaid through programs designed to expand functional literacy, to upgrade the skills of the underemployed, and to promote black consciousness through cultural enrichment. In utilizing their resources to broaden the educational horizons of the urban poor, these alternative educational structures would be encouraging a bootstraps effort to rebuild black America.[47]

Believers in the notion that "the college *is* the community" pointed with pride to the development of institutions such as Malcolm X College of Chicago; Medgar Evers College, a branch of the City University of New York; the Federal City College of Washington, D.C.; Malcolm X Liberation University, located in Durham, North Carolina; and Nairobi College, East Palo Alto, California. Although not all schools of this type were autonomous, most were conceptualized as academic centers for "nation-building." According to Charles G. Hurst, Jr., president of Malcolm X College, each center would "serve as a catalytic agent to synthesize the varied components of the community into a viable force for liberation." Sometimes this process involved totally reorienting young people who had been turned off by the public schools. Malcolm X College, for example, operated a "street academy" for high school dropouts, a work-study program for parolees, and a counseling center for drug addicts. It also employed legal assistants to keep trouble-prone students in the classrooms. Said Hurst: "We've got students bouncing in and out of jail like Ping Pong balls. But I've yet to see a single charge stand up against them."[48]

When in class, students charted their scholastic progress against uniquely focused academic goals. Durham's Liberation University divided its course of study into two approximately year-long sections. The first concentrated on ideological, historical, and cultural topics while the second provided training in food science, architecture, health care, and other vocational skills. In this fashion, students were provided with both a functional black ideology and the expertise needed to become economically self-reliant.[49] At Nairobi College, which had its main office in a shopping center and held classes in churches, homes, and even at a branch office of the Bank of America, each full-time student was required to work on community projects four hours daily. In addition to serving as teacher aides in public schools, assisting in the community health center, or providing legal aid counseling, students immersed themselves in a curriculum that mixed the routine and the unique. The communications sequence, for example, included public speaking, Black English, Shakespeare, and a course comparing African, Greek, Latin and Near Eastern mythologies.[50]

As one college official noted in 1971, although certain courses might be vocational or traditional in orientation, faculty, students, and administrators were determined to make these schools "100 percent black in thinking."[51] To this end, the red, black, and green flag of the black liberation movement was raised over campuses daily. Black music and culture festivals were held to educate and inspire as well as to entertain. A pantheon of past culture heroes graced building walls. Their words were highlighted in college catalogues and pondered during academic forums. At Malcolm X College, even the fallen Muslim leader's shiny black Oldsmobile was placed in the service of racial awareness and pride—exhibited like a treasured work of art within one glass-walled hallway. If, as a critic claimed, Harvard, Yale and the various other "freak factories" had "ruint more good niggers than had whiskey," these culture and community-oriented schools would give black America a new perspective on the possibilities inherent in post-secondary education.[52]

The Black University ideal also was alive and well at the Institute of the Black World (IBW) during the late sixties. Originally, the institute was a component of Atlanta's Martin Luther King, Jr. Memorial Center. Its genesis was closely tied to the controversy surrounding the rise of the Black Studies movement. As Coretta Scott King noted at the time of its founding in 1969, "the whole point of the institute is that black studies just burst onto the national scene. Somebody had to take the responsibility of saying, 'Now, let's get together and sit down and talk about it and try to decide what we're really trying to do.'"[53] Eventually an autonomous operation with offices and seminar rooms located in the former home of W.E.B. DuBois, the Institute aspired to become, in the words of its director, Vincent Harding, "the major black educational creation of this generation."[54]

Faced with this challenge, Harding inaugurated an ambitious program of advanced research, training, and evaluation. Historical studies, social policy analysis, and development of a black aesthetic in the creative arts were encouraged. A publishing program was launched. Staff members served as consultants to Afro-American Studies programs and sponsored workshops for program directors. A national network of IBW research fellows and associates was formed to collaborate on research projects, to aid in the evaluation of Black Studies programs, and to help with fundraising. New teaching methods and materials were tested. Faculty-Student exchanges were established with both black and white colleges. Each of these activities was informed by the notion that the development of Black Studies logically was a black people's task. While some saw the Institute as a black "think tank," others referred to it somewhat less charitably as the "Black Studies Vatican." Whatever their initial impression of the institute, few could deny that the infant discipline needed better definition and further refinement. The IBW's staff and associates believed that their "experiment with scholarship in the context of struggle" would aid measurably in this task. Its existence was additional proof that institutionalized Black Power would conform to no single pattern of expression or development. Instead, it adapted existing institutional forms to the needs of the black liberation movement.[55]

Again and again, as white universities and traditional black colleges experienced student protests (and subsequent curriculum revisions), the concept of a Black University was modified to meet local circumstances. Contemporaries noted that it existed on street corners, in narcotic and alcohol treatment facilities, within liberation schools, at the meetings of community theatre and political action groups, and "within the minds of all Black people."[56] The Black University could be seen in embryo at Cornell's Africana Studies and Research Center, at San Diego's Third College, and on the campus of a re-energized, post-1968 Howard University.[57] If a basic part of this Black Power institution's mission was to challenge the prevailing Euro-American world view while helping young people develop a better appreciation of their own culture, it could be said that the Black University existed wherever black people played a major role in determining educational policy.

While the programmatic measures adopted by the advocates of Black Power in higher education were important steps toward black self-definition and empowerment, the movement could not be contained within campus boundaries. The militants noted that social reform movements in other countries had been sparked by student discontent, but had not been limited to educational issues. Instead, a student vanguard took the revolution home, encouraging parents and other relatives to join in politicizing their local communities.[58] Members of the black American youth culture sought to do the same. They would transmit their values across the generation gap, spreading the Black Power message beyond the academy to the real world. It was there that the vast majority of their age cadre lived and could serve as allies in the cause of restructuring American institutional life.

Black Power in Sports

White people seem to think we're animals. I want
people to know we're not animals, not inferior animals,
like cats and rats. They think we're some sort of show
horse. They think we can perform and they will throw
us some peanuts and say, "Good boy, good boy."

John Carlos, 1968

Insensitive professors and hidebound administrators had their counterparts in the world of big-time sports. During the Black Power era, these
individuals were assailed by members of the college-age youth culture
and their equally militant, if somewhat more senior, allies. Black activists throughout society recognized that both amateur and professional
sports had become important forms of leisure time entertainment.
Sports was big business—a veritable industry founded on muscles,
sweat, pom-poms, and wide-angle lenses. By inventing new and ever
more spectacular media events, the sports-entertainment industry had
the wherewithal to crown and dethrone numerous culture heroes. According to black critics, this arrangement was corrupt. The power relationships were skewed. In most areas of the sporting world, whites
served as kingmakers, blacks as gladiators. It was believed that only
Black Power could improve matters.

The expressed grievances of America's black athletes had multiplied
in proportion to their visibility on the national sports scene. By 1968,
approximately one quarter of all major league baseball players, one third
of professional football players, and slightly more than one-half of all
professional basketball players were Afro-Americans. Within their
ranks stood many of the most prominent and handsomely compensated
athletes in sport. But, while active participation was far preferable to the
exclusion and open hostility of earlier years, black athletes continued to
find fault with the system.

In professional sports, the most glaring insufficiency was to be found
in the managerial ranks. Bill Russell of basketball's Boston Celtics stood
alone. No other black athlete managed a big league team. Moreover, em-
barrassingly few were in training for top jobs. When Dallas met Green
Bay in the 1967 National Football League title game, there were 16 black
players among the 44 starters, but all 13 coaches on the sidelines were
white. Across the league, black assistant coaches were too few in number even to get up a good poker game. What accounted for this skewed
representation? According to NFL running back John Henry Johnson, an
adherance to pejorative cultural stereotypes was at the root of the problem. "It's bad when you give a business twelve, thirteen years of your

life, and then are given no consideration for a job afterward," he lamented, "They've still got the stereotype of the Negro ballplayer."[59]
Supposedly, blacks were fleet of foot, but slow of mind. They folded under pressure. They couldn't motivate white players. Afro-Americans
were to be the entertainers, not the producers or directors of big-time
sports.

Participation without power also was evident at the college level.
Black athletes complained about false recruiting promises, the absence
of effective role models on the coaching staff, and what seemed to be the
preferential treatment accorded white players in terms of media attention. Even after being assigned to demeaning "gut" courses, relatively
few black athletes graduated within four years. Many never graduated at
all. Instead, when age or injury impaired their athletic eligibility, only
the poverty of urban ghetto life beckoned.[60] When asked what he had
received from four years of scholarship athletics at various colleges,
Percy Harris, a coach at Chicago's DuSable High School, spoke for many
when he mused: "Well, let's see. At the University of New Mexico I got a
sweater. At Cameron State College in Oklahoma I got a blanket. At
Southwestern State I got a jacket and a blanket."[61]

During the Black Power era, these and other hurts were articulated
with a vengeance. Influenced by the spirit of the times, militant athletes
made clear their discontent with those who would celebrate—and
market—the Afro-Americans' physical prowess while refusing to tap
their full human potential. The organized effort to boycott the 1968
Mexico City Olympic Games represented, in microcosm, the militants'
attempt to overturn this exploitative system. College-age participants
in the boycott campaign recognized that when separated from campus
demonstrations and violence, issues of educational reform seldom generated headlines. By linking the Olympics with institutionalized racism, they drew considerable attention to the Black Power movement in
the real world beyond the campus.

The Olympic boycott movement was regarded by the media as the
brainchild of Harry Edwards, a black, 25-year-old assistant professor of
sociology at California's virtually all-white San Jose State College. Although the flamboyant Edwards' contributions were essential to the
1968 campaign, neither his expression of discontent with the athletic
status quo nor his technique of withholding services was without precedent. A black boycott of the 1960 Olympics had been suggested as one
way of protesting the treatment of civil rights workers by southern police. Four years later, activist comedian Dick Gregory and 1948 gold
medalist Mal Whitfield, among others, proposed a similar action at the

Tokyo games if black Americans were not guaranteed "full and equal rights as first-class citizens."[62] In the summer of 1967, the more than 1,100 delegates to the First National Conference on Black Power adopted a resolution calling for boycotts of international Olympic competition and of professional boxing. Responding to the treatment of Muhammad Ali following the heavyweight champion's refusal to be drafted into the army, the Newark conference delegates also supported boycotting the products of companies that sponsored commercial boxing matches.[63]

By 1968 both professional and college-level athletes had discovered the utility of this approach. For example, the 1967 American Football League all-star game almost became a non-event when black players refused to play in New Orleans because several had been denied entrance to certain of the local social clubs. Disaster was averted only when the league commissioner succeeded in moving the game out of the city. At the University of California, the demand that a black member of the basketball team trim his Afro-style hair sparked a protest that led to the resignation of both the coach and the school's athletic director. Disgruntled football players at the University of Kansas boycotted spring practice in order to force the integration of the pom-pom squad. University of Texas-El Paso trackmen refused to compete against Brigham Young. In East Lansing, an assistant coach's comment that the assassination of Martin Luther King, Jr. "doesn't have anything to do with practice" inspired a threat by black athletes to pass up the year's sports competition at Michigan State altogether. The mass confusion surrounding these and other campus confrontations made relevant Harry Edwards' claim that, even though given sufficient warning, the American sports establishment was "as unprepared for the revolt of the black athlete as the Virginians had been for Nat Turner."[64]

Edwards did his best to warn of the impending conflict over the Olympics. During the fall semester of 1967, the former San Jose State basketball captain and track and field star presented a list of grievances to the university's president. Speaking for fifty-nine of the campus's two hundred Afro-American students, he demanded that the administration investigate a series of indignities suffered by the school's black athletes both on and off campus. If immediate action was not taken, Edwards and his supporters threatened to "physically interfere" with the playing of the San Jose State–Texas-El Paso football game the following Saturday. President Robert D. Clark promptly called off the event, sparking a statewide debate. Governor Ronald Reagan termed Clark's unprecedented action an "appeasement of lawbreakers" and declared Edwards unfit to

Harry Edwards. From his book *The Revolt of the Black Athlete* (1969). By permission of Dr. Harry Edwards.

hold a faculty position. State Superintendent of Education Max Rafferty fumed: "If I had to ask the President to call in the whole Marine Corps, that game would have been played!" In response, Edwards dismissed Reagan as "a petrified pig, unfit to govern" and said that he and his group would have burned the stadium to the ground if the game hadn't been cancelled.[65]

Early in 1968, Edwards achieved a second major victory when he persuaded scores of black athletes to withdraw from an indoor track meet sponsored by the all-white New York Athletic Club. Again, threats of violence were employed. When, for example, boycott supporters learned that Jim Hines, a world-record-holding sprinter from Texas still planned to compete, Edwards warned: "I hear he wants to play pro football. Some cats in Texas have personally said they'd fix it so he'd be on sticks if he's crazy enough to run in that meet." Eventually, Hines withdrew, hundreds demonstrated outside Madison Square Garden on the night of the event (Edwards claimed more than twenty thousand filled the streets), and fewer than a dozen blacks entered the competition.[66]

The actual organizational infrastructure of the Olympic boycott movement began to fall into place at a black youth conference held in the meeting rooms of Los Angeles' Second Baptist Church on Thanksgiving day 1967. The theme of the conference was "Liberation is coming from a black thing" and, most appropriately, one of the workshops focused on the question of black participation in the upcoming games. About fifty of the two-hundred delegates were college athletes. Following their deliberations, the workshop participants emerged through a protective gauntlet of fifty shaven-headed security guards from the west coast cultural nationalist group, US. Harry Edwards then presented white reporters—who had been barred from the sessions—with the rationale behind the new Olympic Project for Human Rights. For years, he noted, black athletes had been major contributors to the success of their national team. Despite these selfless efforts, they continued to experience discrimination. The boycott supporters weren't purposely banding together to "lose" the Olympics for the United States, they simply, but firmly, were saying that it was time for black athletes to stand up for themselves and refuse to be "utilized as performing animals for a little extra dog food."[67]

In subsequent months, Edwards illustrated his case for black empowerment with gripping vignettes drawn from memories of an impoverished boyhood in East St. Louis. He told of being abandoned by his mother at age eight, of living on beans and spaghetti, and drinking boiled drainage-ditch water. Lacking indoor plumbing, he stayed in high school only because it was the only way he could get a hot shower. Too poor to afford dental care, he pulled out his own rotted teeth. He recalled that some of his peers had frozen to death in their ramshackle shacks with paneless windows and outdoor plumbing. Others, like himself, were jailed for juvenile offenses which they hadn't committed.[68]

And how did these youthful experiences relate to a proposed boycott of the Olympic Games? To Edwards, the relationship was clear. Supporters of the Olympic Project weren't sacrificing their opportunity to win gold medals simply to end their own exploitation. They also were hoping to dramatize and protest the plight of their nonathletic brothers and sisters. After all, he asked, "What value is it to a black man to win a medal if he returns to the hell of Harlem?"[69] The boycotters realized that, for many Americans, sports had become a type of popular culture religion. On weekends between 1:00 and 6:00 P.M. a substantial portion of the country either was in a stadium or in front of a television set tuned to a sporting event. Edwards sought to reach these people, to affect them, to wake them up to the black situation. As he noted in the spring of 1968, "If we can arouse wide publicity by refusing to play Whitey's game, then perhaps those ditch-water drinkers will be remembered."[70]

Self-definition, dignity, and power for every Afro-American in every sector of society was the ultimate concern.

Specific demands made by the leaders of the Olympic Project included expulsion of the International Olympic Committee's "racist" president Avery Brundage; appointment of a black member to the U.S. Olympic Committee (USOC) and an additional black coach to the U.S. team; a ban on competition between Americans and teams from apartheid states such as South Africa and Rhodesia; restoration of Muhammad Ali's heavyweight title; and desegregation of the New York Athletic Club.[71] Initially, these suggested reforms garnered remarkably broad-based support. Following a December 1967 meeting in New York City, Martin Luther King, Jr., of the SCLC, and CORE's Floyd McKissick agreed to serve as advisors to the project. Early in 1968, H. Rap Brown, chairperson of SNCC, pledged the support of his organization. Speaking at a February rally in Oakland, SNCC and Black Panther leader Stokely Carmichael referred to the Olympics as "that white nonsense" and claimed that no black athlete "with any dignity" would go to Mexico City. Support also came from US's Ron Karenga and from scores of lesser-known black activists.[72]

Despite the enthusiasm generated by these endorsements, it was obvious to all that the boycott movement faced a number of significant obstacles. Brundage, a wealthy, 80-year-old, retired engineering consultant who once was quoted as saying he would put his exclusive Santa Barbara Country club up for sale before letting "niggers and kikes" become members, had been associated with the Olympics for 50 years. He was firmly entrenched within its power structure. Moreover, Brundage was placed on the defensive by Edwards' charges of racism. "You can quote me on this" he told one reporter, "I think there should be a qualified Negro on the USOC Board. I think Jesse Owens is a fine boy and might make a good representative. But, you must remember that all must be done according to rules and regulations." The elder statesman of the Olympic movement dismissed Edwards' followers as misguided young people who were "being badly misadvised."[73]

Less polite opposition surfaced elsewhere. Payton Jordan, the U.S. Olympic track coach who explained that his Stanford University team included no black scholarship holders because making a special effort to recruit "colored boys" would discriminate against whites, called Edwards a "commie" and offered to pay his plane fare to Russia. "It's too bad," he lamented, "that the liberal loudmouth gets all the attention, and the person who speaks rationally is not heard."[74]

Encouraged by newspaper headlines which screamed "Negro

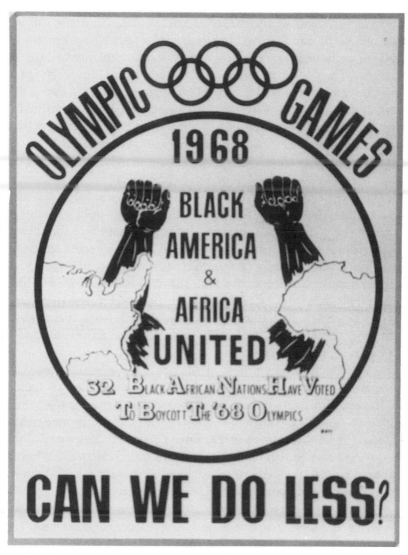

Olympic Project for Human Rights poster. From Harry Edwards, *The Revolt of the Black Athlete* (1969). By permission of Dr. Harry Edwards.

Hothead Threatens Games Boycott," opponents of the movement eventually descended fully into the gutter. Edwards' apartment was plastered with eggs and tomatoes. Sewage was dumped onto the seats of his car and the letters "KKK" scratched into the paint. Returning home late one evening, he found his living room and kitchen splattered with blood and dog hair. An intruder had used an ornamental machete to kill his pet terrier and peekapoo, scattering their remains about the neighborhood.[75]

Soon, hate mail and death threats began pouring into the Olympic Project offices. "Dear Traitor," began one. "I'd rather have our country finish last, without you, than first with you." Others mocked the boycott effort: "Thanks for pulling out of the Olympic Games. Now I can again be interested in our U.S. team. I quit being interested in watching animals like Negroes go through their paces." Still others vilified the boycott proponents and expressed the hope that they would "get [their] bloody heads bashed in."[76] Finally, in what must have been the ultimate insult, bribes of more than $125,000 were offered to Edwards if he would disavow the movement and call off the boycott.[77]

Even before the Olympic trials began, it was apparent that such incidents had taken their toll. Believing that their cause would be harmed by the appearance of disunity, some athletes argued that there should be no boycott without the full participation of all blacks selected to the U.S. team. When it was virtually certain that there was a significant division within their ranks, an alternative to the boycott was developed: athletes could compete, but would wear black armbands and refuse to participate in victory celebrations. Later it was agreed that all participants should protest in their own ways, preferably focusing their actions around the victory stand ceremonies.[78]

Thus, the Black Power protest at Mexico City was manifested in a somewhat different fashion than originally planned. On 16 October 1968, Tommie Smith and John Carlos, two sprinters from San Jose State, mounted the awards platform to receive their gold and bronze medals. Both were shoeless and wore black, knee-length stockings and a black glove on one hand. Smith had a black scarf around his neck. When the band began to play the American national anthem, they sank chin to chest—seemingly to avoid looking at their country's flag. At the same time, their gloved fists shot skyward. Later, in an interview with Howard Cosell, Smith explained the symbolism of their actions. Their raised arms stood for the power and unity of black America. The black socks with no shoes symbolized the poverty that afflicted their black countrymen and women. Black pride was represented in Smith's scarf while the gesture of bowed heads was a remembrance of those like King and Malcolm X who had perished in the black liberation struggle.[79]

Symbolic acts were neither appreciated nor tolerated by Avery Brundage and the IOC. Prior to the opening of the Games, he had warned all competitors that no political demonstrations would be permitted. As a result, the U.S. Olympic Committee moved quickly to suspend Smith and Carlos, ordering them to leave U.S. quarters in the Olympic Village. But this did not end the Olympic Project protest. Following the expulsion of Smith and Carlos, all three U.S. medalists in the 400-meter dash wore black berets on the victory stand, avoiding censure by removing them for the playing of the national anthem. The world-record-breaking 1,600-meter relay team wore black berets and gave a clenched-fist salute. Broad jumpers Bob Beamon and Ralph Boston stood shoeless, wearing long black socks to protest both the black condition in America and the treatment of their teammates. In accepting her gold medal for anchoring the women's 400-meter relay team, Wyomia Tyus announced that their victory was being dedicated to the two San Jose State athletes.[80]

Harry Edwards had harsh words for those who refused to participate in the Olympic protest. Prior to the Games, he labeled them cop-outs—members of "a controlled generation." His office at San Jose State even had a "Traitor (Negro) Of The Week" poster upon which he displayed pictures of former Olympians such as Jesse Owens and Rafer Johnson who had declined to join the Project. Nevertheless, the boycott organizer recognized that the problem was more than generational. It was rooted in the pervasive, compelling influence of the cultural forces which socialized all Americans and which gave them their understandings of the relationship of sports to society. He believed that one of the greatest obstacles to the realization of his Black Power agenda had been Afro-America's own "highly illusionary perspective on sports." According to Edwards, white America had a firm headlock on blacks in the sports arena. Black Americans had been brainwashed so long and so completely about sports' supposedly beneficent role in their lives that the very idea of using athletics as a forum for protest seemed mystifying to some, and criminal or treasonous to others. Most, he said, refused to believe that big-time sports had become a "political and cultural malignancy" whose power and influence inhibited the personal and institutional development of black America.[81]

In the end, had any good come from the black activists' personal sacrifice? Was their campaign worth the effort? It is likely that during times of reflection, Edwards and his allies pondered such questions. Despite many painful memories, they must have been encouraged when they recalled the young people whose perspectives had been altered by their contact with the Olympic Project. These men and women, as well as many others throughout the land, now knew of the game plan constructed by sports' kingmakers, how it operated, and where its weaknesses lay. They also had come to recognize the importance of sports both as entertainment and as a shaper of personal and societal values. Most of all, through the Olympic Project, many had become transformed, empowered individuals. On the eve of the Mexico City Games, boycott spokesperson Lee Evans described the effects of this transformation. "A few years ago," he told a journalist, "I didn't know what was happening. My white junior college coach used to tell colored boy jokes and I'd laugh. Now I'd kick his ass."[82] The Olympic boycott struck a nerve, rudely informing both white and black alike that the Black Power movement would not be confined to matters of politics or education, but would percolate throughout all areas of American social and cultural life.

Black Power and Labor

> DARE TO FIGHT! DARE TO WIN!
> Fight, Fail, Fight again, Fail again—Fight on to Victory!
> Long Live Black People in This Racist Land! Death to
> Their Enemies! Long Live the Heroic Black Workers
> Struggle!
> Dodge Revolutionary Union Movement, 1968

By the late sixties, the athletes' belief that societal kingmakers had to be dethroned was taken up and applied to the larger world of work. During the Black Power era, black labor not only raised its gloved fist in protest, it threw down the gauntlet. Both the corporations for whom they worked and the unions which purportedly represented their interests felt the pressure to alter prevailing power relationships. As a result, the labor movement's traditional rallying song, "Solidarity," took on new meaning for all concerned.

New independent black unions and black caucuses within established unions expressed their members' concerns in dramatic fashion. In 1967, for example, 500 black workers at the Ford plant in Mahwah, New Jersey, shut down production for three days after a foreman called a production worker a "black bastard." Although the United Auto Workers Union (UAW) urged them to return to work, they stayed out until the foreman was removed from the plant. Following this wildcat strike, the United Black Brothers of Mahwah Ford was organized and began a campaign to eliminate all supervisors who were "diseased with racial bigotry."[83] Early the next year in Chicago, members of the Concerned Transit Workers caucus challenged the leadership of their AFL-CIO-affiliated local. Although about 72 percent of the city's 6,800 bus drivers were Afro-Americans, all top officers and 22 of 26 executive board members of Amalgamated Transit Union's Division 241 were white. Feeling that "this is nothing different than the old plantation system," blacks focused their protest on a union rule allowing pensioners (a nearly all-white group) to vote in union elections. Frustrated in this reform attempt, they initiated a series of walkouts—one of which was timed to coincide with the 1968 Democratic National Convention. More than 140 drivers were suspended and 42 were fired for their disruptive actions.[84] Elsewhere, militant workers leafletted at factory gates, picketed convention halls and disrupted production lines. Although specific issues differed depending upon whether one's affiliation was with the United Community Construction Workers of Boston, the Maryland Freedom Union, or the American Federation of Teachers (AFT) national black caucus, the African-American Teachers Association, the black workers' grievances tended to center upon the issue of control. Despite token appointments as plant supervisors and union officeholders, they continued to perceive themselves as second-class citizens within the American workplace. A nondiscrimination clause in union contracts meant little, they said, if white union leaders and company officials neglected to press for its full implementation. Only increased black representation in positions of authority could guarantee that black laborers' concerns would be taken seriously—and even that possibility might vanish if blacks appointed to high posts were estranged from the tenets of Black Power. Without an infusion of this empowering ideology, the nation's factories would continue to resemble modern-day plantations with the second-line black leadership performing the role of house servants and the rank-and-file mired in a field slaves' existence.[85]

Nowhere was the Black Power sentiment more visible than in the auto industry. Job training initiatives spawned by the riots of the mid-sixties lured thousands of unemployed blacks into a new world of foundries, presses, and assembly lines. In some plants, African-Americans came to compose 60 to 75 percent of the work force. Most had little seniority and even fewer emotional ties to their employers. Before long, these young black workers began to challenge established patterns of industrial authority which earlier generations either had learned to live with or had concluded were impervious to change. The Dodge Revolutionary Union Movement (DRUM) and the League of Revolutionary Black Workers were born of this discontent.

Founded in May, 1968, in the aftermath of a wildcat strike at Chrysler's Assembly Plant (Dodge Main) in Hamtramck, Michigan, DRUM moved quickly to establish its priorities. "Our sole objective," its leaders asserted, "is to break the bonds of white racist control over the lives and destiny of black workers."[86] These chains of exploitation were evident, they said, in the practice of assigning the easiest jobs to whites and speeding up production on the lines dominated by blacks.

Discrimination was said to be rampant—in promotion decisions, in the skilled trades, and in the form of racial slurs heard daily throughout the plant. The UAW was perceived as being of little help in resolving these matters because it too was controlled by insensitive whites. The union not only had failed to address their grievances and continually upheld a "racist" seniority system which worked against the interests of young blacks, it also had dared add insult to injury by officially endorsing the annual Detroit Police Field Day.[87]

Certainly, it didn't take a trained sociologist to conclude that the racial and power relationships at the Hamtramck assembly plant had become extremely volatile by the time of DRUM's founding. Said one white worker: "At Dodge Main, there's a young black work force being supervised by reactionary Polacks. Like, you've got a 63-year-old Pole bossing 25-year-old jitterbugs." A black worker agreed, noting somewhat more critically that "everywhere I look there sits some honky, looking down on me."[88]

To remedy this untenable situation, DRUM proposed a series of major affirmative action appointments. After pointing out that 90 percent of the foremen, 99 percent of the general foremen, and all of the plant superintendents at Dodge Main were white, leaders demanded that some 60 blacks be promoted to these positions. DRUM also wanted all security guards, plant doctors, and half of the nursing staff to be recruited from the black community. It even demanded that "a black brother" be appointed head of Chrysler's board of directors.[89]

Other tactics used in the quest for power were somewhat more confrontational. Displeased with UAW representation, DRUM urged black workers to cease paying union dues and, instead, channel the money into the Detroit black community "to aid in self-determination for black people." In an effort to ferret out enemies of all stripes, editors of the militants' weekly newspaper published a damning expose of "Uncle Toms" at Dodge Main. Soon thereafter, DRUM members dressed in greasy overalls and carrying picket signs disrupted a Detroit Urban League luncheon at which League officials had planned to present representatives from Chrysler, Ford, and General Motors with equal opportunity awards. On another occasion, when the organization began to run short of money, it held a combination rally and fund-raising raffle. To symbolize what was deemed the proper perspective on revolutionary change, the group awarded an M-1 rifle, a shotgun, and a bag of groceries as the top three prizes. Finally, to back up claims that "our line is the hard line," DRUM supporters set up picket lines at the entrance gates to Dodge Main in early July 1968. Seventy percent of the plant's black workers were persuaded to stay off the job. As a result of the three day walkout, Chrysler lost an estimated 1,900 units of production. Auto industry executives were put on notice that the volatile combination of unmet black grievances and Black Power ideology invariably sparked internal combustion.[90]

DRUM served as an organizational model for militant associations of black workers such as FRUM (Ford Revolutionary Union Movement), GRUM (General Motors Revolutionary Union Movement), and HRUM (Harvester Revolutionary Union Movement) which formed at other plants. To sustain and give direction to these separate units, the League of Revolutionary Black Workers was established in 1969. Although the League served as an umbrella support organization for the individual workers' units, it was conceptualized on a much grander scale. Black laborers—"the vanguard of the liberation struggle"—would unite with black students, intellectuals, and community residents to "completely close down the American economic system."[91]

To this end, the League organized demonstrations, mounted challenges to union elections, and helped develop revolutionary union movements in other cities and industries. Broadening DRUM's challenge to the establishment, League spokespersons urged the firing of Walter Reuther and the election of a black UAW president. They demanded the opening of skilled trades and apprenticeships to any black worker who applied, the use of UAW investment funds to finance black economic development programs, the shifting of all union strike funds to black financial institutions, and recognition of the League and its affiliates as the "official spokesman" for black workers at both the local and national levels.[92]

Even as it directed these considerable demands to the UAW hierarchy, the League held white unionists at arm's length. It was said that white laborers also were exploited, but retention of white skin privilege diluted their militance. Time and again they had chosen to defend their position of privilege within the proletariat rather than enter into an alliance with militant blacks. This self-serving attitude not only impeded the development of class consciousness, but actually buttressed the prevailing system of racism and exploitation. Thus, according to the League, a multiracial workers' revolution was made unlikely by white racism. Someday, perhaps, whites could be accepted as allies, but first they would have to be radicalized by the black workers' example. The coming revolution against American "racism, capitalism, and imperialism" would be fought and won by black people, led by the black working class.[93]

While the League believed that the best way to organize black America into a powerful force for liberation was first to organize the factories, it did not confine its activities—or concerns—to the workplace. League members, many of whom had been active in community organizing, employed a variety of mechanisms to take their message into the black community. They helped black residents to deal more effectively with their local units of government, supported activist candidates for public office, and spoke out on issues of broad concern—calling for an end to the Vietnam War and the reallocation of defense expenditures "to meet the pressing needs of the black and poor populations of America."[94] Taking to heart novelist John Oliver Killens's notion that a truly liberated black labor movement would have its own Black Studies program, publishing house, and perhaps even a "Black Book-of-the-Month" club, the League established Black Star Press and Black Star Publishing. A book store was opened to market the League's publications. Its Black Star Productions film unit made *Finally Got the News*, a movie on the history of the League, and distributed films about Al Fatah and other revolutionary groups. By entering the cultural sphere in this manner, the League hoped to provide class conscious black laborers with "respite from the total alienation of work."[95]

There was little relief, however, from the organizational problems which continually plagued the League and led to its decline as a force in the auto plants after 1970. Internal disagreements over the scope of the black workers' struggle dissipated group energies. Ideological disputes poisoned personal relationships, festering, and remaining unresolved. Unity of purpose and approach became difficult to maintain when nationalist-oriented members not only rejected alliances with non-black militants, but stated that neither Marx nor Lenin had anything to offer because they, too, were white.[96]

External forces also contributed to the weakening of League influence. The UAW worked hard to meet the black workers' challenge. Even as it blasted the militants as "a handful of fanatics" and sternly warned union members against supporting any group that sought to divide the work force along racial lines, big labor made certain concessions to the League's demands. Having determined that the best way to deal with the Black Power threat was to address the question of representation, the union suddenly found places for a limited number of blacks on executive boards and in staff jobs. This UAW response coincided with a major slump in automobile sales during 1969–70. The impact of the subsequent industry-wide layoffs was felt most severely by young black workers with little seniority—the very group for whom the League's appeal was greatest. Together, the prescient actions of the union leadership and the effects of a slumping economy operated to reduce the attraction of militant ideology among black workers.[97]

Industrial capitalism was not overthrown by the Black Power movement. It was, however, put on notice. The need for a more powerful black voice and a more substantive black presence in the boardrooms and executive suites of big labor and big business was made clear. The UAW leadership's response to the demand for increased participation in decision-making reveals that this most practical of "real world" associations knew exactly what was at issue when existing institutional relationships were challenged. In hindsight, it is apparent that they also were quite adept at determining what it would take to diffuse that challenge.

Nevertheless, to diffuse is not to destroy. The sentiment which propelled the rise of DRUM and the League of Revolutionary Black Workers continued to find expression in the battle against racism in Detroit's public schools; in the continuing effort to improve job opportunities and housing; and in the campaign to wrest control of the city's political life from the white power structure. The spirit of these militant workers also lived on in the various cultural productions which were employed to disseminate their urgent message. One of these, a bold, unpretentious ode in praise of DRUM, speaks of this tenacity:

> For hours and years with sweated tears
> Trying to break our chain. . .
> We broke our backs and died in packs
> To find our manhood slain. . .
> But now we stand for DRUM's at hand
> To lead our freedom fight,
> And now til then we'll unite like men
> For now we know our might. . . .[98]

After the black insurgents declared that "the factories belong to the people and we workers are the people" neither the industrial "plantation" nor its operatives ever could be the same again.[99]

Black Power and "Total Institutions"

I ain't coming back playing "Oh, Say, Can You See." I'm whistlin' "Sweet Georgia Brown," and I got the band.
Marine Sergeant Paul Thomas, 1969

the cage blackman-
there is no hell that can keep him-
no oppression that can surrender him

no pain that can kill the spirit of him-
if his body is ripped off/the spirit of blackness
shall continue to/   ride&right- oN//
From *Cadillac Alley* by Bruce C. Geary

Throughout the 1960s and 1970s sociologists, psychologists, and historians expanded upon the analogy black laborers made between their
work environment and antebellum slavery. Stimulated by Smith College historian Stanley Elkins' controversial "concentration camp analogy," they began to examine the psychological ramifications of life in
"total institutions."[100] In *Slavery: A Problem in American Institutional and Intellectual Life* (1959) Elkins promoted the notion that Nazi
death camp inmates, Afro-American plantation laborers, and others occupying the lower strata of "closed" social systems were beset on all
sides by "the infantilizing tendencies of absolute power." It was said
that victims of the total institution often were bludgeoned into a state
of internalized dependency. Like Elkins' Sambo, the typical plantation
slave, these unfortunate individuals shunned self-directed, rebellious
acts and developed a perverse, childlike attachment to their societal
overlords.[101] Elkins' critics claimed that his concentration camp analogy was overdrawn. The plantation, they said, was not a death camp.
Suggested in its stead were variants of the total institutional model such
as asylums, penitentiaries, military installations, and American Indian
reservations. Initial studies employing these new models held that human personality was far more resilient than Elkins had posited. Moreover, it was shown that the nature and vitality of an affected population's cultural life was of considerable importance in determining the
psychological well-being of individuals who were suffering under conditions of extreme duress.[102] During the Black Power era, the academicians'
theories were tested in a "real world" confrontation between black militants and the two total institutions whose policies and actions most tellingly affected black people. Officials in both the nations' armed forces and
in its correctional system soon discovered how difficult it was to force
culturally aware, militant blacks into an institutional mold.

By the end of 1965, the administration of U.S. President Lyndon B.
Johnson had concluded that the South Vietnamese either were unable or
unwilling to win the war in Southeast Asia. Subsequently, a major U.S.
military commitment was made which mired the nation in a dispirit-
ing, decade-long confrontation with a tenacious and little-understood
enemy. As the fighting escalated, so did antiwar protest. On college
campuses, in factories, and throughout the black community, Afro-
Americans joined in protesting America's rapidly expanding involve-

ment in Vietnamese affairs. A 1966 *Newsweek* poll showed that 35 percent of the black population opposed the war. Three years later this figure had risen to 56 percent. In serious jeopardy was the truism which held that military service provided black youth with far greater opportunities than they could obtain in civilian life. By a two-to-one majority, black Americans in 1969 complained that their young were doing a disproportionate share of the fighting.[103]

Black Power organizations and spokespersons contributed to the spread of this antiwar sentiment with ringing denunciations of a U.S. foreign policy that seemed to bode ill for their own liberation struggles. Some, like the Congress of African Peoples, meeting in Atlanta in September 1970, went on record as being unalterably opposed to the war and urged black troops to cease firing on the Vietnamese.[104] Others, like the Black Panthers' Eldridge Cleaver, talked about destroying the U.S. Army from the inside—sabotaging supplies, turning equipment over to the enemy, and, if necessary, killing any "racist pig" or "Uncle Tom" officer who tried to stop them.[105]

Although such antiwar rhetoric varied greatly both among individuals and over time, much of it was motivated by four specific interrelated concerns. First, in common with other "doves," blacks feared that massive military expenditures would exhaust scarce material resources that desperately were needed to rebuild the central cities and to provide adequate job training and other social services for the nation's poor. It was a matter of priorities, they said—of butter vs. guns. America, not Southeast Asia, was the Afro-American's battleground. The most threatening enemy was the endemic "racism, poverty, oppression and the white man's domination" which afflicted black people at home.[106]

Second, many blacks came to view the Vietnamese—especially those fighting against the U.S.-supported Army of the Republic of Vietnam— as fellow sufferers in a world dominated by exploitative colonial governments. Like other Third World peoples, they long had been oppressed by the West and now were seeking an end to colonial rule. The U.S. military presence was designed to thwart this thrust toward self-determination and, therefore, had to be opposed. "What has a barefoot peasant in Vietnam ever done to you?" asked the antiwar activists. "The man kicks your mother's ass, trains you like a nigger-biting vicious police dog, arms you with his latest shit, and sends you 10,000 miles to terrorize other innocent and defenseless colored women and children. Brothers, what kind of fools are we?" The desired response was for the potential black recruit to state boldly and with conviction: "Whitey, I Will Not Serve!"[107]

Third, black opposition to this war on "darker peoples" was spurred on by reports of atrocities committed by U.S. combat troops. These alleged genocidal acts against the Vietnamese peasants were seen as harbingers of domestic anti-black population control efforts. Indeed, reports of massively disproportionate employment of Afro-American troops on the front lines encouraged the belief that a federally sponsored black genocide campaign already had begun. The "cream of black youth" was being led to slaughter in the jungles of Southeast Asia. Blacks, however, could slow the movement toward full-scale domestic deployment of this heinous plan by refusing to participate in the overseas military effort. By doing so, they also would gain a new source of support in the "war at home." The grateful Vietnamese would become "brothers, friends, and natural allies" who could be called upon in Black America's own time of need.[108]

A final encouragement to anti-war activism was closely related to the hurt and resentment which many blacks felt at being asked to risk a wartime death in order to support the nation's stated goal of winning freedom for Asian peoples. Although not averse to the concept of fighting for freedom, they couldn't understand why their government would expend so much effort to protect the rights of the Vietnamese when it had seemed so indifferent to the lives of civil rights workers in Mississippi. They wondered why full federal power and concern couldn't be applied to the implementation of the 1964 Civil Rights Act or the 1965 Voting Rights Act before it was directed toward the goal of assuring free elections abroad. When they received no satisfactory answer to the question "Where is the draft for the Freedom fight in the United States?" they began to suspect that the persistent cry of "preserve and expand freedom throughout the world" was little more than a smoke screen. Behind this facade, the rich and powerful were plotting to crush any liberation movement that refused to abide by the dictates of U.S. Cold War policy. Recoiling in moral outrage and horror at the inconsistency of their government's position, black activists concluded that efforts to spur Afro-American recruitment via traditional appeals to patriotism were based on false premises. For example, the notion that black soldiers had the same enemies as the Pentagon was said to be both a fraud and a deception. Black people had no quarrel with those Vietnamese or Cambodians who simply wanted to run their countries without foreign intervention. Indeed, they now would stand up and refuse to kill—or to die—in support of Western imperialism. Instead, they would tell their "colored" brothers and sisters, "go to it—get that white man off your back!"[109]

Dissatisfaction with the operation of America's war machine was not confined to those refusing induction. Blacks who had enlisted or who were drafted into the service often found themselves in a hostile, alienating environment. Their grievances were many and deeply felt.

Initial complaints tended to center upon the recruitment process itself. During the sixties, proportionately more blacks than whites from the qualified age cohorts were drafted. In 1967, for example, 64 percent of eligible blacks were drafted. The figure for whites was 31 percent. The chief cause of this racial imbalance was the difficulty Afro-Americans experienced in qualifying for deferments. College students, members of traditional pacifist churches, and those engaged in critical occupations were eligible. In most cases, these criteria benefitted whites. In addition, many more white youths than blacks avoided the draft by taking advantage of National Guard and Army Reserve training options. Whites also were far more successful than blacks in gaining deferments in hardship, dependency, and medical cases. Critics attributed these disparities to the fact that Afro-Americans were grossly underrepresented on local draft boards. In 1967, only 1.5 percent of the more than 17,000 board members were blacks. None served on boards in Alabama, Arkansas, Louisiana, or Mississippi.[110]

Once inducted, other problems surfaced to complicate the lives of the new recruits. They complained of being unable to purchase black-oriented products at post exchanges and of being subjected to repetitive diets of country and western music in mess halls and in off-post clubs. They found flaws in the military justice system, noting that Afro-American officers, lawyers, and judges were harder to find than soul music on the camp jukebox. This fact, they said, helped to explain why a disproportionately large number of blacks ended up in stockades or brigs and, eventually, with "Article Fifteens" (nonjudicial punishment), administrative discharges, or court martials on their service records. Indeed, they found much to be desired in the conduct of their white superiors. Throughout the war, white officers were charged with racial harrassment; discrimination in the assignment of work details; maintaining double standards of conduct; and using offensive, inflammatory language. In the opinion of the black troops, insensitive white officers contributed greatly to the creation of a tense, unhealthy atmosphere in which white soldiers apparently saw nothing wrong with festooning their wall lockers and auto bumpers with rebel flags and Wallace-for-President stickers or celebrating the death of Martin Luther King, Jr. by parading in makeshift Klan costumes, burning crosses, and raising the Confederate flag.[111]

Further hard feelings were generated at the battlefront. Claims that combat assignments were taking a disportionate toll on blacks were proved to be valid. Between 1961 and 1966, when Afro-Americans constituted approximately 11 percent of the general population aged nineteen to twenty-one, they accounted for one out of every five Army combat deaths.[112] The black recruits' lack of formal education and their eagerness to rise in rank and status help to explain why so many undertook dangerous assignments with front-line combat units. Still, the suspicion remained that black lives were being sacrificed. As one black PFC complained: "You should see for yourself how the Black man is being treated over here. And the way we are dying. When it comes to rank we are left out. When it comes to special privileges we are left out. When it come to patrols, operations and so forth, we are first." Another claimed that whenever a black soldier complained about unequal treatment, he was certain to be "railroaded" to an "extremely dangerous area."[113] Had there been more black officers in the field, such charges might have been more easily discredited. But, of the 380 combat battalion commanders in Vietnam in 1967, only two were black.[114]

Prevailing power arrangements made it easy for Afro-American soldiers to conclude that little was being done to promote the sharing of decision-making authority within the armed forces. Like their civilian cousins, they responded by developing various strategies to broach the perimeters of the "closed" system and thereby gain increased access to power. Some chose violence, engaging in fisticuffs with white enlistees and participating in "fraggings" of unpopular officers. Others, like the soldiers from Fort Hood, Texas, who refused assignment to the Democratic National Convention in 1968 out of fear that they might be used against black Chicagoans, simply "boycotted" their orders.[115] Still others modified their pledge of allegiance to include fealty to a Black Power organization.

Mobilizing at stateside installations as well as at those in West Germany and in Southeast Asia, militant soldiers' groups sought to serve both as agents for negotiating black grievances and as promoters of racial pride and unity. If need be, they also would act to defend themselves against white intimidation. In years past, Afro-American soldiers had struggled for equality of treatment within the military. Now, under the influence of Black Power, they demanded official recognition of their distinctive life-style. Groups such as the Moormen, Blacks in Action, the Black Defense Group, and the Unsatisfied Black Soldier held rallies, published underground newspapers, and promoted black cultural awareness. They campaigned for the right to wear Afro hairstyles, declared favorite off-base recreational areas off-limits to whites, and, where pos-

"Wrong salute, Private Jackson."

Cartoonist's view of Black Power in the military. Charles R. Johnson cartoon. Courtesy of *Proud* magazine.

sible, congregated in all-black hootches or barracks. Some promoted the formation of separate, voluntarily segregated Afro-American units within each branch of the military. Others shocked their commanding officers by flying black flags from patrol boats or substituting black berets and shirts for the regulation helmets and fatigues.[116]

The symbols of black solidarity were everywhere. To help counteract the alienating tendencies of military life, the clenched fist black power sign often took the place of the more traditional military salute. One soldier who was stationed at Fort Jackson, South Carolina, recalled that "you couldn't go into the company area without seeing the black power salute." He regularly witnessed clusters of black GIs "giving the fist to colonels." Typically, the officer's response was to stop, get out of his car, and bring the soldiers to attention. Nevertheless, after he returned to his vehicle, the untraditional saluting continued as before.[117] In one survey of enlisted men serving in Vietnam, 56 percent of the black respondents said they used the Black Power salute.[118]

Other culture-based mechanisms were used to promote group cohesion within the environs of the total institution. At Danang, supporters of US designed a special flag for black troops which bore the legend, written in Swahili, "My fear is for you." Its red background symbolized the blood shed both in the war and in racial confrontations at home. A black foreground represented the ethos of black culture while green was used to represent youth and new ideas. Crossed spears and a shield surrounded by a wreath dominated the center of the design. The message here was peace if possible, violence if necessary. Elsewhere, black soldiers added medallions and amulets to their dog tags as badges of unity; constructed special "solidarity" wristbands made of combat boot shoelaces; and devised intricate handshakes which sometimes concluded with a tap on the head (the transmission of knowledge) or a crossing of the chest Roman legion style (a vow to die for one's comrade).[119]

Black troops also selected their own wartime culture heroes. Neither John Wayne nor General Patton was among them. Instead, they chose figures such as Malcolm X, Eldridge Cleaver, and Muhammad Ali. As one black private told *Time* correspondent Wallace Terry in 1969, "I dig the militant brothers. Non-violence didn't do anything but get Martin Luther King killed."[120] Malcolm X was especially revered. The militants-in-uniform recalled his early condemnation of American involvement in Vietnam as well as his critique of government officials who seemingly could mobilize black youth for war in an instant, but were slow to guarantee them the "right to register and vote without being murdered."[121] Throughout the military, Afro-American soldiers studied his *Autobiography*, played tape recordings of his speeches, and demanded that flags fly at half-staff on his birthday. The Black Power organization at Vandenberg Air Force Base was named in his honor because, as a spokesperson noted, "only the ideas of Malcolm were sufficiently suggestive of the continuing struggle for change, cultural mobilization . . . and prevention of our going back to sleep." For these reasons, the fallen Muslim leader was deemed "the most appropriate symbol" for the group.[122]

As could be expected, the formation of organizations such as the Malcolm X Association encouraged rumors among white troops that the Black Power Mau Mau were about to attack. Sometimes they did. During the war years, individual displays of aggression were overshadowed by the actions of groups of blacks bound together through ties of cultural solidarity. In one incident, the character of an interracial brawl at a tank battalion base near Danang changed dramatically when a dozen black Marines, wearing black shirts and gloves and armed with rifles and grenades, arrived to "even the odds." At the Long Binh stockade, more than 200 black inmates donned kerchiefs and African-style robes made from army blankets and proceeded to turn their quarters upside down. Military officials blamed overcrowding and racial tensions for the rampage which left one white inmate dead and scores injured. Aboard the Naval fleet oiler *Hassayampa*, a detachment of Marines was needed to restore order after a group of blacks attacked seven white seamen. In this case, walking sticks whose handles were carved in the shape of a clenched Black Power fist were used to resolve a dispute over a white crew member's alleged theft of money from a black sailor. Outbursts such as these were repeated numerous times in various locales throughout the war. Collectively, they gave credence to the warning issued by Lance Corporal Roddie Latimer, a member of the Mau Mau's, a Black Power group which formed within the Marine Corps. As Latimer told a reporter in 1969, "We want [whites] to know that we are definitely together. Mess with one of us, and you mess with all of us."[123]

Black soldiers fully expected this new, expressive militance to carry over into civilian life. Some 30 percent of Wallace Terry's respondents planned to join a militant group like the Black Panthers upon their release from the service. Said one sailor from Illinois, "The honkies made the Panthers violent like they are. I'd join 'em, and I'd help 'em kill all these honky motherfuckers, because do unto him before he do unto you." Most believed that America would experience additional seasons of racial violence, with nearly 50 percent stating that they too would be willing to take up arms in order to expand domestic freedoms. "Hell, yes, I'd riot," exclaimed one Marine. "If they're kicking crackers' asses, I'm going to get in and kick a few myself. I'm just doing what my grandfather wanted to do and couldn't." More than 45 percent of the black enlisted men interviewed said that they would refuse any order to turn their guns on rioting blacks. "Riots is good," said one. "It makes people wonder what's going on, and they come in and check it out."[124]

During the Black Power era, soldiers such as these refused to abide by rules long ago established to govern total institutions. While in the service, they violently disagreed with opponents of Black Power who, for example, felt that there was "no room in the Marines for any color except green." Returning to civilian life, they provided a potential source of leadership and technical expertise for those who believed that armed struggle was the only cure for impacted institutional racism. With their militant posture strengthened by a firm attachment to black cultural distinctives, they constituted a worrisome threat to American institutions—total and otherwise. The Black Power movement in the military revealed that the vaunted integration of the armed services was perceived by many young blacks as little more than a convenient social arrangement for assembling and running the war machine. Power relationships seemed to have changed little over the years. In their estimation, cooperation between black and white could come about only through a cultural partnership in which Afro-Americans would both share power and be treated as cultural brokers in their own right.[125]

Like the armed forces, America's penal system was perceived by the militants to be in need of drastic reform. As a prototypical total institution, the prison seemed to resemble a concentration camp even more closely than did the wartime army. If physical death was an ever-present possibility on the Southeast Asian battlefields, the inmates of the nation's correctional institutions daily risked an enervation or death of the human spirit. Nevertheless, as the war raged overseas, Black Power slipped through penitentiary bars, providing black inmates with important psychological safeguards against these potentially dehumanizing tendencies. The prisoners' literary and cultural expression strongly suggests that they found no meaningful analogue between themselves and Stanley Elkins' Sambo.

During the Black Power era, black activists provided a detailed critique of crime and punishment in America. Many had firsthand knowledge of the institutions and practices which they described and therefore could provide vivid accounts of the system's threat to internal self-direction. Like Malcolm X before them, the militants held that it was possible for prison to be a transforming experience. "Hard time" could be used to cultivate individual self-awareness, spur intellectual growth, and develop ideological coherence.[126] For many black inmates, however, the prison experience served only as formal recognition that they had been consigned to the very bottom of the American social structure. Their presence—indeed, their overrepresentation in these institutions—was proof of white society's determination to keep black people oppressed and powerless.[127]

According to critics, reform of the nation's criminal justice system would have to begin with the courts. Remarkably little had changed, they said, since the day in 1857 when, in the Dred Scott case, the Supreme Court ruled that blacks "are not included, and were not intended to be included, under the word 'citizens' in the Constitution," and therefore were not guaranteed the same legal rights and privileges as white Americans. By the 1960s, of course, judicial sentiment had been modified. Courtroom bias was not as blatant. Nevertheless, evidence of discrimination on the basis of race and/or class could be seen in prevailing patterns of pre-trial detention, in the time and cost-saving plea bargaining system, and in prosecuting attorneys' use of the peremptory challenge to remove blacks from juries. Critics claimed that the poor were receiving inferior treatment from a system in which counsel often was provided by uncaring public defenders, jurors seldom were their socioeconomic peers, and judges either represented the white establishment or were so overburdened that the task of diminishing their backlog of cases had become more important than dispensing justice. For these reasons, the militants concluded that many blacks were sent to prison largely because of the injustice of the system itself—that "white people are able to get away with a lot of things black people can't."[128]

Once sentenced to a correctional facility, a black prisoner could expect to experience additional instances of differential treatment. Along with ineffective rehabilitation programs and barely tolerable living conditions, advocates of prison reform critiqued both correctional officers and administrators. The guards, they claimed, harrassed and brutalized Afro-American inmates. They also enlisted white prisoners to help enforce their system of internal racial control. Employing the time-honored technique of divide and conquer, they maintained order by providing selected prisoners with knives and zip guns, enforcing segregation in TV and shower rooms, and, if an interracial altercation broke out, levying harsher punishment on the darker of the two combatants. According to "Soledad Brother" George Jackson, such practices proved that racism could flourish even within the stark, regimented confines of the prison. "Overt racism exists unchecked," he wrote to his lawyer in 1970. "It is not a case of the pigs trying to stop the many racist attacks; they actively encourage them."[129]

Prison system administrators were criticized for far more than simply allowing such conditions to exist. They were accused of developing and implementing policies which defined many, if not most, militant blacks as "political" prisoners. Once labeled in this fashion, said the critics, they found their reading material censored, their privileges limited, and their chances for parole greatly diminished. No longer mere criminals, they had become enemies of the social order—to be kept under long-term surveillance by the predominantly white occupiers of the largely nonwhite penal colony. When they appeared before a parole board, their views on contemporary social issues immediately became the primary area of interest. If they were honest and told the truth, they would be termed unrepentant and denied parole. Aware of several cases which seemed to fit this pattern, many critics of "prison politics" agreed with Huey P. Newton's claim that black activists were being "sent to prison for what they did, but they are kept in prison for what they believe."[130] Inmates who felt that they had been incarcerated for political reasons found it a simple matter to equate their situation with that of earlier victims of total institutions. In 1970, for example, striking inmates of California's Folsom Prison issued a manifesto which described the facility as "ONE OF THE MOST CLASSIC INSTITUTIONS OF AUTHORITATIVE INHUMANITY UPON MEN"—a member in good standing of the "FASCIST CONCENTRATION CAMPS OF MODERN AMERICA." To alleviate what was considered an intolerably claustrophobic atmosphere of political and racial persecution, they demanded an end to indeterminate sentences whereby an inmate could be "warehoused indefinitely, rehabilitated or not;" the hiring of ethnic group counselors; reform of the parole system; and vigorous prosecution of correctional officers found guilty of inflicting "cruel and unusual punishment." Prominent "political" prisoners such as Ahmad Evans and Bobby Seale were to be granted asylum outside the United States while all others would see the abolition of a policy which limited prisoners' rights to subscribe to "political" publications. Surely, they said, such reforms would have a beneficial effect on a prison population which had been "victimized by exploitation" and denied "the celebrated due process of law."[131]

Black Power theoreticians agreed that Afro-American prisoners were laboring under physical and psychological restraints reminiscent of other, more universally condemned social systems. According to Huey Newton, prisons not only were "concentration camps where racism is practiced and encouraged by the prison administration," they also could be likened to antebellum slave plantations. In all three, the power of those in authority was total. Inmates were under constant surveillance and were expected to exhibit deference to their tormentors at all times. Long-term personal relationships could be severed instantly through "institutional transfers." Their labor was exploited—often beyond the limits of human endurance. Each system was a case study supportive of the notion that human beings could be terribly brutalized within restrictive institutional environments.[132]

Under such conditions, how could the victims of total institutions hope to avoid the immolation of self—to maintain their humanity while struggling to survive within the belly of the beast. According to the militants, an escape ladder existed which led to individual and group empowerment. The ladder had three rungs, the first of which was overtly political. Prisoners were urged to steep themselves in revolutionary thought. Wherever possible, they were to study the works of Marx, Lenin, Trotsky, and Mao. Recreational reading time was to be spent reflecting on the lives and achievements of Nkrumah, Che, and "Uncle" Ho Chi Minh. Despite efforts at suppression and censorship, they were to maintain contact with sympathetic groups, such as the Black Panther Party, which called for the release of all blacks held in American jails.[133] Strengthened through this radical political union, black prisoners would come to believe that resistance was possible— that they were capable of withstanding the oppression of the total institution.

The second, more treacherous step toward Black Power engaged the inmate in psychological combat. From the prisoners' first day within the walls to the time they were paroled, administrators and their underlings challenged and sought to modify established beliefs and values. Operating on the assumption that, by right of judicial conviction, they had won control of both a prisoner's mind and body, they sought to convince their charges to act and think according to approved institutional standards. When this was accomplished, the battle was won. The prisoner had been "rehabilitated." Black prison activists sought to frustrate this plan. They held that Afro-American "political" prisoners seldom benefitted from this type of therapy. What the authorities deemed a behavioral or character defect was merely a principled refusal to accept the legitimacy of the system. According to the militants, meaningful rehabilitation involved convincing inmates to maintain their personal values, dignity, and sense of uniqueness even as they lived and worked within the total institution's coercive atmosphere. Submission to the dictates of the administrators would result in psychological devastation— condemnation to a living death of the human spirit. If, however, prisoners successfully turned back efforts to corrode their belief system, they could state with confidence that the penitentiary was capable of shackling the body, but not the spirit. Poised on the threshold of revolutionary action, the prisoners now fully recognized that self-direction was a type of empowerment.[134]

In order for this politicized message of spiritual liberation to spread throughout the inmate population, a third and final development—the creation of an effective mode of internal communication—had to be effected. In most cases black cultural expression served as the preferred mechanism of transmission. Because they were compatible with prevailing notions of what constituted acceptable rehabilitation projects, black-run cultural societies, black history study groups, and theatre workshops were tolerated—and even encouraged—by correctional administrators. These self-help organizations conducted classes in black history "so that the good brothers would know we all ain't been hangin' from the trees all our lives." They studied Swahili and Afro-American literature—often pooling their funds to buy books by black authors for the prison library. Some were motivated to work for general education diplomas because, as one inmate noted, "to change the system, you have to get in it first." Others formed singing groups, designed greeting cards with soul messages and even produced their own institutional versions of the dashiki.[135] Through these various educational and cultural efforts, prisoners became creators of culture. With a confidence born of self-direction, they now felt qualified to serve as standard bearers of black awareness. Their mission was to guide others away from the psychological abyss of the total institution. The recently liberated had become the liberators.

The creative cultural expression of "liberated" black prisoners chronicled their experiences, recounted their burdens, and described the advance of Black Power. Their poetry and prose told of the "iron hell" of prison existence and of how their efforts to maintain psychological balance were met at every turn by psychotic guards bent on "taming a nigger." Petty harrassment, mace, electric shock, and the false labeling of prisoners as "freaks, homosexuals and black racist fanatics" were used in attempts to break the inmates. The institution wanted to render them rehabilitated according to white America's image of safe blacks, returning them to society as "white value-loving, incubator-bred humanoid[s]." Fortunately, the creators of prison culture knew that they had to "beware of the flowers of despair." Their mandate was to continue the struggle to remove "the white thorn in the black flesh" of prisoners' minds. Accordingly, they would set their thoughts on more supernal things—the example of Brother Malcolm, the "cosmic beauty" of the "black queen" who awaited them outside the walls, and the prospect of creating a "glorious black nation" for their long-suffering people. To these men and women, it was axiomatic that the drive for Black Power would continue unabated, even behind bars. Its advance could not be stalled because its passion for liberation was "of the people, for the people." Even the skeptical and fainthearted eventually would seek empowerment rather than continue in their submission to whites and their infernal, dehumanizing institutions. Daily, the Black Power revolution was "changing niggers into blackmen— / blackmen into a —
/ blackNation / black Nation into— / blackpower / black power into— / equality / world equality."[136]

Both the startling impact and contagious spirit of the movement was captured in a story written by Indiana State Reformatory inmate Etheridge Knight. The prison poet and essayist recalled the day in August, 1968, when "the young blacks came" and how they "shook up the joint with their blackness and their boldness." The arrival of these youthful militants drew a large crowd of onlookers who crowded the street leading to the admissions building. Suddenly, in through the back gate they marched, chained together like a coffle of slaves—but with important differences. They wore their hair long, in majestic leonine fashion. Tikis and other charms decorated their chests. As the line advanced, they raised manacled hands in the Black Power salute, smiling and shouting to the crowd. Recognizing the potential for disruption, the guards soon broke up the assembly. But, as the inmates dispersed, a dispute ensued. An elderly black prisoner made it clear that, in his opinion, the young militants were troublemakers. "Somebody oughtta talk to them niggers so's they don't make it hard for all of us," he remarked. Immediately, one of his associates responded: "What are you talking about, muthafucka? It can't get no worse. I'm glad they're here 'cause them young niggers just ain't gonna take the shit that we took off the white man."[137]

Despite the fears expressed by some inmates, the presence of the militants seemed to have only beneficial effects. According to Knight, in subsequent weeks there was a perceptible "lifting of the shoulders" among the black prisoners. A "general air of pride" enveloped the black population, fights between "brothers" decreased, and interest in black history and culture became so rabid that copies of Lerone Bennett's *Before the Mayflower* exchanged hands for the princely sum of ten cartons of cigarettes.[138] Black Power had come to the Indiana "pen" manifesting a flair and spirit that refused to be shackled.

Throughout the Black Power era, militant prisoners held that their world of iron bars, guard towers, and "lock-downs" was a microcosm of the larger society.[139] As social systems, both were harsh environments in which to nurture a healthy black psyche. Both sought to remain "closed" to the idea of black empowerment. That neither fully succeeded in suppressing the Black Power ethic is a tribute to the universal human capacity to resist assaults on one's belief system and personhood. The survival of the militant spirit within total institutions also speaks well of the ability of black cultural expression to transmit the message of resistance into even the most isolated corners of the "real world."

four

The Ideologies of Black Power

Both pluralists and nationalists contributed to the ongoing work of the various Black Power groups. While these different activist persuasions could and did coexist within a single organizational framework, there was a pronounced tendency for ideological soulmates to rally around their own leaders, focusing upon issues which they considered to be of most immediate importance. Their individual concerns and specific lists of demands were subsets of the overall Black Power agenda. Pluralists concentrated their efforts in an area broadly defined as "community control." They hoped to generate Black Power within the economic, educational, and political institutions of their communities. Then, using the local constituencies as their support base, they would promote black empowerment and participation at the state and national levels. Within the nationalist camp, territorial separatists, revolutionary nationalists, and cultural nationalists vied for supremacy. The three major factions often were at loggerheads over doctrine and strategy, but all shared a common fatalism. None believed that there was any immediate prospect of blacks gaining significant decision-making power within white American institutions. As an alternative to the mainstream mind-set, they rejected majoritarian values, avoided entering into entangling alliances with "establishment" organizations, and campaigned for long-term sociocultural autonomy.

Pluralism

> Our cities are crime-haunted dying grounds. Huge sectors of our youth—and countless others—face permanent unemployment. Those of us who work find our paychecks able to purchase less and less. Neither the courts nor the prisons contribute to anything resembling justice or reformation. The schools are unable—or unwilling—to educate our children for the real world of our struggles.
>
> From the preamble, National Black Political Agenda,
> Gary, Indiana, 1972

Even before the opening of the Black Power era, Malcolm X had addressed the issue of power relationships in black neighborhoods. "Why should white people be running all the stores in our community?" he asked in 1964. "Why should white people be running the banks in our community? Why should the economy of our community be in the hands of the white man?" His answer, of course, was that white control of the central city was not preordained, but could be altered if black residents made a concerted effort to free themselves from the vise imposed by white institutions. To do so, they first had to recognize the importance of expanding black economic and political power. These were, he noted, the "two kinds of power that count" in America. If black people were to take charge of their own destiny, they had to do a better job of controlling decisions made in these areas. They had to adopt the revolutionary axiom which held that land is the basis of a people's independence. Once in control of the land and its institutions, Afro-Americans no longer would have to "picket and boycott and beg some cracker downtown for a job." The black community would be able to employ its own, to govern itself, and to protect its residents against external enemies. It then could move on to other essential tasks, such as improving public education and eradicating the evils of alcohol and drug addiction, gambling, and prostitution. Buoyed by accomplishments in these areas, a new sense of pride would sweep across the urban landscape, rejuvenating the spirit of black America. Ultimately, this rebirth of self-respect was as crucial as any victory in the economic or political sphere. "We must take pride in the Afro-American community," Malcolm X asserted, "for it is our home and it is our power, the base of our power."[1]

Although they may have needed help in organizing for action, black urbanites of the sixties didn't need anyone to tell them about the effects of skewed power relationships. All that was needed to gauge the nature and extent of the problem was to look across the central city. Many fewer whites were to be seen than in earlier years. Those who could afford to do so had joined the mass Euro-American exodus toward a suburban promised land. So many were involved in this demographic stampede toward suburbia's clean air, spacious homes, good schools, and lily-white social environment that black majorities were forecast for a number of the nation's largest cities within a decade. The émigrés took their tax dollars, skills, and interest in the life of the city with them. Whites did, however, retain administrative and financial control. Urban blacks complained that this arrangement only worsened an already bad situation. The provision of public services seemed less adequate and the process of obtaining assistance more labyrinthian than ever. Educational apartheid was becoming the norm in many public schools. Job opportunities continued to decline in both quantity and quality. With the cities enveloped in this pervasive atmosphere of declining expectations, community pride was a difficult sentiment for any group to foster.[2]

Noting the civil rights movement's lack of success in alleviating the problems of de facto segregation, many blacks saw little hope of improving their lot without altering power relationships within the existing system—a system over which they had little influence. The most skeptical among them claimed that government programs ostensibly established to assist the urban poor actually worked against their best interests. Urban renewal and model cities programs, for example, were said to impede the process of black empowerment. Through massive demolition projects, life-giving ethnic hubs were transformed into "semi-inhabited desert[s]." The majority of the former residents were balkanized and rendered politically impotent through transfer to other areas. By removing people from their old neighborhoods, black population concentrations were, in some cases, decreased. Ties of familiarity were loosened or destroyed. As a result, the possibility that a viable, independent black political movement could be established within the resettlement area was extremely remote.[3]

Even where they retained a solid numerical majority, black people were placed in a strategically defenseless position through urban renewal. Critics claimed that predominantly black high-rise housing projects, such as Chicago's Robert Taylor Homes, were built primarily for ease of population control during riots. Under this interpretation, federal housing programs were seen as little more than cruel deceptions.

Their thin veneer of compassion was insufficient to hide what angry blacks saw as the white establishment's "neocolonization of nonwhite human capital." In league with urban land developers, government contractors, craft unions, and entrenched local bureaucrats, Washington was accused of seeking to maintain and strengthen white political and economic domination of urban black America.[4]

Public opinion polls conducted during the Black Power era revealed the overwhelming desire of these central city residents to escape the ghetto.[5] For most, this hope was not soon realized. Nevertheless, spurred on by Black Power activists and encouraged by government poverty programs which required that officials solicit input from community residents before allocating funds, black urbanites began to organize within their neighborhoods. Their goal: to completely reorient the institutions that were most central to their daily living. They sought to bring schools, hospitals, and government agencies closer to the people by atomizing existing centers of power. It was said that this redistribution of authority was capable of transforming leaden bureaucratic structures into community-oriented vehicles for the provision of essential services. For the first time, the people most directly affected by institutional policies would have a major voice in decision-making. Programs would be monitored by indigenous leaders. Far better equipped than outsiders to define priorities and better able to win the cooperation of local residents, their presence in decision-making roles would mitigate the destructive effects of institutionalized racism. As a result, the special needs of black Americans could be addressed fully and in a sensitive manner. Ultimately, it was hoped that community control of human services agencies would become a widely accepted management technique.[6] According to Boston community development activist Virgil Woods, the immediate goal might be to assure provision of basic services but, over time, the agenda was certain to expand greatly: "Our long range goal ought to be economic independence, educational self-reliance, political empowerment, cultural development and exchange, institutional development—the networking of those institutions."[7] In this formulation, initial victories were viewed as way stations on the road to political and economic control of the nation's major black population centers.

Supporters of the community control concept claimed that their plans for black empowerment were rooted in the pluralistic tradition. Like other ethnic groups before them, Afro-Americans realized that American society functioned through the competitive interaction of its various interest groups. By attempting to form power blocs in the central city, they were not being anti-white, but pro-black. They sought a greater degree of economic and political autonomy—not the rise of a Black Power autarky. Striving to negotiate a viable existence for themselves through self-directed action, they believed that government should be kept as close to the people as possible; that any person of good intentions is capable of administering a public program; and that subgroups within the body politic should be allowed to exercise as much self-rule as possible.[8] The activists' claims that they were seeking no more than an equitable share of the urban economic and political pie were so convincing that the National Urban League and the NAACP adopted strong community control resolutions at their 1969 national conventions. Both rejected the notion that community control was a "separatist" program.[9]

Advocates of neighborhood empowerment defended their beliefs at conferences, in municipal meeting rooms, and on city street corners. Maintaining that human rights should take precedence over property rights, they sought ways to rid their communities of absentee entrepreneurs and administrators. New black-owned businesses, guided by consumer-oriented codes of conduct and staffed by local residents were encouraged. Plans were drawn up for the transfer of established firms from white to black management and control. Demands were made for direct community representation on key government councils, boards, and commissions. The merits of forming tenant and neighborhood credit unions, black banks and employment services, protective associations and development corporations were debated extensively. As the community control movement grew, black America prepared to reorganize the structure of municipal government and city life in general— from bottom to top.[10]

In the economic sector, the fruits of these planning sessions could be seen in the formation of community development groups such as NEGRO, the National Economic Growth and Reconstruction Organization. NEGRO was established in the early sixties as the Interfaith Health Association, a nonprofit corporation which owned and operated a 140-bed hospital in Queens. Its stated aim was to encourage "the self-help concept among the Negro people." By the opening of the Black Power era, it had become a broad-based economic entity. NEGRO owned and operated chemical, paint, and metal-fabricating plants; bus companies in Watts and Harlem; a textile firm which produced dresses and lingerie; and more than six hundred units of housing, many of which had been refurbished by its own Spartacus Construction Company. Following the 1968 riots, NEGRO even opened mobile stores and a farmer's market in the fire-ravaged sections of the nation's capital. By the summer of 1968, NEGRO enterprises employed more than seven hundred, twenty percent of whom were white.[11]

Committed to the development of human resources, NEGRO was both an industrial concern and a training center for the hard-core unemployed. Its directors were convinced that slavery and several generations of welfare dependency had prohibited urban blacks from developing proper attitudes toward work. Many weren't attuned to the demands of the free enterprise system—arriving at the job late and performing their tasks in a lackadaisical fashion. To counteract this attitudinal problem, NEGRO conducted industrial clinics in which new trainees met with teachers, doctors, and social workers in the hope that both the workers' conception of themselves and the workplace would be rehabilitated.[12]

NEGRO was grounded in the ideology of pluralism. Dr. Thomas W. Matthew, a New York City neurosurgeon who had given up a reputed $100,000-a-year practice to become president of the organization, was careful to differentiate the ideals of his group from those of nationalists who were laying plans to withdraw from American society, form a separate black state, or return to Africa. Under NEGRO's "constructive form of black power," economic separatism was not a goal in itself, but rather "a vehicle—a step toward ultimate integration of the races." According to Matthew, blacks neither wanted to be patronized nor dominated. Like the Irish, Italians, and Jews who had preceded them in entering the urban industrial work force, they wanted to be accepted both for themselves and for their accomplishments. In order to reach that point, they would, as the other ethnic groups had done, band together in cooperative ventures, using their own resources to solve common problems. "Our goal is that other people will have genuine reason for respecting us, and we in turn will have the right to respect ourselves," he noted. "The marshaling of all the resources of any particular group is the power of that group. In this instance, since black people are involved, we call it 'black power.'"[13] Supporters of NEGRO favored this expression of the empowerment ethic over more dramatic and volatile separatist versions because it seemed far more relevant to the question of black economic survival in the "real world."

The impact of black activism on economic affairs also was evident in the nationwide debate over the meaning of the newly-fashionable term "black capitalism." Did it refer, as some believed, to the system which would prevail after black entrepreneurs were thoroughly co-opted and had become indistinguishable cogs in the monopoly capitalist machine? Or was it, as others claimed, a term which could be used to describe the

Thomas W. Matthew. From U.S. News & World Report Collection, Library of Congress.

collective or cooperative accumulation of capital by and for the benefit of the black masses? During the Black Power era there was a black capitalism to fit almost any ideological predisposition.

The situation was made especially confusing by the Republican party's employment of the term. In 1968, Richard Nixon forwarded the view that, with proper incentives, private enterprise could be far more effective than government in solving urban America's problems. "With your help," he told television audiences during the presidential campaign, "I will begin a new program to get private enterprise into the ghetto and the ghetto into private enterprise." He joined this tribute to private sector capabilities with talk of investment assurances and tax incentives to corporations that created new jobs in ghetto neighborhoods. Promising black leaders that his administration would do more for their constituents than any other in history, he noted that blacks, too, would have a piece of the action. "It's no longer enough that white-owned enterprises employ greater numbers of Negroes," he said. "This is needed, yes—but it has to be accompanied by an expansion of black ownership, of black capitalism." From this cornucopia of bold initiatives would flow "black pride, black jobs, black opportunity and, yes, black power, in the best, the constructive sense of that often misapplied term."[14] A skeptical black America listened intently to these words and awaited tangible results.

As they assayed the early efforts of the Nixon administration's new economic development agencies—the Office of Minority Business Enterprise and the Minority Enterprise Small Business Investment Companies, blacks were asked to pledge their allegiance to one of several competing plans for the economic rehabilitation of black America. In time, many community control advocates became especially critical of the variant of "black capitalism" whose market orientation appeared to offer the most direct challenge to their own collectivist, participatory style.

As promoted by Andrew Brimmer, the only black member of the Federal Reserve System's Board of Governors, "integrationist economics" seemed to suggest that Afro-Americans should abolish their own economic instrumentalities and become absorbed completely within the white system. "The only promising path to genuine economic progress," Brimmer asserted, was "an accelerated widening of opportunities in an integrated economy." How had he arrived at this conclusion? Brimmer cited data which had convinced him that the black subeconomy was far too feeble even to serve as a base for separate development. For example, in 1966, black Americans constituted 11 percent of the nation's population, but earned on the average three-fifths as much as whites. They received only about 6.5 percent of the total personal income. At the same time, blacks had about two-thirds as many years of schooling as whites; represented one-fifth of the poverty; and owned only 2 percent of the wealth accumulated by American families. Rapid transformation of the ghetto's small-scale retailing and service sector was not likely to occur in this context. He concluded that economic separatism was "dangerous nonsense." It was imperative for blacks to "get *inside* the corporate structure" so that they could learn how genuine economic power is exercised.[15]

Critics of this approach claimed that its proposed panacea for black economic ills was far too competitive and individualistic. It created the impression that the black masses could be integrated successfully into the present U.S. economic system by grafting them onto the infrastructure of corporate capitalism. This was foolhardy, they said. The economic development of the black community necessarily had to proceed via ideas developed within a black theoretical framework. Economic policies had to be based on the experiences and needs of the community. They were not to be mere mechanical applications of the prevailing economic wisdom of white America. The advocates of community control believed that if black people were to be liberated under capitalism, a policy of short-range separatism had to be pursued. Much in the manner of European immigrant groups, blacks would enter a transitional period of "strategic separatism" in preparation for full integration within the American economy. Bolstered by financial assistance from both government and the private sector, the black "sheltered market" would be nurtured until it was powerful enough to interact with the white business community on a basis of equality. Black entrepreneurs could, it was said, accept such aid from outsiders in good conscience as long as they were careful to maintain control of their own institutions. One didn't have to be a committed capitalist (and many claimed that it was far better not to be one) to believe that all of this could be accomplished. One merely had to maintain an abiding faith in the Afro-American people and in their ability to "create *their own black thing*" within an equitable pluralist system. Eventually, trusting in themselves, they would usher in an era of unprecedented urban prosperity. In doing so, they would provide a sound economic base for political independence and a nurturing environment for further cultural development.[16]

Supporters of community control made a direct connection between the ghetto economy and urban education. The acquisition of technical skills and expertise in areas such as engineering, marketing, computer programming, and industrial relations could play a key role in the development of a viable black urban economy. Moreover, a significant expansion of the black skills-base would make "communization" of economic affairs more attractive to all parties. A well-educated central city population would promote the utilization of a wide range of human resources in the cause of community development. Black youth, welfare recipients, ADC mothers, and all other "victims of the systematic degradation and exploitation of American racism" would be provided with the skills and earning power once deemed the exclusive province of the black bourgeoisie. At the same time, outsiders would see that they were not hastening the demise of Western civilization by allowing urban planning and control to be exercised from the bottom levels up rather than from the top down.[17]

Community-controlled public schools were said to have additional benefits. Afro-American educational empowerment would guarantee that all children were being treated as educable beings, endowed with creative capabilities and potential. Schooling would nurture a child's sense of self while at the same time instilling respect for collective responsibility and action. These vital concepts would be instilled by black role models through a completely revamped curriculum. Traditional "See Dick, See Jane, Run Dick, Run Jane, White House, Nice Farm" irrelevancies would be mothballed. In their place would appear new teaching aids, focused on black history and culture. Through the skillful utilization of these materials, educators would resurrect the concept of the public school as a viable and worthwhile cultural institution. Viewing education as an exciting experience in concentrated enculturation, teachers would work in conjunction with other community leaders to transform the present, dysfunctional system into one of relevance and efficacy.[18]

Many advocates of community-based education conceptualized these proposed reforms in pluralistic terms. In the past, they said, very little in the American educational system had dealt with Afro-America from either a positive, realistic, or constructive perspective. Because the schools were structured to meet white needs, black students were treated as if they were out of place. The traditional melting pot approach had emphasized similarities and downplayed differences. From the pluralist perspective, this was wrongheaded and had to be abandoned. As one commentator noted in 1969, "the failure of a round peg to fit into a square hole is not because the peg isn't square, but rather because it wasn't made to fit in a square hole in the first place." Educators had to recognize that schools which promoted cultural homogeneity could not adequately meet the needs of students growing up in a multicultural society. The historical experiences of Afro- and Euro-Americans had differed greatly, said the reformers. As a result, the social and cultural systems of the two groups had developed along separate lines. A truly modern curriculum would attempt to make valid connections between these separate cultures in a climate that respected and nurtured group distinctives.[19]

Was this, as some feared, a form of "reverse segregation?" No, said the supporters of community control. It was merely a way of emphasizing race in a positive way. The goal was not to degrade or subordinate others, but to overcome the effects of the centuries during which race had been used to the detriment of black people. As was the case in many small rural towns and white suburbs, community control of public schooling would bring new accountability and increased citizen participation to the educational process. Parents and school officials then could develop a much closer relationship, working together to attack the complex problems of urban life.[20]

How was all of this to come about? What would be the limits to local authority? How would community-controlled education be structured? During the Black Power era, answers to these questions were numerous and varied. Proposals for educational empowerment often were extremely ambitious, calling for local direction of almost every aspect of public education. The "Twenty Point Program for Real School Community Control," developed for Harlem's I.S. 201 Complex, was among the most comprehensive. It called for citizen control of distinct boundaries, school board election procedures, and construction and maintenance funds. Staff vacancies were to be filled by local residents and all teachers and administrators made fully accountable to the community. Both academic testing and student suspensions would cease until standards could be developed which were "relevant and geared to the requirements of individual communities." School facilities were to be upgraded and more fully utilized for adult education classes. A free community breakfast/lunch program featuring "soul food, rice and beans, and Chinese food" was to begin. Improvements were to be made in medical and health services, drug counseling, and bilingual education. The tracking system would be abolished and a new curriculum developed. Breaking with tradition, it would emphasize "modern day awareness of the real world." Students—who were to have a voice in decision-making even at the junior high level—would study black, Puerto Rican, and Chinese history. They also would grapple with the problems of urban life—"unemployment, poor housing, malnutrition, police brutality, racism and other forms of oppression." The complex nature of this program made clear the activists' desire to institute sweeping changes in a system thought to be mired in "colonial" tradition.[21]

Other proposals for reform also went far beyond the notion that effective decentralization of administrative power could be accomplished through the creation of "demonstration districts" or by appointing blacks to community advisory committees. Some demanded that elections be held for parallel black boards of education. The most fully developed plans of this type would, like the I.S. 201 Complex program, greatly abridge the authority of both educational professionals and the central school board. Administrative control over curriculum, personnel, financing, and student conduct policies would be taken from established authorities and vested in new, local boards composed of students, parents, educators, and representatives of community organizations. These bodies were expected to express "the WILL OF THE PEOPLE—in fact and in deed" and would never, as one 1969 proposal noted, "bargain, compromise, petition, or beg from the present white system of education." It was believed that such policy-making groups would be far more likely than their predecessors to support innovative concepts such as the establishment of black cultural centers and student unions within the public schools.[22]

Even these proposals failed to satisfy activists. Some predicted that busing for desegregation purposes would limit the potential for achieving Black Power in public education. Others feared that their protest efforts might result only in the renaming of a few school buildings or in the expanded use of "Lift Every Voice and Sing" in morning devotional exercises. Skeptical that major educational reforms could be instituted swiftly and without undue compromise, they decided to form their own community schools. Not all were informed by the pluralist perspective, but alternative institutions such as the African Free School of Newark, Urhuru Sasa in Brooklyn, and Boston's Roxbury Community School, were united in the common belief that black students had to be instructed in group values and immersed in black culture before being sent forth to make their way in the larger society.[23]

Serving both pre-schoolers and older youth, these schools evidenced their founders' conviction that true education consisted of more than multiple choice tests and spelling bees. In many respects they were survival schools—preparing the youngest members of the black subculture for later encounters with white parochialism. They introduced children to concepts such as "liberation," "struggle," and "identity." When they taught that there was both beauty and strength in blackness, instructors were sure to note that conformity to the tastes and standards of white America hindered an individual's quest for self-realization. At all times, faith in one's own people was deemed preferable to trust in material possessions. It was hoped that constant reference to these principles would provide each pupil with a reserve of self-knowledge. Supported in this fashion, they would increase the odds of being able to control their own destiny in later years. As one 1968 position paper made clear, like other supporters of black educational empowerment, proponents of independent community schools believed that "to leave the education of Black children in the hands of people who are white and who are racist is tantamount to suicide." By controlling existing institutions and creating new ones to meet their special needs, black parents would counteract the "socialization in whiteness" carried out through traditional schooling. In doing so, they would assure that the concept—and perhaps the reality—of Black Power was passed on to the next generation.[24]

Supporters of educational empowerment recognized that the realization of effective community control depended upon achieving victories against entrenched political foes of one kind or another. Correct in the belief that a flow chart of urban power relationships would surpass many downtown freeway interchanges in its complexity, they were well aware that political considerations influenced all aspects of urban life. As H. Rap Brown observed in this context, there was no meaningful separation between church and state, art and politics, or politics and individual beliefs: "Everything is inherently political. The only division occurs around the question of whose political interest one will serve."[25] Operating on these understandings, they sought to institute a process of political modernization within urban America. By questioning prevailing political processes, constructing new political structures, and expanding the base of electoral participation, black activists hoped to involve the entire community in building a political force sufficiently powerful to solve *all* the problems of black America.[26]

Political activists were convinced that success in the political arena was a prerequisite for black progress in the areas of economics and education. For some, there seemed no other viable course. Political power meant government control and the ability to influence the agendas of all those institutions, agencies, and programs which affected the lives and interests of black people. The politically powerful decided which group would be "last hired and first fired." They mandated that some, but not all, children have access to good schools. They were able to choose which neighborhoods would be bulldozed and who would be warehoused in vertical ghettos. Politics, said Georgia legislator Julian Bond, had a telling impact on every black American. Ultimately, political decisions would determine "whether we rise or fall, whether we work or starve, whether we fight or surrender, or whether we shall have full manhood rights here and now."[27]

According to black activists, Afro-American communities had not received a fair share of the benefits apportioned through the political system. There were several reasons for this unhappy situation. First, they said, the national parties had betrayed black America. Neither Demo-

crats nor Republicans effectively represented black interests. Their dis-
interest was highlighted whenever the black agenda conflicted with or
was perceived as becoming a burden to that of mainstream political elements. For years, Afro-Americans had evidenced an all-too-predictable
loyalty to the party of FDR, but only rarely were they rewarded for their
votes. Recognizing that they weren't likely to garner more than ten or
fifteen percent of the black vote in national elections, the Republicans
cultivated the black electorate even less vigorously. As a result, Afro-
Americans remained a third class influence within the two-party system. Like most other powerful national institutions, it continued to operate almost exclusively for the benefit of whites.[28]

The noticeable lack of black influence in politics also was blamed on
the manipulative practices of the politically powerful. Even after the
passage of the Voting Rights Act of 1965, ancient devices of disfranchisement were being used to limit the impact of the black vote. Requirements for getting on the ballot had been stiffened and filing fees
increased. Elections were switched from a ward to an at-large basis in
counties with heavy black registrations. Elective offices were made appointive. The traditional mechanism of gerrymandering continued in
use as a proven method of fracturing black voting power.[29]

Black political apathy was cited as yet another source of political im-
potence. Wholly understandable, but regrettable and ultimately reme-
diable, black Americans' low rate of participation in electoral politics
was said to have contributed to the major parties' lack of interest in addressing black concerns. It also helped explain why black voters continued to be considered easy prey by the modern-day disfranchisers. In
the presidential election years of 1964, 1968, and 1972, Afro-Americans
voted at a rate of 58.6 percent, 57.9 percent, and 54.6 percent respec-
tively. The figures were even less impressive in off-year elections.[30] A
bare majority of a minority hardly could be considered either a power to
fear or respect. Edward Brooke's 1966 election to the U.S. Senate, the appointment of former NAACP legal counsel Thurgood Marshall to the
Supreme Court in 1967, and dramatic victories by black mayoral candidates in Cleveland, Gary, and Newark encouraged but did not guarantee
widespread interest in governmental affairs. What was needed, said the
politically astute, was a well-considered program for preserving, nurturing, and expanding the black vote until it became a true source of black
empowerment at both the local and national levels.

During the Black Power era, many such plans were considered. Most
were pluralistic in the sense that they envisioned the eventual sharing of
national political power with other interest groups. Recognizing that

proportionate control of the political process had been a crucial factor in the rise of the Irish, Italians, Jews, and Poles throughout urban America, they sought to parlay their own brand of ethnic politics into similar and equally tangible gains. Even those who had trouble agreeing with Adam Clayton Powell that "honest pluralism is a happy fact of American life" found themselves operating within the constraints of the existing system, employing concepts and language more appropriate to a Senate debate than to a separatist revolution.[31]

Afro-American distinctives were, however, extremely important. The black politicos excoriated "establishment" tendencies. Unlike the white candidates whom Dick Gregory accused of being so condescending that they canvassed suburban districts in expensive limousines, but took their campaign into the ghetto "riding a mule . . . that's pulling a wagonload of watermelon," black office seekers promised to conduct themselves with dignity. Their goal was to share political control, not to dominate, humiliate, or exclude other competing groups. Once in office, the welfare of the black politician's constituents would retain a priority over considerations of individual gain. In order to understand the needs of their people, they would shun suburban sanctuaries and live amidst the poor. There, in constant contact with the ultimate source of their political and moral authority, they would promote an ethical value system unique in the annals of American politics. Justice would take precedence over "control," morality over expediency, peace over war, and a livable environment over corporate profits. Black politics, said the true believers, would transform society, not seek a comfortable niche within it.[32]

The individual planks in the Black Power platform were equally visionary, straining and often surpassing the bounds of what pluralism reasonably could be expected to deliver. At various times, black spokespersons called upon the political system to boost funding for community development corporations, increase the minimum wage, overhaul the food assistance delivery system, expand federally assisted child care centers, create new public service jobs, establish a system of national health insurance, and abolish the death penalty. Other items on the agenda included proportionate black representation on juries and in Congress; a government-guaranteed minimum annual income; and free academic and technical education for blacks at all levels. The list was endless.[33]

For some, to make the demands was sufficiently cathartic. Others labored diligently to build functioning political organizations. At gatherings such as the national black political conventions held in Gary in 1972 and in Little Rock in 1974, delegates debated black political strategy and sought to develop new techniques of community mobilization. They established guidelines for endorsing candidates and discussed ways of pressuring the Democrats into supporting black initiatives. Motivated by heady rhetoric and slogans such as "Black Unity without Uniformity," delegates returned to their home districts with new insight into the inadequacies of the existing system and an increased desire to serve as political brokers in the cause of reform.[34]

Black officeholders both joined in these meetings and formed their own organizations to promote the goals of the new black politics. Groups such as the Black Legislators' Association, the National Conference of Black Mayors, the National Black Caucus of Local Elected Officials, and the Congressional Black Caucus served as consultative bodies within their respective national organizations or governmental units. Offering "representative" black opinion on policy issues, the caucus members were determined to increase the political clout of black America. Unlike the early civil rights leaders who had been shut out of public office, they had the potential to become effective internal lobbyists for the black community. Most recognized the strategic value of their position and quickly learned how to survive within the system. "We realize that power politics is the name of the game," said Congressman Louis Stokes. "We comprehend the game and we are determined to have some meaningful input in the decisions. . . . We have reached a point of political sophistication that provides us not only the knowledge and skill necessary to set our own agenda, but to determine our own frame of reference."[35] The basic frame of reference was pluralism; the guiding vision, black empowerment.

Elected officials such as Stokes believed that coalitions with other interest groups could be established if such arrangements would speed implementation of the black agenda. There was considerable debate on this issue within the community control movement. Soured by their experiences with the Democrats, opponents of coalition politics pointed to the tendency of whites to dominate, and thus control the direction of multiracial alliances. Supporters emphasized potential benefits. They noted that politics was a pragmatic enterprise. One needed allies to provide, among other things, votes and money. Instead of rejecting all potential coalitions out of hand, blacks were urged to establish criteria that would secure their independence within the new relationship. This, of course, assumed that they (1) possessed a clear understanding of their own self-interest; and 2) had a well-developed base of support. If these matters had been addressed, Afro-Americans could enter into short-term or issue-oriented coalitions without guilt. As Charles V.

Hamilton and Stokely Carmichael wrote in 1967, the Black Power movement sought to remove the taint of dependency from black politics, but it carried no directive always to "go it alone." Black Power simply taught that blacks should enter coalitions only *after* they were able to stand on their own.[36]

Those who experienced difficulty in locating compatible allies often promoted "independent" or "third party" politics. Most advocates of this approach functioned within the pluralist tradition, but believed that the fielding of an independent slate of candidates was, for the moment, the most promising way to expand black political influence. By boycotting the major parties, Afro-American voters would send a clear message that their grievances merited immediate attention. Moreover, through independent action, considerable media attention would be drawn to their cause. The importance of the black vote would be confirmed.[37]

Support for the concept that blacks must organize separately and bargain with major power brokers from a position of group strength could be seen in the rise of the Mississippi Freedom Democratic party, Alabama's National Democratic party and Lowndes County Freedom Organization, the United Citizens party of South Carolina, and the Party of Christian Democracy in Georgia.

Challenging establishment Democrats for the black vote in local and statewide elections, these groups sought to rid their rural communities of the "rigid system of racial oppression" which had proven resistant to the electoral reforms of the mid-sixties. Like their northern and more urbanized brothers and sisters, they were convinced that the major parties were insensitive to black needs and thus would continue to frustrate their quest for good schools and decent jobs. Some felt that they had no choice but to initiate independent political action. As one Lowndes County resident noted, "It didn't make sense for us to go join the Democratic party, when they were the people who had done the killing in the county and had beat our heads." Most recognized that they were entering the political fray at a distinct disadvantage, but were determined to make life difficult for their opponents until they got what they wanted. Although "ignorant, smelly, with our noses running," as Stokely Carmichael characterized both himself and his Lowndes County allies, they were going to "take that political power because it belongs to us."[38]

Together with their community control counterparts in the North, these black southerners helped create a political climate which emphasized the *possible* in black affairs. During the Black Power era, the pluralists' expectations shifted from gaining access to the political process to forming an activist cadre within government service. Between 1965 and 1975 the number of Afro-Americans elected to public office at all levels climbed from about 100 to more than 3,500. By the end of the period, black representation in the U.S. House had gone from six to seventeen. The number of black mayors reached 135. Responding to the challenge of independent political action, Eldridge Cleaver and Dick Gregory waged spirited presidential campaigns under the banner of the Peace and Freedom/Freedom and Peace parties in 1968. When, following his defeat, Gregory was inaugurated as president-in-exile and drew up plans for a "Black House" to be built across from the White House, many enjoyed the joke, but also pondered the possibilities. A 1974 survey of black political attitudes showed that 62.6 percent of the respondents would support an independent black party in an effort to help communities organize. In politics, as in education and economics, these black Americans knew that their quest for a greater share of decision-making power depended upon two key factors: (1) a thorough understanding of the power-oriented nature of American institutional life; and (2) the ability to establish a lasting sense of group identity and solidarity. With both fully realized, they could bargain with confidence and from a position of strength.[39]

Nationalism

If we are part of America, then part of what she is worth belongs to us. We will take our share and depart, then this white country can have peace.

Malcolm X, 1963

It was a thin line that divided pluralist from nationalist on the issue of community control. During the Black Power years, this narrow demarcation was crossed so many times it became muddied and indistinct. On occasion, all visible shadings of difference between the two ideologies were gray. When, for example, black militants talked of liberating their communities from parasitical colonial rulers, were they thinking of making a permanent break with white society? And if they were, wouldn't the interim period of what surely would be a lengthy process of nation building closely resemble the pluralists' strategic separatism? In discussing variations on the theme of urban statehood within federalism, were the activists promoting or stepping back from black nationalism?[40] Would black students, fresh from preschool training in revolutionary nationalism at Philadelphia's Freedom Library Day

School, be "living a lie" when they enrolled in the public system?[41] These and other related questions merited in-depth study and careful analysis. Rarely was it given. Most often, black spokespersons simply and honestly stated what they believed without placing their views firmly within any of the classical political traditions. Likewise, harried reporters saw no need to take a crash course in political ideologies just because the civil rights movement had changed into something . . . well, different. At times, the nationalist expression of Black Power seemed intriguingly unfamiliar to almost everyone. Writer Theodore Draper was not far off the mark in asserting that it was "much easier to be a black nationalist than to know what black nationalism is."[42]

In part, this condition existed because, to most Americans, the notion of a black American nationalism *was* unfamiliar. As applied to the modern-day issues of community control, the term resonated with importunate connotations. Mere mention of "black nationalism" made the imagination soar and the juices flow. For most, becoming a committed nationalist was a developmental process. Since many future nationalists had been acculturated to believe that their destiny was inextricably linked to the larger society, they initially were attached to the pluralist assumption that black America's problems could be solved through group political action. At some point, however, doubt would creep in. Each summer it seemed that the festering ghettos provided more jobs for social workers and national guardsmen than for black youth. No one appeared to be working on a way for people to get off the welfare dole or to maintain both personal dignity and a public assistance check. For every black "first," scores languished in the backwaters of American society, their path to a better life blocked by the dual monoliths of caste and class. Critics of the American Dream added their own discouraging words to this depressing scenario and began to talk about "autonomous city-states" and "national homelands." Their interest aroused, wavering pluralists asserted that it would be a useful intellectual endeavor to demonstrate the utility of the black nationhood concept. Certainly, it was unnecessary to close out other options. Shortly thereafter they were heard to say that Afro-Americans should organize *as if* they were building their own separate nation. The die was cast. Soon they would abandon all efforts to operate within a political system which they viewed as being inherently racist and irredeemably insensitive to human needs. Instead, they would adopt a political stance oriented toward the creation of an independent state or some still unspecified form of local self-government. Community control had grown fangs.[43]

Those who sought to use neighborhood empowerment as a stepping stone to black control of the major cities, of the national government, or of a self-governing state developed a full panoply of meanings for the term "black nationalism." Either directly or by implication, most incorporated the concept of separatism into their definition. Some talked of minimizing racial friction by partitioning the United States into black and white living areas. Others saw merit in exploring the possibility of exchanging populations—perhaps swapping the blacks of North America for the whites of South Africa and Zimbabwe. Still others believed that cultural affairs too often were subordinated to politics or economics and that a thoroughgoing separatist cultural revolution was needed. Then, black Americans could establish spiritual independence wherever they might call home.[44] Whether their primary motivation came from urban poverty, Marxist theory, historical example, or a new-found appreciation of black cultural distinctives, nationalists tended to agree that: (1) Separatism differed greatly from segregation. The former was far more ennobling. Its motive force came from within black America and was not imposed by an external power. (2) Both separatism and nationalism were well adapted for use in the black freedom struggle because they were grounded in social reality. Each recognized the essential racial dichotomy of American institutional and cultural life and sought to turn it to black advantage. (3) Since there was little reciprocity of interest or expectation between black and white America, accepted channels for inducing societal change were heavily biased toward maintenance of the status quo. (4) Majoritarian interests almost always were inimical to the welfare of blacks. (5) To survive as a people, Afro-Americans first had to establish a corporate consciousness and sense of collective responsibility. Then, informed by shared group values, they would attempt to chart their own destiny. This was to be accomplished through the formation, preservation, and control of their own institutions and means of expression, independent of white influence. (6) Although strengthened by the geographic consolidation of the black community, their nationalism was not to be defined solely in terms of a struggle over land, but also was to be seen as a struggle for natural resources, social justice, and human dignity. (7) Whatever their preexisting political beliefs, all blacks were to be considered potential members of the black nation.[45]

While not as popular with a broad cross-section of black Americans as were the pluralists, nationalists were more influential than surveys indicated.[46] During the Black Power years, they swelled the ranks of the vanguard—composing a large percentage of those militant blacks who always seemed to be in front of a microphone or television camera. They made the most outrageous demands and received the harshest punishment for doing so. Their intimidating presence within the movement helped black moderates win concessions from white power brokers.

TERRITORIAL NATIONALISTS

For the fruition of black power, for the triumph of black nationhood, I pledge to the Republic of New Africa and to the building of a better people and a better world, my total devotion, my total resources, and the total power of my mortal life.

Oath of Allegiance, Republic of New Africa

Of the three major divisions among nationalists, territorial separatists monitored the debate over community control most closely. Development of the separatist position on this issue can be traced in the ideological and programmatic changes which occurred within the Congress of Racial Equality during the Black Power era. The details of CORE's evolution from moderate civil rights activism to strident black nationalism reveals that community control was an extremely malleable concept, easily shaped and adaptable to almost any ideology or plan promoting group empowerment.

Founded in Chicago during World War II as a nonviolent, direct-action protest organization, CORE gained national recognition during the early 1960s for its southern "freedom ride" campaign and for conducting demonstrations at the 1964 New York World's Fair. By 1965, CORE chapters also had become engaged in a variety of more traditional community development projects. As evidenced by their convention theme, "Black Ghetto: An Awakening Giant," CORE leaders recognized that the central cities faced staggering problems against which their traditional anti-discrimination, equal opportunity emphasis now seemed hopelessly ineffective. With new vigor, CORE entered the ghetto and began organizing the black lower classes.

After door-to-door canvasses were conducted to determine neighborhood concerns, CORE helped form tenants' councils and launch rent strikes. Community centers were opened, offering tutoring, sports, and craft programs, job counseling, and information on health care, family planning, and voter registration. In some cities, unemployed youth were assembled for clean-up campaigns; in others, they formed patrols to watch for police brutality. Some chapters assisted black workers in organizing for better pay and work conditions and lobbied for increased grass roots representation on local antipoverty commissions. As National Director James Farmer noted, the freedom ride experience had taught CORE to employ local citizens in their demonstrations whenever possible. This practice encouraged dispirited blacks to "take their lives into their own hands." "We are turning inward to the core of the Negro community," he wrote, "where ultimately the strength of our people must lie."[47]

CORE's shift away from high-visibility, direct-action demonstrations to the more tedious, less showy work of community organization, was due in part to significant membership growth and a subsequent increase in staffing and other resources. By 1965, CORE had 80,000 members and a staff of 137 who worked through 220 full-fledged or affiliated chapters. The active membership had become predominantly black as had the leadership in most chapters and on the National Action Council. Recognizing the trend, Farmer remarked that CORE had "ceased simply serving Negroes and has become a Negro organization."[48]

Both the "darkening" of CORE and its new community orientation were conducive to the development of a separatist Black Power perspective. For some, black separatism and community organization seemed to go hand in hand. Compared to the earlier civil rights thrust, organizing the ghetto required far less contact with the white power structure. As one longtime west coast member asserted, within this predominantly black environment Afro-American activists "felt confident not only in excelling whites, but even being able to do without any whites at all."[49] This confidence seemed to increase within CORE following James Farmer's resignation late in 1965 and the election early the next year of Floyd McKissick to the organization's top leadership post.

Under McKissick, CORE moved its national office from downtown Manhattan to uptown Harlem. Convenient to the problems of the ghetto, CORE now operated out of the third floor of a roach-ridden walkup at 135th Street and Seventh Avenue, right across the street from Jennie Lou's Restaurant and the Truth Coffee Shop. From the new leader's desk (to the right of which hung a banner proclaiming "BLACK POWER" in large, bold letters) came new initiatives. A major "Target City" project was begun in Baltimore. Conceived as a showcase demonstration of how the urban poor could be mobilized for their own advancement, the program organized welfare mothers and tenants. Staff members developed the Maryland Freedom Union, which campaigned for better wages for black workers in white-owned ghetto stores. With the assistance of federal funding, CORE began a program to train high school dropouts as gas station attendants and managers. Moving beyond economic issues, "Target City" workers initiated a movement to redistrict the city and thereby create an effective power base for black politicians.[50]

Not long thereafter, the National Action Council approved an (overly) ambitious 15-point plan which contained a number of key cultural components. In addition to launching a major resettlement and community development drive and starting up a "country cousin" program to welcome and help settle displaced black farmers in urban areas, CORE sought to expand the teaching of African languages throughout the black community. The leadership also hoped to develop black cultural centers and craft workshops. An art fair was planned for Harlem. Partial funding for these activities would be provided by mail order sales of books and craft items. It was believed that CORE's cultural program eventually could be expanded to include the establishment of a black university.[51]

The 1966 national convention bode ill for pluralism. Those attending heard Stokely Carmichael declare: "We don't need white liberals. . . . We have to make integration irrelevant." McKissick added that as long as whites had "all the power and money" nothing would be accomplished. In his opinion, nonviolence was "a dying philosophy" which had "outlived its usefulness." The only way to achieve meaningful change was to "take power." Despite warnings that an organization like CORE could not survive without white support, delegates eventually endorsed the Black Power slogan and discarded their longtime commitment to nonviolence. Following these meetings, CORE became more explicitly separatist. The word "multiracial" was dropped from the constitution in 1967 and, before long, the national director could be heard talking about blacks living as a "nation within a nation." White members responded by fleeing to safer shores. In resigning from the national advisory committee post which she had held for twenty years, southern white supporter Lillian Smith spoke for many of the disaffected when she complained that "CORE has been infiltrated by adventurers and by nihilists, black nationalists and plain old-fashioned haters, who have finally taken over."[52]

Floyd McKissick was not, however, a nihilist. He wasn't even a very predictable "bourgeois" nationalist. McKissick's personal leanings were revealed in his innovative plans for black independence through economic development. In the fall of 1968, he left the directorship of CORE and established his own consulting firm. Floyd B. McKissick Enterprises operated on the principle that black Americans should be provided with the means to "become a part of the American capitalist system and thereby achieve social and economic parity with the white community." Claiming neither to support nor condemn capitalism,

McKissick simply recognized the existing system as "a power fact of life." If blacks were to share in the wealth of the nation, they had to become good entrepreneurs. They had to establish black-run enterprises "on every level of the capitalist structure" if they were to improve the trade imbalance which continued to plague the nation's black "colonies." With black people controlling their own industries "from beginning to end," whites would be forced to invest in black corporations if they were to reap any economic benefit from their relationship with Afro-America. To these ends, McKissick sought to join black economic development with social commitment to the black community.[53]

McKissick's model for community development was "Soul City," a completely new town to be created in Warren County, North Carolina, just south of the Virginia border. In the early seventies, Warren County had a population of some 15,000, 63 percent of which was black. Almost one-third of its residents were unemployed or underemployed agricultural workers with few industrial skills. There were no black elected officials. The general nature of race relations could be summed up in local newspaper editor Bignall Jones' response to a news service reporter's query: "I carry all the nigger weddings," he said. "It's a fully integrated paper." It was here, in the ninety-eighth–poorest of the state's 100 counties, that Soul City would rise.[54]

With the support of the Small Business Administration, the Department of Housing and Urban Development, and the Chase Manhattan Bank, McKissick hoped to build a prosperous "free standing community" that would differ in important respects from such posh developments as Columbia, Maryland and Reston, Virginia. Located in a completely rural area, it would not be dependent on population spillover from a major urban center. Although employing an integrated staff, Soul City would be conceived and managed by blacks. Industry and affordable housing, not campus like clusters of expensive homes would be the developer's first priority. These were the major distinctives, said McKissick. The emphasis was on "social gains and building something for minorities in the Black Belt," not on "siphoning [people's] income to put them into great big houses." Projected over 20 years and an eventual 5,000 acres, Soul City was to become a community of 50,000 with an economic base of 18,000 industrial jobs.[55]

McKissick saw Soul City as a grand experiment to prove the efficacy of Black Power and the value of black capitalist economics. Eventually, spurred by the success of the Warren County venture, other new cityscapes would appear. Each development would be controlled by blacks, with technical assistance provided by government and private

Floyd McKissick. From U.S. News & World Report Collection, Library of Congress.

industry. It was not mandatory that they be located exclusively in rural areas. Land in places such as Harlem or Bedford-Stuyvesant could be transferred to community corporations whose trustees would be elected by local residents. Ownership of businesses also could be transferred, with the present absentee owners retained by the government as advisers to the new black owners. As this "reclamation" program advanced, all government facilities in the black living areas would be operated by black people. Provided, at last, with the resources to address the task of urban renewal—resources earned but never collected "over years of toil and oppression"—the Afro-American community would be able to solve its own problems. Within one generation, said a hopeful McKissick, this process of ever-expanding economic and political control could result in the creation of "two or three states that are Black led, Black controlled, and predominantly Black populated." Then, with Black Power fully realized in at least a few, presumably southern, locales, the Afro-American people would be able to exert unprecedented influence within the federal system. This newfound clout could be used to improve the quality of life in black communities nationwide and, through a revision of foreign policy guidelines, in black households throughout the world. According to McKissick, whites had little alternative but to relinquish a significant portion of their power, money, and resources to blacks in this dramatic fashion. "The continuation of present policies can inspire only disaster," he wrote in 1969. "As mighty and as powerful as is America, it could not withstand the total onslaught of the oppressed."[56]

If McKissick's discourse on federalism and the free-enterprise system—as modified by Black Power—caused some to wonder exactly where his pluralism ended and his nationalism began, there was no such problem with his successor at CORE. One of Roy Innis' first press releases as national director proclaimed that CORE had become, "once and for all," a black nationalist organization with "separation" as its goal. He deemed this course of action "a necessary and pragmatic way of organizing two separate and distinct races of people." Unlike the "pie-in-the-sky" supporters of integration, separatists were said to be capable of recognizing the importance of manipulating power relationships. Their program would enable Afro-America to bargain with whites at a distance and from a position of strength. No longer merely one of several minority supplicants at the altar of white control, blacks would show that they could stand on their own. Their successful independent endeavors would convince even the most skeptical critics that the two races could coexist if each controlled their own institutions.[57]

In the summer of 1968, CORE officially excluded whites from membership. As the spirit of nationalism grew, delegates to the annual convention in Columbus, Ohio, avidly discussed the concept of a black nation-state. Some demanded that the seaboard states from Maryland to Florida be emptied of whites and turned over to black separatists.[58] Under Innis' leadership, CORE unveiled a three-part program for the national liberation of black America.

Phase I involved support of the Community Self-Determination Act introduced in Congress in July 1968. Backed by a bipartisan group of 26 senators, the bill promoted the establishment of community development corporations. If enacted, federal loans and tax incentives would be used to help the corporations run profit-making enterprises. Earnings would fund community health and education programs. Through this initiative, blacks would be given a chance to operate their own businesses. National corporations would be motivated to locate black-managed plants in the central city. With this mechanism in place, said Innis, black Americans would have an effective "economic instrument" to assist them in gaining control of their own communities.[59]

Ultimately, Innis hoped that blacks would be able to call all the shots. After they had established plants in the ghetto, white capitalists would sell them to blacks and move out. By "seal[ing] the border" and placing a "membrane" around the black community, residents would have full interaction with outside business interests, but at the same time would be able to set preconditions and guidelines for those who sought to engage in mutually beneficial economic relationships. This black nationalist approach to economic development would protect black interests, maximize the flow of money into the community, and bring about a "geometric progression toward economic well-being." Why would whites support such stringent limitations on their earning power? Innis claimed not to have "an unshakable faith in white people," but was confident that one underlying assumption would hold true in the long run—that those who had the most power and thus the most to lose from racial chaos would, however grudgingly, go along with his proposal.[60]

The second part of the program adapted the community control theme to non-economic areas of concern. Innis held that all people in America's heterogeneous society lived in natural sociological units known as communities. White communities also served as political subdivisions of county, state, or federal government. This was not true for black communities. They existed as politically impotent "colonial appendages" of the white units, whose power brokers controlled the flow of goods and services into the colonized areas. As a result, like exploited and underdeveloped Third World nations, the black communities suffered from high unemployment, poverty, and an unfavorable balance of trade. Even the most impoverished Third World country exercised a greater measure of national sovereignty and had more autonomy in economic and political dealings than did black America. This had to change, said Innis. Blacks had to gain those missing ingredients—sovereignty and autonomy. The control of goods and services flowing through a distinct geographical area inhabited by a distinct population group had to be in the hands of the indigenous people. Afro-Americans had to control their own schools, health care facilities, law enforcement agencies—in short, "every single institution that takes our tax moneys and is supposed to distribute goods and services equitably for us."[61]

Phase III, the long range component of CORE's plan, followed logically from this. When blacks ceased to relate to the larger nation as a

Roy Innis. From U.S. News & World Report Collection, Library of Congress.

dependent people and began to assert power through control of their community institutions, the black colonies would in fact compose a "nation within a nation." In Innis' conceptualization, the black nation could be said to exist wherever and whenever black people were able to "redefine the turf" upon which they lived. The areas which had been removed from white control need not be contiguous. The black nation would be "the sum total of all the black parts"—a collection of black enclaves joined together as a separate political entity with parallel institutional systems. As Phase III progressed, the United States constitution would be revised. A new protective social contract would redefine the relationship between whites and blacks, at long last recognizing the latter as a "major interest group." Densely populated black areas of the country, especially those in urban centers, would lose their unofficial status as sub-colonial appendages of the cities and become political subdivisions of the state. Then, as other interest groups always had done, black people would control the basic institutions within their individual spheres of influence.[62]

CORE had journeyed a long way from its roots in the American pacifist movement. By the late sixties, the founding generation would find its ideological preachments strange and its rhetoric all too abrasive. The saga of CORE and its evolving leadership elite reveals the difficulty that blacks and whites, integrationists, pluralists, and nationalists had in working together within the same organization during the era of Black Power. Nevertheless, CORE's continuing emphasis on the issues of community control and economic development revealed that fundamental concerns could survive shifts in leadership and ideology. The manner of expressing these concerns and the specific programs designed to address them changed considerably during the 1960s, but bold proposals designed to reduce black America's power deficit continued to be forwarded, sparked by the creative tension released through intra-group rivalry and the bravado of CORE leaders. As Roy Innis once observed, since only instruments of white-imposed segregation, but not of black-controlled separatism, had received legal sanction during this country's long history, who honestly could say that CORE's plans wouldn't work?[63]

During the years 1965–1975, other voices elaborated upon and expanded Innis' dream of a city-state federation composed of "a series of islands with land separating us."[64] Members of the Nation of Islam and the Republic of New Africa were especially vocal in presenting proposals for the acquisition of sovereign territory. In truth, the former group served as inspiration for the latter, while the latter helped carry the torch of territorial nationalism on to a new post-Malcolm X generation.

The separatist stance of the Nation of Islam had been made clear to initiates since its founding in the midst of the Great Depression. Patriarch Elijah Muhammad taught that all Americans of African descent belonged to an "Asian Black Nation," more specifically to the tribe of Shabazz. It was the mission of the North American branch of this ancient clan to redeem the Black Nation from centuries of unjust white rule. Short of divine intervention, the best solution to black people's problems was thought to be relocation to a "state or territory of their own—either on this continent or elsewhere." Elijah Muhammad maintained that this separatist approach met with Allah's approval and was more than justified by past history. On this point he was adamant. It was "FAR MORE IMPORTANT TO TEACH SEPARATION OF THE BLACKS AND WHITES

IN AMERICA THAN PRAYER." Certainly, only fools willingly would choose to integrate with "400-year-old enemies," thereby making perpetual beggars of their progeny. No, there was no such thing as living in peace with white America. There could be no peace—or true freedom—in the world until "every man is in his own country."[65]

The Nation's leaders were less willing to make definitive statements concerning matters of time, place, and method of implementation. Often, their position on territorial separation was couched in eschatological language or hidden in cryptic references to "the earth that originally belonged to us." Members of the Nation would serve as the separatist vanguard, but where was the Muslim Zion? At times, Elijah Muhammad seemed not to care whether the new black homeland was located in North America or on "an isle in the Pacific or Atlantic Oceans." The important thing was the acquisition of "some land" that was fertile and rich in mineral wealth. If the U.S. government refused to countenance the surrender of a fair share of its territorial assets, blacks would not start a war to seize the land. Neither would they beg. Instead, the Nation would demand federal support for voluntary resettlement in a foreign land—giving "to . . . Caesar what is Caesar's" and moving elsewhere, preferably "back where we came from, where you found us." The price of this relocation would be steep, however. Black Muslims held that the federal government was obligated to finance and maintain the expatriate settlement for a period of up to twenty-five years.[66]

Should whites consider this price too dear, Elijah Muhammad was perfectly content to consider partition of the United States into white and non-black sectors. Here, the Muslim plan for territorial separatism became somewhat more specific, encouraging the belief that this was a preferred option. Spokespersons repeatedly called attention to the Black Nation's inherent right to land in America. Their claim was based on two key considerations: (1) white settlers originally stole the country from a nonwhite people, and (2) blacks had worked for centuries as chattel slaves and even longer as exploited wage laborers, thereby legitimately earning a share of the nation's assets. "We helped you to get what you have," Muhammad told whites, now it was time to repay the favor. The scope of the proposed territorial cession varied over time and according to speaker—from "two or three states" to more than two dozen. "We have well earned whatever they give us," said Muhammad. "If they give us twenty-five states, we have well earned them." However large, it was claimed that great things were in store for those who elected to settle the new homeland. Separation would enable black people to escape the "mental poisoning" of their former slave-masters. They would

Transporting Nation of Islam produce to market. From U.S. News & World Report Collection, Library of Congress.

Elijah Muhammad. From U.S. News & World Report Collection, Library of Congress.

"discover themselves," learn to think on their own, and then work to create a vibrant Islamic civilization "beyond the white world."[67]

According to the political economy of the Nation, separatism was designed to lessen the psychological impact of white domination and to enhance black community control. Even without full-blown statehood, much could be accomplished toward these ends. Indeed, by the dawn of the Black Power era, Muhammad's followers had taken his advice to heart and created an incipient nation within a nation. Determined to become an independent people, they pooled their resources, spent money among themselves, and created their own institutions. In the words of one such supporter, Brother Leonard IX, they would "keep on building the little nation that we now have . . . until we get enough of our people together so that the Messenger will not have to beg for any agreements."[68]

The magnitude of the Nation's assets were shrouded in secrecy, but they included such trappings of independent statehood as an Islamic flag, said to be several trillion years old; a communalistic tithing/taxation system known as the "Duty"; the University of Islam—primarily an elementary and high school system; a paramilitary self-defense corps, the Fruit of Islam; and a wide-ranging economic infrastructure of businesses, factories, and farms. Beyond all of this was a unique theology which transcended normal religious boundaries, greatly influencing all group economic and cultural activities.

Public awareness of the Nation's program and of Elijah Muhammad's belief that "this is the time in history for the separation of the so-called Negroes and the so-called white Americans" increased following Mike Wallace's five-part television documentary "The Hate That Hate Produced" (1959) and the media's subsequent discovery of the outspoken and charismatic Malcolm X. Soon mainstream organs like *Time, U.S. News & World Report*, and *Reader's Digest* were informing readers that "purveyor[s] of . . . cold black hatred" were skulking about the land. Although he likened the situation to "what happened back in the 1930s when Orson Welles frightened America" with his broadcast of an imaginary alien invasion, Malcolm X would not be quieted simply to calm white people's nerves. He continued to promote the Nation's separatist program, sometimes joking that it would be nice if the Messenger would choose someplace sunny, like California or Florida, for the Muslim Zion.[69]

More than any other spokesperson, Malcolm X convinced members of the Black Power generation that it was foolish to accept white America's halfhearted and deceitful offers of "integration into her doomed society." His suggestion that the only permanent solution to the nation's racial dilemma was "complete separation on some land that we can call our own" frightened whites but emboldened blacks. Even after his break with the Nation and subsequent assassination, Malcolm's militant reproach to white society continued to strike deep chords within Afro-America. His image and message encouraged many to conclude that moderate civil rights organizations "spent most of their time planning the annual brotherhood dinner" and were capable of delivering but a single message to whites: "the harder you kick my ass the more I love you." To many, only Malcolm X seemed to understand the depth of the abyss separating the races.[70]

Nowhere was the Muslim leader's message more influential than within a nationalist organization known as the Republic of New Africa.

Co-founder Milton Henry, a Yale-educated Detroit lawyer, had accompanied Malcolm X on his African travels. At first, Henry couldn't fathom his touring companion's belief that separatism was the basis of a people's independence. Then, while visiting government officials in West Africa, his eyes were opened. He saw former college classmates, now high-level dignitaries, "sitting in their offices making decisions" and realized that neither he nor most other black Americans had "the kind of power that permits one to make a real decision." Henry concluded that Malcolm was right. Power could come only through independence. Reflecting further, he came to believe that black Americans constituted a nation—a "community of suffering" whose differences were overshadowed by a wealth of shared experiences and a common relationship to the powerful ruling race.[71]

In 1967, Henry and his brother Richard joined in the organization of Detroit's Malcolm X Society, helping to shape its program of self-defense and separatism. Soon, like Malcolm, they dropped their "slave names." Milton became Brother Gaidi Obadele. Richard designated himself Imari Abubakari Obadele and began to call for government reparations in partial compensation for centuries of slavery and injustice. A portion of the reparations were to be paid through the cession of five southern states which then would be organized into a new black nation. In March 1968, the Obadeles and several hundred other nationalists from around the country met in Detroit to solidify their plans for black statehood. A declaration of independence, written by Imari, was circulated and signed, thereby bringing into existence the Republic of New Africa. Shortly thereafter, local branches or "consulates" were established nationwide. New members became "citizens of record," transferring their national allegiance to the black government.[72]

The RNA's position on territorial separatism was clear and unambiguous. The states of South Carolina, Georgia, Alabama, Mississippi, and Louisiana constituted "the *subjugated territory*" of the black republic. The basic objective of Afro-Americans should be to liberate this land upon which black people long had lived and, with their blood and sweat, had helped develop. Once sovereignty was achieved, the RNA's present "government-in-exile" would work to "consolidate the Revolution" by constructing new institutions guaranteed to improve the lives of black residents. *Ujamaa*, the Tanzanian model of cooperative economics and community self-sufficiency, would serve as a guide for the structuring of the Republic's economy. When, in late May 1968, Brother Imari hand delivered the outline of this program to the U. S. State De-

Leaders of the Republic of New Africa. Photograph by Adger Cowans, which first appeared in *Esquire* magazine, ca. January 1969. Courtesy of the Hearst Corporation.

partment and requested the opening of negotiations between the two "nations," administration officials must have wondered where their community development initiatives had gone wrong.[73]

As they waited (in vain) for a serious reply to their proposal, officers of the Republic planned for the future—and for all possible exigencies. What, for example, would be the course of action taken if the United States was unwilling to cede the five states or provide the $400 billion in start-up money which the RNA demanded as part of the reparations settlement? Although Gaidi Obadele referred to the funding package as "chump change," he knew that federal officials likely would view the matter in a somewhat different light. As a result, the RNA's first contingency plan was based on the power of the black ballot. If land and money were not immediately forthcoming, the RNA would purchase farmland in rural Mississippi to serve as a prototype "New Community" settlement and future national capitol. It would be named El Malik in honor of Malcolm X and be operated much like the land of any business corporation in the state. Having gained a territorial base, the group then would organize black voters. Through legitimate political processes, blacks would ascend to power in county after county. Eventually, Mississippi and the other four contiguous states destined to form the Republic of New Africa would come under black legislative and police control, greatly increasing the RNA's ability to bargain with the U.S. Congress. Like the Jews in Palestine, Afro-Americans would have a power base from which they could say, "We have land and we want to change the sovereignty."[74]

But, what if the American government proved actively hostile to the building of a RNA power bloc? In such an eventuality, the Republic would fight a "people's war" on two fronts. First, a formally organized army, the New African Security Force, would meet the enemy as it invaded RNA territory. In active support of their troops, the Republic's civilian population would harass the invaders, leaving "not one drop of water that is not poisoned, not one ounce of gasoline that is usable, not one bridge left standing." Prepared for indefinite combat through training in the RNA's peacetime police corps, the Black Legion, southern blacks would prove formidable opponents in a struggle for control of the homeland.[75]

As the battle raged, RNA sympathizers throughout the urban North would act spontaneously to open a second front. Although operating outside the direct control of the RNA, these urban guerrillas would possess a "second-strike capability" potent enough to divide the U.S. forces. Northern industry would be brought to the brink of total collapse by this underground army composed of "bank clerks and street cleaners and college professors and housewives and filling station attendants and doctors and ministers and little old ladies." Paraphrasing James Baldwin, Imari Obadele claimed that the scene in the industrial heartland would be one of incredible destruction: "no more the corner cleaners but the factory next time."[76]

According to the Obadeles, the combined onslaught of the guerrillas and the RNA Security Force would bring U.S. representatives to the bargaining table on their knees. If the Vietnamese could force an American retreat from Southeast Asia "without ever being able to land a single bomb on a single American city," certainly the RNA and its allies had the potential to win far greater concessions. As Brother Gaidi told a reporter in 1968, "They can't shoot all of us. They can't shoot enough to discourage others. . . . This country will either talk to the separatists today or will talk to them later."[77]

Presuming then that a sovereign black nation would be established, either through peaceful negotiations or by force of arms, what would life be like within the new land? Leaders of the RNA once again consulted their oracle and concluded that it would be marvelous. Since the five-state area already was equipped with roads, factories, and harbors, the Republic would begin its existence without many of the handicaps which burdened developing nations. White technicians, granted resident visas, could contribute to the running of industry, but would have far less authority than in earlier years. After being subjected to a rigorous entrance examination, white immigrants would be put on notice that their continued presence was to be determined by the needs of the nation. Whites deemed unacceptable, either among prospective immigrants or within the nonblack population resident at the time of statehood, would be sent to the United States or re-educated. Their places would be taken by Afro-Americans from the North eager to vacation at the black resorts in Biloxi and Gulfport.[78]

Although political rights and freedom of the press would be limited, unions discouraged, and military service made compulsory for both sexes, black citizens could appreciate the fact that they were not, as Brother Imari phrased it, recreating America "all over again but in technicolor." Assurance that they were, indeed, developing a truly *New Africa* would come through an outpouring of creative cultural activity. Energized by the experience of winning independence, black theatre, dance, and art would thrive within the altered social context. As "false and alien ideas and institutions" were discarded, both citizens of the Republic and those abroad would witness the "cultural realigning of a whole people." Uncontaminated by white standards of acceptability, blacks would be free to develop their own definitions of aesthetic excellence. According to RNA Minister of Culture and Education Baba Oseijeman Adefunmi, full development of the nation-state concept would allow black America to become "a completely separate nation mentally, spiritually, politically, even in ways of marriage and burials."[79]

The RNA's detailed blueprint for exercising their territorial imperative in the Deep South discounted the possibility that competing nationalist plans could become viable approaches to black liberation. The Republic's leaders rejected proposals that blacks work toward forming a nation within a nation by setting up independent city-states in urban areas. This was unacceptable, they said. Whites would "have us surrounded," controlling the food supply, transportation, and utilities. Urban residents would remain at the mercy of external forces. Even if such polities were established as an intermediate step to true nationhood, the whole process would be slowed. No, the best approach was to get out and get away as soon as possible. Having taken this position on the city-state federation concept, the RNA was willing to give up claims to the land-locked urban "reservations" in exchange for the contiguous two-ocean, five-state territory in the southland.[80]

A second nationalist approach rejected by the RNA was pan-African emigration. Reasons for opposition to resettlement in Africa ranged from the logistical ("It's easier to put furniture on a truck than to get it across that ocean") to the tactical (a sovereign state located in North America would be more effective in lobbying the superpowers on behalf of beleaguered African brothers and sisters). Members of the RNA were interested in expanding diplomatic and commercial relations between black America and Africa. Some even talked of reintroducing African so-cial forms—including polygamy—into the former American South. But, they would not countenance relocation to the African continent, closing the door on a concept that had become the subject of consider-able debate within the international black community.[81]

Like the domestic separatists, supporters of repatriation made selec-tive reference to the writings and speeches of Malcolm X when seeking approval for their beliefs. During the Black Power era, pan-Africanists of all stripes echoed the Muslim leader's view that black Americans had erred in neglecting to establish "direct brotherhood lines of com-munication" with African peoples. This was only to be expected in the American sociocultural context. As Malcolm had explained, the white-dominated media continually bombarded blacks with negative images of Africa: jungle savages, pagan idolaters, cannibals. A constant diet of this bitter fare had caused Afro-Americans to disassociate themselves from the "Dark Continent". Early in life they learned to hate the African people and, by extension, the very "blood of Africa" that was in their veins. In this manner, whites had brainwashed most black Americans into conducting their daily affairs as if they were more American than African. Subconsciously, said Malcolm, blacks knew that the reverse was much closer to the truth. To end the deception and promote correct understanding, they had to "return' to Africa philosophically and cul-turally," developing a working unity within the framework of pan-Africanism.[82] For those who understood the term to have connotations beyond the philosophical or cultural, pan-Africanism might mean an ac-tual physical return to the ancestral homeland.

Promoters of emigration anticipated that black Americans would re-ceive a warm reception from their long-lost African kin. Like Malcolm X, upon whom Nigerian admirers had bestowed the Yoruba name Omowale, "the son who has come home," those who were prepared to make a contribution to the developing African states would be welcomed with open arms.[83] According to the emigrationists, this long-delayed reunification of African peoples would benefit both parties. Afro-Americans would gain a land base on "the richest continent in the world"—a territorial foothold far more secure than they would have in any black nation-state located in North America. In Africa they would neither be surrounded by hostile whites nor burdened with "the collective failures of American capitalism." Instead of living in constant fear of a neighboring white majority, settlers would find their spirits rejuvenated through association with the free-spirited, uncorrupted Africans. Although busily engaged in infusing post-colonial society with indigenous values, their hosts would assist the newcomers in adapting to a social system that was oriented to people rather than to things. Provided such a setting, the American expatriates would be able to develop their maximum human potential. In return, they would employ their technical expertise in the cause of national development. By assisting the African states to increase in strength, all African peoples—including those of the diaspora—would gain new status and pride. Then, as Malcolm X had forecast, even the black American who elected not to emigrate would be "respected and recognized because he has a country behind him, a continent behind him. . . . some power behind him."[84]

Not so fast, said skeptics, applying the brakes to the emigrationists' runaway enthusiasm. There were a number of matters which had to be addressed before those of the nationalist persuasion could abandon plans for a North American nation-state and return en masse to the "motherland." Black critics of separation conceded that blood was thicker than water, but were less certain about their relationship to blood brothers and sisters who had been separated by a very large body of water for centuries. Except for aesthetic and historical concerns, was there really any profit in believing that "we are all Africans?" Some indigenous leaders cast doubt upon this contention. According to Tom Mboya, Kenya's minister for economic planning and development, the only thing the visitors had in common with native Kenyans was their color. Beyond that, black American travelers quickly discovered that they were in "a totally foreign and strange community" with "a strange culture, strange habits and strange attitudes of mind." He found it disconcerting that they believed it was possible to shed their American culture and become instantaneously African. Some even held the most ridiculous views of native culture, thinking for example that to identify with the Africans one should "wear some cheap Japanese or Hong Kong-made textiles [and] a shaggy beard or a piece of cloth or skin on the head." African culture, said Mboya and like-minded commentators, was much deeper than this. It was "the sum of our personality and our attitude toward life." It could not be mastered in a day, as many from the United States seemed to believe. Realistically, the black expatriates were the African's nieces, nephews, and cousins—of Africa, but not fully African. Culturally, they could be categorized as "sub-American, and extremely little African." Indeed, said the harshest critics, they were Americans born and bred. They talked, thought, and behaved like Americans. Typically, they assumed too much and were "very brash."[85]

These concerns were echoed by black Americans who had lived in Africa or had studied the customs of its varied population. Most black visitors, they said, knew little about the continent, its history, or its traditions. Many only recently had begun to understand *themselves.* Some seemed to think that their longtime residence in the land of electric toothbrushes, garbage disposals, and men traveling in space somehow made them wiser and more able than their African hosts. Others were far too eager to enlighten Africans with their visions of proper revolutionary consciousness or definitive readings of the black historical experience. Instead, the newcomers should have been listening to the Africans and mining their storehouse of wisdom acquired over centuries of colonization and neocolonization.[86]

The most perceptive recognized their shortcomings and felt ill at ease in a social context where one couldn't "crack a joke and have someone . . . *really* understand it." In their longing for American conveniences and desire to fathom the unique characteristics of African society, the visitors arrived at a new appreciation of their own, distinctive black American culture. Upon reflection, some concluded that cultural misperceptions had contributed to their sense of alienation. As one expatriate confessed, their concept of Africa all too often was formed in America—an Afro-American Africa "based primarily on a reaction to the white man's Africa and what we thought Africa would be like." Upon arrival, they were disappointed because what they were seeing and experiencing failed to conform to their preconceptions. In essence, the black Americans' view of the continent was a projection of their own psychological and emotional needs.[87]

African commentators agreed with this assessment, adding that such misunderstandings were not confined to the Western Hemisphere. While it was true that the pejorative view of African society forwarded by Hollywood had caused generations of black Americans to believe that Africa was "a mere curiosity, a jungle country of primitive people," Africans, too, had been affected by the popular media's disinformation campaign. Many knew of their black cousins only through their image in films and had concluded that this was one branch of the family tree that could be pruned without great loss. According to Ugandan writer John Nagenda, few Africans were eager to claim a pan-African brotherhood with filmdom's "flashing-teethed, eye-rolling, broken-shouldered, perpetually perplexed nigger" whose only distinction in life was that he "brought drinks to Clark Gable." Certainly, Afro-Americans had to rid themselves of the notion that Africans "live even now in a bygone era." But, Africans also needed to understand that the black Americans' brusque and sometimes overly assertive demeanor was, in part, a response to the fact that whites long had treated them as if they *were* the stereotypical shuffling incompetents seen on the big screen. Until both sides addressed these matters of culture and cultural stereotyping, pan-African relationships were bound to remain tenuous and filled with tension.[88]

Despite the many problems involved with extending racial solidarity on an international basis, committed emigrationists continued to believe that the joining of two separate black nationalisms was an obvious solution to the relative powerlessness of dark-skinned peoples worldwide. Through their return to "Mother Africa" they hoped to convince skeptics that Black Power actually meant African Power. Convinced that pan-Africanism was the highest political expression of the separatist ethic, they studied African history and culture, worked to divest the continent of remaining neocolonial appendages, and formed organizations to promote travel, technical assistance, and repatriation. Those involved with groups such as the African Nationalist Pioneer Movement and the African-American Repatriation Association were convinced that once their people were in the homeland, *they* would not add to the Ugly (Afro) American image. Instead, they would provide yet another alternative for territorial separatists seeking a locale whose political climate was conducive to the forging of a black nation.[89]

REVOLUTIONARY NATIONALISTS

There are two forms of violence: violence directed at you to keep you in your place and violence to defend yourself against that suppression and to win your freedom. If our demands are not met, we will sooner or later have to make a choice between continuing to be victims or deciding to seize our freedom.
Eldridge Cleaver, 1968

Many nationalists felt that any African "return" had to be accompanied by a thoroughgoing socialist transformation of society. They recognized

that black Americans could not escape the effects of white power by fleeing to Africa. Even after independence, African states continued to be
entangled in exploitative economic relationships within the world
capitalist system. To remedy this situation, nationalists would support
guerrilla movements against the remaining European settler governments and work to strengthen progressive black nation-states against
capitalist subversion. For some, true African independence could be
achieved only through continent-wide socialist revolution. For others,
the specific theatre of confrontation mattered little. No black person
was free until all were free. The fundamental problem facing black and
other Third World peoples was American-led, capitalist control of international economic affairs. The fundamental solution then, was to make
the entire world a battlefield—to organize both nationally and interna-
tionally for the overthrow of the prevailing system. To those staying in
the United States, this would mean mounting a socialist revolt in the
very maw of the enemy.[90] During the Black Power era, the most militant
advocates of this position were convinced that all efforts toward building black nationalism should be subordinated to this task. It was either
"unite or perish" under a racist and fascist regime.[91] "For Black people it
is not a question of leaving or separating," said the revolutionaries,
"given our historical experiences, we know better than anyone that the
animal that is america must be destroyed."[92]

As explicated during the Black Power era, the basic tenets of black revolutionary nationalism held that the right to self-determination was inherent in all nations, including the black "internal colony of the United
States." In order to end their exploitation, Afro-Americans had to gain
control of land and political power through national liberation, establishing revolutionary socialism as their operative creed. Since a nationalist revolution would be considered reactionary if concerned only
with the problems of blacks, it was incumbent upon participants to recognize the international character of capitalist oppression and act accordingly. Control of the black nation-state had to be viewed as part of
the world liberation movement, not as an end in itself. There could be
no separate peace with the oppressor. Instead, alliances would be made
with Third World peoples, and, after careful scrutiny, with white radicals. Within these working relationships, the black "peasantry" (variously defined as the laboring class or the underclass) would compose a
leadership vanguard. Through revolutionary struggle, the downtrodden
would banish neocolonial imperialists from the globe and usher in an
era of unprecedented gains for humanity. With the consolidation of the
revolution, "black internationalism" would prevail, eliminating the

need for aggressive forms of nationalism. The new world society would bring universal law, order, and justice to all people.[93]

As a result of these cataclysmic events, a "New Black Man" would be created. Guided by a fresh conception of morality and social ethics, these reformed individuals would be devoid of all selfishness, egotism, and "me-firstness." Finding their greatest satisfaction in working for the benefit of the collective, they would consider every day a "revolutionary work-day," continuing the struggle against injustice wherever it might lead. After socialist liberation, the "reign and rape of capital" would cease. The "New Black Man" would put a quick end to the practice of poisoning the earth's precious atmosphere with the "Frankenstein byproducts" of capitalism's industrial machine. In the place of capitalist-induced scarcity and planned obsolescence, a worker-controlled economy would appear in which all citizens could have their needs met without "hoarding, hustling or hiring others."[94]

This multifaceted, anti-capitalist ideology, expressed in numerous variations throughout the period, was a melange of the theories of Marx, Lenin, and Mao; DuBois, Garvey, and Malcolm X; Nkrumah, Nyerere, Toure, and Cabral. International in scope, but Afrocentric in its promotion of black Americans ("America's Achilles' heel") as the liberating vanguard, it was flexible enough to be adapted to the needs of a wide variety of black leftists. All felt that they were reading history correctly by linking their cause to Third World liberation movements. The problems of Afro-America, they said, were the result of "the flow of global history" over the past several hundred years. Therefore, it was proper to view the black nationalist struggle as one of both race and class. Both had been used by imperialist exploiters to consolidate their worldwide colonial domination.[95]

This reading of world history and of the contemporary political order set the revolutionary nationalists apart from those whom they derided as "black militants." To their way of thinking, a black militant was an Afro-American who was "angry at white folks for keeping him out of their system." These poseurs could be seen regularly on television in their Afros and dashikis, giving press conferences, scowling, and threatening whites with all manner of property damage if their constituency wasn't placated with low-paying jobs and dependency-breeding poverty programs. Having gained the attention of white authorities, the so-called militant tended to be placed on a government commission, given a $30,000-a-year job, and used by the power elite to "cool off" the ghetto. In contrast, they said, black revolutionaries wanted to tear down and destroy the entire system of oppression. It was impossible for a black revolutionary to be bought off. They were far too committed to the model of the "New Black Man" and the socialist dream of a new world order. According to revolutionary nationalists, the country was "crawling with black militants," but there were all too few black revolutionaries.[96] Their numbers were, however, sufficient to form the vanguard that would bring about an epic reformulation of caste and class relationships both in this country and throughout the world.

The revolutionary nationalists' commitment to socialist revolution was accompanied by a willingness—even eagerness—to achieve their goals through violent means. Resistance was not enough. Aggression was the order of the day. Although they sometimes claimed that there would be no exultation "for the blood that [will flow] in the gutters"— that they would destroy only "so we may be more human"—the revolutionary nationalists left no doubt that the apocalypse was imminent. Intrinsically, violence was neither good nor evil. It was necessary. America always had shielded itself through military might, employing counter-revolutionary violence to maintain the established system. To win their freedom, the oppressed would have to defeat the monster with its own weapons. When the conflict broke, the victim would become the executioner. Then there would be "bloodshed, bloody, bloody bloodshed" such as the world had never seen. The war would be more violent than the Chinese Revolution and last longer than Vietnam—perhaps as much as a generation of struggle lay ahead. But the true revolutionary could not be deterred by the enemy's staying power. They would keep on fighting and "destroy them as sure as the night follows day!" In such an encounter, willingness to die in the cause of right was considered the ultimate expression of a liberated consciousness. Death was the price of revolution—an authentic articulation of the revolutionary struggle. Those who perished in the conflict would be given a hero's burial—a gala upbeat affair with "home-brewed wine and revolutionary music." Relatives would kiss their loved ones goodbye and smile—saddened only by the fact that it had taken so long for the black world to produce such self-sacrificing warriors.[97]

During the late sixties, no revolutionary nationalist group received more publicity than the Black Panther Party. Founded in Oakland in 1966 with a core membership of less than a hundred, the Panthers' penchant for the dramatic soon carried their image and influence far beyond the Bay Area. Chapters formed in England, France, and Israel and in such unlikely North American locales as Des Moines, Iowa and Halifax, Nova Scotia. By the fall of 1970, the Party was operational in some thirty-five cities in nineteen states and the District of Columbia.[98] Both the Panthers' notoriety and their attractive power among young blacks stemmed from the group's militant panache and the response they garnered from the (black and white) establishment. Whether rallying to guard Malcolm X's widow on a West Coast visit or making a dramatic appearance on the floor of the state assembly to lobby against gun control legislation, the typical Panther cut a dashing figure.

They were youthful. In 1968, for example, the top-ranking leadership ranged in age from twenty-six to thirty-four while second-level leaders were between twenty-one and twenty-six. Sixteen- to twenty-one-year-olds predominated among the rank and file.[99]

They were splendidly outfitted. The original Panther uniform—black leather jacket, slacks, shoes, and beret; powder-blue shirts with scarves or turtleneck shirts; dark glasses optional—had great symbolic value. Their very appearance spoke of discipline, organization, unity, and deep commitment to the cause of black liberation.

They were outspoken and, to say the least, vivid in their expression of grievances. Whose ears wouldn't literally *burn* upon hearing Panther children sing "Free Huey Newton" and "We want pork chops, off the pigs;" or Eldridge Cleaver proclaim "total liberty for black people or total destruction for America;" or Bobby Seale's account of younger days spent extorting lunch money from "little white liberal[s]" by threatening to "cut [their] guts out" with his pocket knife; or Panther minister of religion Earl Neil's characterization of the Statue of Liberty as "a cold marble figure of some dyke woman covered with pigeon droppings sitting in a polluted Bay in the Atlantic Ocean"? The Panthers termed such phrasings "political rhetoric," "metaphor" and "the language of the ghetto." Outsiders called it intimidation.[100]

Above all else, they were armed to the teeth, employing their arsenal both as a self-defense mechanism and as an aid in recruiting "the brothers on the block" to the organization. Panther leaders maintained that the gun was only a strategic political tool and not a fetish or an end in itself. They quoted Mao's axiom that war could be abolished only through war. In order to "get rid of the gun," it was necessary to "take up the gun." At the same time, they pointed out that California law made it perfectly legal for any citizen to carry a loaded, unconcealed weapon. Exercising their citizenship rights, they would make sure that each member family had enough firepower to protect itself.[101]

Panther chapters conducted classes in the use of firearms, engaged in close order drill, and studied literature on guerrilla warfare techniques. Recognizing that they wore the Panther reputation for armed militance whenever they donned their uniform and strapped on a gun, recruits

Black Panthers at Free Huey Newton rally, Oakland, 1968. From Ruth-Marion Baruch and Pirkle Jones, *The Vanguard* (1970). By permission of Beacon Press.

made certain that they knew how to defend themselves against all comers. Along with proper weapon care and "righteous political education," they received instruction in the manufacture of firebombs, pipebombs, and hand grenades. Some chapters included information on how to disable enemy vehicles by using spike-studded boards to deflate automobile tires. Upon leaving the training session, a typical Panther delegation might have in their possession several shotguns, a couple of M-1 rifles, and all manner of handguns. If challenged by the police, they coolly would recite the applicable legal codes to the officer as an interested crowd of prospective members assembled, eyes bulging at the sight of bold, dignified young blacks facing down armed white authority figures.[102]

The Panthers noted that they did not use their guns to "go into the white community to shoot up white people," but only to defend themselves against unjust attack. Party rules stated that no member could point or fire a weapon at anyone other than an advancing enemy. They couldn't even have a gun in their possession if "drunk or loaded off narcotics or weed." After all, the name and symbol of the Black Panther Party *for Self-Defense* originally was adopted because it was not in a panther's nature to initiate attack. But, when backed into a corner, the sleek animal would strike back forcefully. Black America, said the Panther leadership, was backed into a corner and had to respond. Their response would be considered defensive in nature because oppressed peoples never legitimately could be termed aggressors. All of the actions were taken in self-defense. Certainly, Blacks had no death wish, only the ardent desire to live with hope and human dignity. They would chance physical death rather than endure those forces which lead inevitably to a death of the spirit. In risking their lives, there was at least the possibility of changing the intolerable conditions created by their "capitalistic, imperialistic exploiters."[103]

According to the Panthers, the police were the armed guardians of the oppressive social order. They served the same function within the black community as foreign troops occupying conquered territory. It was their duty to keep the peace and protect the way of life of those in power. More specifically, they were to keep "the peace of the Bank of America and General Motors" by maintaining black oppression. This was called "keeping the niggers in check"—making sure that blacks were intimidated, locked in mortal fear, and paralyzed in their bid for freedom. Under this system, security was the byword. Justice was secondary. For black liberation to occur, the power of the police had to be neutralized by a countervailing force. How could this be accomplished?[104]

The Panthers sought to effect a change in the behavior of all "racist pig cops" by organizing armed citizens' patrols of black living areas. The patrols were designed to make the police "start to riding shaky and scared," thereby discouraging brutality and abuse of authority. Each day, fully armed teams would crisscross the ghetto, shadowing individual squad cars and monitoring the officers' actions. They hoped to put an end to petty harrassment of blacks by standing nearby and reciting relevant portions of the penal code in a loud voice. The Panthers also composed and distributed a "pocket lawyer" which provided a similar introduction to basic legal rights. If a subject was arrested, the Panthers would follow and post bail at the station house. Thus, with weapons in their hands and law books in their cars, the Panthers put the police on notice that blacks no longer could be considered victims, but were to be treated as equals under the law. Eventually, it was hoped that legislation could be enacted stipulating that all officers who patrolled a particular community had to live in that community, serving only at the pleasure of its people. Until that time, they would continue their patrols and public information campaign, all the while humming the catchy ditty:

"There's a pig upon the hill/If you don't get 'im, the Panthers will."[105]

As one might expect, any black militant group that patrolled the police, hawked copies of *Quotations from Chairman Mao Tse-tung* to fund firearms purchases, and called a gun an "extension of our fanged teeth that we lost through evolution" was bound to gain the attention of the media.[106] Reporters smelled a story in the Black Panthers and dogged their every showy movement. The media, perhaps unavoidably, dwelt on the Party's seeming preoccupation with weaponry, often failing to explain the group's rationale and raison d'etre. They were "black racists" and, according to the FBI's J. Edgar Hoover, the number one threat to the internal security of the nation. As Panther officials noted, many outsiders seemed to believe that their ultimate goal was "to go out in the streets with five hundred black people lined up with guns and shoot it out with a thousand policemen." No, this wasn't the plan at all, they complained—to no avail. The stigma of armed militance had been imprinted on the public consciousness. Harris surveys conducted in 1970 and 1971 showed that some 60 percent of whites and 20 percent of blacks considered the Panthers to be a "serious menace" to the country.[107] In the long run, the Panthers' utilization of the gun as a recruiting device and "political tool" worked to their disadvantage, inflaming public opinion, skewing news coverage, and spurring a deadly response to their presence by law enforcement personnel

Beyond the rhetoric of the gun, the Black Panther Party stood for community control and black self-help. Their community-oriented social welfare efforts were not entirely altruistic. Panther ideologues conceptualized them as part of a revolutionary, socialistic program that would educate the masses to "the politics of changing the system." To declare a spontaneous revolution and hope that it would succeed was a fantasy, they said. The peoples' trust first had to be won, their consciousness raised, the present system's contradictions made clear, and *then* they would have the wherewithal to "seize the time and deliver themselves from the boot of their oppressors." To this end, the Panthers sought to institute a "survival program" which would help organize and sustain black America until the revolution could be launched. In contrast to government-administered handouts or the food pantries and free clinics operated by white counterculturist groups, the Party's attempts to "meet the needs of the people" could in no way be considered palliative or "reformist." They were nurturing the development of a potential revolutionary juggernaut.[108] As minister of defense Huey Newton observed, before any organization could aspire to revolutionary action, it had to organize the people. "You have to have some sort of spark to set the prairie fire," he said. And for the Panthers, "The programs are the spark. The people are the fire."[109]

The Black Panther survival program involved members in a dizzying array of social service activities. Individual chapters provided breakfasts for children, free shoes and clothing, legal assistance, medical care, and screening for sickle cell anemia. They operated liberation schools where black youth were taught that "Revolution Means Change; Revolutionaries are Changers; Liberation means Freedom" and that they were part of a "BIG FAMILY working, playing, and living together in the struggle." The Party gave away upwards of 20,000 bags of groceries through its nationwide Angela Davis People's Free Food Program. There also was a Free Busing to Prisons Program, an Intercommunal News Service, and even a People's Free Plumbing and Maintenance Program designed to improve housing conditions. These community services were staffed by volunteer labor and funded by contributions from local businesspeople.[110]

On a somewhat more ad hoc basis, the Panthers promoted voter registration as a way to place more black and poor people on juries, thereby facilitating the dispensation of "revolutionary justice." They protested the eviction of black tenants, counseled welfare recipients, and accompanied community residents as they sought redress of grievances from school or government officials. On one occasion, Huey Newton informed authorities that armed Panthers would begin to direct traffic at a dangerous intersection in the Oakland black community unless a signal was placed there to insure the safety of neighborhood children. Within days, city workers installed the light. In all such endeavors, the Party kept its social service and ideological goals in perspective. They would not, said Newton, regard the survival program as a definitive answer to the problem of black oppression. Revolutions were made of sterner stuff. Nevertheless, since "the people and only the people make revolutions," the goals of the revolution could be achieved only if the people were kept from perishing from lack of care and sustenance.[111]

The ideology which guided the Panthers evolved through several stages, each of which was accompanied by fissures, fractures, and defections. By the end of 1970, the Party leadership had moved from a purely black nationalist stance to the advocacy of revolutionary socialism and then on to "intercommunalism." Under intercommunal theory, the world's people formed a collection of communities. Either directly or indirectly, all were dominated by the "United States Empire," a cruel, power-hungry entity whose tentacles of control had made the concept of

Huey P. Newton. From Ruth-Marion Baruch and Pirkle Jones, *The Vanguard* (1970). By permission of Beacon Press.

a truly sovereign nation-state anachronistic. The Black Panther Party would end this oligarchic rule by leading the downtrodden masses as they seized the means of production. Then, under the new international order, wealth, technology, and political representation would be distributed in an egalitarian fashion among the world communities. Wars would end and the state-as-oppressor would cease to exist, being replaced by a system of "true communism" where "all people produce according to their abilities and all receive according to their needs."[112]

In arriving at this revolutionary vision, the Panthers interpreted, deleted, and modified classical Marxist-Leninist tenets at will. They paid close attention to the experiences of other revolutionaries, but they would not, for any length of time, follow in lockstep. The Panthers could admire "all the people that held up the light before" and still evidence self-direction. Surely, *their* new world order would evidence considerably more attachment to civil liberties than had past "revolutionary" governments. Theirs was, as Eldridge Cleaver termed it, "a Yankee-Doodle-Dandy version of socialism" designed to address the specific problems of a black minority living in a highly urbanized, industrialized society.[113] As such, the Panthers placed considerable emphasis on the central role of the lumpen underclass in carrying out the revolution. According to Party belief, workers displaced by the present regime's rush toward a cost-cutting technocracy gradually would swell the ranks of the lumpenproletariat, assuring ultimate victory over "all the enemies of the wretched of the earth." Led by the Black Panther vanguard, they would end the tyranny of both class and race.[114]

Believing that their ideology allowed them to speak to racial and class oppression at the same time, the Panthers felt comfortable in sharing their plans with non-black allies. Capitalism was a white-dominated economic system which exploited blacks and promoted racism, but it also hurt many whites. Moreover, the Party believed that it would be fruitless to install socialism in a black enclave—or even in a five-state subnation—without destroying the rest of the capitalist superstructure. What was needed then was liberation in the black colony and revolution in the mother country.[115] To reach this stage of revolutionary development, the Panthers sought to make as many linkages as possible with groups who were equally dissatisfied with the present system. As a Panther conference poster stated, "Yippies! Political Parties! Workers! Students! Peasant-Farmers! You the Lumpen! Poor People! Black People, Mexican-Americans, Puerto Ricans, Chinese" were all invited to join in forming a "united front against fascism."[116] In attempting to achieve revolutionary solidarity, the Party walked an ideological tightrope be-

Eldridge Cleaver. From Ruth-Marion Baruch and Pirkle Jones, *The Vanguard* (1970). By permission of Beacon Press.

tween the popular demand for Black Power and the communal ideal of "people power" devoid of racial exclusivity.

The Brown Berets (Mexican-Americans), Young Lords (Puerto Ricans), Red Guards (Chinese-Americans), and Young Patriots (poor whites), established alliances with the Party. The Peace and Freedom Party, which consisted mainly of white antiwar activists, agreed to put Panthers on their state ticket in California and made Eldridge Cleaver their 1968 presidential candidate. The Panthers also worked closely with black student unions and, on occasion, the SDS. They established caucuses within trade unions and invited supporters of the gay, peace, and women's liberation movements to their conferences and rallies. Certain of these efforts at coalition-building were, like their 1968 "merger" with the Student Nonviolent Coordinating Committee, brief, unhappy affairs, filled with rancor. Nevertheless, despite grousing and disaffection, the Panthers maintained that such alliances were, in the long run, more productive than any conceivable union with "bourgeois procrastinators." After all, they asked, hadn't John Brown done a lot more for black freedom than the present generation of black college-educated intellectuals? "We judge everybody by what they do," said the Panther leadership. And, besides, "the hippies weren't the enemy."[117]

The Black Panthers' willingness to form alliances with non-blacks was rooted in revolutionary nationalist ideology, but made possible through group self-esteem, strength, and confidence. The Panthers were no "fellow travelers." They saw themselves as the vanguard—the Black Power vanguard. As Huey Newton noted, the Panthers had a mind of their own and would utilize it to its fullest—both in formulating and in implementing revolutionary theory.[118] The Panthers derided those who would "quibble about color" in matters such as the use of white defense lawyers in court cases. They held that there was nothing to fear from the "white mother-country radicals." Not only was there a qualitative difference between white people and *revolutionary* white people, but the Party's position as the key "vector of communication" between the black and white radical camps also assured that it would remain independent of white control. It was the "duty" of whites to aid in the revolutionary struggle, not to burden the movement with their hang-ups about controlling its direction. To those potential allies who were put off by the Party's refusal to sacrifice its integrity or waiver in its "rock-bottom allegiance to the black masses," they would say, "well, right on racists, right on enemies." The Black Panthers would count them as defectors and continue on, providing leadership for all oppressed peoples.[119] As Fred Hampton noted, "It's up to us what happens. We paid the cost of being the boss. We were the ones in this class that were oppressed the most."[120] In viewing potential alliances from a Black Power perspective, the Panthers revealed that class consciousness and the concept of black self-rule need not be mutually exclusive. The black self-determination ethic could continue to exist even within the framework of an interracial leftist coalition.

Should the Panthers falter in their commitment to the revolution, there were other militant groups anxiously awaiting their chance to rise in the revolutionary nationalist hierarchy. During the Black Power era, the line literally stretched around the block. While they didn't exactly push the Panthers into a centrist position or make them seem like pussycats by comparison, these pretenders to the top slot on J. Edgar Hoover's list of dangerous "black-extremist" groups were ready, willing, and able to bring actual guerrilla warfare to America's cities.[121]

The Panthers had warned that domestic guerrilla activity would escalate if black America's "basic demands" were not met. Like Malcolm X, who once advocated sending armed guerrillas into Mississippi to protect black lives, they believed that the masses respected and would imitate those who threw a Molotov cocktail in support of black freedom. This peoples' resistance movement would, they said, amount to a second Civil War, plunging America into "the depths of its most desperate nightmare." Far more effective than random rioting or practicing "revolutionary romanticism" by parading about the ghetto in combat boots and fatigue jackets, strategic guerrilla resistance could carry the day.[122]

According to the Panthers, a vanguard group had to maintain a visible presence until it was driven underground by the enemy. Its members had an educational mission to fulfill and an obligation to serve as role models within the black community. Although this approach had its risks, the Panthers preferred it to a situation in which the vanguard party operated as a secret organization about whom the masses knew little and with whom they had few contacts. As Huey Newton noted, underground parties logically could not distribute leaflets announcing underground meetings. If they did so, they were considered ideologically inconsistent. If they failed to do so, they either remained unknown within the community or risked charges of cowardice. Inevitably, someone would accuse them of fearing exposure to the very dangers they were asking the people to confront.[123] During the Black Power era, the supporters of the Revolutionary Action Movement, the Black Liberation Front, and the Black Liberation Army, among others, chose to risk censure by adopting elements of this more covert approach to revolution.

Domestic guerrilla groups recognized the Panthers' position on combining consciousness-raising with the provision of community social services via an above-ground "program of practical action." They also recalled Huey Newton's claim that the vanguard party's activities on the surface necessarily would be short-lived. All too soon, the establishment's repressive response was bound to drive the militants underground. Furthermore, they remembered Malcolm X's assessment of the situation: whites couldn't win a guerrilla war. Without the bomb, America was essentially toothless. Nonconventional warfare demanded that a combatant have "heart"—and white America was, he determined, woefully lacking in that essential quality. White soldiers couldn't cope with an "unseen" enemy. Combining these insights, the domestic guerrillas concluded that (1) majoritarian oppression already was of such a magnitude that an underground response was merited; and (2) black revolutionaries could be successful if they adapted the techniques of Third World freedom fighters to their own situation.[124]

The domestic guerrillas put white America on notice that they meant business. They called for the creation of a Black Urban Army, adopted anarchistic slogans such as "Kill, baby, kill," and laced their correspondence with talk about meting out justice "in the tradition of Malcolm and all true revolutionaries." Interspersing their public pronouncements with salutes to the power of the people, they said that the United States was about to reap what it had sown. It was too late to save the racist state. America was about to become the "Blackman's Battleground."[125]

According to guerrilla spokespersons, the people possessed the latent ability to disable the machinery of government, disrupt agriculture, and cause mass chaos throughout urban America. Striking by night and sparing none, the guerrillas planned to neutralize white America through fear. The oppressors' communication and transportation systems would be among the first targets. Initially, telephone lines, radio and television stations, newspapers, subway systems, rail stations, and airports were to be sabotaged and rendered useless. Then, steel, chemical, and auto plants would be put out of commission by guerrilla mortars. Slowed by sniper fire and strategically placed walls of burning gasoline, police and emergency personnel would be unable to respond to "terror raids" conducted against key business executives or to control the numerous fires set by incendiaries. Before long, Wall Street would crumble, Washington, D.C. would be torn apart by riots, and public officials everywhere would be seen running for their lives. Summoned by the cry, "It's on!," thousands of blacks would fill the streets, confident of victory. Unafraid of dying in this high stakes confrontation, some would feel cheated if they weren't killed attempting to wipe the white American ruling class "off the face of this planet." Others, however, would begin to organize a revolutionary Afro-American government in the liberated areas, eventually employing their resources to help topple "U.S. lackey governments" overseas. As announced to the presumably dry-mouthed and trembling American public, the guerrillas' itinerary spelled the end of white world supremacy.[126]

The historical context in which the militants operated magnified their every threat and made it appear that Armageddon was as near as they claimed. The unprecedented scourge of civil disturbances which took place during the mid-sixties convinced many that every ghetto contained hundreds—even thousands—of irreconcilable extremists whose singular goal was to foment rebellion. Terrified whites conjured up visions of campus radicals, Muslim separatists, and black teenage gang members banded together in an unholy pact to kill whitey or force him to his knees. To many suburban refugees, the black ghetto seemed a vast, uncharted sea which only the guerrillas knew how to navigate. Fear of the unknown caused these outside observers to vivify reality and to enlarge the threat of guerrilla war beyond the bounds of reason. As the NAACP's Roy Wilkins observed, practically every black-white confrontation was attributed to black-inspired, anti-white conspiracies. Despite the failure of authorities to authenticate the existence of wide-ranging conspiratorial activity, the charge was repeated after each interracial conflict. The persistence of these claims, he said, revealed the high level of "fear and paranoia" present within white America.[127] Thus, despite militants' complaints that all too many blacks living in the riot zones "wanna loot—they don't want to shoot," many believed that the urban "insurrections" had definite revolutionary overtones.[128]

As a paraphrased summary of contemporary news stories demonstrates, accounts of guerrilla activity reaching suburban homes did nothing to alleviate white fears that somewhere in the recesses of the ghetto there was a Molotov cocktail with their name on it:

> [New York City, 1965] Police and FBI agents uncovered a plot to dynamite the Statue of Liberty, Liberty Bell, and Washington Monument. Masterminded by a six-month-old group known as the Black Liberation Front, the terrorist plan also included a surprise air attack on the White House and simultaneous nationwide assaults on police stations, airfields, and industrial plants. A police informant who had infiltrated the BLF later tes-

tified that the leader of the cabal had received training in guerrilla tactics and weapons construction from a North Vietnamese army major stationed in Cuba.[129]

[Philadelphia, 1967] Informants told police that members of the Revolutionary Action Movement were in possession of nearly 300 grams of potassium cyanide and had tried unsuccessfully to initiate a riot on July 29. Had they succeeded, the cyanide would have been placed in the food and drink distributed to police assigned to quell the disturbance. An FBI analyst reported that the dosage could have killed as many as 4,500 people. Earlier raids on RAM units had uncovered numerous weapons (including a machine gun and steel-tipped arrows), literature on guerrilla warfare, and plans to assassinate moderate civil rights leaders, blame the murders on whites, and thereby spur nationwide racial uprisings. Police also speculated that RAM members were acting as advisors to ghetto youth gangs. J. Edgar Hoover encapsulated the nature of the RAM threat by informing a House Subcommittee on Appropriations that the "highly secret all-Negro, Marxist-Leninist, Chinese Communist-oriented" organization had units in several cities and was "dedicated to the overthrow of the capitalist system in the United States, by violence if necessary"[130]

[New York City, 1969] A group of 21 Black Panthers were charged with conspiring to blow up police stations, department stores, and other buildings in the city. The accused circulated an open letter through the underground press praising "righteous urban guerrilla military actions" and criticizing the national leadership for "tripping out," "throwing seeds of confusion," and being insufficiently militant. They claimed that mere readiness to die for the cause—to commit "revolutionary suicide"—would only make martyrs. The Panthers desperately needed "more revolutionists who are completely willing and ready at all times to *KILL* to change conditions."

Only continuous confrontation and armed struggle would destroy the "Amerikkkan machine and its economy."[131]

[Chicago, 1972] Six young blacks were arrested and accused of taking part in nine recent murders throughout Illinois. At their arraignment, the suspects appeared with their arms extended in the Black Power salute. Police told reporters that they were part of a nationwide league of embittered black combat veterans who had to "kill a whitey to get into the gang." Cook County officials claimed that the arrests thwarted the group's plan to begin a systematic cop-killing spree. Dashing any sense of relief this news may have encouraged, *Tribune* headlines screamed: "MURDER GANG 3,000 STRONG. DE MAU MAU TAKING OVER FOR THE PANTHERS."[132]

Throughout the Black Power era, reports such as these heightened interracial tension. Rumors that the militants were assembling a vast arsenal via army surplus store buying sprees or that female guerrillas were hiring on as maids in order to "liberate" handguns hidden under white folks' mattresses led many to believe, against both hard evidence and common sense, that conspirators were everywhere.[133] "You can just about bet," said a special investigator from one metropolitan police department, "that these people have the circuit diagrams of the underground power-cable systems in many of the major cities." Fearing that there existed a well-oiled conspiracy to kill agents of the establishment, an off-duty New York patrolman added, "I've become so paranoid that when I go out for a container of milk, I take my gun." This dangerous situation moved police union officials to call for increased firepower and bulletproof squad cars for their members. Patrol officers donned protective flack jackets and carried extra guns in defiance of regulations. Reports of "suspicious persons," rumored weapons caches, and guerrilla organizational activity were thoroughly investigated. This response to the guerrilla's covert threat virtually guaranteed that police-community relations would be slow to improve and that charges of police brutality and excessive use of force (which originally had moved many blacks to militancy) would continue unabated.[134]

Although very real to all parties at the time, much of the foregoing scenario seems the stuff of fiction today. Indeed, the guerrillas' vows to end black oppression through revolutionary armed struggle and the establishment's counterefforts to stave off imminent disaster formed the substance of a good deal of the Black Power era's most vivid popular literature. During the late sixties and early seventies, America's historical fear of both blacks and radical ideologies magnified the revolutionary nationalist "conspiracy" far out of proportion to its actual size, degree of organization, and potential for success. The "New Black Man" never made an appearance. Instead, white America's response to the revolutionary nationalists resulted in a narrowing and popular distortion of Black Power's meaning. This distortion contributed to the maintenance of a high level of interracial misunderstanding and to the imposition of new cultural stereotypes on the black American people.

CULTURAL NATIONALISTS

Dress the muse in black . . .
　　No!
　　　Kill her!

Carolyn F. Gerald, 1969

During the Black Power era, there also was a great deal of misunderstanding between revolutionary nationalists and those fellow militants whom they disparagingly referred to as bourgeois or "pork-chop" nationalists. Uncharitably portrayed as posturing "jiving dudes" prone to parading about "with naturals on their heads and nothing on their minds," cultural nationalists vigorously defended themselves and their approach to liberation against all comers.[135] Convinced that Afro-America's quest for dignity and power would fail if led by "neo-leftist bloods" intent on wearing "some dead 1930's white ideology as a freedom suit," they, instead, proposed a black cultural renaissance as a key component of the revolutionary struggle for Black Power.[136]

To the cultural nationalist, picking up a gun without first reaffirming the beauty and uniqueness of black culture was the height of foolishness. A "straight-up, no monkey-business Nationalist perspective" rejected the notion of pinning black people's hopes on "foreign" ideologies promoted by a few confused revolutionary nationalists "high on marijuana and white women." The liberation movement was to be grounded in the understanding that Afro-Americans composed a separate entity—an "alien Nation/Race" ensnared by white-sponsored ghetto colonialism. Their unique cultural contributions reflected their "special consciousness" or worldview. Neither European nor African, the black aesthetic, as evidenced in literature, art, and music, was Afro-America's most important national resource. It was the veritable soul of their nation—the essence of their collective psyche.[137]

As the embodiment of the national spirit, black culture was said to be of signal utility to the Black Power movement. Its vitality and grandeur challenged white cultural particularism and invalidated claims of European racial-cultural superiority. Its depth and scope provided a blueprint for the development of an authentically black value system. Diverse in format and mode of presentation, cultural expression could carry the revolutionary message to all manner of blacks. Moreover, unlike the ideology forwarded by certain "misguided jew oriented revolutionaries," black culture was organically connected to the lives and traditions of the African-American people. And the people, not some self-appointed neo-Marxist vanguard, would make the revolution.[138]

For cultural nationalists, black culture *was* Black Power. By asserting their cultural distinctives via clothing, language, and hairstyle and by recounting their unique historical experiences through the literary and performing arts, cultural nationalists sought to encourage self-actualization and psychological empowerment. Their celebration of blackness elicited charges of racial chauvinism, but promoted racial unity and provided both impetus and direction for the expansion of the black liberation movement's "political" thrust. It was believed that the subordination of culture to economics or politics would eviscerate the revolution by denying its supporters access to the movement's life-blood.[139]

No group better conveyed the spirit of militant cultural nationalism than the Los Angeles–based US Organization. No individual provided a more suitable lightning rod for anti-cultural nationalist sentiment than its leader, Maulana Ron Karenga. US embraced every aspect of the cultural renaissance—leading the West Coast "back to black" movement in clothing and hairstyles; championing the teaching of Swahili as a "non-tribal" language of "self-determination";[140] sponsoring community-based arts events; and inaugurating the celebration of black holidays such as *Uhuru* Day (August 11, commemorating the 1965 Watts riot) and *Kuzaliwa* (May 19, celebrating Malcolm X's birth).

Inspired both by Malcolm X and the writings of Sekou Toure, Julius Nyerere, and Kwame Nkrumah, Karenga took his adopted Swahili name literally.[141] He would be "keeper of the tradition," seeking to wean his black brothers and sisters from Euro-American cultural forms and the unhealthy values they reflected. In their place, he would substitute a cultural system which continually generated heroic, Afrocentric images. In Karenga's formulation, to return to tradition was the first functional step toward a greater Afro-American future. Recognition and celebration of a common cultural heritage would minimize "Negro hang-ups" while providing access to new wellsprings of racial identity and individual self-respect. Surely, the actions of the black "cultural nation" would be legitimized and its people guided by the positive values promoted through the vibrant separatist culture.142

In seeking to "take things which were traditional and apply them to the concrete needs of Black people," Karenga developed the *Nguzo Saba*, a set of seven key values by which blacks seeking liberation were to "order their relations and live their lives." It was held that each of the principles—*Umoja* (unity), *Kujichagulia* (self-determination), *Ujima* (collective work and responsibility), *Ujamaa* (cooperative economics), *Nia* (purpose), *Kuumba* (creativity), and *Imani* (faith) reflected recurring value emphases found in traditional African cultures. The Nguzo Saba would promote the growth of "a new world and a new people" within contemporary Afro-America.143

He also instituted the celebration of *Kwanzaa* as an alternative to the "economic entrapment and alienated gift-giving" that characterized white America's approach to the Christmas season. Initially observed in Los Angeles from 26 December 1966 to 1 January 1967, this Afro-American holiday of the "first fruits" was derived from the harvest-time festivals of African agriculturalists. In the more urban context of black America, participants sought to recapture and to honor their communal heritage through symbol and ceremony. As they wished each other "Kwanzaa yenu iwe na heri" ("Happy Kwanzaa"); poured *tambiko* (libations) and drank from the *kikombe cha umoja* (Unity Cup); lighted the black, red, and green candles (*mishumaa saba*); participated in the *karamu* (feast); and exchanged "heritage symbols" (African art or talismanic objects, pictures of black liberation heroes, etc.), Kwanzaa celebrants reaffirmed their collective commitment to the work and struggle of their ancestors.144

The Nguzo Saba and Kwanzaa were constituent components of the ideology and practice of *Kawaida*, the theory of cultural and social change adopted by US. Kawaida theory held that black Americans needed to carry out a cultural revolution before they could mount a successful political campaign to seize and reorder established institutions of power and wealth. Infused with a value system capable of providing the Afro-American people with a new appreciation for activism, the cultural revolution preceded and made the political revolution possible. It also would secure the gains of the political struggle. To be led by transformed, self-conscious agents of liberation, the cultural revolution was conceptualized as an ongoing process designed to establish, refine, and reinforce a distinctive black national culture.[145]

According to Karenga and his followers, black liberation was impossible, by definition unthinkable, without breaking the white culture's domination of black minds. It was imperative that Afro-Americans "overturn" themselves, rejecting the values of the dominant society while beginning to "redefine and reshape reality" in their own image, according to their own needs. If blacks rejected this approach to liberation they would be self-condemned to continue their senseless consumption and imitation of white cultural forms—a debilitating condition which vitiated political activism and made the Afro-American people and their cultural expression "only a set of reactions" to the colonizer's worldview. Possessing "elements of a culture," but not the unified value system needed to move forward, they would languish in shameful mental torpor amidst the "self-deforming and self-destructive values and views" of their oppressors.[146]

Personal testimonies as to the transforming effect of Karenga's ideology approached the evangelical. US converts were loyal, even devout. Some stood awed at the boldness of his attempts to desanctify received cultural imagery—"talking about Jesus as a faggot, and Mary as a whore, and all sorts of things about the white man." Others credited Karenga with initiating life-style changes which permitted them to substitute black culture and language studies for unproductive "slave" habits such as "smoking reefers, and dropping pills, and drinking wine." As one follower recalled, Kawaida provided identity, purpose and direction—an attractive alternative to acculturation as a black white man. After accepting Karenga's message, he no longer was driven to "wear some shark skin suit I had to buy from a Jew." A *buba* now seemed perfectly appropriate attire. Never again would he lust after those "stringy haired, colorless, white women." Instead he had begun to develop a new appreciation for the natural beauty of black womanhood. Surely, all praise was due Maulana, "the Blackest Panther, the eye-opener." Karenga was "saying what needs to be told" and leading Afro-America down the "Path of Blackness."[147]

Not all who heard the US leader's message were equally ecstatic. Although he spoke often of achieving unity without uniformity and maintained that perceived divisions between revolutionary and cultural nationalists were, in truth, greatly exaggerated, Karenga's insistence upon "cultural reconversion" as a precondition for political revolution alienated many potential allies.[148] When he opined that "the international issue is racism not economics"; that US members in good standing "do not accept the idea of a class struggle"; or that non-cultural approaches to the problems of race were "necessary but not sufficient," revolutionary nationalists became livid.[149] Angered by his apparent disregard for their ideological heritage, they tagged Karenga and his shaved-headed, toga and tiki-bedecked followers as counterrevolutionary cultists—"those niggers with the bongos in their ears."[150]

Disagreement over Karenga's claim that "to go back to tradition is the first step forward," soon deteriorated into open warfare between US and the Black Panthers.[151] By early 1969, several shoot-outs between members of the two groups marked the degree to which an ideological and methodological dispute within the nationalist camp had been transformed first into name-calling and then into a deadly power struggle over organizational "turf", control of community institutions, and the direction of the west coast movement. To many revolutionary nationalists, Karenga became an enemy of the people, an "afro-cosmic lunatic" whose passion for "weird rituals and strange fashions" stultified rather than advanced the cause of black nationalism.[152]

During the Black Power era, many such charges greeted the ears of practicing cultural nationalists. Unlike Karenga, most were forced to dodge these verbal barbs without the protection provided by a wedge-shaped formation of stolid *Simba Wachanga* (members of Young Lions, the US security corps). They were called every name in the Little Red Book: "black racists," "a new type of Tom," "non-persons," "murderous turncoat idiots," "cowardly fat-mouths."[153] Their motives, sanity, and parentage were questioned. Believed to be more interested in ego gratification than black liberation, cultural nationalists were criticized for adhering to a "puritanical concept of blackness" which denied revolutionary political thought its rightful place within the black cultural dynamic. They were accused of commercializing and making a fetish out of African-inspired cultural forms, causing the celebration of Old World traditions to become an end in itself. In doing so, it was said that they encouraged escapism—a mythical flight from real world socioeconomic realities.[154] Thus, for those who posited a dialectical contradiction between the variants of black nationalism, cultural awareness and observances by themselves were incapable of subverting White Power. The movement needed "some stronger stuff."[155] Cultural nationalist "posturing" was seen as a tellingly inadequate substitute for the revolutionary culture which would be generated through popular struggle. As the Black Panthers' Bobby Seale asserted, "I have a natural and I like it, but power for the people doesn't grow out of the sleeve of a dashiki."[156]

Nationalist infighting disrupted the political unity of the Black Power movement, causing potential birds of a feather to be perceived as tenacious birds of prey. This need not have happened. Had these emotionally charged years allowed more ample time for reflection, both sides might have recognized that territorial and ideological disputes within the nationalist camp had a tendency to obscure underlying commonalities. In truth, although they utilized cultural forms in various ways and to differing degrees, all manner of activists employed culture in the cause of black empowerment.

Ideological enemies may have been opposed to the cultural nationalists' ordering of priorities, but they were not against incorporating cultural elements into their own definitions of Black Power—or of writing a poem, song, or short story as time and talent permitted. Overly rigid labeling and categorization of "isms" could become farcical—and counterproductive—when "political" figures behaved as if they belonged in the "culture" sphere or when individuals commonly associated with black cultural expression became active in the political arena.

Were Black Panther leaders condoning counterrevolutionary tendencies when they selected a Minister of Culture, commissioned a cartoonist for their paper, issued a set of seasonal greeting cards, or sang along with "The Lumpen," their political education/musical group? Did the poetic effusions of Huey P. Newton, H. Rap Brown, James Forman, or the Black Liberation Army's Albert Washington ("Rather to live with the shame / Of a bullet lodged within my brain / If we were not to reach our goal / May bleeding cancer torment my soul") signal disenchantment with other modes of activist expression?[157] How far was Karenga straying from the Kawaida path in predicting that 1971 would be "the year of guerrillas"?[158] What sort of ideological fence did Stokely Carmichael straddle when he defended the "cultural integrity" of non-Western peoples against an "imperialist . . . system" that engaged in both economic and cultural exploitation?[159] Was CORE's Roy Innis downgrading the importance of community control and black economic development when he claimed that an accurate picture of black nationalist strength could be obtained only by counting both individuals committed to a "conscious ideology and philosophy" and those more "passive nationalists" who evidenced their beliefs by shunning bleaching creams and hair straighteners.[160] Did Minister Louis X of Boston compromise the Black Muslim position on territorial nationalism by recording the calypso-like tune "White Man's Heaven Is Black Man's Hell"?[161]

During the Black Power years, the answers to these and other similarly vexing questions more often than not were blowing in the ill winds of angry revolutionary rhetoric. Nevertheless, perspective gained by the passage of time allows one to say, with some degree of confidence, that much of the cultural nationalist coda was utilized and accepted as valid by a remarkably broad cross section of black activists. All that most required was that it be tinctured with their own essence. Inextricably involved in culture-creation, they found cultural expression valuable both in the conceptualization and in the promotion of Black Power.

When viewed in this manner, the chief preoccupation of the cultural nationalists can be seen as a central concern of the movement as a whole. Often pigeonholed as one of the more esoteric, even aberrant expressions of the black liberation ethic, cultural nationalism actually provided much of its thrust and dynamic. Moreover, both their search for a meaningful African past and their concept of unifying the black nation with mortar drawn from a vibrant Afro-American culture had broad appeal and widespread application. Certainly, such notions were much more than the wild-eyed ramblings of some west coast fringe group wearing strange garb and fixating on a mythical racial past.

Time and events also reveal that the most definitive incarnation of the Black Power movement's tendencies toward cultural cross-pollination and the invalidation of inflexible, ideology-bound schematic models was Newark-born, Howard University-educated poet/dramatist Amiri Baraka. During the early sixties, as LeRoi Jones, his credentials as an essayist and playwright had been established with the publication of *Blues People* (1963) and the Obie Award-winning off-Broadway production of *Dutchman* (1964). Well known in Greenwich Village avant-garde circles, his poetry, *Preface to a Twenty Volume Suicide Note* (1961); *The Dead Lecturer,* (1964); fiction, *The System of Dante's Hell* (1965), and biting social commentary, *Home* (1966) soon won the young literary lion a much larger audience and offers to teach poetry and creative writing at a number of universities. It was during one such assignment at San Francisco State College that he discovered the Nguzo Saba as "the key to the new Nationalism."[162]

Impressed by Karenga's commanding presence, the well-disciplined nature of his organization, and the "depth and profundity"—as well as the cultural emphases—of Kawaida doctrine, Jones quickly assimilated US beliefs.[163] One of Kawaida's chief proselytizers for almost a decade, he hoped to bring credit to the new name given him by Karenga and Heesham Jaaber, the orthodox Islamic priest who had buried Malcolm X. Imamu (spiritual leader) Amiri (prince) Baraka (blessed one) would seek to develop the aesthetic that delineated what he termed "an absolute gulf " separating the Afro- and Euro-American racial and cultural spheres.[164]

For him, race was defined by a feeling—an identity—which culture preserved and art expressed. To be racially conscious was to be cultured—that is, consciously black. It was this consciousness—and the racial unity which it both promoted and revealed—that would lead to the resolution of black America's many problems. With culture as their guide, citizens of the black nation would be able to move beyond the constricting boundaries of Western thought, reordering the world.[165] As an inscription prominently displayed above the stage of his Newark cultural center read: "The minds of the people are the most important factor of any movement; without them you have nothing else."[166]

Believing that the dissemination and acceptance of his message would be hindered by isolation and excessive individualism ("the white boys' snakemedicine"), Baraka contributed more than his fair share to making certain that the cultural nationalist infrastructure was "hooked up through organization."[167] In 1965 he dedicated the Black Arts Repertory Theatre/School in Harlem "to the education and cultural awakening of the Black People in America." Although short-lived, it served as a model for the many community theatre-workshop-schools that promoted cultural expression and "hard-core nationalism" during the late sixties.[168] Within a year he moved his base of operation to Spirit House in downtown Newark. Here he combined repertory theatre with an African Free School whose curriculum was developed around the black value system of Kawaida. Soon thereafter, Baraka organized Newark's first Afro-American Festival of the Arts, began a literary magazine, *An Anthology of Our Black Selves*, and launched Jihad Publications with a volume of poetry entitled *Black Art*.

In all of these endeavors, Baraka sought to take *both* nationalist cultural concepts and political ideas to the black masses. His definition of culture was broad and inclusive: All activities were cultural. Social and aesthetic values were inextricably wedded. Art was politics and politics art. In line with this conceptualization, Black America was "a cultural nation striving to seize the power to become a political nation." To reach this goal, the politically-minded needed to become "culturally aware." Black politics had to utilize key symbols and images from the black past if it hoped to gain the confidence of the people and become energized by "their strivings at conscious blackness." For their part, more culturally-oriented blacks were obliged to create a pragmatic politically-involved art. Their poetry, music, and drama had to translate the nationalist political impulse into cultural forms equally suitable for

Amiri Baraka/LeRoi Jones on Black Power–era poster. Courtesy of Robin's Book Store.

converting unbelievers or demystifying and emasculating enemies. To Baraka, black nationalism was more than a pastiche of political rhetoric and literary functionalism. It was a remarkably unified, empowering ideology, eminently useful in the "deathbattle" being waged by two opposing cultures.[169]

Believing that "BLACK ART IS CHANGE, IT MUST FORCE CHANGE, IT MUST BE CHANGE," Baraka wore the hats of political organizer and cultural theorist wherever he went.[170] Whether as spokesperson for the US-inspired Black Community Development and Defense Organization, the politically-active United Brothers of Newark, or the "united front" coalition, Committee for Unified Newark, he sought to promote electoral participation both as a consciousness-raising exercise and as a mechanism to wrest political power from the unsavory assortment of "stooges, thieves, and toms" long entrenched in public office.[171] His goal was to create a black world that reflected black soul—to "take over our own space in these same shitty towns transforming them with our vision and style to be extensions of swiftshake and stomp sound."[172]

In this nationalist vision of fully-realized community control, Newark, Gary, Detroit, Harlem, Bedford-Stuyvesant, East St. Louis, and other black dominated "city-states" were destined to become "beautiful thrones of man"—testaments to the "ecstatic vision of the soulful." On the national level, this transformation of economically depressed, white-ruled colonies into life-affirming, parklike living areas complete with neo-African designed homes and shops was to be supported by an Afro-American political party. Eventually a World African Party would rise to unite the long-separated people of the black diaspora in a pan-African struggle for liberation. Ultimately, with the creation of an International African State, descendants of slaves would win recognition as "one of the most powerful people in the world, everywhere in the world they are."[173]

Positive proof of black capacity for self-rule, this newly realized power also would reveal that their value system, the essential repository of group identity, purpose, and direction throughout the years of nationalist struggle, was superior to that of the whites. Kawaida was to be celebrated as "the atom hot nucleus of positive political movement," a vitally rejuvenating force in black politics. In Baraka's world, black art forced change, enabling blacks to recreate themselves "as African Philosophers, African Historians, African Politicians, African Economists, African Artists, . . . as new people."[174]

To these ends, Baraka employed a diverse array of organizational techniques and forms, stirring them into a veritable nationalist gumbo of

cadre creation and culture consciousness. He played a major role in organizing the broad-based Congress of African Peoples in 1970 and served
on the steering committee of the first National Black Political Convention, held in Gary, Indiana in 1972. In Newark, he opened Spirit House to
political meetings, walked picket lines, and distributed leaflets at his
plays. He stenciled the Black Power fist on building walls and challenged
those he met on the street with the consciousness-raising greeting,
"What time is it?"—anticipating that his query would elicit the spirited
response: "It's Nation time! The land is gonna change hands!"[175] Indeed, Baraka's voter registration and performance-oriented fund-raising
activities contributed greatly to Kenneth Gibson's successful 1970 bid
to become the city's first black mayor.[176]

On occasion, Baraka's culturally-manifested activism transgressed
the boundaries of "polite" political behavior. For example, while still
living in New York, he was taken to a precinct house for encouraging
looters during the Great Blackout. He had been adding to the confusion
by cruising Lenox Avenue in a sound truck, shouting "Now's the time.
They can't see you. Rip these stores off. Take everything. Come on out
and get it!"[177] Later, during the 1967 riots in Newark, he was arrested
and tried on charges of resisting arrest and unlawfully carrying firearms.
Although his subsequent conviction was reversed on appeal, Baraka received an important lesson in culture and politics courtesy of the Essex
County Court system. During the initial sentencing proceedings, Judge
Leon W. Kapp read aloud from one of the black poet's creations entitled
"Black People!" A bold statement of militancy which counseled ghetto
residents to intone "magic words" ("Up against the wall mother fucker
this is a stick up), take "magic action" ("smash the windows daytime,
anytime, together"), and do a "magic dance" in the street ("take the shit
you want. Take their lives if need be"), the poem visibly angered Kapp.[178]
He called it a "diabolical prescription to commit murder and to steal and
plunder"—good reason to suspect that Baraka had participated in "formulating a plot . . . to burn the City of Newark." The severe prison sentence imposed by the judge, ($2\frac{1}{2}$–3 years, versus 18 months received by
his codefendants) convinced Baraka that he was "being sentenced for
the poem."[179] Undoubtedly, the episode also served to increase his
awareness of the unmistakably "political" nature of black creative expression. As he once noted in describing the developing beliefs of his
militant/artist fellowship in Harlem, nationalist ideology was not
easily divided into district "cultural" and "political" components. It
was formed from "an eclectic mixture of what we thought we knew and

understood. What we wanted. Who we thought we were. It was very messy."[180]

During the Black Power years, cultural nationalists were prominent in the development of another "eclectic mixture"—the Black Arts movement. Although Baraka has been credited by some as being "the Merlin of the movement," the black arts concept needed no cultural nationalist warlock's potion to attract devotees.[181] The era's pervasive Black Power dynamic moved creative talents of varying political persuasions to manifest the existence of a distinctive black worldview through cultural expression.

As conceptualized by its participants, the Black Arts movement was the "spiritual sister" of Black Power. Exhibiting the commonly felt need to define the universe in their own terms, the poets, playwrights, and artists of the late sixties and early seventies, sought to speed black empowerment via "a radical reordering of the western cultural aesthetic." Their major goal was to spur the growth of a dynamic, functional black aesthetic that (1) emphasized the distinctiveness of African-American culture—along with its unique symbols, myths, and metaphors; (2) extolled the virtues of black life-styles and values, and (3) promoted race consciousness, pride, and unity. If successful in this quest, they would bring about "the destruction of the white thing," putting an end to the "alien sensibility" that long had tainted black creative expression. No longer limited by "white ideas, and white ways of looking at the world," both the artists and their audience would move several steps closer to complete liberation.[182]

Novelist Ronald L. Fair detailed the mental processes involved. As he related in 1965, halfway through writing a novel populated largely by white characters, he came to the realization that he was "distorting reality" by apotheosizing a make-believe lily-white America. He was selling out, becoming just another literary "Tom" who sought acclaim by denying the existence of black people. Furious with himself, Fair tore the manuscript into tiny pieces, lit a match, and "watched it burn with all the ceremonial intensity of an early Christian witnessing the Last Supper." He felt free for the first time. Proud to be black and "not afraid to shout it," he had been released from the aesthetic stranglehold of white literary tradition. No longer driven by the need for white approval, he would begin to create true-to-life black characters, and relate meaningful black experiences. There was "just too much that had to be said that couldn't be said by white writers," for him to continue in his old ways, estranged from the black cultural aesthetic.[183]

But, what, exactly, was this magical, mystical, potentially potent "black aesthetic"? Like "Black Power" itself, the term was most easily identified by its physical manifestations. "Institutions of Blackness" either inspired or given new life by this race-specific concept ranged from cultural workshops (Organization of Black American Culture, Watts Writers' Workshop), to conferences (Black Arts Convention, World Black and African Festival of Arts and Culture), journals (*Black Dialogue, Black World, Journal of Black Poetry*), publishing houses (Jihad, Broadside, Third World), and even a Black Academy of Arts and Letters dedicated to "affirming the existence of creative excellence in places where we are not accustomed to look for it."[184]

Although many who invested their time in these new organizations were eager to praise African-American cultural achievement—and equally quick to condemn both the "white racist press" and those "black lackeys" who had "adopted its white attitude toward black literature"—most were far more tentative in their explication of the black aesthetic. As the normally voluble poet Don L. Lee noted in 1968, "a blk/aesthetic does exist, but how does one define it? . . . or is it necessary to define it? I suggest, at this time, that we not try."[185]

Those who did grapple with the term's ultimate meaning tended to digress quickly from commentary on the aesthetic as a type of cultural sensibility, philosophy, or ethos. As members of an activist generation they were more interested in pointing out what the aesthetic could *do* for black people. Beyond its recognized utility as a conceptual and critical tool for the evaluation of cultural forms, the black aesthetic was valued as a means of "helping black people out of the polluted mainstream of Americanism."[186] Thus, for Black Arts participants, the chief concern of contemporary black artists and critics was not the relative beauty of a particular melody, play, or poem, but rather the degree to which the work helped transform an American Negro into a Black American. Viewing themselves both as inheritors and architects of a black aesthetic tradition, Black Arts activists sought to define the role of the artist in an age of social change. Stunningly bold and ambitious in conceptualization, these portrayals of creative artists as high priests and necromancers, teachers and social analysts, firemakers and bomb throwers, accorded them responsibilities no less central to the realization of Black Power than those typically assigned to "political" figures.[187] They were to serve as "hammers" against racial oppression, recasting the long-distorted Afro-American cultural image in a consciously black mold. Speaking to the needs and aspirations of everyday blacks, they would create a literature of celebration and uplift. Employing core values resident within the black community, they would inspire and affirm, leading their audience to psychological liberation. Refusing to stand aside from the contemporary fray in order to pursue their Muse, they would serve as the consciousness, coagulant, and coadjutor of Black America—important facilitators of black empowerment.[188]

To succeed in this role, several prerequisites had to be met. First, each individual had to critique and reject major tenets of the dominant white aesthetic. Few Black Arts loyalists experienced significant difficulty in this area. During the Black Power years, white culture was widely perceived as arid, stagnant, and debilitated. "They stop and say the greatest happens to be Shakespeare or Bach or Michelangelo," noted one commentator. "They stop around the 15th, 16th, 17th or 18th century, and only once in awhile will somebody [more recent] sneak in."[189] Having run its course, the Western aesthetic was considered an anachronism. It no longer seemed possible for anyone, black or white, to create meaningful art within its moribund, decaying structure.

Any vitality evident in white culture more often than not could be traced to theft or plagiarism from other traditions. Left to their own devices, whites tended to throw together a "dry assembly of dead ideas based on a dead people," calling it "high culture." Allegedly, this principle could be seen most clearly in the "static" nature of classical music—an "artifact" from a bygone era that lacked relevance for the contemporary world.[190]

Considered as a whole, white culture was said to reveal an unfortunate separation of art from life; artists from their audience. The Euro-American aesthetic was far more concerned with the preservation and veneration of artifacts than with the creative act itself. It negated expression in favor of reflection, aptly mirroring the hollowness of white life. From this perspective, it was easy to agree with Amiri Baraka that, "The white man is not cultured. He knows neither James Brown nor John Coltrane."[191]

To avoid the taint of this outmoded aesthetic, black artists were urged to reexamine the notion of universality as it applied to their craft. White critics' demands that they move beyond a preoccupation with black subjects to become interpreters of universal human experiences had to be seen for what they actually were—thinly veiled attempts to impose "Anglo-Saxon" definitions and values upon others. In truth, it was the white Westerner who most often failed the test of universality. The world was three quarters nonwhite and their depiction of it was 99-44/100% Euro-centric. To demand that Afro-American artists begin the creative process by focusing on ill-defined universals would rob them of the opportunity—and obligation—to depict the life experiences they knew best. They were not to perceive themselves as actors or poets or painters who just *happened* to be black. First and foremost, they were black "brothers and sisters" creatively engaged in explicating the folkways of Afro-America.[192]

In order for "Caucasian idolatry in the arts" to end, it was believed that black culture-creators also had to divest themselves of the "art for art's sake" mind set. A key element in the white aesthetic tradition, this hallowed principle was considered antiquated and dysfunctional in an age of social revolution. To some, it seemed like "something out of a Shakespearian dream." Others claimed that the term was a misnomer. All artistic expression was value-laden—and much of it created primarily "for esteem, competition and MONEY's sake."[193] Instead of being lulled into social unconsciousness by "art for art's sake," blacks were urged to create art that was functional, inspirational, committing. Creative expression was to be "social first and aesthetic second." As Maulana Karenga noted: "We do not need pictures of oranges in a bowl or trees standing innocently in the midst of a wasteland. If we must paint oranges and trees, let our guerrillas be eating those oranges for strength and using those trees for cover."[194] To Baraka, the needs of the hour were equally clear. As he wrote in "Black Art" (1966):

> We want poems
> like fists beating niggers out of Jocks
> . . . .
> We want "poems that kill."[195]

No odes to grecian urns, beatific sunsets, or forest glades would suffice.

After divesting themselves of this Euro-American cultural baggage, black artists were encouraged to meet two additional prerequisites of cultural "priesthood." It was essential, said Black Arts spokespersons, for all participants to view black culture as distinct from the mainstream. In addition, they had to reject the "protest" tradition in Afro-American letters. Looking inward, they were to focus on individual and group self-discovery.

"When Black Art happens, it is different" was a commonly-accepted viewpoint. More than a cultural "index of repudiation" or the grudging recognition of unwilling "separate development" within segregated institutions, this expressed desire to celebrate the uniqueness of racial culture was said to be rooted in the belief that the ancestors of slaves were an African people still estranged from white America. No manner of integrationist rhetoric could disguise the fact that the "high, thick dividing walls which hate and history have erected" made laughable the notion of one country, one people, one "melting pot" culture. Throughout history, blacks had been subjected to treacherous "push and pull" forces generated by the majoritarian society. Lured by the siren call of a white-inspired and -dominated consumer culture, they were urged to wear the same clothes, drive the same automobiles, and become eye-glued to the same television programs and film fare as whites. At the same time, the black culture-consumer was confronted with indescribable acts of inhumanity daily. To maintain equilibrium, Afro-Americans ever more tightly embraced their own forms of cultural expression, molding them into a unique group "style." No more able to express their "Peopleness" in a white cultural context than a barnyard fowl could "find his chickenness in an oven," blacks knew that the opposite also was true. No other group could duplicate their culture, lifestyle, or worldview unless its people were "willing to drink from the same cup."[196]

Given this historical perspective, it was understandable that white culture held little meaning for those influenced by the Black Arts movement. They were acclimated to white culture, but felt no need to assimilate into it or to honor or value it as a personal standard of reference. Lacking the need to press for integration into the cultural mainstream, African-American artists could focus their energies on the celebration of blackness. Certainly there would be sufficient opportunity to distance oneself from the conscienceless majority population by ridiculing their mores, but compared to earlier years, relatively few words would be wasted on white people. Little interest was expressed in talking to whites about what they had done to blacks. Both parties knew the ugly details all too well. There would be no more humble appeals to morality. Instead, black poets and dramatists were urged to speak directly to their own communities, championing a new sensibility of self-acceptance and a corresponding "psychic withdrawal" from values and assumptions promoted via white culture.[197] By abandoning the fruitless "protest" posture, both black artists and their audiences could, in the words of poet Lance Jeffers, enter upon a "journey into the vast Afro-American soul . . . a journey whose destination is self-discovery and psychological freedom."[198]

It was on this spiritual pilgrimage that artists would begin to manifest the black aesthetic sensibility in their works. Although there was no universally recognized litmus test for this trait, it was widely believed that Afro-American aestheticism involved matters both of form and substance. Black art was to be created out of the experience of black life and conveyed to black audiences in a language they could understand.

As a result of these beliefs, artists sought to become cultural anthropologists of soul. Convinced that "there is no better subject for Black artists than Black people," they utilized their own street experiences and on-site interpretation of communal mores as subject matter. Their goal was to create meaningful rituals of ethnic identity and self-worth—to teach their people about themselves so that they could view blackness as a unique blessing.[199] "We look at what we've got," wrote one young poet, "and instead of allowing that to oppress us, we affirm it because its parts of our experience."[200]

But if black expression truly was to be organic, the folk collective had to do more than provide the raw materials of anthropological inquiry. It was given the additional duty of helping shape the contours of black creative vision. The Black Arts movement held that "the people" could "sustain, assist, and inspire" art. Often they dictated its form and content. Ultimately, they would pass judgement upon its worth. In this view, the community was both the essential source and the chief critic of the artists' work. Moreover, within its communal boundaries lay a seminal understanding lost on white outsiders: the souls of black folk were valuable, worthy, even sacred. It was this appreciation for the beauty of black life that most clearly defined the black aesthetic—a unique cultural sensibility that was thought to be most evident where the artist/community bonding was most complete.[201]

To increase the likelihood that artist and audience would unite in support of black empowerment, the Black Arts movement forwarded its message in the patois of the people. To some, it seemed that Black Arts participants spoke only the language of people just like themselves—or in the vernacular of the people whom they emulated and aspired to become. None, however, could deny that the language they utilized was vivid and compelling, well suited to their chosen mission: "to turn people on, to wake people up, make them conscious of themselves and their environment and hopefully push everybody to the stage where their very lives are poetry."[202]

Having declared the oppressor's aesthetic to be clinically dead, Black Arts writers abandoned "proper" literary style, creating their own communicative medium. Poets, for example, attempted to capture the flavor of black American speech—its sounds, rhythms, and style—in verse that was written for performance. Presented with all the improvisational spirit and flair of a back room jam session, the new black expression often lapsed into exultant screams and jazz-like scats:

> dig the mellow voices
> dig the Porkpie Hat
> dig the spirit in Sun Ra's sound
> dig the cosmic Trane
> dig be
> dig be
> dig be
> spirit lives in sound
> dig be
> sound lives in spirit
> dig be
> yeah!!!
> spirit lives
> spirit lives
> spirit lives
> SPIRIT!!!
> SWHEEEEEEEEEEEEEEETTT!!!
>
> take it again
> this time from the top[203]

Thunderous reverberations of black empowerment issued forth from the necromancer's lips:

> blackman be the wind, be the win, the win, the
> win, win, win:
>   wooooooooooowe boom boom
> wooooooooooowe bah
>   wooooooooooowe boom boom
> wooooooooooowe bah
> if u can't stop a hurricane, be one.[204]

More concerned with rhythm than rhyme, verse such as this gave feeling precedence over form, reflecting the poet's belief that "Feelings need not make sense. / Feelings are sense. / Pure high sense intelligence / undisciplined, pinnacles of our knowledge / tabernacles of Blackness."[205] Perhaps, they suggested, "nonsense" was needed to create new sense—a liberating sense—one that had no link to oppressive tradition. If conveyed in the proper manner—in the musical cadences most familiar to the people—anyone with "street smarts" could understand the message.

The use of polyrhythms, short and explosive lines, delayed rhymes, and other techniques borrowed from verbal rituals of the street such as the rap, the toast, scatting, and signification assured audiences that black writer/performers no longer cared about "talking white." Instead, they would utilize a distinct lexicon, syntax, and phonology.[206] Rejecting traditional grammatical paraphernalia as "tools, symptoms of the honkie's ORDER," they wrote in what novelist John Oliver Killens called "Afro-Americanese."[207] Here, "befo" replaced "before," "thang" was substituted for "thing", and "be" (also "bes" and "bees") was treated as a finite verb. To the uninitiated this was "bad English". To Black Arts writers, it was a reflection of their close identification with the unique expressive style of their people. What whites believed was immaterial. Time and again the shallowness of their commentary had proven that white critics possessed "neither the right nor the authority to proclaim themselves 'experts' on Black literature." Certainly, *they* were not capable of writing "like be-bop musicians play."[208] Motivated by the demands of the times, black creative artists would invent new names, new rules, a new language. As Hunter College/NYU-educated poet Sonia Sanchez noted proudly, "we bes the moral / keepers / cultural / bearers, the true believers."[209]

If, in their mind's eye, the highly literate aesthetes of the Black Arts movement could conceive of bonding with the black underclass, it took only an additional step of faith—albeit a major one—to conceptualize the symbiosis of all variants of Black Power under the banner of cultural union. Despite obvious temptations to do otherwise, a surprising number of black activists—including both cultural nationalists and their "political" opponents—expressed a desire to link politics and culture in support of national liberation.

For some, especially pan-Africanists, culture defined a unique community, widely dispersed by the diaspora, but joined by virtue of its ancestry, its value system, and its struggles against white colonial domination. It was Africa that provided blacks in this hemisphere with a much-needed reference point within the pageant of world civilizations. It also supplied many of the essential elements of their New World cultures. Neither tradition separated art and life and politics as fully as did the European-American. In return for these gifts, black Americans would remind their cousins on the continent that most of the divisions and antagonisms evident in modern black society were the result of European intermeddling. In truth, the universals of black culture transcended local differences and geographic boundaries. Recognition of this principle not only would enable those of the African heritage to better appreciate black cultural distinctives, but also would encourage them to cultivate the liberating egalitarian and communalistic principles of political and economic organization embodied in the pan-African culture.[210]

Others, including many attracted to revolutionary nationalism, felt that whatever their theoretical or ideological relationship, culture and politics were anything but antithetical in practice. The white power elite always had understood how to manipulate language and art in order to forward political views. Certainly, every cultural act was political in some sense. The essential question was whose political interests would be served. In this context, Black Power could be seen as a challenge to the whites' modus operandi—a movement of reaction against white cultural domination concomitant with political domination. If prevented from becoming too "otherworldly," black culture possessed revolutionary possibilities. Properly cultivated, it could help raise and maintain the nationalist spirit. As a tangible expression of revolutionary consciousness, it was capable both of posing an alternative to white values and of revealing to Afro-Americans the way in which their oppression must be brought to an end. Lacking sufficient cultural consciousness, even a successful political revolution stood in danger of erosion, or even total reversal, through an infiltration of white culture-borne values.[211]

Still others, especially those of the cultural nationalist persuasion, believed that if isolated, one from the other, neither black politics nor the black aesthetic were likely to free the black nation. The revolution was not only at the point of a gun, it also was concerned with matters of spirit and intellect. Culture, like politics, was an instrument of change. On the other hand, uninformed by nationalism, the creative output of a black artist rightly could be considered "white art"—reactionary and supportive only of the political status quo. In truth, Black Power was both a cultural and a political revolt, each thrust reinforcing the other. To free the nation was to free the culture—and vice versa. Since culture could be seen as a "whole way of life" encompassing the economic, political, social, and aesthetic aspects of a people's existence, the work of black artists was capable of accomplishing liberation in the temporal as well as in the "spiritual" realm. Certainly, on an individual level, it would be difficult to become involved in the revolutionary process without simultaneously beginning to look both at oneself and others in a new light—with a revised vision of self and society provided by an empowering black aesthetic.[212]

Guided by their cultural nationalist conscience, African-American artists reached many new understandings during the Black Power era.

"Impact Africa" cultural exhibit at the Studio Museum in Harlem. From *The Art Gallery* magazine, April 1970. Courtesy of William C. Bendig.

Recognizing that culture sometimes took the role of politics among the disfranchised, they hoped to reconcile ethics and aesthetics. Serving as a communication link between advocates of various "political" persuasions, they articulated and popularized a new black consciousness. By doing so, they raised political awareness and intensified popular commitment to social activism.

Useful for more than identifying cultural landmarks on the political map of a hoped-for black nation, black art carried the essentials of the

Black Power message from the priest/necromancers to their intended audience. If well conceived and executed, artistic and cultural expression could inspire black people to undertake meaningful personal change, committing them to action on behalf of the group. Grounded in the collective spirit of Afro-America, black art—the cultural nationalists' most treasured possession—was deemed capable of unifying Black Power enthusiasts, and of propelling them to ultimate victory over the purveyors of demeaning cultural clichés.

Taken together, the three major variants of African-American nationalism provided the Black Power movement with much of its ideological distinctiveness, many of its most compelling spokespersons, and a considerable share of its dynamism and attractive force. Members of the culture cadre were major players in the nationalist program for group empowerment and thus can be said to have performed central roles in the sociodrama which shaped the larger movement. By focusing upon cultural nationalist tenets and techniques, one gains new perspective on both the origins and the ultimate meaning of Black Power.

five

Black Power in Afro-American Culture: Folk Expressions

*The way we talk (the rhythms of our speech
which naturally fit our impulses), the way we
walk, sing, dance, pray, laugh, eat, make love,
and finally, most important, the way we look,
make up our cultural heritage. There is nothing
like it or equal to it, it stands alone in comparison to other cultures. It is uniquely, beautifully
and personally ours and no one can emulate it.*
Barbara Ann Teer, 1968

Throughout the Black Power years, Afro-American
activists—in tune with the anti-institutional tendencies of their times—brushed aside the obscur-
ing veil of White Power to reveal to the entire
nation what most of its black citizenry already recognized: black people possessed a distinctive
group culture which reflected unique themes,
values, and ideals. To such individuals, Black
Power became a revolution of culture which utilized all available forms of folk, literary, and dramatic expression to forward its message of self-
actualization. Fully cognizant of the transforming
potential of cultural self-definition, they called
upon the "spirit of blackness" ever-present in their
folk heritage to assist them in doing battle with

all forms of oppression. If it was in their power, they would free American culture from white hegemony.

Black folk expression (here defined to include the visual, linguistic, and culinary arts; folklore, music, and religion) mirrored the impact which "living black" in a white-dominated land could have on a people. Their unique cultural expression was by no means racially exclusive in the sense that it was transmitted through the genes. Nor was it, as the black psychologists revealed, induced solely by poverty and low socioeconomic status. Black culture was not deficient or deviant or a pathological perversion of mainstream culture. Its special character originated in the ancestral past. In modern times, the inheritors of these African traditions continued their attachment to a group culture which emphasized the collective and maintained a preference for oral forms of expression—traits that had been reinforced by the cultural isolation and proscription of New World slavery and segregation.

Although frequently romanticized or overstated, thereby making its very existence suspect, the black-white culture gap was real. While black Americans both contributed to and imbibed from the mainstream, they continued to retain and to cherish black cultural distinctives. Modified by time and contact with the white world, Afro-American culture, like most ethnic American subcultures, retained a unique set of values, life-styles, orientations, and shared memories. Black culture coexisted with a majoritarian culture which sought sustenance and rejuvenation from the Afro-American heritage even as it mocked black humanity through gross caricature and distortion.

Some blacks had little choice when it came to determining their placement in relation to the "culture gap." As any number of social science surveys conducted during the Black Power era revealed, black and white respondents evidenced significant differences of opinion on contemporary issues such as the delivery and quality of municipal services, degree and frequency of police brutality, or the pace of movement toward a fully integrated society.[1] The differential weighting of those responses reflected the continued existence of major societal roadblocks to socioeconomic integration. These, in turn, resulted in quantifiable black-white disparities in educational attainment, job status, and overall standard of living. For individuals trapped in inner-city poverty, the black subculture was both a vivid social reality and an important resource for survival.

But what about those who had greater choice? Did blacks who to all outward appearances had become part of the mainstream possess a

racial memory? If so, did it allow them to retain an attachment to traditional forms of cultural expression? Although certain exceptions
sometimes seemed to prove the rule, the answer in most cases was an
affirmative one. Like survivors and heirs of the Nazi Holocaust, these
upwardly mobile blacks sought to honor and preserve what was theirs.
Their cultural inheritance, as they defined it, had aesthetic as well as
functional dimensions. Both were found to be useful in maintaining psychological and emotional equilibrium. While aspiring to the good life,
they remained wary of unabashedly embracing a culture whose values
and practices long had denied their own humanity. To varying degrees,
they distanced themselves from the dominant culture for protection of
self. Believers in a black aesthetic which revealed the worth and beauty
of all black people, they agreed with their less well-to-do brothers and
sisters that to equate the Afro-American with the Euro-American experience was "fraudulent behavior."[2] To abandon totally their ties to the
ancestral culture would place them in an untenable position. Many
would be cast adrift amidst a hostile, alien people who continued to evidence little respect for—if a great deal of curiosity about—black folk life.

The Black Power constituency contained a contingent from each
group. Some either had little choice but to "live" the culture or purposely elected to do so. Others venerated it and promoted its ideals from
a somewhat more secure vantage point. All were joined in the belief that
their common racial heritage gave meaning to black life, providing an
important sense of identity for the children of the diaspora. They also
understood that to possess a unique racial culture was a valuable asset in
the group struggle for empowerment. Each individual who desired to
cultivate the black Muse could become a creator of culture in support of
liberation.

Soul Style

But do all blacks have 'soul'—and could nonblacks become 'soul
brothers and sisters'? While not the most crucial questions posed during
the Black Power years, they were among the most often repeated. Why
was this true? Perhaps it was because Afro-Americans loved to ponder
the implications of their preferred responses ("most likely, yes";
"highly improbable, no") while whites had a great deal of trouble coping
with the resulting rejection experience.[3] In any case, controversy over
the locus and ultimate meaning of "soul" made this quintessential in-
group concept one of the most compelling elements in contemporary
black folk expression.

Soul was the folk equivalent of the black aesthetic. It was perceived as being the essence of the separate black culture. If there was beauty and emotion in blackness, soul made it so. If there was a black American mystique, soul provided much of its aura of sly confidence and assumed superiority. Soul was sass—a type of primal spiritual energy and passionate joy available only to members of the exclusive racial confraternity. It was a "tribal thing," the emotional medium of a subculture. To possess a full complement of soul was to have attained effective black consciousness. Since every Negro was a potential black person, this experience was available to all Afro-Americans, but try as they might, most whites were incapable of reaching the same state of awareness. Because few outside the culture sphere knew what it was like to grow up black in an experiential sense, their strivings toward soulfulness invariably fell short of the mark. For outsiders, soul defied both codification and imitation. Often, even an adequate definition of the concept was hard to come by. It wasn't as literary as "Negritude" or as threatening as "Black Power." It was more like red beans and rice, nappy hair, and James Brown at the Apollo. As comedian Godfrey Cambridge noted, "You can't learn it, because no one can give you all those black lessons." You just had to be black.[4]

As a cultural concept, "soul" was closely related to black America's need for individual and group self-definition. During the Black Power era, the self-defining capabilities of soul were nowhere more evident than in the soul style that originated in and was authenticated by the urban black folk culture. In this sometimes crazy quilt world of the cool, the hip, and the hustle, stylized forms of personal expression were developed which not only conveyed necessary social information, but also could be utilized to promote a revitalized sense of self. At its most fundamental, soul style was a type of in-group cultural cachet whose creators utilized clothing design, popular hair treatments, and even body language (stance, gait, method of greeting) as preferred mechanisms of authentication. To reflect the uniqueness of Afro-American culture in one's person, it was not necessary to be a trained artist or musician; to create a new black theology; or to cook up the spiciest pot of gumbo in town. One merely had to be open to the unstudied, spontaneous expression of blackness. Ideally, this receptivity would result in a distinctive display of panache that fellow blacks would be inspired to emulate.

To the Black Power generation, urban soul "style" was a no-holds-barred, swaggering conceptualization. The truly soulful made an effort to appear in control of every situation. They cultivated aloofness and detachment, radiating an aura of emotional invulnerability. They shook

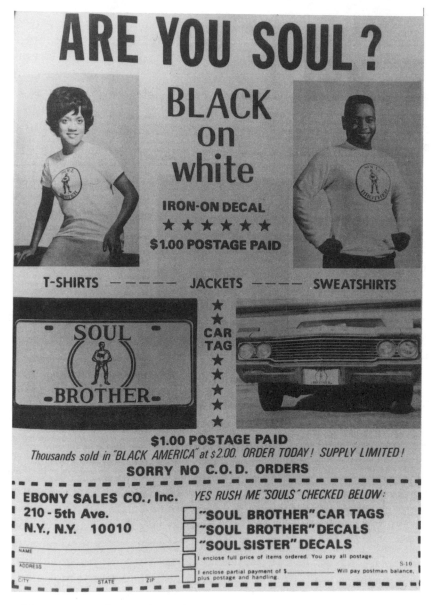

Advertisement for "soul" products. From *Sepia* magazine, October 1968.

off charges of arrogance and racial particularism like water off a duck's back. Instead of a begging plea for empathy and understanding, the message they sought to convey was more along the line of "Don't mess with me. I'm into my own thing." However powerless one might be in relation to the larger society, this sometimes inscrutable persona was well suited to neutralizing all opposing forces on the block.

Uninhibited in their manner of self-expression, the soulful were urban exhibitionists par excellence. They didn't simply *walk* down the street. They bopped, chopped, strutted and *flowed* from place to place in a manner that said "This is *me*, muh-fuh. Dig it!"[5] As described by their contemporaries, the sight of the accomplished soul stylist in motion was a thing of rhythmic perfection:

> You look at one cat, he may be doin' bop, bop-bop,
> bop, and another one goin' *bop*-de-bop, *de*-bop.
> Beautiful, man. Those are *beautiful* people. . . .
> *Polyrhythms.* That's what it is. Like a flower
> garden in a breeze.[6]

To "walk that walk" was to be hip, super-cool, and so fine.

Other forms of nonverbal communication provided equally striking counterpoints to the rigid, purportedly robot-like mannerisms of "uptight" white people. Handshakes, for example, became far more than perfunctory rituals of introduction. "Giving and getting skin" came to be viewed as a personal art form as well as a mark of communal solidarity. It could be used as a gesture of agreement and approval; to pay a compliment; or as a type of kinesic exclamation mark. Existing in a multitude of variants, "soul" handshakes could be accomplished with right hand/right hand, right hand/left hand, left hand/right hand, left hand/left hand, fist-to-fist, or back-of-hand-to-upturned palm contact. Some, such as the stylized Black Power greeting, were executed in rapid-fire sequence. First, there would be a mutual encircling of thumbs, signifying togetherness. Then, to evidence strength, hands were grasped with bended fingers. These fluid movements would be followed by a mutual grasping of wrists and the placing of hands on shoulders—revealing close comradeship. Finally, to symbolize black pride, solidarity, and power, arms were raised, biceps flexed and clenched fists formed for dramatic emphasis. Such rituals held far more meaning for participants than the traditional "hello, nice to meet you," handshake. Whatever the specific form, soul greetings were physical symbols of two individuals sharing the same feeling.[7]

Distinctive clothing also delineated the soul style, separating it from the drab polyester mainstream. Flashy and flamboyant, the soulfully attired took their fashion cues both from the African past and from the sartorial standards of inner city hustlers. Seeking to create a personal signature by wearing "some nice threads," young blacks donned floppy wide-brimmed hats, "Soul Brother" and "Soul Sister" berets, long, full-cut jackets, platform shoes, leather vests, and tight-fitting bell slacks with three-inch cuffs. When in the mood, they might choose to switch to a pan-African theme. Here, gold and ivory beads and earrings, cowrie shell belts, "African heritage" medallions, and elephant hair bracelets proliferated. Bubas, caftans, agbadas, djellabas, and geles, appeared in colors and fabrics that would have seemed exotic even to their most resplendently attired forebears.[8]

Eventually, the self-affirming, self-referential spirit evident in these creations influenced design considerations for more typically "western" garb. One clothing firm, New Breed, Ltd., promoted its line of suit-coats by noting that although traditional suiting materials were utilized, the garments were designed to complement the unique dimensions of the black physique. Since African-American men were "customarily heavy of chest, thinner of waist with a slightly protruding backside," these jackets were cut shorter than ordinary with wider lapels, deep vents, and an elevated waistline. Most important, trousers were gently tapered with the "New Breed slant," thereby accenting the "capital assets of the black male."[9] Gone was the day when a major fashion consideration was the selection of dark shades of clothing to make very black folk appear lighter-skinned. Now, Flori Roberts nylons ("This is not a black woman's version of a white woman's pantyhose") could be purchased in colors designed to flatter *all* shadings of black skin.[10] The Black Power generation was eager to accentuate and to promote what they considered to be favorable group distinctives. They remained relatively unconcerned whether such distinctives were physiological or stylistic, "real" or heavily colored by the idealism and romanticism of the era.

The most suitable complement to a soulful wardrobe was the "natural look" in hair styling. During the late sixties, white American youth used their hair to make a variety of political and philosophical statements. Young blacks were not excluded from this trend. Although most would agree that an individual (bluesman B. B. King, for example) could possess a fair quotient of soul without growing an Afro, the new style was perceived as having so many advantages that to remain content with a "process" brought both one's intellectual savvy and political wisdom into serious question.

What was so "righteous" about the natural? While some variants of

Black Power–era fashions. From *Sepia* magazine, March 1974.

African-influenced fashions. Courtesy of *Proud* magazine.

the new grooming technique may have been simpler to care for and cheaper to maintain, the fundamental attraction went beyond convenience and utility. A natural hair style served as a highly visible imprimatur of blackness; a tribute to group unity; a statement of self-love and personal significance. "We have to stop being ashamed of being black," asserted Stokely Carmichael in 1966, "A broad nose, a thick lip and nappy hair is us and we are going to call that beautiful whether they like it or not. We are not going to fry our hair anymore."[11] Rejecting the continued dictation of white-influenced beauty standards, black Americans abandoned the "konk," the "do" and the "fix," cleared hot irons, chemical straighteners, and permanents from their medicine cabinets, and filled the shelves with Raveen Hair Sheen, Frazier Blow Out Combs, and Head Start vitamin and mineral capsules ("for the healthiest possible hair").[12]

As they responded to Hank Ballard's urgent musical query, "How you gonna get respect when you haven't cut your process yet?", the Black Power generation searched the black cultural tradition for styling tips. Some treatments appeared purposely "bushy" in remembrance of "the first Afro natural," the black American slaves' ungroomed coiffure which, when matted down, was said to resemble "tramped-on hay." Others were so fully teased, sprayed, sparkled, and shaped that they seemed more a trick on Mother Nature than heartfelt homage to the ancestors. Still others were inspired by traditional African techniques. In addition to Karenga-style baldness as modeled on the Masai, these New World interpretations included cornrowing ("the living art form of millions") as well as more rarified styles like the Ayanna (Yoruba for "beautiful flower"), Ashia (a short natural adapted from Kenya), and Afro-Pyramid ("conceived through the influence of Amenhotep"). Certain treatments were so intricate—having small beads or shells wrapped or sewn into the hair—that three or more hours were required to complete a styling.[13]

Given the time and effort involved, it is understandable that a brisk business soon developed in easy to maintain Afro wigs made from "Afrylic" or "Afrilon" and marketed under sobriquets such as "Super Afrique," "Afro Bunny," and "Nubian Queen." If even this was too much trouble, various types of headwraps were available as "a pleasant change from wigs."[14] In the end, whatever the configuration or chemical composition, the natural look in hair styling became an important symbol of black cultural autonomy and psychological "debrainwashing." As one middle-aged visitor to Atlanta SNCC headquarters remarked upon entering a room full of Afro-topped workers in 1967, "I ain't never seen

"Natural" wigs. From *Sepia* magazine, May 1974.

nothin' like this. Y'all sho' are some new Negroes."[15] More correctly, the young activists were *ex*-Negroes, now endowed with a full quotient of dynamic soul style.

The culinary analogue to soul style was soul food. This, too, was a distinctive form of folk expression, delineating an important sphere of

Afro-American cultural achievement. Like the assortment of trendy college students and spaced-out rock musicians who attempted to replicate the natural hair stylings of blacks and wound up looking like Little Orphan Annie in a wind tunnel, whites who sought to create authentic soul delicacies often found themselves serving up a pale imitation of the real thing. Certainly, the most ambitious could search out and assemble the correct ingredients, cast aside their Teflon and Silverstone for cast-iron and earthenware, and follow all the necessary directions in a soul food cookbook. But there was no guarantee that the resulting dish would be considered soulful. Double blind taste tests might prove otherwise, but to the taste buds of black America, white folks' cooking almost always lacked that indefinable "something."

Like the "soul" concept itself, the preparation of soul food was said to be closely related to the presence of certain ill-defined feelings or attitudes. To determine whether a particular dish was soulful one had to be provided with a general introduction to the chef's mind-set as well as the list of key ingredients. As Obie Green, Georgia-born proprietor of one of Harlem's soul food eateries told a reporter in 1968, "Soul means love. And I cook with soul and feeling. I couldn't be a dollar-sign cook if I tried."[16] Individuals such as Green claimed to cook by "vibration," constantly improvising and altering their recipes to suit the mood or the moment. Other than mother wit and common sense there were no absolute standards established for creation of their cuisine. "The look and smell of it" was the accepted medium of authentication. Fellow blacks were the only acceptable arbiters of taste.[17]

The inexact nature of soul food preparation was held to be a byproduct of the black American's slave heritage. Lacking both literacy and appropriate measuring devices, the southern bondsmen somehow managed to transform cast-off ingredients—hog maws, neck bones, ham hocks, chitterlings—into "a gourmet's delight."[18] But to the modern day descendants of these ingenious slave chefs, soul cooking most definitely was not southern or regional.[19] Although collard greens, black-eyed peas, hush puppies, deep-fried chicken, and catfish may have appeared on both white and black tables in the antebellum South, it seemed to take a black hand in the kitchen before any recipe could be considered "soulful."

Authentic dishes were distinguished from the "thin, white man's parody" by a strong diasporan element. It was held that the soul style in cooking was developed but did not originate in the white-ruled South. It began in Africa. There, prior to Euro-American contact, the slaves' forebears used hot peppers to make the unique sauces that became such an essential part of the soul food menu. African fish stews served as models for New World gumbos. Collard and mustard greens, okra and other "slave food" was eaten with great relish in the ancestral homeland. Even the lowly yam and sweet potato provided an unbroken dietary link to the African past. In this conceptualization, the Atlantic slave trade initiated an important "culinary exchange" which eventually led to the flowering of an "international African cooking style." Surviving the Middle Passage, these distinctive dietary preferences and food preparation techniques were passed along and preserved by plantation bondsmen from different regions who "tasted each other's cooking and verbally exchanged recipes" in the quarters.[20]

During the Black Power years, the "tantalizing flavor" and "solid, lasting nourishment" of soul food not only was credited with sustaining black folk throughout the centuries of oppression, it also became an important aid in nurturing contemporary racial pride. White chefs, cookbook authors, and food section editors might continue to "act like they invented food and like there is some weird mystique surrounding it." They even could try their hand at preparing "Nat Turner's Favorite Crackling Bread," "Grits A La Soul," "Redneck Ragout" or any of the other recipes included in the newest cookbooks. But, ultimately, it would become apparent to all that a white chef lacked that most rare and precious ingredient—"blackness." The Black Power generation believed that only the originators of the soulful style knew intuitively that the African-American contribution to American cuisine amounted to more than providing the inspiration for "black bottom pie" and "niggertoes." Black people knew that "soul food ain't frozen collard greens." The genuine article was fresher and far more natural—the inimitable creation of a living pan-African folk culture.[21]

Soul Music

While in their kitchens preparing barbecued ribs, corn dodgers and sweet potato pie, soulful cooks often found themselves swaying and snapping their fingers to the latest hits from the black music charts. Broadcast by black-oriented radio stations which ceaselessly boasted about how many watts of "heart rockin' and soul sockin' super soul" sound they were capable of sending over the airwaves, songs such as "Memphis Soul Stew," by saxophonist King Curtis, "Too Many Cooks (Spoil the Soup)" by 100 Proof, the Soul Runners' "Chittlin' Salad", and Johnny Watson's "Soul Food" ("Girl if you want a friend right till the end, just put some neckbones on my plate") were well suited to inspiring culinary greatness.[22]

As acknowledged in a song by Marvin L. Sims, during the Black Power era everybody was "talkin' 'bout soul." Boosted by heavy airplay from ultrahip "Soul Brother" disc jockeys, the new, infectious style of music became a national pan-racial passion. Both brown and blue-eyed groups (Soul Children, Soul Clan, Soul Survivors) sang about the joys of listening to a "Soul Serenade" while doing the "Soul Limbo" at a "Stoned Soul Picnic." They offered up musical tributes to "Soul Power" and to the men and women ("Soul Brother, Soul Sister") most visibly infused with "Soul Pride." Little wonder that rhythmically entranced whites longed to get down to the "nitty gritty" and become one of the "Soul People."[23]

But it wasn't that easy. Soul music was claimed as the aesthetic property of blacks. In both structure and conceptualization it was said to be part of an African musicological continuum. As an indigenous expression of the collective African-American experience, it served as a repository of racial consciousness. Transcending the medium of entertainment, soul music provided a ritual in song with which blacks could identify and through which they could convey important in-group symbols. Music was power and considered to be supremely relevant to "the protracted struggle of black people for liberation." To some, it was "the poetry of the black revolution." If the group was to be liberated, the authenticity of this cultural form had to be preserved at all costs.[24]

Outsiders had trouble understanding these things. To black observers, most were either clumsy imitators or crass exploiters of the soul style. Intellectually, whites could appreciate that soul's attractive power was derived from the tension and electricity created by joining gospel's joyful devotional fervor with the bluesman's tales of worldly despair and sexual anguish. On select occasions, they might even experience the emotional catharsis provided by the music. But they seldom seemed to advance beyond superficial understandings. Allegedly, some "soulful" whites simply wanted to learn "how to shake their asses again"—an expertise supposedly lost when the Puritans escaped worldly corruption by leaving "the terrors of the Body" to "primitive" Africans. While blacks listened to the message in each song, whites were content to boogaloo blindly to the beat.[25] Others were said to be more concerned with swag than with swing and sway. As previous generations of entrepreneurial types had done with "race music" and "rhythm and blues," they hoped to label, package and thereby commercialize and "whiten" the sound of soul for personal gain. In either of these scenarios, Afro-

Americans faced the threat of becoming "cultural slaves." If whites were successful in appropriating both the soul style and the music itself, they would control the cultural essence of the people.[26]

The possibility of whites growing rich and racially rejuvenated through the prostitution of black folklife was distasteful, but anticipated. As noted by a sarcastic LeRoi Jones, "the more intelligent the white, the more the realization he has to steal from niggers." In this view, contemporary white music was so lacking in imagination and spontaneity it was imperative that *something* be done, even if it involved pillaging black culture.[27] After all, how many more Bobby Vinton albums could the record-buying public tolerate?

Initial attempts to breathe some life into mainstream music involved electronic gadgetry and ear-piercing amplification. With stages bending under the weight of massed speakers, drum sets, cables, keyboards, and controls, groups such as Iron Butterfly, Blue Cheer, and Vanilla Fudge tried to simulate what black musicians accomplished through the "electricity and power of *human* magnetism." According to Afro-American critics, most failed dismally. To them, white rock seemed more a technology than a felt experience. Despite their affections and pretentious preening, white groups were said to be sustained by gimmicky stage props, not talent. The rock stars' utilization of modern audio technology allowed them to create a wide variety of "visual-electronic novelty effects," but this brought them no closer to the authenticity of black music. They were merely substituting "artificial, simulated, canned musical pollutants" for natural, organic musical expression.[28]

A second approach was to cast caution—and credibility—to the wind and blatantly attempt to copy the performance style and repertoire of black rhythm and blues and soul artists. Blue-eyed soulsters like the Righteous Brothers, Mitch Ryder, Eric Burdon, Janis Joplin, and the Young Rascals strutted, screamed, sweated, and swallowed syllables in an awkward and sometimes humorous attempt to approximate the speech patterns and inflections of blues shouters, plantation field hands, or ghetto hipsters. Although their melding of blues and soul with Vietnam era white nonconformity was a huge commercial success, in the main black critics remained unimpressed. Said veteran drummer Max Roach when asked if whites were capable of playing his kind of music: "Yes, anybody can play something that's already been set out there. If a painter paints a certain thing, I can imitate it. But no whites have ever contributed to the creative or innovative aspects of black music." LeRoi Jones was even more blunt. Affirming Roach's opinion with a historical observation, he recalled that the "minstrels never convinced anybody they were black either."[29]

African-American commentators such as these rejected the notion that imitation was a sincere form of flattery. They were troubled by the probability that, as soul music became ever more popular, it would be expropriated and bowdlerized by whites. Although "beholden to a life experience based primarily upon European cultural tenets," these performers nevertheless sought to co-opt blackness. If possible, they would savor the sweet without tasting the bitter. In their feverish quest for cultural invigoration, popularity, and profit, whites were willing to push the real "soul people" off the stage and far into the background. According to the black critics, if they were successful, innovative blues, soul, and jazz stylings would be replaced by a wholly derivative form of musical expression that forever would remain a pale imitation of its original models.[30]

Exactly what was it that made the black version of a soul or blues song so special? For black audiences the answer was simple: the performer. In truth, "soul" was more than a musical category useful for charting black-oriented music in *Billboard* and *Jet*. It also was a performance term.[31] As sung by the Beatles, "Eleanor Rigby" and "Day Tripper" were prime examples of clever mid-sixties Euro-American pop. The music was engaging, but contained not a hint of soulfulness. Versions of the same songs performed by Ray Charles and the Vontastics had it in abundance. The same could be said for Aretha Franklin's interpretations of hits by Simon and Garfunkel and Dusty Springfield. The singer, not the song, determined whether a tune would be considered soulful.[32]

Like soul food cooks and their cuisine, musical performances were awarded one, two, three, or four stars largely on the basis of "attitude" and "feeling." To be successful, the would-be soulsters had to convey human experience and emotion in an authentic manner. They could not be content merely to reflect upon people and events from afar. Their job was to *project* the black aesthetic, not to categorize, analyze, and intellectualize it. Sometimes a proficient soul stylist didn't even need words to get the message across. The experienced performer could capture a mood through instrumentation or convey it via emotion-laden falsetto screams and broken cries of ecstasy. According to one Chicago disc jockey, some popular artists of the day were "almost unintelligible." But "the emotion, the feeling still gets across, the message is across."[33] Indeed, who could deny that the "Godfather of Soul," James Brown, was *communicating* when he chanted and moaned:

You've got to feel,
Just—you got, got to—
I've got to feel, give it to me.
You got to, let me.
Uh—uh, uh—let me. Let me have it.[34]

Whatever the song's lyrics or the artist's preferred synthesis of blues, jazz, and gospel, music performed by a truly soulful individual was soul.

Successful communication between soul people required that the audience heed the singer's demand for emotional involvement. If moved emotionally, they would reaffirm the artist's sentiments, clap and shout loudly: "Good Gawd," "Ain't that the truth," or "That's what's happenin', baby." To achieve this sought-after union, skillful practitioners of the art of soul drew upon the black musical heritage and employed every trick in their considerable repertoire. These included call-and-response song structure, use of colloquial and slang phrases, dazzling theatrics, and direct entreaties to

"get off your seat,
And get your arms together and your hands
    together,
And give me some of that old soul clappin'."[35]

When authentic soulmen asked if they could "get a witness" or begged an audience to "let me year you say yeah," they were nudging listeners toward a feeling of oneness that, in a somewhat different venue, might be adapted to more "political" ends.

During the Black Power years, Afro-American recording artists not only served as conduits for the vital message of racial unity, but they also became significant role models for many young blacks. One didn't have to be a committed cultural nationalist to believe that successful composers and performers functioned as "modern PRIESTS and PHILOSOPHERS" of the black nation.[36] You simply had to listen to their music. According to the Hues Corporation, for example, those in need of direction in life would do well to "talk to the man who takes all the time and makes all the rhymes." He knew "the right way." This was his hour, they said, and "he's got the power."[37] Many agreed. And for these committed fans, the soul singer became a true culture hero—the embodiment of soul style and the repository of folk wisdom. As novelist William Melvin Kelley noted in discussing soul's "Godfather," a "mere" singer was indeed capable of accurately transmitting the core values of black folk culture across the generations. "A hundred years from now," he wrote "if people want to find out what black people were in this country they will be listening to James Brown's

Advertisement for James Brown album. From *Jet* magazine, January 17, 1974. Courtesy of Polygram Records.

James Brown on trading stamps. Courtesy of *Proud* magazine.

records rather than reading Ralph Ellison. Ellison is too far from them."[38] To put it another way—in the words of a black teen leaving the Apollo Theatre after witnessing a James Brown concert—"The dude is as down as a chitlin'."[39] No higher compliment could have been given.

The attractive power of the soul singer rested on two major areas of accomplishment. First, and most obvious to all, they put on a darn good show. Accompanied by blaring horns, a pace-setting rhythm section, and a gaggle of bespangled, hyperkinetic backup singers, accomplished stage acts sought to drive both themselves and their listeners into a veritable frenzy of emotion. "Working up a sweat" was a prerequisite to a successful performance. As Sam Moore of the popular duo Sam and Dave noted, "Unless my body reaches a certain temperature, starts to liquefy, I just don't feel right."[40] If all went well, by the end of the show, the audience would be drained, but willing to follow the soulster's star wherever it might lead.

Second, despite a disposition toward conspicuous consumption and the attainment of a lifestyle far more glamorous than that of the vast majority of their listeners, soul artists generally were perceived as remaining "unspoiled," "natural," and close to the people. The record buying public's demands were simple, but weighty. In the words of Little Junior Parker, "They expect what you are."[41] To meet these expectations, black performers worked hard to maintain their image as soulful populists. No matter how many creature comforts they had acquired, they remembered to pay homage to the ancestors. At the 1972 Wattstax benefit concert, for example, Kim Weston linked past and present by leading some 100,000 spectators in the singing of the traditional black national anthem, "Lift Every Voice and Sing"—an emotional moment that was followed by a mass Black Power salute and the bowing of heads and joining of hands in an affirmation of racial unity.[42] They also made sure that their public was made aware of personal struggles encountered on the way to the top. "I never knew my papa's name," intoned Tony Clarke in "Ghetto Man." "My ma scrubbed floors to keep me clad, / And me and three brothers had to share one bed, / When I was young I felt ashamed."[43] To many inner-city blacks, Clarke seemed a true soul brother, fully capable of understanding their situation in life.

As they urged listeners to "Be What You Are" (A "Natural Woman" or an "Ordinary Man"), the soul singer sought to meet a deeply felt need of their Black Power era fans. When they sang "together we stand, divided we fall" these musical populists, in effect, were providing grass roots cultural leadership to a constituency made eminently receptive by soul's galvanizing, unifying power.[44] In providing "down home" role models that were both similar (cultural and socioeconomic background) and different (acquired status and wealth) from the masses who idolized them, the stars of soul both personified and strengthened the peoples' desire for "me" power.

Many black performers relished this role and sought to transform the bandstand into a bully pulpit of empowerment. There was nothing improper in this, they said. Success in such endeavor not only forestalled the commercialization and "whitening" of their music, but also facilitated black psychological liberation.[45] The "painless preaching" of a well-known activist/musician could result in transformed lives. After their pulse had been quickened and their consciousness raised by the soul artist's empowering message, attentive listeners would be moved to question received wisdom. No longer would they believe themselves incapable of creativity or of greatness. Now, they too could become "somebody." As Curtis Mayfield of the Impressions noted in lending his support to this militant musicological endeavor: "If you're going to come away from a party singing the lyrics of a song, it is better that you sing of self-pride like "We're a Winner" instead of "Do The Boo-ga-loo!"[46] The beauty of soul music was that it educated as well as entertained.

Like "soul" itself, the lesson plans created by these black musician-educators were both joyfully and painfully true to life. Whether conveyed via the driving dance sound of a James Brown, the sophisticated stylings of a Roberta Flack, or the ragged avant-garde "New Jazz" compositions of an Archie Shepp, the most compelling music of the day went beyond the preoccupations of traditional romantic balladry to influence opinion on affairs more weighty than those of the heart. Although certain of the more visionary improvisationalists seemed intent upon subverting Western musical conventions by creating an elaborate "hidden language" which excluded whites, most of the sentiments expressed by artists still attached to conventional standards of tonal beauty were suitably clear to all but the most obtuse.

If not specifically directed to white listeners, many of these musical offerings gained their attention by "talkin' about a change" that would be "more than just Evolution."[47] Such songs were more akin to the folk-oriented ballads of the civil rights movement than they were to the traditional blues repertoire. Like "Go Tell it On the Mountain," "Up Above My Head," and other sacred songs that had been adapted to the purposes of the southern freedom movement, James Carr's "Freedom Train" employed gospel imagery ("C'mon y'all, we gotta ride the freedom train, / We ain't gonna live this way again") in the cause of worldly freedom.[48] Echoes of "I Ain't Scared A' Your Jail" and "Freedom is a Constant Struggle" could be heard in the Impressions' "Keep on Pushing," the Chi-Lites' "(For God's Sake) Give More Power to the People," and Willie Hightower's ode to the rebirth of black pride, "Time Has Brought About a Change." The creators of this music claimed the ability to "see the face of things to come" and some predicted that it "won't be water but fire next time."[49]

These updated protest songs lacked the aura of loneliness and isolation, world weariness and resignation, the "hard luck and trouble" that characterized a traditional blues lament. As in the 1960 Sam Cooke hit "Chain Gang," the subjects of Black Power era music might sometimes feel that they were in danger of "moanin' their lives away," but more often than not they now employed adversity as a reference point and a goad to activism.[50] The revised message was that while it still might be, as Edwin Starr sang, "hell up in Harlem," black residents no longer were willing to live out their years in a "concrete reservation."[51] Despite attempts to hold them back, black people would "keep on, keep on keeping on."[52] When, in "Message From a Black Man," the Temptations told whites, "I have one single desire, just like you / So move over, son, 'cause I'm comin' through," the sentiment was unequivocal.[53] Soul people meant to revolutionize history. As noted by an angry Gil Scott-Heron, it was unlikely that this forthcoming revolution would be a glitzy, staged media event with musical entertainment provided by Glen Campbell and Engelbert Humperdinck. It would not be "brought to you by Xerox in four parts without commercial interruptions." There would be no instant replays of "pigs shooting down brothers." The coming struggle, he predicted, certainly would be no "rerun." The revolution would be live and in living color.[54]

In addition to affirming that "time is running out on bullshit changes," Black Power era soulsters conducted two- to three-minute mini-courses in the techniques of empowerment.[55] Following cultural nationalist guidelines, they taught that in order to alter social conditions, blacks first had to change the way they looked at themselves. Like more prominent soul people, the average Afro-American had to stop mimicking white ways and strive to be "natural." If successful in casting off the psychological burdens imposed by Euro-American pretensions to cultural superiority, their true soulfulness would be revealed— radiating outward for all to see. As the Impressions sang, "If you got soul, / Everybody knows, / That it's alright." Convinced that their culture was worthy and that they could "make it with just a little bit of soul," Afro-Americans would be better able to direct their energies toward "moving on up."[56]

Through personal example, black singers and songwriters revealed that recognition of one's natural soulfulness often was accompanied by a newfound proclivity toward braggadocio. This, too, was "natural." It was to be expected from individuals who only recently had succeeded in demolishing ancient sociocultural truisms. Moreover, said the soulsters, it was the stone truth. African-Americans deserved respect because they were a beautiful people, "so beautiful it makes you cry."[57] In the words of a Nina Simone song, they were "young, gifted, and black/And that's a fact!"[58] According to Dyke and the Blazers, they set standards that few outsiders could equal:

> When we walk,
> We got more soul, we got it,
> When we talk,
> We got more soul, we got it,
> When we sing, Lord have mercy,
> We got more soul. . . . [59]

The message of these lyrics was explicit. If you were one of the soul people it was legitimate to claim "I am somebody, you are somebody."[60] By first acknowledging and then putting their natural gifts on display, they proved their receptivity to the "me" power, "us" power message. Firm believers in their own worth and value, the beautiful, gifted, soulful ones were not at all self-effacing. Eagerly joining James Brown in a heartfelt personal tribute, they declared, "You're all right and you're out of sight, / Say it loud, I'm black and I'm proud."[61]

Lest overweening pride lead to a disastrous fall, some recording artists took it upon themselves to warn the public of various pitfalls to be encountered along the road to Black Power. The most memorable of these admonishing musical prophets were The Last Poets, an ensemble of streetwise performance-oriented improvisationalists from New York whose record albums and appearance in the film *Right On* spread their message nationwide. Believing that, in their current state, many black Americans couldn't "get it together until it's 'up against the wall' time, until they see the 'man' coming down the street, until he's kicking their doors in," they forecast the apocalypse. The Poets' abrasive doomsday-droning recitations warned listeners that time was running out. Plans to extend the sway of White Power and, through birth control and other means, decimate the black population, had to be thwarted by a Black

Power revolt. The musicians' role, as they saw it, was to "turn people on, to wake people up" before black folk found themselves "drowning in a puddle of the white man's spit."[62]

A major hindrance to this crucial awakening was said to be the "Niggers"—blacks who feared revolutionary change. In the Poets' vision, such individuals formed a dangerous fifth column within the black community. "Niggers" were "very untogether people."[63] Most were poseurs and actors who might, on occasion, speak of their commitment to social change, but in truth spent most of their time seeking personal gratification. Their mental processes corroded by oppression, many, it was said, sought nothing more out of life than to be provided with an adequate supply of alligator shoes, El Dorados, and white lovers.

The Poets' great fear was that when the revolution began and the shooting started, "Niggers" still would be "shootin' the shit." "Niggers," they said, were very adept at shooting craps, pool, dope, and sharp glances at white women, but they were "scared of revolution." This had to change. As musicological harbingers of this portending but avoidable doom, the Poets were determined to harass, threaten, and shame "Niggers" into changing their unproductive ways. As they noted in "Black People What Y'all Gon' Do," in the face of impending disaster it was essential for all members of the black community to rid themselves of oppression-induced entropy and stand up for themselves and for their people in a meaningful way. If they did so, the Poets' version of the Negro-to-Black conversion process would be deemed a success. Rifles and revolvers would take the place of songs and poems as black America formed a united front against white aggression. In time, they said, African-Americans—the first people—would be the last. Until that day, the Last Poets vowed to continue their assault upon the ears and conscience of black America, warning against complacency, backsliding, and disloyalty to the cause of empowerment.[64]

During the Black Power years, Afro-American musicians provided a running commentary on the state of the folk culture. Through their musical messages and dynamic performance style, they both mirrored and directed their people's struggle for empowerment. They meant to be—and were—successful entertainers. But they also served as standard bearers of a separate, avowedly superior culture. Although their less danceable, more overtly political music often made little impact on national record charts, the message of these songs was spread underground via a modern-day "grapevine telegraph." But it really wasn't necessary for black music to contain strident, anti-white lyrics to be considered revolutionary.[65] There were as many successful approaches to the encour-

The Last Poets. Courtesy of Celluloid Records.

agement of black unity and pride as there were variants of the soulful performance style. When they moved the peoples' feet to dancing, authentically soulful artists also opened black minds to new possibilities. As Malcolm X once had suggested, there was no reason why black people's proven ability to create and to improvise musically couldn't be adapted to the formation of new social and political structures.[66] Their music offered essential instruction in mental decolonization and self-definition at least as cogent as any "political" broadside of the day.

Soulful Talk

The lyrics of the soul songs comprised a veritable lexicon of mid-sixties street talk and slang. When black performers implored their audience to "get down," "do it right," "tell it like it is," "dig it," or "show me where it's at," they were seeking to establish a rapport based upon shared linguistic understandings. Initially, this was an in-group dialogue, inextricably connected to other forms of urban black folk expression. But as this music became more popular, the choicest colloquialisms were "borrowed" by outsiders, filtered through the popular culture, and eventually treated as part of the public domain.

Afro-Americans resisted these co-optative tendencies and struggled to maintain their linguistic distinctives as a mark of cultural uniqueness. As whites sought ever greater access to the "hidden language," blacks became increasingly possessive of the black vernacular. Believing that linguistic independence was essential to group self-definition, they were determined to quash the seemingly inexorable movement toward cultural homogenization.

This phase of the battle for Afro-American cultural integrity was fought in the mass media—a battleground made especially treacherous by the fact that it long had been controlled by whites. From a black point of view, early reports from the field were discouraging. Catchy phrases that had originated within the folk culture were being wrenched out of context and used to sell a wide variety of products. Hoping to win the loyalty of black consumers, advertisers claimed that Eve menthol cigarettes could "cool a stone fox;" that L & M Super Kings tasted so good they were "Super Bad;" and that one sip of Johnnie Walker Red Label could convince any whiskey drinker that "Red is Beautiful too." In this manner, black cultural expression was placed in the service of commerce with the lion's share of profit-making to be enjoyed by those who knew the black vernacular only as a "second language." An unusually forthright ad placed in *Essence* by Oriental Wig Imports of Atlanta encapsulated the whole process. The caption next to a picture of their newest model read: "No price is too high to pay for your FREEDOM. This particular FREEDOM is $6.72."[67]

Particularly attractive to marketing moguls was soul's emphasis on authenticity. Chevrolet Vega ads, for example, promised potential buyers that there would be "No jive. No phoniness. No foolishness. No nonsense." The General Motors compact was "one honest car." In similar fashion, magazine advertising for Kraft Barbecue Sauce urged readers to "Act Natural," thoughtfully including a recipe for "Soul Ribs N'Rabbit Slaw" for those who needed guidance in such matters. Following the trend, the makers of seemingly "unnatural" products, such as Nice n' Easy hair color and Bonne Bell Ten-O-Six Lotion, also claimed to be promoting authenticity—in this case "honest-to-you color" and "Honest Skin." As a spokesperson for Nice'n Easy asserted, it was possible for her to recommend the hair treatment to other soul sisters because "It lets me be me." Even the U.S. military eventually climbed on this new marketing bandwagon with ads informing prospective recruits that "You *can* be Black *and* Navy too" because the Navy "lets you do your own thing." In this manner, commercial exploitation of the black vernacular removed a unique mode of expression from its nurturing environment within the urban folk culture, ultimately exposing it to all manner of trivialization, misinterpretation, and degradation.[68]

As they witnessed the passage of "black talk" from the streets of Harlem to the Manhattan offices of account executives and then on to the sound stages of Hollywood and into mainstream parlance, Afro-Americans developed a variety of mechanisms to preserve essential elements of the once "hidden" language for themselves. In effect, they made the black vernacular a moving target—frustrating and confusing whites by refusing to play by the rules of assimilationist gamesmanship. Had a Black Power primer been written on these obfuscating techniques, it would have included the following guidelines:

1. Alter the meaning of "standard" English words and phrases, placing them in a black-controlled context whenever possible. Disregard deprecatory connotations of "nigger." But don't discard the word itself. Given the proper nuance and context, it is capable of conveying either sentiments of hostility or of fondness between soulful people. On the other hand, make "pig" a part of your "political" vocabulary. It should become synonymous with the brutal urban cop, not the common barnyard animal.[69]

2. Abandon the use of a term if it consistently has been misused, skewed, and made part of the whites' "rhetoric of oppression." Describe "urban renewal" accurately. It is "Negro removal." Substitute "trippin" for "jazz." The former is a descriptive performance term. The latter relates to white sexual fantasies about black people and their music. Refuse to designate either Harriet Tubman or Marcus Garvey as a black "Moses." To do so removes them from an African-American frame of reference—and therefore from black history.[70]

3. Avoid white folks' hangups with diction. If they insist on saying "my" instead of "mah," "your" instead of "yo," or "man" instead of maee-yun," let them. But don't copy their style. A soulful expression "perfectly" enunciated by the hopelessly unhip no longer can be considered soulful.[71]

4. Define white people just as they have defined you. Use names they wouldn't be caught dead using themselves. Options include but are by no means limited to the following: blue-eyed devil, beast, Chuck, cracker, gray, honky, The Man, Miss Ann, Mr. Charlie, paddy, peckerwood, o-fay, red neck, whitey.[72]

5. Employ a judicious amount of violent and/or profane language in oral expression. Don't be embarrassed. Like "soul" itself, impassioned speech conveys genuine emotion. It is the "idiom of the oppressed." Angry phrases like "up 'ganst the wall mo' fucker" are more true to

life and yet more powerfully symbolic of the people's struggle than "We shall overcome." Besides, profanity always frustrates and confuses mainstream print and broadcast editors.[73]

6. Reform literary expression. Spell phonetically, turning the tables on several generations of writers who utilized dialect to denigrate black characters. Capitalize "We" and use the lower case "i" to emphasize that the community is more important than any single individual. Substitute "k" for "c" in "Africa," liberating the continent from linguistic colonialism.[74]

7. Finally, Never, NEVER allow non-blacks to define key concepts such as freedom, integration, or Black Power for you. Why not? If you don't know, you either haven't been paying attention or you are one of "them."[75]

Given the efforts involved in keeping the argot of soul a mystery to outsiders, one also might wonder why the Black Power generation was so protective of dialect that most whites considered "bad" English. The reason was readily apparent to those socialized within the folk culture. Although most Afro-American defenders of the black vernacular were not formally trained in linguistics, they understood the basic relationship between language, society, and culture. Many would agree that "free people are comfortably expressive people. And comfortably expressive people speak a language that they have given birth to, a language they control."[76] Both the linguist and the soulster recognized that language was an indispensable vehicle for the transmission of social mores. Utilizing a vocabulary that served as an index to a people's worldview, language was capable of conveying the values, symbols, and definitions accepted by their culture. By mastering a specific language, one not only learned how to communicate, but also how to think and reason within the group context. Thus, to speak was to assume a culture. To speak in the black argot was to establish both a personal identity and a bond between oneself and one's soul mates.[77]

Like other forms of black expression, language can be viewed as being both "political" and "cultural." It either promotes group strength and cohesion or contributes to the spread of disunity and confusion. Like a campaign slogan or national flag, it could become a rallying point for group advancement. In times of adversity, language served as a survival mechanism, unifying the people, reaffirming the correctness of their worldview and providing an unconscious defense against the incursions of opposing value systems. This was critical because any external assault on the validity of a people's language threatened their very existence as independent culture bearers. By abandoning one's language, either willingly or through coercion, one risked permanent dislocation, rootlessness, and estrangement from the protective natal culture.[78]

During the Black Power era, the maintenance of linguistic distinctives was of signal importance to black activists. Those who fought most vigorously to preserve the black idiom felt it unlikely that a vigorous group culture would be able to survive and flourish if, in the words of poet June Jordan, black people began to imitate the "double-speak/bullshit/non-think standard English of the powers that be."[79] Cultural independence could be bolstered by defining the world in terms familiar to the group even while making a conscious effort to learn and understand every nuance of the oppressor's language.

Definition, in fact, was the name of the game—and "naming" a cultural practice that transcended purely linguistic concerns. The problem centered upon the capacity of language to transmit the value judgments and biases of its users; to impute value; and to authenticate human experience. If language provided a "window" through which to view the world, blacks held that "standard" English perpetuated the racial hierarchy of that world. By defining all things black as either negative, subordinate, or inferior, it reinforced inequality and hindered the spread of the empowerment ethic.

A quick thumbing of *Webster's* tells the tale. Words such as black sheep, black market, blackmail, black magic, and blacklist all had decidedly negative connotations. White elephant, white sale and white heat did not. As had been pointed out by Dr. King and others, of the 134 synonyms for whiteness listed in *Roget's Thesaurus*, 44 (bright, clean, chaste, upright, just, etc.) conveyed positive images while only ten (such as ashen, pale, and wan) could be considered somewhat negative. On the other hand, fully half of the 120 synonyms for blackness (baneful, dirty, foreboding, sinister, etc.) carried unfavorable connotations. None were positive. In effect, African-Americans schooled only in "standard" English were provided with 60 reasons to despise themselves, but few, if any, to encourage the development of self-esteem.[80]

In an attempt to avoid psychological damage, they could, of course, insist upon being referred to as a "Negro," but this only created additional problems. Not only did the word lack geographic, linguistic, or cultural specificity—thereby denying the pan-African heritage—but it, too, had become a derogatory epithet.[81] Stokely Carmichael placed the naming issue in historical perspective:

> When we were in Africa we were called Africans
> or blacks; when we were in Africa we were free.

> When we were captured and stolen and brought to
> the United States, we became Negroes. So negro
> is synonymous with slavery. . . . if you say you're
> a Negro, what you're saying is that your begin-
> ning is in slavery. If your beginning is in slavery,
> the best you can hope to be is a good slave.[82]

According to Carmichael, in order for group aspirations to reach a higher plane, blacks had to stop "talking this junk" and begin to seek their true identity in the pre-diasporan world of their freeborn ancestors.

This critique did not originate with contemporary Black Power activists. Dissatisfaction with "Negro" was evidenced as early as David Walker's *Appeal* of 1829 and continued to be manifested throughout a lengthy twentieth-century campaign for universal acceptance of the capital "N."[83] Malcolm X brought the issue to the attention of a new generation by prefacing "Negro" with "so-called" and by promoting the notion that the word was no more than a deceptively polite, polished form of "nigger." By the time of Malcolm's death, Muslim and non-Muslim alike were starting to investigate his contention that the appellation made blacks "non-existent." As long as they identified themselves as "Negroes," he said, black people could claim no country, no language, no culture as their own.[84]

Eventually, many Afro-Americans, especially the young, came to view "Negro" as a déclassé designation. Refusing any longer to answer to a name that transformed a soulful people into the "reflection of another man's fantasy, a nonentity, a filthy invention," they developed a list of preferred alternatives. Whether one chose to use Black, Afro-American, African-American, or Americans of African descent, the goal was the same—to shape a new identity through self-definition.[85] Believing that "only slaves and dogs are named by their masters," black activists saw that these revised terms could have an important bearing on their racial destiny. Placed under black control, the cultural practice of "naming" would become a conscious political act of resistance. For example, when defined outside the white tradition, it was possible for "black" to have alternative meanings, such as beautiful or proud. No longer was it simply a derogatory social label or a skin color. Given a positive connotation, the word literally became a "concept." As such, it provided the psychologically downtrodden with a semantic tool capable of generating a radically altered perception of one's self and one's world. To replace Negro with Black or Afro-American might not, in the short run, do a great deal to transform societal power relationships. But it was a beginning.[86]

The debate over who had the right—and the power—to "name" black Americans raised an even thornier pedagogical question: Given their determination to define both self and society in their own terms, how much longer would Afro-Americans continue to accept the imposition of "standard" English in inner city classrooms? For some, supplementary African language study provided the necessary psychological and cultural distancing from white linguistic imperatives.[87] But for others not even this would suffice. Claiming that "the masses of black people . . . have never spoken the European's languages," they demanded that "black English" be recognized as the lingua franca of the black nation. The most outspoken advocates of this position held that mainstream American English, not Swahili or Hausa, was the proverbial "barbarous" foreign tongue, to be treated, at best, as a "second language" elective in black schools.[88]

The campaign to legitimize black English was buoyed by its supporters' unassailable confidence in the superiority of "black talk." Denigration of the black idiom was viewed alternately as (1) yet another manifestation of American racism; (2) part of the whites' plan to force their middle class mind-set on others; and (3) a clumsy attempt to camouflage cultural jealousy.[89] But who could believe what white people said about language anyway? One minute they were badmouthing the black vernacular as a social deficit—part of the supposedly pathological "culture of poverty"—and the next they were slurring their syllables and "gettin' down" in a vain attempt to be "with it" and find out "where it's at." Black folk didn't need their advice on how to speak. They weren't "sloppy talkers" who had "lazy lips." What they had was a soulful manner of communicating that served their cognitive needs perfectly. Indeed, in an Afro-American cultural context, it was standard English that was dysfunctional. Black English was far more capable of accurately expressing black feelings and experiences—and far less likely to insult their intelligence and dignity.[90]

To drive home the point that black English was "one of the highest expressions of black culture" as well as to silence critics' charges that it was little more than a random accumulation of linguistic errors uttered by the undereducated, advocates sought to show that their everyday speech was blessed with both function and form. It possessed an artistry and informal elegance lacking in the more utilitarian "standard" variant. It also had structure. Black English was to be considered a bona fide language and conceptual *system* with its own rules and conventions.[91]

While far more flexible than standard English, there was a correct way to pronounce words and a correct grammar to be used in speaking. It was believed that the core elements of this system could be heard in the unaffected oral expression of black people from all social classes, living in all parts of the country. One study claimed that approximately 80 percent of the Afro-American population spoke black English.[92] Specific to Afro-Americans, but not limited to urban black youth, distinctives in intonational contouring and syntactical variation made black English speakers ethnically identifiable. This was said to be true no matter how much exposure to mainstream society an individual had experienced. Even the most skilful Afro-American practitioner of standard English could find their internal black English converter spontaneously activated when they "got with the brothahs." It was whites' lack of acculturation into this linguistic "deep culture" that made them sound so ridiculous when they tried to "talk black."[93]

The speech of the soulful was difficult for outsiders to master and hard for *anyone* to understand when described in academic jargon. But there was no shortage of attempts. Blacks seeking to justify and non-blacks attempting to fathom the unique language system offered considerable, sometimes conflicting, advice on the subject. Lexicons and dictionaries of "black jargon" were compiled.[94] Linguists attend "Ebonics" conferences and debated the findings of new research into possible pidgin and creole roots.[95] Texts, novels, and culture-specific I.Q. tests written in black English became available.[96] Attempts were made to codify a "universal Pan-African language."[97] There was much talk of "idiolects," "paralinguistic features," "co-occurrent adverbial expressions," and "basal language equations." But, exactly what did anyone learn as a result of all this feverish activity? Well, it was discovered that:

1. "The Hawk definitely ain't jivin' outdoors today" meant the same thing as "the air is crisp."[98]
2. If it had been written in black English, the Twenty-third Psalm would have begun: "The Lord is my main man; I can't dig wanting."[99]
3. The Double Pronoun Reflexive Principle, as evidenced in "*Ahma* have to get *me* a drink uh some of that coffee" and "*I'm* gonna get *me* one of them" was related in some fashion to self-esteem.[100]
4. In the black English present perfect singular, the conjugation of "to throw" went as follows:
   I done throwed
   You done throwed
   He, she, it done throwed.[101]
5. On the multiple choice section of a culture specific I.Q. test, "to travel" most definitely did not correctly answer the question "What is the meaning of the phrase 'to get down'?"[102]

Of course many of the soul people knew these things already. Others couldn't have cared less what the linguists' studies revealed. They knew from personal experience that the black vernacular was an essential part of the Afro-American's cultural identity. Black dialect could be dissected, diagramed, and analyzed endlessly, but the essential wisdom remained the same: you simply couldn't be soulful talking white standard English.[103] Moreover, black English speakers were well aware that whatever claims were made regarding the structure and cohesion of black expression, *they* were the ones who had final authority in matters of linguistic convention.

African-Americans understood that their language system had both oral and physical components. They knew that words alone did not guarantee effective communication. Here, the master of the metaphor was king and a diverse array of gestures and inflections added texture and meaning to any conversation.[104] In this respect, black English was a true art form. But it also served as yet another example of the "me" power inherent in Afro-American culture. It promoted the validity and worth of group distinctives while muting the voice of those unable to get inside the folk culture well enough to learn its hidden language. In their own organic speech patterns, black Americans found an effective model of self-definition. And they thought it was "boss," perhaps even "tough," and most certainly "bad" and "out of sight."

Soulful Tales

Nowhere were the oral and physical aspects of black expression more visibly intertwined than in the modern urban folktale. Like their unnamed forebears who had formulated the original trickster tales, the Black Power generation understood that a good storyteller needed no elaborate stage set, makeup, or costume. If well versed in their art, they could become creators of culture utilizing only soulful speech, native wit, and body language. The skilful melding of these elements entertained, informed, and helped shape a cultural identity different from that of their white contemporaries.

The tales, jokes, and anecdotes of urban black America were part street-corner amusement, part acculturative coming-of-age ritual, and part blood sport. Ingenuity, originality, and verbal dexterity were highly valued social skills that had to be developed through constant practice. The ability to recite a lengthy narrative poem (the toast), to best ones' peers in verbal duels (sounding, signifying, playing the dozens), or simply to talk with a high degree of style (rapping) brought recognition and status. An adept wordsmith could influence the beliefs and actions of others. Through taunt, boast, and banter, the storyteller could become the controlling agent of any social situation.[105] Viewing their folkloric heroes—and by implication themselves—as superior to the heroic representatives of all other peoples, black urban storytellers claimed the authority to name, describe, and indict; to contravene the mores of "polite" society; and to take power whenever the opportunity arose. If the average black person on the street was only one-tenth as obstreperous as their folk heroes, there was little doubt that they would succeed in maintaining cultural integrity—and perhaps be successful in achieving political independence as well.

The tales of an earlier day were brought up to date by placing the Brer Rabbit, slave trickster John, and "Bad Nigger" characters in the garb of urban hustlers and mackmen (pimps).[106] Instead of Brer Bear and Brer Fox, their adversaries were Goldberg, Vanderbilt and other members of the white power structure. Like their more rural predecessors, modern-day black folk heroes successfully opposed, ignored, or circumvented the social roles assigned them by "outsiders." In doing so, they displayed a mental agility, physical strength, and sexual prowess that elicited both fear and awe. Their exploits often surpassed the capability of most mortals. But, in the realm of the folk imagination, anything was possible.

African-American folk heroes turned the tables on real-life socioeconomic relationships. In effect, they became crude and colorful representations of black wish-fulfillment. With great gusto they toasted the "good life" and the luxuries they had acquired. Long-Shoe Sam, for example, boasted:

> I had a sharkskin vine in a powder blue,
> Black wingtips from Bendette's, sparkling new,
> My shirts were from Brooks'; my socks cost a
>   pound;
> I wore solid gold cufflinks—I knew I was down.
> I wore a hat from Disney with a fifty-dollar tag,
> And my snakeskin billfold was loaded with
>   swag.[107]

Hophead Willie, on the other hand, invested his considerable disposable income in real estate and durable goods:

> I bought the east side of New York City and the
>   west of dear old Chi,
> I bought airports in California that Henry Ford
>   had tried to buy,

. . . .

Now I got me a yacht on every ocean and just a
    flock of seaside grills,
I bought me fourteen furniture companies and
    twenty-eight lumber mills.[108]

Whatever their preference in creature comforts, the urban folk hero knew that to display great wealth with soulful panache helped establish a reputation as a "hipcat stud."

The hipster's distinctive élan also caused him to be awash in attractive and pliant women. Whenever he tired of material things and began to feel lonesome or "a little bit blue" there always seemed to be "five or six bitches" around with whom he could "spend an hour or two." Sometimes viciously misogynic, such tales portrayed women as little more than sex machines—income producing whores or submissive pawns in marathon "fucking contests."[109] That they commonly neither sensed nor objected to their victimization can be attributed to the decidedly male orientation of the genre. But, if the stories themselves were to be believed, the explanation was somewhat different: women didn't complain because they had an insatiable craving for sexual gratification.

In the urban folk tale, the size of a male's penis determined his potency and hence his attractiveness. Here, bigger most definitely was considered better. As a young woman named Sally exclaimed in one of the tales, "They don't come too long and hard for me, baby!" To thoroughly satisfy such a woman, one had to have roughly "eighteen pounds of red-hot meat." Fortunately, the typical male folk hero met these requisites handily. Some were said to keep in top physical shape by using their member to chop down trees, to crack coconuts open, and to impregnate a wide variety of animal life. Like the well-endowed "Pimping Sam," who claimed to be "the biggest in the field, / The man you girls need and the master at the wheel," they sought to be recognized as black America's premier "back-binder, booty-grinder, sweetspot-finder."[110]

Sex appeal and conspicuous consumption were not the only mechanisms used to gain power over others. To a man, the urban folk heroes were clever individuals who used wit, cunning, and dexterity to get what they wanted. On occasion, they would challenge an unwary opponent to a contest of skill—which, in truth, was no contest at all. In one story, the black hero won a boasting contest with a white man by tossing an apple into the air and then peeling, coring, and dicing it with his knife before it hit the ground. Another recounted how the popular trickster Shine met the challenge presented by a hungry shark. Menaced by the creature as he departed the sinking *Titanic,* Shine bragged: I outswim the white man, I outswim the Jew, / I know motherfucken well I can outswim you." Making good his claim, "he passed the cruisers, destroyers, the sea-goin' plane, / he passed the battleship *Luxion,* the *Washington,* and *Maine,"* easily outdistancing the shark and reaching dry land long before the doomed ship came to rest on the ocean floor.[111]

Often, however, urban folk heroes simply bullied, intimidated and then *took* what they desired. Apparently, this trait was present at birth. A character named Dolemite, for example, was said to be a "ramping, scamping young fellow from the day he was born." At the age of one he started drinking whiskey and gin. At two, he began "eating the bottles they came in." By the time Dolemite was a teenager, it took one hundred strong men to constrain him. Special television bulletins alerted the citizenry of his comings and goings. Undoubtedly aware that he had "swimmed across bloody rivers and ain't' never got wet," even the Rocky Mountains took heed and parted to let him pass.[112]

Other black folk heroes were similarly adept at winning through intimidation. Certainly only the brash or the foolhardy would question the authority of a man who was so self-confident he could proclaim, "I measure forty-two inches across my chest / and I fear not a livin' sonofabitch between God and Death"; or who proudly boasted of his ability to "put chains on lightning and shackles on thunder"; or who declared that he could make "Astaire dance and/Sinatra croon"—and, if he felt like it, even make the Supreme Court "eat shit from/a spoon." Such an individual probably *did* "kick ass morning, noon, and night" and therefore was a force to be reckoned with. "Mentally free" and endowed with an "adding-machine mind," great physical strength, and extraordinary wealth, these heroes of oral lore were more than a match for Paul Bunyan, Mike Fink, Davy Crockett, or any other competition the Euro-American folk culture could offer.[113]

Neither the characters of urban folklore nor the streetwise storytellers who recounted their fantastic exploits were hesitant to speak black English or to "tell it like it is." Too "raw" for mass consumption, the tales could be "marketed" to the mainstream only as academic research in cultural anthropology or linguistics. From a black perspective, this was all according to plan. Few of the stories reached the tender ears of whites in the original idiom, thereby preserving their essence and function. Whites were, however, allowed access to basic storylines via certain black comedy albums and national magazines such as *Ebony.*

Gatekeepers of their own culture, Afro-Americans shared just enough of the folk heritage via black humor for whites to receive the central message: Euro-American assumptions of superiority were a joke.

During the Black Power era, laughter provided a much-needed leisure-time respite from the tensions of the day. But it also served as a forum for the airing of social grievances and as a popular culture platform upon which to introduce a new self-image for Afro-America. Black humor was used to reveal and mock white hypocrisies and foibles, thereby robbing the prevailing caste system of its legitimacy. It also was useful in passing along the message of empowerment. Hearty laughter from a black audience solidified the bond between comics and their audience, transforming personal into collective expression. In effect, the views of one were tested, approved, and amplified in the giggles and guffaws of many.

Social satirists such as Dick Gregory, Flip Wilson, Moms Mabley, and Godfrey Cambridge were remarkably adept at deflating white authority. No audience, for example, could continue to view world history as a triumphant Eurocentric pageant after listening to Wilson's parody of the excitable Queen Isabella ("Chris goin' to find Ray Charles! Chris gonna *find* Ray Charles!") or after hearing his uppity Prissy character tell Scarlett O'Hara: "Look, honey, we may have come over in different ships. But we's all in the same boat now!" Even simple one-liners such as: "Have you heard, Spiro Agnew recently set a new ground speed record—running through Harlem" or "The answer to the racial problem is simple—it's give and take. If they don't give it, we're going to take it" presented a significant challenge to white egos.[114]

Cartoonists also joined the fray, sharing their vision of a world in which people of color controlled their own destiny and whites spent most of their time mimicking the quakes and shudders of Stepin Fetchit and Willie Best. In a *Black World* cartoon, a huge African pointed an intimidating finger at the chest of a much smaller, bug-eyed white man. The caption read: "You're Tarzan, king of *what* jungle?" In *Ebony*, a sheepish-looking white motorist gingerly raised an arm in the Black Power salute as he was approached by a black patrol officer, ticket book in hand. In *Negro Digest*, an Afro-American woman with a large natural made small talk at a cocktail party. "I'm liberal," she noted, "I think some whites are as good as blacks." Despite the passing of the years, black tricksters had lost none of their ability to induce laughter by inverting customary social relationships.[115]

Black humorists instituted role reversal at all levels, among all classes and age groups. A truly wise person, they seemed to say, treated every Afro-American as powerful. Some, like Richard Pryor's "Clark Washington"—

mild-mannered custodian for the *Daily Planet*—revealed their true nature only when absolutely necessary. Then, in the wink of an eye, they were transformed into "Super Nigger." In Pryor's conceptualization, such an individual was "faster than a bowl of chitlins" and capable of leaping tall buildings full of white folks at a single bound.[116] Others chose to display their power—and their soulfulness—openly. A 1974 *Ebony* cartoon, for example, pictured a group of whites uncomfortably pinned against the walls of an elevator by the huge natural which graced the head of a black passenger. Wearing platform shoes, bell bottoms, and an ultraconfident expression, he was the embodiment of Afro-"cool" in the midst of white folks' discomfort.[117]

Still others possessed neither clever disguise nor resplendent attire. They simply called upon the ever-present power of blackness to aid in turning the tables on whitey. In the comics, even a small child could make a cogent statement about Afro-America's collective mental health by spray-painting a snowman black or by frightening unsuspecting whites with blood-curdling shouts of "Black Power." By becoming aware of their own self-worth and then standing up for themselves and their people, such characters were capable of forcing a change in white behavior with relatively little additional effort. "My son joined the Black Panthers," said an elderly man in one story. "I can't say I go along with everything they do, but at least they are making the whites act more courteously to our people. Only the other morning, I was in an elevator and a banker turned to the black operator and said, 'I'd like to get to the fifth floor—if it isn't out of your way.'" Apparently, all that was needed to begin the process of revamping traditional power relationships was for soul people to recognize the power they already possessed—and to display it proudly. Maybe force and violence wouldn't be necessary. On the other hand, did you hear the one about the correspondence school principal who became so nervous reading reports of campus riots and disorders that he was afraid to open his mail?[118]

Artist Murry DePillars' pen, ink, and pencil composition, *The People of the Sun*, would have caused this troubled individual to become apoplectic. Here, an extremely angry Uncle Remus is shown bursting forth from a book of folk tales as Brer Rabbit raises his fist in a Black Power salute. Beneath them lay the detritus of a decomposing American society. Although more subtle, Betye Saar's *The Liberation of Aunt Jemima* was equally capable of stirring emotions beyond accustomed limits. Her mixed-media work transformed the well-known symbol of nurturing and domestic service into a still-grinning, but now rifle-toting black liberation warrior. Zip-a-dee-do . . . Say what? While neither can be considered the ultimate representation of the black aesthetic, these vivid examples of Black Power era art revealed their creators' determination to link the folk heritage with contemporary activism.[119]

Speaking the language of the palette and easel, black visual artists recalled tales of Afro-America's confrontation with oppression. Although there was no single "soul style," much of this creative expression had a hard edge. It allowed a brief but telling glimpse into the soulful culture's "dark side," revealing the pain occasioned by what Faith Ringgold termed "the unmovable reality" of living black in white America for more than three and a half centuries.[120] Utilizing the African-American pantheon of folk and culture heroes as subject matter, black artists sought to redefine and redirect history by reeducating the people about their past. To capture and preserve this story on canvas was to affirm faith in blackness and to serve as a helpmeet in the cause of group mental decolonization. Eventually, the pain would have a positive value. For the viewer, soulful black art provided both a social studies lesson and inspiration for living. As artist Tom Lloyd noted, "When they see me and they see my work, I know what they say. They say, 'Dig it, a Black cat did that.' And that means something to them, I know it does."[121]

Like their cartoonist cousins, Afro-American visual artists utilized the technique of role reversal. Role rejection would be a more accurate term. They refused any longer to play the part of cultural cipher, wandering aimlessly throughout history. Many of their most iconoclastic portrayals of the African-American historical pageant were executed on a scale that was itself heroic. Painted on building and playground walls, on fences around construction sites, and in the halls of community centers and schools, these "walls of dignity and respect" appeared in one form or another in major cities from coast to coast. Offering a colorful corrective to white-authored history books, they intertwined images of bold and determined Afro-American heroes with depictions of African kings, black liberation flags, and ranks of marching blacks breaking chains, pointing guns, and raising fists. More inclusive and up-to-date than most textbooks, the murals memorialized cultural figures like John Coltrane, Nina Simone, Gwendolyn Brooks, and W. E. B. DuBois as well as recently anointed "black saints" such as Medgar Evers, Dr. King, and Malcolm X.[122]

Community murals and storefront galleries in black neighborhoods brought the artists' heroic imagery close to the people. Here, far removed from the "closed society" of the white-dominated art world with its "presumptuous, temerarious canons" and its "castrating" standards

Murry N. DePillars, *The People of the Sun: Uncle Remus* (1972). Courtesy of
Murry N. DePillars.

of evaluation, black people could evaluate and honor black talent in their
own way.[123] They could determine for themselves, in both aesthetic and
ethical terms, what constituted black art. As noted by Jeff Donaldson of
the Chicago-based African Commune of Bad Relevant Artists (AFRI-
COBRA), "Art for people and not for critics whose peopleness is ques-

William Walker, "Peace and Salvation: Wall of Understanding," Chicago. From Alan W. Barnett, *Community Murals* (1984). By permission of Associated University Presses.

tionable" was the essential guideline.[124] When provided with artistic images "THAT THEY CAN FEEL, THAT THEY CAN SENSE, THAT THEY CAN KNOW"—images generated by an experiential knowledge of the relevant folk culture—even the least likely homeboy could develop an understanding and appreciation of black art. After honing their aesthetic sensibilities a bit, they might even be able to "tell just by looking which works were really by black [as opposed to white or "Negro"] artists." Although lacking formal training, such individuals were deemed legitimate critics and valued guardians of the black aesthetic tradition.[125]

More often than black humor, the art of the Black Power years focused on the grim process as well as the soul-satisfying results of "turning the tables" on white society. And it was the *process* of social change that most fully required the motivation and intimate involvement of the people. Exhibits presented at the Studio Museum in Harlem, San Francisco's BlackMan's Art Gallery, or Art & Soul community workshop and gallery on Chicago's west side were populated with canvas-backed tales of feverish revolutionary activity. Works such as Frederick Campbell's *Burn, Baby, Burn*, William Curtis's *Riot: USA*, and *Molotov Cocktail* by Vincent Smith told of black estrangement from white American society in stark images of attack dogs, burning cities, and interracial confrontation.[126]

Others employed depictions of readily recognizable contemporary figures to impart the militant message. Dana C. Chandler Jr.'s *LeRoi Jones—House Arrest* and *Fred Hampton's Door*, for example, reminded viewers that real-life revolutionary acts could be hazardous or deadly. Paintings and drawings of this type, such as Black Panther Minister of Culture Emory Douglas's *Free Huey Newton* and *The*

Eugene Eda, "Wall of Meditation," Chicago. From Alan W. Barnett, *Community Murals* (1984). By permission of Associated University Presses.

Lumpen sometimes were reproduced in poster form to aid in fund-raising or recruitment efforts.[127]

Still others carried their message in slogans incorporated within the work: "Our Nation Calls Now"; "Black Men—Preserve Your Race. Leave White Bitches Alone"; "Resist Law and Order in a Sick Society." In this manner, all possible misunderstanding and misinterpretation was avoided.[128]

Whatever their chosen medium or technique, these artist-activists knew that black liberation was a goal not yet realized. Believing that "a really great revolution will have a great picture," they hoped that their didactic depictions of folk and culture heroes engaged in daring deeds would inspire revolutionary ideals.[129] While black art by itself might not create a new world, it could provoke thought. Its message prepared the people for the full realization of black empowerment by liberating them from Euro-centric notions of the (im)possibility of Afro-American heroism. If a picture was worth a thousand words, Black Power-era artists authored a lengthy treatise on how cultural expression could be utilized to symbolize and project, celebrate, direct, and interpret the historical strivings of black Americans for wider recognition of their true heroic nature.

Twenty-one black artists, "Wall of Respect," Chicago. From Alan W. Barnett, *Community Murals* (1984). By permission of Associated University Presses.

Dana Chandler with *Leroi Jones—House Arrest* (1969). From *Dana Chandler Retrospective, 1967–1987*. Courtesy of Dana Chandler.

Soul Theology

The ultimate cultural joke which Black Power generation tricksters played on white folk and their misguided notions of superiority involved heroic tales which contained elements of role reversal and postulated a radical revision of received history. All was presented on an epic scale. In the language of the Scriptures, the last had been determined to be first. God, Jesus, the Virgin Mary, and a host of supporting characters were said to be black and beautiful, not white and just alright. Black activists discovered that they had soul brothers in the spiritual world who could be called upon to assist them in the quest for temporal empowerment.

In truth, this was no revelation. Afro-American artists such as William H. Johnson, whose 1935 work *Jesus and the Three Marys* depicted a black Christ on the cross, had been creating images of a black Messiah for years.[130] Motivated by the same spirit which moved literary lights such as W.E.B. DuBois and Countee Cullen to long for a Savior who would not have to be conceptualized as "a pale, bloodless, heartless thing," black painters made their racial loyalties clear by dipping brushes into dark pigment when portraying key biblical figures.[131] In doing so, they paid homage to those African forebears whose art also was created for religious purposes.

This practice continued during the Black power years as Afro-American artists shared their melding of theological and ideological beliefs with the community. In the stately romanesque dome of Detroit's St. Cecilia Roman Catholic Church, Devon Cunningham's twenty-four-foot-tall, purple-robed, black Christ accompanied by a multiracial band of angels, gazed down upon worshippers. Above the altar of the First Baptist Church of Melrose Park, Illinois, Douglas R. Williams created powerful images of a haloed black Christ and his disciple Peter. Martin Luther King, Jr. and Malcolm X were used as models. At St. Dominic's in Chicago, Keithen Carten helped parishioners from nearby housing projects identify with the faith by stressing its universality; the figure who took Jesus' body from the cross in one mural panel appeared in the next as the resurrected Christ. Outdoors on Brooklyn's Fulton Street, passersby could view Floyd Sapp's vision of a divine black Guide and Protector following an African-American family down a woodland path. Other artists placed the black Messiah in urban ghetto settings or used his image as a "philosophical symbol of any of the modern prophets." Some sought to reach an even larger audience—and in the process abjure earlier vows of poverty—by marketing their works on holiday cards or through mail order ads placed in *Essence, Sepia,* and *Jet.* Collectively these artists let it be known that they no longer would spend six days of the week saying "I'm black and proud" and then on the seventh blindly worship a white Christ.[132]

The concept of a black Messiah was popularized during the late sixties and early seventies by Rev. Albert Cleage, whose Shrine of the Black Madonna in Detroit was graced with a thirty-foot high mural of a plump, sad-faced Mary with babe in arm. Once dominated by a large window depicting Pilgrim elder William Brewster, the chancel of the former Congregational church served as the thematic focal point of Cleage's Black Christian Nationalist movement. From this religious hub, Cleage hoped to convince his people to "come in out of the wilderness" and unify, forming "one black community, one Black Nation."[133]

To this end, he developed a Black Power theology. According to this nationalist creed, human history began millions of years ago when God created the first man in his own image in the heart of Africa. Eventually, the Creator—who was "a combination of black, yellow and red with just a little touch of white," but who would have been considered black by American standards—presented his own Son to the world. God's chosen ones were the black Israelites, a people whose complexion had become darker and darker during their lengthy sojourn in Africa. Jesus came to them not as a whitened "spiritualized" lamb, but as a black revolutionary Zealot whose mission was to rebuild Israel, liberating its people from the exploitation and brutality of white gentile Rome. Forwarding a message of unification as he went from village to village preaching, teaching, and performing miracles, Christ sought to build a movement, not a church. His blood was shed because he posed a serious threat to the white power structure of his day.[134]

How did Jews become "white"? And how did Christianity come to have such an "otherworldly" focus? According to Cleage, the former can be attributed to conversion, the latter to perversion. Modern-day "Jews" were converted to the faith 1,000 years after Jesus. They could claim neither Abraham nor Moses as kin. The Old Testament was the history of *black* Jews—a people who were "guided and loved by God." Paul, "the evangelist of individualism," corrupted Jesus' nationalistic teachings in an attempt to conform to the pagan philosophies of the gentiles. He transformed a revolutionary message addressed to a black nation by a black Messiah into a doctrine of universal brotherhood which would appeal to those seeking an individual escape from sin and death.[135]

The contemporary relevance of this complex story was clear to Cleage's followers: Rediscovery of the black Messiah was intimately related to black Americans' rediscovery of themselves. Once freed of the

Albert B. Cleage, Jr. Courtesy of Benyas-Kaufman Photographers.

self-hatred fostered by worshipping a white God, they could reclaim their religious heritage by struggling to rebuild the disunited Black Nation just as Jesus had 2,000 years ago. With philosophy and direction provided by the reconstructed black church, the people would become "welded together" in revolutionary unity. One day, they again would be able to exercise the "Black God-given Power" one expected a chosen people to possess.[136]

Shrine of the Black Madonna. Courtesy of Benyas-Kaufman Photographers.

Cleage's claim that "almost everything you have heard about Christianity is essentially a lie" generated controversy both within and outside the community of black Christians.[137] As the debate raged, activist ministers and religious commentators added their own emendations to the Black Christian Nationalists' account of biblical events. In doing so, they proved that like Black Power itself, a race-specific theology of liberation was not easily molded into a singular form.

Communicants could pick and choose from this lengthy list of alternative theological conceptualizations, assembling those deemed most relevant into a personalized testament of empowerment. For example, it was not necessary to debate the existence of a historical, physically black Messiah with the same fervor that earlier religionists had debated the relationship of angels to heads of pins. Whether taken literally or utilized as a symbol, it was the *concept* of a black God that was of profound importance to contemporary blacks. Like the indigenous Christian voice in the Third World, it decolonized theology, particularizing religious experience and making it meaningful. As Christ was perceived as a "black presence" in their midst, all would see that God never leaves the side of the despised and downtrodden. He was with the poorest of the poor both in Pharoah's Egypt and in Richard Nixon's America.[138]

If the historical God of the oppressed was concerned with achieving social justice and if Afro-Amricans had been selected as God's target group in the United States, then it was legitimate to conceptualize black theology as a present-minded doctrine of empowerment. Proponents of an activist theology held that Christianity always had been the story of God's liberating activities on behalf of those who were enslaved by "principalities and powers." Jesus' ministry had been in the streets, among those reviled and rejected by the establishment. He offered them comfort, leaving them with the revolutionary promise that the last would be first—a promise that was meant to be redeemed within the earthly lifespan of the believer. The mission of the black church was to copy his example, forwarding the message that people of color were due the dignity of sons of God in the here-and-now as well as in the great by-and-by. Recognizing that the concept of power was not foreign to Yahweh, black clergy were to articulate a theological self-determination that would provide the black revolution with ethical and religious dimension. In this context, black liberation was both a secular task and a sacred duty—a union of cultural and political initiatives that could be viewed as an essential part of God's plan for creation.[139]

Thus, Black Power was not heretical. Neither were the Black Power activists' methods and practices those of the Antichrist. Their goals had been approved by a God of love *and* power—one who proclaimed deliverance to the captives and then supplied them with resources sufficient to accomplish the task. But did this include violence? For many, the answer was a definite "yes"—if the violence was directed at a persistent evildoer. Although love was a central element of the Christian faith, the extent to which it would be shared with oppressor groups was up to each individual. Responses varied depending upon the vividness of one's conceptualization of God as a divinity of wrath.[140]

Some saw violence as the only effective counterpoint to conscienceless power. To appeal to the conscience of those who benefitted from an ungodly, unequal concentration of power was deemed senseless and self-defeating. Since their position was maintained through violence, it became a question of whose violence would be supported. Only through a show of force, a legitimate instrument of freedom, could oppressors be made to share their power and to end their crimes against the humanity of others. Since all forces and laws contradicting human dignity violated the Creator's purpose for humankind, the ending of such coercion rightly could be seen as a manifestation of God's active involvement in the protection of His people's most sacred rights. Liberated from the power of the conscienceless, they again could concentrate on establishing community. They were free to cultivate self-love. Both activities would serve to negate the spirit of violence. Eventually, some type of fellowship might be established with a former bondmaster, but never at the expense of justice or through the ceding of power.[141]

White Christians seemed unaware of this divine plan. Perhaps this was due to the fact that they spent an inordinate amount of time trying to usurp the place of the darker-skinned chosen ones at God's right hand. Black Power theologians developed a stinging critique of this obtuse, yet presumptuous mind-set, using their own theology as a reference point.

What, exactly, was wrong with white folks' profession of religion? It was said to have emanated from an alien culture sphere. Ever since Cotton Mather and Jonathan Edwards, American theologians had interpreted the Bible according to the economic and political interests of white society. Identifying closely with the dominant power structure, white religionists—like the culture from which they took their intellectual cues—were theologically corrupt. Most were more concerned with assuaging the guilt of fellow oppressors than with offering the thirsty a cup of cold water. Moreover, they knew little about cultural pluralism. Whenever whites "shared" their faith with other groups, what they actually were doing was attempting to impose their assumptions of racial superiority. In the process, new converts risked being robbed of their own cultural distinctives. Grounded in the inegalitarian beliefs of an idolatrous, slave-mongering people, white religion was most unsoulful and almost totally culture-bound. In language, interpretation, and application, it was a gross distortion of the original gospel. It had far less than "universal" application, standing condemned by its very whiteness.[142]

Unfortunately, said the Black Power theologians, throughout history most Afro-Americans had bought into the white vision of Christ as a flaxen-haired, middle-class supporter of the status quo. The gift of free will was a terrible thing to waste and these people had misused it by allowing themselves to be taken in by the whites' otherworldly theology of pacification. As a result, the contemporary black church was dominated by an individualistic, integrationist mentality that sapped the black community's will to join in united social action. Those who through custom or religious blindness had accepted the preachments of this church were spiritually sick.[143] As agents of white Christianity, they needed to reject the teachings of their nonintellectual, authoritarian ministers and join in confessing their sins, saying:

> "I have been an Uncle Tom and I repent. I have
> served the interests of my white oppressors, have
> identified with them, and have wanted to be
> accepted by them. Because of self-hate I did not
> recognize my enemy. I have failed to realize that
> nothing is more sacred in God's sight than black
> liberation. I now pledge total commitment to that
> cause, recognizing that there is no other way to be
> saved."[144]

By refusing to allow whites to define their existence, black Christians now could claim the biblical promise of freedom. Recognizing their blackness as a "special creation" of God, they no longer would be ashamed to accept themselves as they were. They would be reborn into blackness.[145]

Invigorated by its newly race-conscious membership, the black church would become what God intended it to be—a soulful community-based organization with the potential for generating collective power. Revitalized and rooted in an Afro-centric theology of liberation, the church would serve as spiritual helpmeet, custodian of the African-American cultural heritage, and chief promoter of the empowering doctrine which holds that even Harlem, Watts, or Newark could become the New Jerusalem.

The movement to define and to win acceptance for a black theology spurred a flurry of activity among white church leaders who sought to reform their institutional professions of Christianity. Believing that increased sensitivity to race was needed to stem a projected black exodus from the faith, they entered into numerous dialogues with their Afro-American counterparts, instituted pulpit exchanges with black congregations, and authorized the use of *Soul Food*, a special annotated edition of the *Living Bible* designed for black readers.[146] But whites could soul search all they wanted. Black theologians had more on their minds than white spiritual renewal. They had a political agenda to develop.

Like black artists' conceptualizations of a black Messiah, this union of religious and secular reform had ample historical precedent. Even during the antebellum era, black condemnatory prophets appeared who were determined to call down the wrath of God and man on a sin-soaked white society. Linking earthly and heavenly forces in support of freedom, activist ministers such as Henry Highland Garnet, militant laymen such as David Walker, and slave preachers like Nat Turner hoped to speed the arrival of a new age in which black agents of messianic destiny would accomplish the providential goals of history.[147]

This vision was carried into a new century by a diverse group of neo-black Messiahs who claimed for themselves the ability to lead the African-American "chosen" into the resplendent realms of spiritual purity and earthly power. Like African Methodist Episcopal (AME) Bishop Henry McNeal Turner, a former Reconstruction-era legislator from Georgia and the first Afro-American clergyman of note to define God as black, they would address controversial "political" issues such as African emigration, disfranchisement, and lynching because "the good Jehovah, in his allwise providence, had made a distinction in color, but not in political or social status of the human race."[148]

During the 1920s, for example, followers of Noble Drew Ali's Moorish Science Temple of America were taught that "before you can have a God, you must have a nationality." They were so taken with this notion that they refused to be called "Negro," claiming that its negative connotations robbed them of power. Instead, they adopted the supposed ethnicity of Jesus ("Asiatic" or "Moorish"). Distinguished by their fezzes or turbans, beards, and "nationality and identification" cards bearing a star and crescent logo, believers sang the praises of their Prophet and talked of signs in the heavens foreshadowing the destruction of white civilization.[149]

Members of another black sect, Universal Hagar's Spiritual Church, favored the designations "Black" and "Ethiopian." Led by Father George

W. Hurley, "the God of the Aquarian Age," Hurleyites began celebrating an alternative Christmas in 1934, had their own version of the Ten Commandments ("Thou shall not pray for God to bless your enemies;" "Thou shall ask God to give you power to overcome them," etc.), and believed that the "black man at one time reigned supreme and he is bound to reign again." If legitimate demands for justice were not met, said Hurley, there would be "destruction on the earth and all over the world."[150]

In similar fashion, Father Divine's depression-era Peace Mission denounced not only those who questioned its leader's omniscience and power, but anyone deemed a "segregator" or "discriminator." A favorite song, "The Mills of God Are Grinding On" recounted the Afro-American struggle for racial justice and warned white sinners of the certain punishment awaiting them:

> Let them come in "dust and ashes",
> Let them moan and seek GOD's Face;
> Let them feel the bitter lashes,
> And of their own evil, get just a taste.
> Let their blood help pay the price
> Of centuries of sorrow and blinding pain
> They dealt to others in their arrogance;
> Let them feel GOD's cold disdain.[151]

Peace Mission members did not await this day of judgment on bended knee. Shunning spiritual escapism, they established churches in hitherto exclusively white neighborhoods, pressured white-owned business to hire and promote blacks, and demonstrated on behalf of individual victims of southern justice, such as Angelo Herndon and the "Scottsboro boys." On one occasion, Divine's followers gathered 250,000 signatures on a petition urging the enactment of federal antilynching legislation. By actively campaigning for desegregation of all aspects of American society, the Peace Mission made clear its belief that the struggle for earthly justice was a high religious calling.[152]

Even Marcus Garvey, better known for his pan-African nationalism than for his connection with the black church, had considerable interest in the "whole person." Religion, for Garvey, was eminently political. For many followers, Garveyism *was* a religion. Indeed, his Universal Negro Improvement Association (UNIA) meetings possessed many of the characteristics of a church service. Garveyites worshipped a "Black Man of Sorrows" and had their own *Universal Negro Catechism* and *Universal Negro Ritual.* Apotheosized as "the reincarnated Angel of Peace come from Heaven to dispense Political Salvation" to an oppressed people, Garvey employed biblical imagery (i.e. "No one knows when the hour of Africa's Redemption cometh") to further his program of self-reliance and race pride.[153] As was noted in the UNIA catechism, black political nationalism was seen as the fulfillment of prophecy:

Q. What prediction made in the 68th Psalm and
   the 31st verse is now being fulfilled?
A. "Princes shall come out of Egypt, Ethiopia
   shall soon stretch out her hands unto God."
Q. What does this verse prove?
A. That Black Men will set up their own
   government in Africa, with rulers of their own
   race.[154]

If, during his lifetime, this objective was not met, Garvey pledged to rise from the dead to help create an autonomous black world. Even in death he would be "a terror to the foes of Negro liberty."[155]

Elijah Muhammad, Malcolm X, and the Nation of Islam kept this vision current by sharing their own messianic beliefs with a new generation after World War II. To the devout, Muhammad was the "last Messenger" of a black creator God. Divine by nature, black people were "the first and last, maker and owner of the universe." Unfortunately, four hundred years of "masterful brainwashing by the slave master" had convinced many that they should view blackness as a curse, Jesus as pale-skinned, and God as a colorless spirit. Nevertheless, the perverse sweetness of this master stratagem for keeping "so-called Negroes" subservient was about to lose its savor. The time of judgment for "blue-eyed devils" was fast approaching. Sometime before the year 2000, Allah would reappear, signaling the beginning of a new and glorious epoch in which black people would inherit power over all of creation. Prior to that great day, the Nation would help sustain the chosen people by actively promoting economic nationalism and by continuing to harass the federal government until, through territorial cession, it provided Afro-Americans with "back pay" for "four hundred years of slave labor."[156]

Ironically, poignantly, the Black Muslim's most effective spokesperson for this cosmic mix of religious, economic, and territorial nationalism entered the realm of the prophets on the very eve of the Black Power revolt. In death, Malcolm X was beatified—elevated to the status of a martyred but soon-to-be-triumphant redeemer. Speaking in terms that would have been understood by Garvey, Hurley, or Father Divine, memorialists called their fallen leader the "Fire Prophet." And they were more than willing to be guided by his light. Adopting his encapsulation of the Afro-American messianic tradition as their own, his followers talked of "the beauty of blackness, of black unity" and pressed their demands for temporal empowerment even as they awaited "the second coming of MALCOLM."[157]

Often criticized for their theological "aberrations," "militant" political agendas, and worldly "excesses," prophets such as these were excluded from the American religious mainstream. But, by continually raising the cry for Black Power, they provided an important service to more orthodox believers. Their activism kept the notion current that the black church was the proper judge of white America's collective sins and the legitimate arbiter of its own members' racial destiny. When "nation-building time" arrived, it was recognized that no "plantation" theology would suffice. Only a revolutionized faith could provide Afro-Americans with the spiritual insight needed to see them through to the promised land.[158]

High on the traditional black Church's list of priorities during these years was the development of an effective political voice. If this could be accomplished, the faith would remain relevant to a people seeking rapid socioeconomic change. All manner of Afro-American Christians, professing a variety of opinions on the legitimacy of a race-specific theology, participated in this effort. In an attempt to spur church renewal, black caucuses were established in the Protestant Episcopal Church, American Lutheran Church, United Church of Christ, and other predominantly white denominations. In 1967, a black caucus within the National Council of Churches' Division of Christian Life and Mission called upon Afro-American congregations to establish freedom schools, train lay leaders in community organization, and offer financial support to "self-determination" groups. A year later, black Baptists demanded that the American Baptist Convention devote 10 percent of its investment portfolio to the capitalization of black-owned businesses. Meeting in Cincinnati in 1968, some 250 black United Methodist ministers adopted a "Black Paper" in which they confessed to having accepted a "false kind of integration" and condemned the use of "white power" to keep blacks in a subordinate position both within and outside the church.[159] At New York City's Riverside Church in 1969, SNCC leader James Forman interrupted Sunday morning services to read a 2,500 word "Black Manifesto" which claimed that the nation's "racist churches and synagogues" owed black Americans $500 million in hardship reparations. This, he said, amounted to a mere "fifteen dollars per nigger." He later upped the ante to $3 billion.[160] Elsewhere, groups such as the Interreligious Foundation for Community Organization and the National Committee of Black Churchmen issued equally strong statements calling for church support of southern African freedom-fighters and an end to the deployment of black soldiers as "Executioners" of their "black, brown and yellow Brothers."[161]

Collectively, these impassioned voices challenged all members of the religious community to be "reborn into involvement in the liberation of black people." Like the theology student who attempted to intimidate his professor with the pointed query, "Before I sign up for this course, what does Kierkegaard have to do with the Black movement?", black activists sought to make white Christians aware of their historic failure to grant people of color full and equal status as children of God.[162]

With the same sense of urgency and conviction, they scored black congregations for their inability to become effective, culture-based instruments of empowerment in their local communities. They said that if the black Church was to regain its soul, black religion had to be redefined and reformed. It was to be an activist faith solidly rooted in the folk tradition, but given contemporary relevance by its ability to address both the spiritual and the political dimensions of the African-American condition. In their determined efforts to make black religious expression both distinctive and truly liberating, these activists made one point especially clear: just as the concept of the soul was central to Christian theology, the soulful folk culture of black America was seen as central to the success of the Black Power movement.

The soul styles, music, talk, tales, and theology of the Black Power era reveal a great deal about the determination of Afro-Americans to preserve cultural distinctives, to define the world in their own terms, and to promote group psychological wellness. By recounting their heroic, comedic, and messianic representatives' victories in power struggles between competing culture spheres, they succeeded in creating a visionary Afrocentric society where heroic deeds had become everyday acts. It was a world turned upside down, perhaps the world of the future. God was black and the devil white. "Lazy lips" made the sweetest sounds. "Bad" was good and "Bad Niggers" like the liberated Uncle Remus grinned madly as they torched the plantation. Seemingly, the prophecy of the Black Muslim song had come to pass—in reverse. In Afro-American folk culture, the black man's heaven became the white man's hell.

Black Power and American Culture: Literary and Performing Arts

You don't know nothin' about my life. But I know all about yours.

Amiri Baraka's Rochester
to Jack Benny in *Jello*, 1970.

The cultural forms which African-Americans defined as "uniquely, beautifully and personally ours" conveyed images of black humanity that were well suited to the nurturing of individual and group pride.[1] This could not be said for most white cultural expression. Racial caricatures and stereotypes which originated long before the Civil War continued to perplex and anger blacks throughout the 1960s and 1970s.[2] Striking at the very roots of the self-definition ethic, variants of these demeaning images were nowhere more numerous and visible than in the literary and performing arts. Just as black tricksters and badmen could be found throughout the modern black folk culture, images of blacks as comic minstrels, obsequious servants, and uncouth "primitives" continued to be forwarded in theatrical films, television sitcoms, stage shows, and popular novels. The Afro-American response to these mainstream conceptualizations confirmed the existence of separate black and white cultural worlds. In this context, black-authored literature and drama served as an oppositional and defensive mechanism through which creative artists could confirm their identity while articulating their own unique impressions of social reality.

Could the appearance of Sambo's wide-grinning countenance still spark gales of belly-bursting laughter? Was it possible that Uncles Tom and Remus were content to truckle to Miss Ann for another generation? Did tragic mulattos, superstitious, melon-eating plowhands, and natural-born cooks and musicians continue to provide local color for white authors of the Black Power era? Were Zip Coon, Jim Crow, and Dinah from Carolina waiting in the green room for yet another curtain call? Not exactly. Contemporary white folks weren't quite as crude and insensitive as their forebears. But sometimes the differences between the old and new characterizations were slight.

Despite the wider acceptance of black-authored works by major publishers and an increase in the number of appearances on stage and screen, the imprint of earlier practices was difficult to erase. For example, a study of prime-time television shows conducted over a two-week period in 1962 revealed that no blacks appeared in 309 of 398 half-hour units of programming. Of the remaining units that did contain blacks as cast members, about one-third featured Afro-Americans as singers, dancers, or musicians.[3] By 1968, however, media analysts noted that "black actors are popping up all over the place." As Cal Wilson, a graduate of Watts Writers Workshop, gleefully told one reporter, "Black people are hot! You could almost go roller skating in the street and they'd put you on television!" Due in part to the increased awareness of black society brought about by urban racial unrest, the 1968–69 TV season boasted 21 prime-time series with at least one regular Afro-American cast member.[4] Especially noteworthy were Greg Morris' portrayal of electronics expert Barney Collier on *Mission: Impossible*, Clarence Williams III as undercover cop Linc Hayes on *The Mod Squad*, and former singer Nichelle Nichols as Uhura ("freedom" in Swahili), communications officer aboard the starship *Enterprise* on *Star Trek*. Still, a 1973 survey showed that blacks appeared on television less frequently than their distribution in the population (6.3% vs. 11%) while whites remained overrepresented (75% vs. 70%). Even Britishers were more visible (6.6%).[5]

Moreover, as the appearance of blacks on TV became more commonplace, the manner in which they were portrayed came under ever closer scrutiny. Critics claimed that outside of a few well-publicized exceptions, the networks persisted in consigning most black actors and actresses to minor, bit part roles. Seemingly reluctant to develop this wealth of black talent, producers seemed content to employ their services as mute, shadowy background figures devoid of emotion or personality. To psychologist Kenneth Clark, this tendency indicated "a deep wish that the Negro did not exist in society." It perpetuated the notion that black Americans were "non-beings," incapable of relating their feelings or life experiences to others. Such, indeed, seemed to be the case when Kurt Vonnegut's black protagonist Bokonon was made white for the television version of *Between Time and Timbuktu* or when Tracy Keenan Wynn's screenplay of the Ernest J. Gaines novel, *The Autobiography of Miss Jane Pittman* introduced a white narrator/reporter to tell Pittman's story.[6]

It was said that certain carefully-selected blacks were given starring roles in dramatic or comedy series only to "keep the other niggers quiet." Such shows were perceived as little more than "a front behind which to purvey age-old stereotypes."[7] For example, on *Sanford and Son*, Los Angeles junk dealer Fred Sanford waged interminable Kingfish/Sapphire-like battles with his departed wife's sister, the formidable Aunt Esther, constantly demeaned son Lamont by calling him a "dummy", and spent his considerable leisure time boasting and bickering with pals Bubba, Melvin, and Grady—all unreflecting fellow victims of white economic power.

More often validating than dispelling racial stereotypes, the *Flip Wilson Show*'s one man repertory company brought old-style, in-group ethnic humor to a large, heterogeneous audience through its star's vivid characterizations of, among others, Reverend Leroy, a dishonest, lecherous preacher, Sonny, the janitor, and a sassy, impulsive vamp named Geraldine Jones. It was the immensely popular Jones character who made "the devil made me do it" the nation's preferred cop-out for months.

In like manner, *Good Times* employed Jimmie Walker's trademark "Dyn-O-Mite!" expression to tickle the public funnybone, thereby sugarcoating the harsh reality of southside Chicago tenement life. His far more socially aware and militant sibling, the 12-year-old Michael, was too young and cute to spoil the fun or be perceived as a threat by white viewers. As media critic Tony Brown said of Walker's coon-like minstrel portrayal, "If you can't tell the difference between the old Stepin' Fetchit character or the Amos 'n' Andy genre and J.J. on *Good Times*, it's because there is none."[8] The same could have been said for the depictions of blacks on other popular sit-coms. Too often this TV genre portrayed Afro-Americans as loud, ill-bred simpletons who found great pleasure in insulting one another and being "colorful" for the entertainment of a white majority audience.[9]

Police and detective shows of the Black Power era also received unfavorable reviews. Here, the major complaint was that the electronic medium was being utilized as an instrument of social control. Like a video version of the old "good cop/bad cop" ploy, dynamic, attractive actors and actresses such as Robert Hooks of *N.Y.P.D.* and *Get Christie Love!*'s Teresa Graves were shown as determined protectors of white society. A 1975 study concluded that Afro-Americans were being cast as police officers more often than any other occupation on television.[10] These were the new preferred role models for potentially disruptive black youth—the media's counterproposal to images of militant black activists appearing on the nightly news.

This message seemed to be everywhere. On *Dragnet*, an African-American officer delivered it clearly—and with a straight face. He told a class of would-be recruits why he had chosen to be a cop:

> I wanted to do something for my country . . . I
> wanted to do something for my own people . . .
> And I'll tell you something else, some of our
> people talk about white man's law. There's no
> such thing, not when Black men like you and me
> wear this uniform—it's everybody's law.[11]

In other series, the presentation was more subtle. For example, Diahann Carroll's pert and proper *Julia* had far more in common with Doris Day than with Angela Davis. She was employed as a nurse by the Defense Department. Her husband had been killed in Vietnam. Her best friend's husband was a policeman. At the other end of the sweetness-and-light spectrum, Jemal David (Otis Young), the sullen ex-slave bounty hunter of *The Outcasts*, was shown to be both self-sufficient and combative. He was a "bad dude" who distrusted whites and was bitter about his slavery experiences. Nevertheless, to the ever-observant Stokely Carmichael, he was "still a cop"—a character whose main purpose in the series was to promote the image of "a black man who fights for law and order—*their* law, and *their* order."[12] No matter what the time frame or setting, Black Power activists were keen to recognize those who willingly served as overseers for the establishment.

Ultimately, dissatisfaction with the black image on TV transcended concern over specific genres. Critics claimed that accurate depictions of black social and cultural life were rare throughout the entertainment spectrum. Reality, it seems, simply wasn't very entertaining. As *Julia*'s creators asserted in defending the series, "Who wants to see poverty and despair week after week?" Just because Ms. Carroll happened to be black didn't mean that she had to concern herself with the "problems of all black people." The show simply wasn't "politically oriented." This narrow, but pervasive perspective diverted attention from pressing contemporary social issues even as it denied the existence of black "community." What emerged was "the usual slick, well-packaged slop" in sepia-tone.[13]

Too often the perspectives, values, and goals of black television characters seemed virtually indistinguishable from those of white co-stars. Their color—and cultural roots—were incidental to the action. To no one's surprise, most delivered no "heavy rap" on race, provided no contextualization for black life experiences, and, in effect, denied the existence of a black-white cultural gap. Untroubled by their estrangement from the real world, they seemed content to mouth soulless white dialect and bond primarily with non-black "buddies." To critics, they were the "mod version of the old house nigger."[14] By neglecting to highlight racial distinctives, they not only were lying to themselves, but also misinforming their viewers as to the nature of black society.

Much of the blame for this state of affairs was laid at the conference room door of network executives and the myriad writers, producers, casting directors, and technicians whose behind-the-scenes labors helped to determine whether or not a new series won an audience. During the Black Power years, these key managerial and craft positions were monopolized by whites. At best, the majority had only the most tenuous connection with the real-world black experience. Those who lived and worked in the west coast film colony faced additional problems of geographic and social class insularity. As a result, their view of society was decidedly Eurocentric.[15]

As long as the medium was (mis)-informed by this mind-set, commercial television's scrutiny of the Afro-Americans' world was destined to remain cursory. The one-dimensional characters seen on prime-time TV were unable either to reveal or to celebrate the African-American lifestyle. Beyond an occasional Sammy Davis Jr. variety show appearance, "blackness" was deemed to offer little in terms of cultural or educational enrichment. The lack of respect accorded black folkways suggested that there was no lasting commitment to black representation on TV. If "the times" demanded it, there would be black-oriented comedies and detective shows. If not, goodbye *Shaft* and *That's My Mama*, hello Sammy, Harry (Belafonte), and Pearl (Bailey). As veteran actress Ruby Dee acknowledged in 1968, "We are the most commodity-conscious nation in the world. The Black man is the commodity this year. If Black people sell, they'll be back. If they don't, they won't."[16] It was all commerce.

To creative artists such as Dee, this perspective was as absurd as it was dangerous. Perhaps television executives could be forgiven for attempting to create a make-believe world of escapist entertainment for their viewers, but to encourage black professionals to deny or to falsify their own life experiences for the furtherance of commerce constituted a political act. According to novelist James Baldwin, the manner in which they were being asked to participate in the "national fantasy" guaranteed that it would be "left unchanged and the social structure left untouched." Whites didn't *want* to hear what the black actor knew—and, he added, "the system can't afford it."[17]

Similar concerns were voiced over white control of black portraiture on stage, in theatrical films, and in popular literature. During the Black Power years, movie audiences continued to be treated to big screen appearances of blacks as uncivilized and incompletely human beings. Not even Sidney Poitier's many dignified, sensitive (some would say antiseptic) portrayals could atone for the embarrassment caused by films such as *The Naked Prey, Dark of the Sun,* and *Up the Sandbox.* Here, African people were presented as ferocious jungle creatures, devotees of "primitive" religions, and practitioners of ritual murder. Ooga Booga! It was enough to make a black activist like Stokely Carmichael wish that someone would "beat the hell out of [Tarzan] and send him back to Europe."[18]

Apparently, these traits were difficult to shed because the slave characters in Hollywood plantation films such as Dino DeLaurentis' *Mandingo* and its sequel, *Drum,* were at least as barbaric as their Old World relatives. Advertisements warned potential viewers to "expect the savage, the sensual, the shocking." Seemingly these antebellum blacks enjoyed nothing more than a full day's schedule of miscegenation, flagellation, nymphomania, incest, sadism, and other deviations from the Old South social norm. While their emotion-driven, havoc-wreaking behavior may have provided youthful black moviegoers with a brief, vicarious venting of frustration against white authority figures, more reflective viewers realized that the slaves' crude antics made even the screen's most backward white ignoramus appear to be a world-beater.[19]

Broadway, too, had its problems. Although, incredibly, *Mandingo* did enjoy a brief run as a play, its preoccupation with promiscuity and property damage failed to establish standards of plot and characterization for stage productions purporting to deal with black themes. But what *was* the norm? So few Afro-Americans appeared in Broadway shows that this often was difficult to determine. In spring 1968, for example, only 57 of 523 actors, 14 of 664 production employees, and 2 of 381 stagehands working on Broadway were black.[20]

According to Black Power-era critics, especially those associated with the Black Arts movement, white control of stage reality made the theatre both an alien and an alienating medium for Afro-American creative artists. This was held to be true irrespective of the subject matter or focus of a particular theatrical vehicle. Whether appearing in *Hello Dolly, Hallelujah, Baby!*, or *Golden Boy*, black cast members were subjected to white expectations that once the music began they *all* became Mr. Bojangles. Others were restricted to dramatic recreations of occupational roles their directorial overlords felt black people played in real life. Exploration of the Afro-American condition was discouraged except to provide commentary on its supposed tragic nature. Critics held out little hope that such approaches to black theatre either would "civilize" whites or aid blacks in gaining a better understanding of themselves.[21]

Deeply enmeshed in time-honored conventions, Broadway eschewed radical change. It was said to subvert the creativity of Afro-American artists and bolster the societal status quo. The Off-Broadway and university theatre stages were different, but no better. Their main bill of fare was, in the words of one black playwright, "intellectual and esoteric crap" directed primarily at "alienated middle-class whites." Even at its best, said critics, the contemporary white American stage was irrelevant to most black people. It was a "theater of the Bourgeois, by the Bourgeois, about the Bourgeois, and for the Bourgeois"—a cultural institution whose controlling interests rarely embraced broader frames of reference or more inclusive concerns. Providing only mildly entertaining diversions and social palliatives, its musical and dramatic offerings were filled with "belles-lettres pomposity, . . . hasty-pudding hi-jinks, pseudo-absurdity and closet avant daring." Black people were advised to enter at their own risk. Whatever characterizations of black life they might find there were bound to detract from, rather than enhance, their cultural I.Q.[22]

White-authored literature also fell short of rising black critical standards and expectations. Books produced for young adults were scored for their inauthentic portrayals of Afro-Americans and their culture. Although the number of volumes including one or more black characters in text or illustration doubled during the Black Power era, (6.7% in 1962–64 compared to 14.4% in 1973–75), many ignored all differences except obvious physical ones. In seeking to promote the ideal of an integrated society, childrens' authors created a make-believe world of melting pot homogeneity. In certain cases, readers would have had no way of knowing that the story concerned people of color were it not for accompanying illustrations. The text revealed no distinctive African-American experiences, traditions, or institutions. Often, even the drawings offered little guidance. As one commentator noted, since some books showed only one or two darkish faces in a group or crowd scene, readers were left wondering "whether a delicate shadow indicates a racial difference or a case of sunburn."[23]

Sometimes additional attention to detail caused even more troublesome problems. Dick and Jane may have been making some new black friends, but what *were* they like? Those who were not cultural clones of whites were delineated by racial attributes which stereotyped at least as often as they authenticated. They had odd names: Leroy, Jasper, Fat Ernest, and Rufus.[24] They misused *both* standard English and the Black vernacular. Some were prone to headscratching, shuffling, and eye-rolling. Others had "shiny" faces. If light-complexioned, they were intelligent and attractive to members of the opposite sex. If dark, what a shame![25] Critics deemed such portrayals condescending and ignorant— "cloying little books."[26] Seemingly it was easier for their authors to re-create hackneyed stereotypes and to forward paternalistic platitudes than it was to construct honest portraits of black life.

Afro-American portraiture in adult fiction was greeted with similar scorn. A burdensome legacy of incomplete or distorted black characterizations tempted the critics to throw up their hands, totally giving up on white writers. Asking the modern inheritors of this tradition to pen full-blooded, realistic portraits of black folk seemed to be demanding the impossible. Many, they thought, were neither culturally or emotionally equipped for the task.[27] In lieu of hands-on, in-depth understanding of the black world, white novelists would continue to draw upon familiar images of African-Americans as, among other things, existentially alienated victims who offered little effective challenge to white hegemony. "Somewhere," lamented one commentator, ". . . there is a white-created black character who resembles real live blacks. But I have yet to find him. And given the myopia of most white Americans, a realistic image of blacks in white literature will be a long time coming."[28]

This negative impression of Euro-American literary capacity was so-lidified by the Black Power era controversy over William Styron's *The*

Confessions of Nat Turner. While white reviewers praised this Pulitzer Prize winning best-seller for its accuracy and insight, most black critics saw it as a purposeful misrepresentation of the Afro-American past. The novel was, they claimed, "an anathema," a "witches' brew of Freudian psychology," a "throwback to the racist writing of the 1930's and 1940's." Although drawn from its author's own "sick and bigoted fancies," it revealed the larger white society's attempt to "escape the judgement of history."[29]

Nat Turner offered something less than an ennobling depiction of Afro-Americans struggling against adversity. Styron's slave insurrectionist was a man victimized by the "madness of nigger existence." Part of his life was spent playing "the good nigger a little touched in the head with religion." At other times he fell under the spell of troubling visions which foreshadowed his 1831 revolt. When the moment came to spill white blood, he was "nearly torn apart by frights and apprehensions" and stole away "to retch dry spasms in the bushes." Indeed, slavery was shown to have been so effective in mentally hamstringing Turner that he could be sent into "demented ecstasy" just by imagining himself to be "white as clabber cheese, white, stark white, white as a marble Episcopalian." This, certainly, was not the type of historical role model activists sought to promote during an era of "nation-building." While author Styron dismissed as a "metaphysical fantasy" the notion that the Virginia insurrectionist was a black Paul Bunyan, Afro-American critics weren't so quick to discredit folk wisdom. In their opinion, Nat Turner was still "one of our great heroes." It was the white contemporary writer who seemed more than a little touched in the head.[30]

Were the creators of these pejorative images of blacks affected by the madness of *white* existence in an increasingly alienating, technocratic society? Could their desire to relieve their own frustrations and insecurities explain this continuing fascination with ancient stereotypes? Or was the misshaping of reality inherent in any popular entertainment medium? Were the screenwriters and novelists simply giving the public what it demanded? In the context of the Black Power era, each perspective was valid.

Popular cultural expression is not simply imposed on an audience from above. Neither is the mind of the screenwriter or novelist a *tabula rasa,* subject to complete creative control by external elements. A completed teleplay, film, or short story is the product of a confluence of forces. It is a reflection of the individual creator's beliefs, but it also symbolizes society's values, and to some variable degree, shapes and confirms those values. If their entertainment vehicles are to be well received, producer/artists must join their own vision of reality (and fantasy) with that of their consumer/audience. If profits are to be maximized, the basic task becomes one of responding to the concerns of a segmented, but decidedly white middle-class public.[31]

During the Civil Rights/Black Power years, both white creative artists and their public exhibited a deeply felt desire for reassurance in matters of racial hegemony. They sought continued confirmation of self and of their own world view. To meet these needs, popular entertainment forms were employed as a type of cultural security blanket. Through the repetition of familiar formulae, anxiety over radical societal change could be eased. Traditional black (and ethnic, class, and gender) stereotypes provided psychological comfort, helping the majority population cope with change. Thus, even though surviving stereotypes conveyed the essence of a reality that had passed (and, indeed may never have existed in the first place), they continued to serve current needs. Reflecting the desires, fears, and fantasies of a society that found it difficult to accept Afro-Americans as equals, the popular culture offered escape from the inescapable. It sheltered whites from the truth that black folk were non-stereotypical, highly differentiated individuals who had little in common with either Styron's Nat Turner or Good Times' J. J. Evans.[32]

Refusing to accept white popular cultural opinion of themselves as valid, Afro-Americans addressed the issues raised by the continued dissemination of demeaning black caricatures. As they saw it, entrenched White Power lay at the root of the problem. Throughout the literary and performing arts, whites served as gatekeepers to critical acceptance, manipulators of public opinion, shapers and authenticators of racial imagery. If blacks were portrayed as comic buffoons and hapless losers by Hollywood, it was because white producers, their backers, and their mainstream audience willed it. The image makers acted out of fear—the fear of losing, perhaps forever, the power to define. For this group, being forced to relinquish their hold upon the world of imagination would be only slightly less cataclysmic than witnessing the transfer of total societal hegemony. Indeed, reversals in one area very well could lead to major upheavals in the other. Western civilization seemed at risk. And black people knew it.

Invigorated by this subversive understanding, Afro-American poets, playwrights and novelists set out to discredit old stereotypes, to develop alternative group imagery, and ultimately to gain controlling influence over black portraiture. Some would work to create a theatre of the Spirit and of shared experience. It would express the voice of the black community, not simply the voice white audiences wanted to hear. Others sought to forge a new world of black letters, revealing both the black writers' deep self-love and their determined hatred of the oppressor. Still others attempted to refocus Afro-American theatrical images so that heroes, not flunkies, predominated. Their small screen counterparts would aid the cause by assuring that future generations could laugh *along with* and not just *at* black characters on TV. If black creative artists were successful in any aspect of this crusade for popular cultural empowerment, the larger Black Power movement would be strengthened and an important bulwark of White Power severely damaged, if not destroyed completely.

As they prepared to do battle with entertainment industry image-brokers, the creative artists developed new institutions and transformed old ones into beacons of black cultural education. The appearance of the National Black Media Coalition, Black Citizens for Fair Media, the Aldridge Players/West, Blkartsouth, the Dance Theatre of Harlem, and the Black Theatre Alliance, among others, signaled the determination of Afro-Americans to disseminate their rapidly rising sense of racial consciousness throughout the popular culture. Collectively, they would counsel black patrons of the arts to straighten out their minds instead of their hair.

While not all such organizations conformed to a strict nationalist definition of financial, technical, and administrative autonomy, they were united in the belief that numerous uncharted aesthetic frontiers beckoned. For those most intimately involved in such endeavor, success was not to be measured solely by the critical reception of a play, poem, or novel. The act of institution-building in itself was deemed socially desirable and potentially empowering. It could facilitate the promotion of a broad cultural awareness which, in turn, would help individual blacks discover important truths about themselves. No longer forced to view the world through a white interpretive lens, they could proceed to chart the future with confidence, knowing that they were supported by a strong, self-affirming, and distinctive culture.

With personal resolve strengthened and creative juices stirred by contacts made within these supportive, community-oriented groups, Afro-American writers proceeded to develop a series of major themes centering upon the contemporary black condition and the vital message of empowerment. In doing so, they provided their public with a unique literary/performing arts guide to the Negro-to-Black conversion process. By examining these themes, one gains important insight into the nature, motive force, and meaning of the Black Power movement as a whole.

Advertisement for "soul" programming on early 1970s television. Courtesy of *Proud* magazine.

Defining "Whitey"

Black writers understood that there was great social utility in knowing the enemy. Like their ancestors who had used the Brer Rabbit and John stories to warn of White Power's many dangers—and to suggest ways of triumphing over them—modern-day novelists and playwrights told tales on white folk. They pulled no punches in relating their fellow countrymen's character flaws. Black survival very well could depend upon understanding white Americans well enough to predict their collective response to the Black Power agenda.

What was whitey *really* like? In most cases, it was not a pretty picture. Black-authored fiction and drama suggested that a people who pretended to be the crown of creation actually were the scum of the earth. It was possible that whites weren't even fully human. If they were, ice water filled their veins. It was said that from earliest times, whites had exhibited a vast array of unflattering traits. And they seemed to have left none of their bad habits behind in Europe's caves. Technological achievement provided no measure of their humanity. Those who "first set foot on the moon," noted poet Gil Scott-Heron, also had given explicit meaning to "war, rape, murder, adultery, / and hell / where they shall all someday reside." Theirs was a horrible history of "mass murder and inflicting pain."[33]

Under the pretense of spreading their corrupt version of religion among the heathen, these "pink faced monkeys" had looted the riches of wealthy African kingdoms, polluted native value systems, and enslaved innocent black people.[34] Exhibiting the same degree of immorality, inhumanity, and greed as their forebears, modern-day members of this "diseased species" behaved like "colorless wild savages" ceaselessly seeking "quick kicks / sensational sex / and immediate murder." White male characters created by black writers cannibalized the remains of lynch-mob victims, raped sheep, and were responsible for introducing both drug addiction and venereal disease to the black community. Females of the species were shown to be morally and physically impure "bitch devils." Likened by poet Ted Joans to a stinking, stopped-up sink, the white woman's greatest desire was to seduce and infect Afro-American men with disease—even going to the extreme of paying them for sex.[35]

Together, these degraded beings had created an evil empire, a "Dangerous Germ Culture" ruled by the almighty dollar. According to Nikki Giovanni, white people worshipped money so intensely that they transferred this feeling to anything even remotely resembling it. "That's why you see those goddamn KEEP OFF THE GRASS signs," she wrote, "Not that [the white world] cares about grass but that it's green." Enslaved by the desire to acquire ever more "materialistic fetishes" and "consumer produced nothingness," they had ruined nature, polluted the environment, and made their homeland "the cockroach of civilization."[36]

So grotesque and foreboding was this highly undifferentiated Euro-American image (depicted in one Melvin Van Peebles play as a huge, beady-eyed, hideously grinning white masked figure perched high above the stage) that Black Power era writers warned of genocide. Incapable of generating compassion for others, the "rhythmless hearts" and hate-dulled minds of these pale-skinned creatures were said to harbor only thoughts of death and destruction. There was no middle ground. They wanted black people enslaved or buried.[37]

Giving voice to recurring contemporary fears that Washington was about to implement a program of black population control through family planning and "preventive detention" initiatives, creative artists developed a variety of "early warning" scenarios.[38] In Floyd McKissick's "Diary of a Black Man," the tipoff that the black pogroms were about to begin came with congressional passage of strict gun-control legislation. After police and national guardsmen had disarmed the Afro-American population, a National Registration Act ordered all blacks to carry special identification cards. Then, in a television address, the President urged implementation of a National Heritage Act which would declare subversive all overt expression of "alien" cultures. At about the same time, the government announced development of a new "pill bomb." No larger than an aspirin tablet, it could destroy limited areas without danger of widespread fallout. After testing in Bedford-Stuyvesant, charred black bodies were to be cleared away and the bombed-out district redeveloped by major corporations.[39]

Other fictionalized approaches to the problems brought upon white society by "nigger unrest; nigger demands; nigger population; niggers period" were somewhat more subtle, but no less insidious. In Ben Caldwell's short play Top Secret or a Few Million After B.C., "Operation Pre-Kill" was adopted by federal authorities only after proposals such as establishing concentration camps or A-bombing Harlem had been rejected as "too barbaric." The approved plan centered upon a crash program to develop and market, via a massive advertising campaign, an inexpensive birth control pill. In the words of McNack, head of the President's Inner Space program, the pill would "kill the nigger babies before they're born! Fast as them black bucks can shoot 'em in! Simple as that!" If Operation Pre-Kill was a success, the government no longer would have to worry about marches on Washington. The Boy Scouts could handle any future riots. Within twenty years, he predicted, there would be a severe—but most welcome—shortage of black people.[40]

Alternative depictions of the nation's movement toward an African-American final solution told of plans to engage the minority population in an all-out domestic race war; to commit "double genocide" by assigning black troops to combat duty in Vietnam; to promote "behavior and aspirational changes" through psychobiochemical mind control; and to implement a Pentagon-sponsored "Forget-for-Peace" program that would induce mass amnesia and erase "militant" racial memories. One writer even predicted that all black folk eventually would be shipped to the moon, "whether they like it or not." But only if the moon proved unfit for white habitation.[41]

The instigators of these genocidal schemes tended to be high-status public officials, military officers, and scientists. But this by no means assured black people that they could look to the "average" white American for their salvation. According to black writers, the various white social classes were only slightly different versions of the same basic, inhumane model. All had been hopelessly corrupted by early socialization into a society which had "reached its cultural apex/with the perfection of murder." As poet Nikki Giovanni wrote, "the worse junkie or black businessman is more humane/ than the best honkie." None could be trusted.[42]

Upper-class whites were said to have been instrumental in shaping the fundamental institutions of "the frozen impersonal west." Some, such as a character named Mr. Mann in Ed Bullins' The Gentleman Caller, had risen to the top by mouthing patriotic platitudes while dealing death to all who stood in their way. Mr. Mann may have worn star-spangled socks and had a dresser drawer full of flag-striped boxer shorts, but his true nature was reflected in his choice of decor. Mann's comfortably furnished living room was lined with mounted, stuffed heads of blacks, American Indians, and Vietnamese.[43]

Others, even though wealthy and accorded high social status, revealed major character defects through their sexual preference. Convinced that "regal faggots crowd the/ white man's history," many Afro-American writers depicted whites as limp-wristed homosexuals. In these works, "highvoiced fags," such as Jack Benny's friend Dennis Day, J. Edgar Hoover and assorted members of the "faggot b.i." (alternatively, the "Federal Bureau of Faggots" or "Faggots Bullying Indirectly"), Santa Claus (that "ho ho hoing . . . red suited faggot"), and even the traditional white Christ figure were utilized as metaphors for racial weakness.[44]

Additional Euro-American shortcomings were revealed through characters who were shown to be consumed by a feverish passion for heterosexual coupling. LeRoi Jones' *Experimental Death Unit #1*, for example, provided a sordid picture of brutal, libidinous white men fighting among themselves for a few minutes of "greasy pleasure" with a cheap whore. To the black writers, this uncontrolled lust and penchant for violence was most uncivil, but typical of those socialized in "charlieland." Such behavior was not to be emulated. As Henry Adams, an Afro-American character in Barry Beckham's 1972 novel *Runner Mack*, noted upon making a narrow escape from seduction and unwilling participation in a drug-fueled sex orgy: "Let's get out of here, Mack. This is not us." His companion agreed. "Right on," said Mack, fleeing the steamy scene. "These muhfuckahs are ca-ra-zee." Black manhood adhered to higher standards and would not be ruled by passion.[45]

Some whites, on the other hand, seemed to be ruled by their funny bone. According to black writers, white folks' proclivity to unwitting displays of humorous behavior was legend. That their shtick was providing clownish comic relief could be seen in characterizations of the red hot Mamma Too Tight, a laugh-provoking white prostitute in Ed Bullins' *Goin' a Buffalo* and, at least at first glance, of the rotund, baldheaded, polka dot-suited judge which Herbert Stokes created for *The Man Who Trusted the Devil Twice*. Black dramatists even created "white" characters for the stage by tearing a page from the annals of burnt-cork minstrelsy. They rubbed black faces with chalk. White people, they seemed to say, were very corny.[46]

But, this was a very deceptive and "black" humor. In some cases, the slapstick characters' toothy grins disguised the fact that they were power-mongering killers. Despite the greasepaint, they were not to be dismissed as "ca-ra-zee." Certainly, it would be a grave mistake to rest easily in the presence of such powerful and dangerous fools.[47] As Nikki Giovanni warned:

> You would not trust your life to a wolf or tiger
> no matter how many tricks they can learn
> You would not turn your back on a cobra
> Even if it can dance
> Do not trust a honkie
> They are all of the same family[48]

Barnum and Bailey were both the end men and the power behind the white supremacist throne.

Although white liberals, with their many foibles, could be quite funny, they too were greeted with a great deal of suspicion. Black writers typically defined them as "revolt-on-weekend-yung whi-T's" who were attempting to "dig by-proxy what a mental ass-kicking they received thru n-sti-2-shun-al-eyezed everything." While professing concern for black people and their problems, they had "no real stomach" for true revolutionary action and could be expected to withdraw proffered support if asked to take up arms.[49]

Addicted to tokenism and filled with hypocrisy, they were not merely cowards. They were cowards who also happened to be closet racists. As revealed in Douglas Turner Ward's one-act play, *Brotherhood*, the white liberals' behind-the-scenes lifestyle often contradicted their egalitarian rhetoric. One evening, after black guests had left the suburban home of a seemingly exemplary white couple named Tom and Ruth Jason, a most remarkable transformation occurred. False masks were removed. As "Old Black Joe" blared from the phonograph, the Jasons began to work feverishly, repositioning cherished furnishings that either had been disguised or hidden. Soon, a staggering array of "Niggerphalia" was unveiled. Within minutes, the room spilled over with the Jasons' grotesque collection of crimson-lipped, white-eye rimmed jockey and mammy statuettes, bare-bottomed ashtray blacks, and ebony "pissing-stanced" lamps. Relieved that the masquerade of interracial camaraderie had ended and that things were back to normal, the happy couple settled down to drink their mint juleps and relax to the soothing strains of "Swanee River."[50]

When combined with other alleged personality flaws, such as arrogance and cultural insensitivity, the white liberals' disposition made it all but impossible for them to be accepted as trustworthy allies. Not even white ethnics with a long history of service to the traditional civil rights coalition remained above suspicion. "All white folks are pricks," noted Dave Trent, a black newspaper editor in Chuck Stone's novel, *King Strut*. "Scratch one and a bigot'll bleed."[51] What then, one might ask, was the role of whites in the Afro-American freedom movement?

Black power-era writers taught that, at least for the immediate future, white people should be kept at arm's length. Fearing that assistance offered by this motley assortment of "beatniks, misfits and neurotics" might irreversibly harm the movement, they opted for independent action. At their most charitable, they suggested that white liberals could "go amongst the peckerwoods" and help other white people to "cast the beast from out of themselves."[52] As noted by the chorus in Joseph A. Walker's musical epic *Ododo*, the times called for black initiative and self-direction:

> I don't need no LSD,
> Or guilty hands to set me free,
> For my destiny,
> For my destiny,
> For my destiny,
> Depends on me![53]

In effect, like their "political" brothers and sisters, Afro-American creative artists had defined whites *out* of the movement and, in some cases, outside the bounds of humanity itself.

This "cultural" act involved more than white exclusion. In turning the tables on time-honored popular cultural stereotypes, black writers revealed the outlines of a distinctively Afro-American world view. By caricaturing white people as savages, deviants, clowns, and killers, they demystified the oppressor. Their vivid tales of inhumanity and immorality described what the majority population was capable of doing to preserve racial hegemony; revealed the absolute necessity of overthrowing white power; and suggested that to do so would require considerable mental agility, might, and staying power.

Black Power-era poets, novelists, and playwrights understood that, by itself, determining the nature of the enemy would not solve black America's many problems. But it was a beginning. The very act of defining whitey could contribute to the development of black self-esteem, confidence, identity, perhaps even total psychological liberation. And with this increased mental freedom would come even greater insights and ever-bolder initiatives. Then, when black folk had moved beyond what poet Mari Evans has termed the "need to scream," they would be "ready for other things"—to share black love, to develop black strength, to build a powerful black nation.[54]

Identifying "Toms"

Afro-American writers who were so bold as to forward unflattering depictions of white behavior did not shy away from suggesting appropriate standards of conduct for members of their own racial group. After all, growing up in a largely segregated society, much of their information about the white world had come from viewing television soap operas, westerns, and detective shows. The "evil tube", as one of LeRoi Jones' characters termed it, helped shape their impression of whites as "some sick type folks" living a "nasty sterile bullshit imitation life."[55] On the other hand, most of what they understood about black people was derived from a lifetime of firsthand experiences, observations, and interpersonal relationships. Certainly no one knew more about Afro-American personality types than Afro-Americans. And none were more concerned that their kinfolk refrain from imitating white ways than activist black writers.

During the late sixties and early seventies, Black Power truth squads sought to expose the most acculturated of black Americans, the Uncle Toms. Tomish behavior—defined as that which reflected the internalization of majoritarian values—was unequivocally condemned. Black writers alleged that this was *learned* behavior, traceable to close contact with corrupt whites. In literary and dramatic portrayals, they showed these unfortunate creatures being created through laboratory experimentation, classroom and media indoctrination, white liberal flattery, and outright bribery. Through these various processes, normal Afro-Americans were transformed into zombie-like beings. Eager to do their masters' bidding, they were considered racially disloyal and dangerous.[56] They had to be identified and rooted out of the black community with all deliberate speed. What specific traits did one look for in seeking out members of this Afro-American fifth column? How could they be spotted within the general population? As a public service, the black writers provided a detailed field guide to Tom-hunting.

First, they offered a brief introduction to Tomist history. Antebellum blacks conclusively identified as Uncle Toms included traitors who compromised slave uprisings in return for an "extra [pork] chop" as well as subservient bondsmen who refused to believe that slavery was an absolute evil. Typically, these shufflers could be seen, hats in hand, telling their beloved white owners, "I'se happy as a brand new monkey ass, yassa, boss, yassa, Mass Tim, yassa, Massa Booboo, I'se so happy I jus don't know what to do." They danced and sang, scratched themselves and bowed deeply—all to win massa's favor.[57]

In later years, Tom's descendants moved North, adopted to a new group of white overlords, and taught their children to "accept their limited progress as the end of the evolutionary pattern." Having developed neither fortitude nor courage, subsequent generations displayed little interest in pressing militant demands. Upon reaching the top of their truncated caste-based world, the Toms retreated within shag-carpeted ranch-style tract homes, venturing out only to display a new barbecue grill or big-finned car. This behavior, said black writers, was rooted in their powerlessness and marginality vis-a-vis white society. They were "scared shitless" of losing this (very tiny) piece of the rock.[58]

Uncle Toms were said to be concentrated in several high visibility occupations. These inheritors of the Tomist tradition were easy to spot. It seemed that a good number were attracted to the entertainment world. Their ranks included actors Stepin Fetchit, Sammy Davis Jr., and Hattie McDaniel as well as vocalists Harry "the Black Caucasian" Belafonte and Diana Ross and the Supremes—those svelt singers of "whiter than mr./clean songs" and "wearer[s] of other people's hair."[59]

A second occupational category consisted of black bureaucrats and police officers. The former were said to offer the average Afro-American little more than the momentary thrill of seeing "black faces in high places." In reality, they were white collaborators, junior partners, and puppets.[60] Members of the latter group were termed "nappy fuzz infiltrators," "Uncle Peeping Toms" and "traitor niggers." Allegedly, they would gun down their own mother to uphold "De Law" and receive a commendation from Mr. Charlie.[61]

Other Toms could be identified by their allegiance to the ideology of nonviolence. Membership in any of the mainline civil rights organizations was a dead giveaway. Unlike the more militant characters created by Black Power era writers, they seldom spoke of the need for armed self-defense against white violence. More accustomed to turning the other cheek than striking out against the oppressor, Toms retained an unassailable faith in white allies, big government, and the efficacy of civil rights legislation. Moreover, they were said to be oblivious to the teachings of history, not realizing that their cherished laws rang as hollow as treaties made with the Indians. An unclouded view of the American past would have revealed that very few whites had ascended to the heights of societal power through "Love Your Brother" fundraisers and marches.[62]

Unfortunately, the minds of nonviolent Toms were anything but unclouded. Black writers claimed that the civil rights leaders' mental processes were at near-gridlock with grandiose plans for self-aggrandisement. Certainly, the heads of "SNICK, FLICK, RICK, TICK, KOR, POOR, [and] SNORE" made a splendid show of marching with "the people" and of listening to their "beloved" brother's and sister's heart-rending lamentations with bowed head and furrowed brow. But, in truth, their deceptively hidden agendas had little to do with either public policy issues or humanitarian concerns. As was revealed through the character of Rev. Abraham Lincoln Brown in Joseph White's play *The Leader*, a primary goal of nonviolent elites was to position themselves within the movement in such a manner that their followers wouldn't be able to "wipe they behinds unless you there to tell 'em to." One day, Brown predicted, his name would be so well known that "when I cut my toenails, it'll be in the news." Recognized by all as the "one *official* black leader," the former pastor of Holy Disciplines Baptist Church, in Rocky Mount, North Carolina, would be acclaimed "the black man's Julius Caesar," the most famous Afro-American in the history of the world.[63]

Until such time as human events caught up with the egocentric aspirations of Rev. Brown and other members of the fictional civil rights establishment, they would occupy themselves with the numerous and costly creature comforts granted to those who had succeeded in making a lucrative career out of nonviolence. And herein was located the Achilles' heel of all who were disadvantageously affected by what LeRoi Jones termed the "Gandhi syndrome." Within the civil rights aristocracy, a plush office, hefty travel budget, and expensive wardrobe may have denoted rank and status. But to the Black Power activists, these regal trappings constituted incriminating evidence, possibly conclusive proof that an individual was in an advanced state of Tomism.[64]

Even if not noticeably afflicted with this condition, Toms almost always could be identified by their speech, mannerisms, and habits. Through their literary and dramatic portrayals, activist writers compiled a handy check list to be used in ferreting out those who were not card-carrying nonviolent elites. Questions to be asked of suspected Uncle Toms included the following:

1. Are you prone to using "big horseshit doctor words" and an affected Oxfordian accent normally heard only on certain Ivy League campuses during fraternity rush?[65]
2. Is there enough face powder and bleaching cream in your medicine cabinet to bake a three-layer cake? If not, do you claim that at least one of your grandparents was a "genuine, full-blooded, qualified, Seminole Indian"?[66]
3. Have you ever refused to read a black newspaper or periodical because of the mispelled words?[67]
4. Would you become confused if asked to explain the relationship between the terms "your bag," "your thing," and "your stick"?[68]
5. Do you worry about "lazy, dirty, triflin', raggedy-ass" Negroes moving into your neighborhood and lowering property values?[69]
6. Is "integration" defined as having your children be the only black students in a white private school?[70]
7. Do you claim to be a "Negro professional" when a more accurate designation would be "Assistant Negro Assistant to the Associate Vice

President's Assistant"? Irrespective of the answer, did you marry white in the hope of advancing your career?[71]

8. Have you ever been known to say: "Ain't no chile o mine gon walk around with no nappy head," or "I'm gonna go to Spelman so's I can marry me a Morehouse man," or "We got nothing to do with them African savages," or "Niggers ain't shit"?[72]

9. Do you refer to "Black" as "that awful militant word"?[73]

If the majority of their answers were in the affirmative, a respondent could expect to be considered a prime candidate for recognition as Tom-of-the-Year.

When located, it was advised that Toms be approached with extreme caution. Like "a monkey with [a] straight razor" they were a danger both to themselves and to others. Black writers portrayed them as enemies of the revolution, helpmeets in the holocaust. In Charles Oyamo Gordon's play, *The Breakout*, a Tom received the President's National Hero Medal for helping eliminate "divisive factors in the Negro community." Toms formed an elite, antirevolutionary special forces unit called the Exterminators in Ed Bullins's *Night of the Beast: A Screenplay*—and never took prisoners. LeRoi Jones not only made blacks with white brains and "mindsouls" the assassins of Malcolm X, but also showed how a single symbolic Tomish act could kill the spirit of an entire generation. It seemed that their unrestrained urge to become "white as snow" could lead only to death and destruction.[74]

Much of this abhorrent behavior was attributed to cultural dislocation. The further Toms strayed from their folk roots, the greater threat they posed. As they adopted majoritarian behavioral traits and values, they became slaves to white aesthetic imperatives. Substituting integrationist ideology for that of racial empowerment, they came to the conclusion that "blackness is a Dirty Disgraceful ugly thing." A major hindrance to black psychological liberation, Toms were said to constitute a bourgeoisie in blackface who were leading Afro-Americans in "the opposite direction of peoplehood." There were two schools of thought on how to meet this challenge. One advocated force, the other forgiveness.[75]

As one of Ed Bullins' militant characters asserted, there was none more vicious than "a nigger who is threatened by the Blackman with losing his imaginary place beside the whiteman." Once the violent revolution began, these treacherous "Uncle Thomas Wooly Heads" would be the first to go. In their tales of intraracial retribution, black writers told of how ages old scores were to be settled. Chanting "Death to the house niggers," militants would swoop down and round up each and every "bushwa" malefactor. If adjudged guilty of keeping the race down, carrying out the slavemaster's will, or any other common Tomish crime, the accused's traitorous tongue would be removed. Those posing the greatest threat to the revolution faced summary execution. The message was clear: "NEGROES THAT LEAN WHITE, LOVE WHITE, WILL HAVE WHITE/NIGHTS OF DEATH."[76]

But this course of action was fraught with adverse consequences. What if the black Anglo-Saxon could be reclaimed and converted to activism? As if afraid to confront the *real* enemy, black folk always seemed to be killing their own, diluting their power. If the Uncle Toms suffered from cultural disorientation, why couldn't a cure be found through cultural reeducation? After all their ill-advised behavior was learned, not genetically determined. Upon reflection, some black writers urged restraint in dealing with the Toms, suggesting that it was possible for all but their most heinous crimes to be forgiven.

Affirming Stokely Carmichael's faith in the activist potential of each and every Afro-American, the authors of black fiction and drama asserted that "all Black People are Black in one way or another." According to poet Raymond R. Patterson, there was enough "Grief- / Energy in / The blackness / Of the whitest Negro / To incinerate / America." This being the case, it was the duty of creative artists to help the unfortunate Toms "straighten out the shit in their heads." As was taught in Marvin X's dramatic parable, *The Black Bird*, after being jolted from their stupor and forcibly removed from the white world's "burning house," even those mentally caged creatures who had "forgotten what freedom was" could find their way "home." After recovering their misplaced identity, once despicable "knee-grows" could be expected to join in common cause against the white oppressor.[77]

Black writers claimed there were many more educable Toms than most militants imagined. In fact, some downright "together" individuals seem to have been judged unfairly. For example, the only "crime" committed by certain of those who were charged with exhibiting Tomish behavior was that they had been born on the wrong side of the generation gap. And this fabled chasm, said novelist Toni Cade Bambara, was nothing more than "a white concept for a white phenomenon." In less confused times, all would have acknowledged that "old folks is the nation." The parental generation would have been praised for standing the storm and paying the dues, for serving as a sturdy black bridge over which their children could march with determined stride and raised fist. It was to be lamented that many younger folk had chosen to disregard these contributions and enter into an adversarial relationship with their elders.[78]

Instead of treating members of this group, out of hand, as "the enemy", it was suggested that they be seen as potential allies. Perhaps these oldsters weren't very well versed in the latest styles, but they understood adversity and could relate countless stories of the struggle against it. None could deny that they composed a fair share of the "black masses" for whom the revolution was being waged. Moreover, they were to be valued as living repositories of African-American folk wisdom. As noted by poet Alice Walker, they "knew what we / Must know / Without knowing a page / Of it / Themselves." If, on the surface, some might seem a bit Tomish, it nevertheless was possible that they could become invaluable assets to the movement, instructing the younger generation in familial love. Certainly, the capacity "to love, to protect, to cherish, our young, our old, our / own," could not be considered the least important attribute of any activist seeking to promote group solidarity and empowerment.[79]

Another reason for sparing suspected Toms was that they might be fellow revolutionaries in disguise. Black Power-era fiction and drama described how militants could beat the system by going "underground"— pretending to be loyal, thoroughly acculturated members of the black bourgeoisie. This ploy had the advantage of utilizing the element of surprise to good effect. (Who ever heard of a malevolent minstrel?) It also provided participants with an energizing psychological boost. In fact, the whole scam was downright *delicious*. To immobilize and destroy the white world with fake versions of its own Frankenstein-like creations would be poetic justice of the highest order.[80]

As was made clear in Ed Bullins' 1965 play, *How Do You Do*, even an "authentic" Tom only recently released from spiritual servitude could be used to defeat whitey. Continue to "scratch your head, shuffle, pray to his gods until you decide what day you'll call Judgment," counseled a musician-poet named Paul. "Imitate him; become an alter-ego Superman . . . in blackface, but really turn into the Shadow." Here, clownishness and servile imitation was transformed into a most deadly simulation of the former reality. "Tell your victim you are goin' to kill him," advised Paul, "but giggle, buckdance and break wind before you pull your razor." By successfully carrying out this important covert mission, the former Tom would gain redemption. He would be recognized by his new, militant friends as a "guerrilla warrior of ideas."[81]

Certainly, not all fictional Uncle Toms were what they seemed. And the creators of black drama and literature did their best to provide Afro-America with a useful cultural guide to their history, habitats, and characteristic behavior. They suggested ways in which to meet the Tomist threat and, most significantly, kept the hope alive that one day all Toms would be able to transcend their inglorious past and integrate into blackness.

Understanding Black History

Having warned of the dangers presented by Tom and whitey, black writers proceeded to place racial relationships into a larger historical context. Their poetry, plays, and novels portrayed the grim work of the oppressor, extolled African-American heroism, and highlighted the continuing need for group unity. In celebrating the values which had allowed their forebears to endure, black creative artists denied any interest in creating a historical fiction. Firm believers in the notion that "to revere one's past/ is to rule one's present," these New World griots sought to reveal the black truths of the ages to all members of contemporary black society—even to Uncle Tom and his kin.[82]

According to the black writers, some type of curse seemed to have been placed upon their lineage in ancient times that had yet to be exorcised:

> as it was
> in 1619
> is now
> and ever
> shall be
> SHIT
> without end[83]

Somber tones were most appropriate.

The nature of this curse could be seen in Black Power-era depictions of the African diaspora. After being locked for weeks, even months, in "the bowels of a floating shithouse," forced to watch as family members were tormented by rats and "eaten away by plague and insanity," the accursed ones were introduced to life in the colonies. Here, freedom had meaning only for whites. By some mysterious, unspecified virtue of their melanin deficiency, the lowest, most ignorant rogue only recently released from an English prison was considered a lord—intellectually, culturally, and morally superior to any of the kidnapped Africans. Driven by dollar signs and delusions of grandeur, these pale-skinned brutes proceeded to treat their black charges with unspeakable cruelty.

The Africans' descent from human to chattel, person to property, had begun:

> They are gone to the new world
> They are gone to America
> Into hell they have been hurled

As poet Gil Scott-Heron noted, with biting sarcasm and considerable understatement, "slavery was no smiling, happy-fizzies party."[84]

But from a black perspective, neither was the Civil War—or Reconstruction—or the Gilded Age—or the Progressive Era. New Deals, New Negroes, and New Frontiers might come and go, but the activist writers' vivid descriptions of "asphalt plantations" and Klansmen "sailing like white-hot ghosts" through the New South night suggested that scholarly attempts at historical periodization were ill-informed.[85] For most black Americans, time had a way of standing still. Although rooted in the slave era, white power and black powerlessness continued to be significant facts of modern-day Afro-American life. "Grampa, will you settle a argument for us?" asked a young character in 'Sippi, John Oliver Killens' novel of the civil rights movement. "Who won the Silver War? The North or the South?" The elderly man replied as if the answer was all too obvious. "White folks won it," he said without hesitation. "That's how come you ain't free yet."[86] Old Massa still held title to the land, controlling access to the nation's storehouse of riches.

A close reading of such works reveals that the authors were not simply crying in their beer or rubbing salt into an open wound when they spoke of oppression. There was a method to these portrayals of societal madness. Afro-American writers utilized black suffering as a springboard to greater racial awareness. They were not about to wallow in self-pity. Instead, they would help their people reconstruct and "reexperience" the terrors of the past, awakening them to the necessity for unified action in the present. As playwright LeRoi Jones noted, the black revolutionary theatre was by definition a "theatre of Victims." It viewed the world through their tormented eyes so that audiences could understand that "they are the brothers of victims, and that they themselves are victims if they are blood brothers." This realization, he said, "will cause their deepest souls to move, and they will find themselves tensed and clenched, even ready to die, at what the soul has been taught."[87] Such a clear-eyed, cathartic approach to the grim legacy of the past stripped history of its fatalism. By enumerating black misfortunes, the writers transcended them, opening the way for a new appreciation of their ancestors' capacity for survival. They focused on cruelty only long enough to make a point: Afro-American history was a study in adversity. But, it also was an ennobling account of the many heroic struggles against it.

Interspersed within their commentaries on life's general brutishness were numerous exemplary encouragements to black empowerment. As they worked to revise the canon of historical fiction and drama, Afro-American writers posited four major requisites to a correct understanding of the past: making the pan-American connection, venerating black heroes, celebrating the beauty of black life-styles, and acknowledging the importance of black culture. White authors had left these important elements out of their accounts. As a result, black folk had been given "false comic images." By reclaiming their collective history, these presumed heirs of Mantan and Buckwheat would let it be known that they conceptualized themselves as "lovers and the sons / of lovers and warriors and sons / of warriors."[88] Indeed, in the view of some writers, the black Americans' many trials had made them well-nigh indestructible.[89]

Hoping to reinstate an Afrocentric vision of the world, black novelists, poets, and playwrights posited the existence of a pan-African continuum of thought and experience which bound black Americans to their forebears even as it distanced them from stereotypical images of Africans as primitives or savages. In this view, black history did not start with the first benighted Jamestown slave. It began in a "time . . . before the beginning of time," in the very "cradle of all creation," among an accomplished race whose color was the same rich brown as the earth from which they sprang. Africa, not the United States, was the true home of this strong, but exiled people. They never had "stopped being Africans." Lest the present generation forget this fact, Black Power era writers made a determined effort to convince the diasporan population that there was a living "Afro-Soul" connecting Harlem and Timbuktu via "the drums of mental telepathy." Believing this, every person of African ancestry would be able to say, "I am all of them, they are all of me, I am me, they are thee."[90]

To encourage pan-African unity, black writers turned away from European cultural models and looked to Mother Africa for wisdom. Calling upon the same old world spirits that had strengthened their ancestors during times of trouble, they advocated the use of ancient rituals in support of contemporary black empowerment. In Richard Wesley's play *Black Terror*, for example, young revolutionaries danced, chanted, and burned incense to the Spirits of the Black Nation before launching a bloody war of liberation. "Come forth / Reach into our hearts / And remove the fear," they sang. "Guide our lives / Make us strong / Place steel in the marrow of our bones / Grant us inner peace / To fulfill our terrible missions." In like manner, the solemn, robed supplicants in Robert Macbeth's *A Black Ritual* entreated the ancestral gods to provide them with the inner strength needed "to withstand the beast, to withstand the devil and to finally overcome him." As noted in a short story by Akbar Balagoon Ahmed, even if they failed in their efforts to defeat the white oppressor, black revolutionaries would continue to express their gratitude to the spirits for allowing them to experience "the warmness of the sun"—for helping uphold the dignity of the African bloodline both in ancient Cush and on the not-so-ancient battlefields of America.[91]

Activist writers paid homage to mere mortals, too. While the ancestors' spirits may have watched over them, providing inspiration and guidance, it was understood that the responsibility for carrying out the Black Power revolution rested upon the shoulders of the living. Even as they sought to cast the spell of the continent across black America, Afro-American writers used their "African imaginations" to create literary and dramatic vehicles that would celebrate black heroism, past and present. They hoped the contemporary diasporan population would be inspired by—and succeed in emulating—their heroes' daring deeds.[92]

"Rip those dead white people off/your walls," urged Los Angeles poet Jayne Cortez. Replace them with a "Black Hall of Fame."[93] During the Black Power years this was a widely shared sentiment. No longer would Afro-Americans tolerate the refusal of white culture-makers to elevate black folk to heroic status. They would honor their own movers and shakers, selecting those individuals who best represented qualities deemed essential to group advancement. But, who were the favored role models?—and what purpose did they serve?

Not surprisingly, this pantheon of notables contained many historical and folkloric figures. Black-authored poems, stories, and plays recounted the exploits of Shine, Stagolee, and Railroad Bill.[94] They told of how Gabriel Prosser, Nat Turner, and Harriet Tubman had stood up to "the Man", teaching by word and example that Afro-Americans were "a fantastic race of people."[95] Having in common the ability to thwart whitey's attempts at dehumanization, the black heroes looked their societal overlords straight in the eyes and disputed assumptions of racial superiority in strident tones. "I ain't got no white kinfolks," stated one of John Killens' outspoken female slave characters." I'm pure black ain't-been-messed-with, and I'm damn proud of it!"[96] Although delivered in an antebellum setting, bold speeches such as this were timeless. Their message for the modern day came through loud and clear:

> Hero with an Afro
> Mojo in indigo
> Gonna overthrow
> The status quo.[97]

And whites were well advised to stand back.

More recent inductees into the Hall of Fame included Black Power era "political" figures such as the "tall, fair and wiry-haired" Angela Davis; El General—better known as George Jackson—who had gone to an early rest in "the world of gods, / heroes, tall men, giants;" Bobby Hutton, celebrated as the Denmark Vesey of "our now / time;" and of course, Brother Malcolm, the "black Messiah" who taught his people that they were "their own salvation."[98]

Shoulder to shoulder with these political activists stood representatives from the culture sphere. Literary greats Gwendolyn Brooks and Langston Hughes were memorialized as "weaver[s] of black dreams." Their "kisses of verse" had motivated a generation of readers to "search for light." Musicians John Coltrane, Jelly Roll Morton, Lester Young, and Charlie Parker were said to be far more than "mean horn blowers/running obscene riffs." They were latter-day John Henrys who had "descended from Black Olympus" with an empowering message of brotherhood and redemption. Boxing champion Muhammed Ali and Olympic Games' boycott leaders John Carlos and Tommie Smith won acclaim for their athletic prowess. But they also garnered praise for providing "a new/current, a new/exchange, a new/vision" for all people of color.[99]

On occasion, black writers went so far as to grant themselves honorary membership in the pantheon of notables. Don Lee, for example, toasted fellow poet Ted Joans as "a worldman, / a man of his world," known to all as being "badder than bad." Joans returned the favor, in a roundabout fashion, by penning a poem which touted LeRoi Jones as the rightful "king" of the black movement: "LeRoi Vive le Roi." Unselfconsciously referring to himself as "the man who walked the water and tied the whale's tail in a knot," H. Rap Brown even became his own urban folk hero in "Rap's Poem." Verses such as these were part braggadocio, part recognition of the capacity of *all* blacks for heroic action.[100]

Irrespective of their age cadre or field of endeavor, these heroes were considered representative Afro-Americans—or, at least, representative of what black people could become. As a character in Charles H. Fuller Jr.'s play *The Rise*, said of his hero, Marcus Garvey:

> Sometimes, I think of somethin' I want to tell 'em
> myself, and before I can say it, Mr. Marcus done
> got it out, and is shouting it from the stage! It's
> like he says what we all been waitin' so long to
> say, and jest couldn't git out! He's like all of us put
> together—and when you follow a man like that,
> you follow yourself.[101]

Such individuals were honored for the way in which they had shared the "Living Word" of blackness with those less fortunate than themselves— black folks who had not yet completely shed the "white plaster of . . . 'negroness'." Literary and dramatic depictions of Garvey, Turner, Shine, and the others provided their people with a vision of the collective future, a cultural roadmap through the swamp of lies promoted by white writers. "Black in thought, and Black in deed," these heroes transcended the limited, often demeaning roles assigned to most blacks by the majoritarian society. By refusing to become victims, they taught important truths about racial unity and cultural independence. Their bold acts and signal accomplishments revealed the limitless possibilities of black history.[102]

It was held that the blackness radiated by these heroic men and women was reflected in the lifestyles of "average" Afro-Americans. According to activist writers, historical oppression had destroyed neither the viability nor the beauty of black community life. They acknowledged no incurable pathology of deprivation—recognizing only the strength accrued through generations of struggle. So-called "ghettos," such as Harlem, long had been the "target for thousands of lies, cruel epithets, verbal assaults." In truth, they were far from being urban wastelands, filled with the detritus of black humanity. More correctly, they were complex, diversified environments populated by some of the world's most soulful people—black folk who pursued life with vigor and feeling. "Where my grandmother lived," wrote poet Doughtry Long, "there was always sweet potato pie / and thirds on green beans and / songs and words of how we'd / survived it all." Although "poverty-stricken" in a material sense, most black communities were governed by the maxim, "Black love is Black wealth." They were seen by residents as richly endowed repositories of group strength—places where the culturally disaffected could receive care and spiritual rejuvenation.[103]

To popularize this notion, black writers moved beyond a literature and theatre of "oppression" to focus upon the intricacies of black "experience." Works such as Ed Bullins' *In the Wine Time* and *Clara's Ole Man* plunged audiences into the depths of community life, revealing its richness and internal dynamism.[104] In the language of the street and to musical backdrops drawn from the contemporary soul/jazz/gospel repertoire, they recreated the "scarred and comic, dangerous and tender" multifaceted composite of urban black life. This grit-laden, other-side-of-the-tracks environment provided an appropriate setting in which to showcase *real* black folk struggling with the basic issues of human existence. As Bullins noted, here was "a group of people, honestly and realistically depicted, in real life experiences. They start at one point; things happen; and, their lives are changed by these happenings."[105]

Whether shown perched on the crumbling stoop of a row house, holding court in a seedy bar, or semi-permanently ensconced on a well-aged living room sofa, these creations of the black writer's memory and imagination joined black art and life in a fashion rarely seen in white-authored works. Such characters were more than vehicles for the display of local color or mouthpieces for their creator's political views. While many *were* colorful, peppering their talk with a diverse array of expletives or strutting across the boulevard with a rear-end sway which observers likened to "babies fighting under a blanket," they taught by example, not proclamation. Utilizing communal patterns and rituals of communication, they boasted and squabbled, shared aspirations and failures, and discussed relationships both budding and broken. Their central message was forwarded in a soliloquy presented by one of the characters in Melvin Van Peebles' play *Aint Supposed to Die a Natural Death:*

> Poor ole black people always got to be dealing in
> reality, not that they don't love daydreams and
> cotton candy. . . . One of the first lessons a blood
> must get together is how to roll with the impact
> of the concrete of life.[106]

Black history, the writers said, was not a study of impoverishment and misery relieved only by fanciful dreams of future heroics. It was a richly textured tale of black people, in black communities, coping with the "concrete of life" by living life to its fullest.

The literature and theatre of "experience" held that Afro-American culture played a major role in the history of black communities. Over the centuries, it had sustained the people, enriched their existence, and provided a showcase for their many talents. Black culture unified the black nation, endowing the lives of the "insignificant" with meaning by linking them to a glorious racial past. In a sense, all black history was cultural history, a proof text for the richness and beauty of Afro-American life.

Like the good cultural nationalists many of them aspired to be, black writers were convinced that theirs was a superior culture. Drawing their evidence from history, folklore, and the rituals of everyday life, they sought to show that "black is best." For example, they boasted that no African god would have "let his own son get / Lynched over there in / Jerusalem Land;" that white people might be able to stride or saunter, but they couldn't *strut;* that the art of Charles White was more vital than that of Picasso; and that if placed on the same stage in fair musical competition, Martha and the Vandellas could beat Mahler hollow, any day. Surely, wrote a culturally confident LeRoi Jones, when the first spaceships landed, it would be seen that these "long blue winggly cats" from outer space had journeyed all this way in search of Art Blakey and Albert Ayler records.[107]

According to the black historian/writers, this rich cultural mix could be likened to an umbilical cord that "stretched across an ocean from the hot sidewalks of Harlem and red-dirt roads of Georgia to the tangled green jungles of the Congo." Throughout their shared history of sorrow and celebration, black culture had served as a life-sustaining link between the widely-separated peoples of the Afroworld. In like manner, the activist writers attempted to narrow the psychic distance—"that nigger space"—separating artist from audience and black folk from each other.[108] They would utilize cultural expression to unite the present generation in support of black liberation.

Evidencing firm control of their own aesthetic priorities, black poets, dramatists, and novelists were unafraid to equate Black Power with brotherly love or to show how a single poem or session of "unity music" could spur black brotherhood.[109] Some described "soul" as a natural power and blues as a feeling that only black folk could understand.[110] Others contrasted black and white American cultural expression and spoke of the necessity of achieving unity across (black) caste and class lines.[111] All, in one way or another, believed that it was possible to transform bookstores into cultural communication centers and theatres into interactive forums dedicated to the creation and celebration of communal experiences.

To such individuals, culture was both history's lifeblood and an essential element in the contemporary quest for Black Power. As noted by poet Don L. Lee (Haki R. Madhubuti):

> A people without their culture
> are a people without meaning.
> a people without their culture
> are a people without substance.
> a people without their culture
> are a people without identity, purpose and
>   direction.
> a people without their culture
> are a dead people.[112]

United through their culture, with perspective gained from their history, black Americans understood why they could not be broken by oppression. At the end of white history, it was said, all would know the importance of black culture.[113]

According to the black writers, people who were well versed in African-American history could recount many past horrors, but they also had learned to value ancestry and heroism. They could appreciate the beauty inherent in black lifestyles. Perhaps most important, they had succeeded in locating the cultural wellspring of group strength and staying-power. Knowing all these things about the past, they were thought to be well prepared to chart the direction the black nation would take in the future.

Achieving Liberation

For many Black Power writers, historical themes had utility only if they promoted modern-day black empowerment. As able representatives of an exceedingly present-minded generation, they were eager to move beyond the past. Focusing pens and typewriters on the societal revolution that was going on all around them, they created numerous fictional scenarios involving movements in support of black liberation. Some story lines seemed to have been taken directly from (or to have inspired) the plans of revolutionary and territorial nationalist organizations. These grim tales tended to focus on guerrilla warfare and the eventual overthrow of white political hegemony. Others were less bloody, but equally compelling. They related an individual's or group's quest for psychological self-determination. Still others attempted to combine the two forms. Irrespective of story type, black culture and black cultural expression were considered vital to the acquisition of both political and psychological freedom.

Like their real-life counterparts, the paramilitary street gangs and urban guerrillas of the black imagination forwarded lists of demands that were both lengthy and varied. Delivered to both white officials and representatives of the black bourgeoisie, most could not be met without a significant reallocation of socioeconomic power. Some, like the Cetewayo militiamen depicted in Chuck Stone's novel *King Strut*, were passionately committed to the establishment of a black state in the American South. Other groups sought the withdrawal of military forces from Southeast Asia, U.S. disinvestment in South Africa and Rhodesia, or the creation of modern, black-run Black Universities. In one plan, to be funded by "Fear Money" (reparations) from the Federal government, every needy black family would receive "ten acres of land, one intermediate-sized car and five thousand dollars." Collectively, the militants were telling the establishment to "Get off every black man and woman's back! / Get off! Get Off! / And if you don't, / We're going to push you off!"[114]

The ideologies guiding these literary and theatrical activists were as varied as those of the writers who created them. In Julian Moreau's *The Black Commandos*, spokespersons for the Black Liberation Front promoted armed self-defense—a "Strategic Violent Movement"—to meet the continuing threat of white terrorism in the South.[115] Modifying this doctrine until it became, in effect, one of self-sacrifice, a fiery, quick-tempered Richard Wesley character named Geronimo was so committed to black liberation that he couldn't see beyond revolutionary suicide. "To fight and die for the revolution. I won't live beyond it! I don't want to," he proclaimed. "I don't care what goes down after we win. . . . I seen my death. I'm gonna die like a revolutionary with the blood of the enemy on my hands."[116]

With a somewhat more steady eye on the political future, Amiri Baraka's *The Motion of History* taught that significant societal change could occur only through a multinational, multiethnic revolution "to end Capitalism and build Socialism." According to this plan, oppressed working-class peoples would put aside petty differences and unite to "smash the degenerate system." Eventually, guided by "Marxism-Leninism—Mao Tse-Tung Thought," they would usher in the glorious dictatorship of the proletariat.[117] Barry Beckham's *Runner Mack* countered with the opinion that while black militants might wish to work with white radicals (who could provide money and contacts) to "change the country," no long-term alliance should be contemplated. It was hoped that after the revolution, blacks would "get it together" and regroup along racial lines.[118]

For those attracted to cultural nationalism, a "fo/real / revolution" involved the initiation of intense mental as well as physical combat. As noted by a character in Ed Bullins' *Night of the Beast*, the task was one of epic proportions—"revolutionizing our entire culture." In order to teach the next generation "to love their blk/selves," these rebels vowed to abandon "yesterday dreams" and to herald the wonders of African-American lifestyles throughout the length and breadth of "this/white/assed/universe." Nevertheless, a certain amount of circumspection was advised. According to poet Don L. Lee, no matter how strong one's faith in black culture, it was never to be forgotten that "no poems stop a .38 . . . no stanzas break a honkie's head . . . no words kill." Until "similes can protect me from a night stick," he wrote, "i guess i'll keep my razor / & buy me some more bullets."[119]

Whatever form the future revolution would take, one thing was certain. After reading these accounts it was clear that oppressors were going to be *punished*. During the Black Power years, angry black writers evidenced their rejection of the civil rights movement's nonviolent ethic by creating characters who vigorously called for whitey's eradication. Some, such as Dan Freeman, the CIA officer cum guerrilla warrior of Sam Greenlee's novel, *The Spook Who Sat by the Door*, expressed regret about being placed in the role of societal executioner. Others seemed to enjoy their bloody work. All-too-real fictional militants pistol-whipped hostages, beat cops bloody, and methodically slaughtered enemies of the people "like a sadist stomping on an ant train." "It's such a kick," said one black protagonist, "to feel my knife slicing into white meat." For such hate-driven individuals, it was indeed "spiritual ecstasy" to see the bodies of their once-powerful adversaries "shattered and broken apart, cast into death."[120]

On occasion, the black writers seemed to be cheering their fictional creations on to ever greater acts of retribution. Nikki Giovanni, for example, asserted that history was filled with examples of black people dying to further white interests. Now, they had to show that they could kill in support of their own:

> Do you know how to draw blood
> Can you poison
> Can you stab-a-Jew
> Can you kill huh? nigger
> Can you kill

> Can you run a protestant down with your
> '68 El Dorado
> (that's all they're good for anyway)
> Can you kill
> Can you piss on a blond head
> Can you cut it off[121]

According to the black poet, contemporary politics proved that the barrel of a gun was the best voting machine; a dead honkie the most effective protest vote.[122]

Holding to this notion that it sometimes took an inhuman act to end inhumanity, Afro-American writers defended social violence as necessary to self-defense and nation-building. Through a show of deadly force, they eventually would be able to "build up a Black world . . . where there will be no more killing." Just as important, they said, blacks killed in order to "rebegin" psychologically—to alter the "nigger mind." In this view, terrorist bombings and political assassinations had both tactical and psychosocial consequences. Such acts chipped away at White Power, but they also helped purge black folk of their slavery-induced mind-set, wiping away the "skid marks of oppression and / degradation" in dramatic fashion. As Julius Lester wrote at the time of the Newark rioting, "Even as we kill, / let us / not forget / that it is only so we may be / more human." After shedding white blood in revolutionary action, blacks would find their own flowing far more freely through spiritually rejuvenated bodies.[123]

These rituals of expiation and release took several forms. In Sonia Sanchez's play, *The Bronx is Next,* African-American revolutionaries practiced role reversal on a white cop. Noting that it was going to be a long night, "maybe the longest of your life," they forced him to experience what it was like to be singled out and verbally brutalized. After humiliating the officer, ("You ain't shit boy. You black.") the militants evacuated and then torched the ghetto in a symbolic act of purification.[124]

Black rebels in Blyden Jackson's *Operation Burning Candle* sought to meet the "collective psychotherapeutic need" of their people through selective assassination. Their targets were "the living continuum of slavery"—key elected officials from the deep South, including all who held major House or Senate leadership posts. The death of these politicians would end a long-term roadblock to the enactment of progressive legislation. Moreover, by dramatically altering traditional power relationships, this "symbolic uprising" would sever forever the chains of psychological bondage. In future years, whenever a white person saw a young black boy sitting on a curb eating ripe watermelon, instead of visualizing him grinning and shuffling, grateful to be tossed a penny, they would begin to worry that at any time he might "leap up with a blazing submachine gun" and strike them down. As stereotypical images of black people changed, so would blacks' perception of themselves.[125]

The therapeutic nature of violence was nowhere more simply or effectively taught than through Ed Bullins' aptly titled *Short Play*. Although it involved neither ghetto cops nor southern racists, its message could be applied to either type of oppressor. The only action in the play involved a black actor going into the audience and "shooting" whites in the face at point-blank range. Through this violent ritual, black viewers were freed from the intrusive white presence.[126]

Symbolic acts such as these taught that decisive revolutionary action was both possible and beneficial. Recognizing that many in their audience had to experience the revolution vicariously before they could agree to its feasibility, Black Power-era writers utilized what Blyden Jackson termed "creative violence . . . cleansing violence" both to exorcise the psychological past and to direct the political future.[127]

They also employed culture as a weapon. Recognizing the tenacity and resilience of black culture, Afro-American writers showed how folk, literary, and theatrical forms could complement any militant's arsenal. There was more to the revolutionary stratagem than "Tick, tock, toe / Three whiteys in a row / Bang, Bang, Bang." In their opinion, one of the best ways to fight representatives of an alien culture was to imbibe from one's own fully and deeply.[128]

Holding up their experiences as exemplary case studies, black novelists, poets, and dramatists touted the ability of culture-makers to serve as conduits of revolutionary wisdom. By diligence, they said, it had been possible to uncover foundational truths about the past. With considerable bravado, they were continuing to dispute white assumptions about the present. Through artistry, they would construct and forward empowering visions of the future. When, in addition, a black writer took an African name, put on a buba, or grew "uncompromising / untamed / not straightened / natural / protesting / kinky / nappy / Revolutionary hair," they extended the Black Power communication net even further. Utilizing cultural forms and expression to convey militant messages, they "plug[ged] into the ghetto grapevine," thereby becoming a significant threat to White Power. Even if the only "weapon" at their disposal was a "beat-up typewriter and some cheap rag bond," the potential for disrupting white folks' world was great. Black writers were unafraid to tell others about the sickness within American society—or about the strengths within themselves.[129]

Having made a case for the centrality of their role, activist writers engaged their imaginations fully, in unwavering support of the revolution. Their stories, poems, and plays told of guerrilla warriors sending signals via African "talking drums," booby-trapping watermelons, and terrifying whites with their wall art.[130] They intoned rootworkers' curse / prayers ("that disease and death shall be forever with them. . . . that all about them will be desolation, pestilence and death") against the enemy, causing considerable chaos in both domestic and foreign affairs. According to one tale, in the period of a single month, tactical use of "super juju" was responsible for three airplane crashes, five hijackings, three floods, four tornadoes, and an influence-peddling scandal that threatened to topple the government.[131] Black music was equally deadly. The shock waves from an ancient Egyptian "Afro-horn," for example, were said to be able to kill whites instantly. At the same time the music drowned out their death screams.[132] The moral of these incredible stories was obvious. When "armed" with their own powerful culture, black folk had little to fear from whitey. Surely, as Ted Joans noted, white Americans had good reason to "get UPTIGHT and . . . COWER" when a black poet even *whispered* Black Power.[133]

In an important sense, these literary activists were merely fighting fire with fire or, more correctly, trading poem for poem. According to the black writers, their counterparts within the white culture sphere long ago had perfected the use of culture as a political weapon. They consistently misinterpreted Afro-American cultural expression and attempted either to alter or silence any dissonant black voice. Mainstream publishers, they said, had manipulated writers for generations, accepting their work only if it spoke with unreasonable fury or recounted debilitating pain. They never allowed a black author "to soar, to sing golden arias."[134] Record industry moguls exploited black talent, shamelessly marketing singers "like cornflakes" and robbing them of their hard-earned royalties. In quest of a hit record, these Frankenstein-like beings would create white James Browns or black Tom Joneses as the market required.[135] TV and movie executives treated ethnic culture with great insensitivity. Most of their "product" distorted black lifestyles for the greater good of entertaining mass audiences and generating revenue. So pervasive was this practice that even the most world-wise brother on the block stood in danger of being brainwashed by Hollywood's inaccurate depiction of contemporary urban life.[136] To the black writers, these white misappropriations of what once truly was soulful were blatant, politically motivated acts of aggression. It was their intent to meet each one with a powerful blast supplied by their own undiluted cultural expression.

More often than not, Black Power-era writers were able to declare victory over the oppressor. Their works showed how culturally transmitted messages unified the people, enabling them to overcome a numerically superior enemy. All manner of black Americans contributed to the cause. From maids and mail carriers to militant medical students and college professors, they cast aside class-based differences to fight as one. Despite desperate white attempts (martial law, public executions, concentration camps) to save the tottering regime, these black folk of fiction achieved liberation, ushering in a new post-revolutionary world.[137]

And what a splendid place it was. After driving most of the survivors into Stone Age caves, the now fully empowered black leadership established new ethical and aesthetic standards. With words and music by Amiri Baraka and Pharoah Sanders, their national anthem spoke of the societal changes wrought by the revolution. The air was clean and the water pure. Hunger existed only in history books—which were so little concerned with "whi-tness" that white people's accomplishments were remembered only on "anglo-saxon american history day." Money was abolished and war removed from the national vocabulary. Dedicated to black pride, unity, and freedom, the new millennial kingdom honored past greats with renamed landmarks such as Huey Newton street, Muhammed Ali square, the city of Marcus Garvey, and the state of Malcolm X. Here one could find "black angels / in all the books and a black / Christchild in Mary's arms." There even were black Easter bunnies, black santas, and black ice cream. Indeed, it now was a crime to be anything *but* black. White America's once-dominant school of acculturation had been placed in permanent recess.[138]

But what about the fictional revolutions that failed? Like cautionary antebellum folktales, a fair number of these black-authored works told of valiant efforts falling short, of rebels being forced underground or into exile to await another day.[139] In such cases, was anything gained from the bloody struggle? To ask an even more probing question of stories drawn outside the revolutionary context, could black characters win psychological freedom without experiencing the catharsis of violence? Could black protagonists, in effect, acquire "me" power before their group had won "us" power via armed rebellion? Black writers gave an affirmative response to each of these questions. Black people, they said, could achieve psychological liberation in almost any setting.

Some characters began the journey to greater black consciousness as a result of contact with an already "converted" individual—a person who, like James Baldwin's Christopher Hall, was "black in color, black in pride, black in rage." Others were led to examine their lives more closely by external events or after receiving the self-definitional message from an unanticipated source. In one story, a nonviolent minister was convinced that the time for "cheek turnin'" was over by a clever burglar masquerading as the Almighty. In another, the instrument of conversion was a persistent roommate who kept bringing "those beautiful Black people home, . . . talking that talk." The words of Malcolm X moved many.[140]

No matter how they were introduced to "the new blackness," Black Power acolytes soon found themselves engaged in a life-transforming process unlike any they had encountered previously. Afro-American writers described the Negro-to-Black conversion experience with a stylistic flair that most psychologists could not hope to match. They equated liberation from whiteness to "walking out of shadow / And going forth in sun." "WE are the New!", they exclaimed. "We are the Rivers of the Spring breaking / through / the cold, white ice of Dying Winter." Like a sedated lion that awakened from its stupor and ate the trainer, they had succeeded in smashing the "white plaster" that had clogged "mental pores." As the "Black Spiritual Oil" within their minds was released, they felt "an easing at the core" and a "Keener taste / For life." Vowing to carve out a new existence "within the Black Flame," they became their own "necessary blackself." Newly endowed with self-esteem, they walked with head high, knowing that envious passersby were likely to be thinking "AIN'T THAT BLACKMUTHAFUKKA BEAUTI-FUL."[141]

Unfortunately, just as the black psychologists had predicted, some individuals had trouble moving beyond the "blacker than thou" stage of their personal odyssey. Often seen in the so-called blaxploitation films of the era, these Super Blacks were victims of arrested psychological development. Close kin to larger-than-life Hollywood heroes (such as Jim Brown, Jim Kelly, and Fred Williamson in *Three the Hard Way*, or Coffy, Friday Foster, and Foxy Brown as played by Pam Grier) who accomplished near superhuman feats in support of noble ideals, they exhibited certain elements of the Black Power style, but little of its substance.[142] Super Blacks outmuscled and outsmarted whites, took their women, and stole their money—all with a suitably "bad" attitude. But, in doing so, they displayed many unfavorable character traits. Instead of materially assisting in the decolonization of black minds and the renewal of the black spirit, they provided little more than fantasy release. Stopping short of addressing broader issues, Super Blacks sensationalized and celebrated individual acts of revenge against whites as if, by themselves, these isolated confrontations could bring about group empowerment.

By creating skewed, black macho versions of James Bond—a cinematic hero LeRoi Jones once described as a "suave, unbeatable fascist"— black writers and directors seemed to be selling their rich, complex, soulful culture short. In limiting display of the more joyous aspects of the black spirit, they offered viewers a one-dimensional definition of soul style. To the Super Black character, life was *all* scowling, sneering, bravado, and glitz. As the ads noted, Superfly and Trouble Man definitely had a plan to "stick it" to whitey. But, one had to ask, did this involve anything more than renting a luxury apartment and riding off into the sunset in a new Rolls Royce?[143]

However shallow their commitment to the revolution, Super Blacks served a useful purpose when used as negative role models or as foils for more "together" characters. By satirizing the Super Black lifestyle, black writers hoped that real-life counterparts might be brought to their senses. Then, recognizing their folly, such individuals would move beyond the blacker-than-thou mind-set and complete the transition to authentic blackness. Super Black traits to be avoided included the following:

Ideological vacuousness.—Super Blacks "knew everything about everything" and never lost an argument. They claimed to be natural-born champions of nationalism and uncrowned princes of the black government in exile. But, in truth, they were bogus blowhards addicted to empty rhetoric. Poet Edward S. Spriggs described one such individual, noting that despite his incessant mouthing of militant maxims, he seemed incapable of "finishing the sentence." Content to scream "revolution means change . . . ," he had no conceptualization of post-revolutionary life. In The Breakout, playwright Charles Oyamo Gordon parodied the ideological immaturity of this type of pseudomilitant by describing the code of conduct which he had composed for his group, the Royal Order of Tiger Liberators. The first, presumably most important, rule was: "There will be no spitting on the floor during Liberator meetings."[144]

Ostentation.—Black writers skewered the Super Blacks' habits of conspicuous consumption. As they noted, there was nothing wrong with a little pride properly cultivated. But when flaunted through lavish displays of material wealth, it could become a hindrance to liberation. The "double-natural . . . triple-hip" lifestyle alienated potential allies and sowed jealousy among the brothers and sisters.[145] A case in point was Omar, a swinging Super Black revolutionary drawn by Mae Jackson. Not only did he have a closet full of "really hep danshikis" and a "fro so high that it almost touched the clouds," but he also was the proud owner of a specially designed tiki. To startle and impress his peers all he had to do was push a button and out from its center "would pop a blade sharper than lighnen."[146]

Vanity.—Super Blacks were exceedingly self-centered. In Henry Van Dyke's *Dead Piano*, one such character was said to be so taken with his own physical beauty that "he used his body and his face in the way a homely man uses his wits." After delivering an angry harangue, Fargo Hurn experienced a rush of power, but at the same time felt cheated. If only his speech could have been taped, he mused. More concerned with attitude and appearance than with conveying revolutionary wisdom, Hurn longed "to *see* himself acting, playing his role."[147]

White women often stood behind such blacker-than-thou characters, adding heft to their already bloated egos. After a lengthy stint of clenched-fist posturing and podium pounding, what better way for a tired militant to end the day than to be greeted at his apartment door by a blonde, blue-eyed charmer in a filmy negligee? These pale innocents from Oberlin, Harvard, or Wisconsin who had gone south one Freedom Summer and wound up as long-term bedmates of the Super Blacks were said to be treated as sporting trophies, spoils of the white wars. Money, fame, "and his own white broad" were the showcased perks most avidly sought by such "maker[s] of the Black revolution." In truth, said the black writers, these "loudmouth boasters" were making a career out of the revolution—and loving every minute of it.[148]

Ideologically vacuous, ostentatious, and vain, the typical Super Black made a perfect late night talk show guest. In a John Oliver Killens parody, one such figure was introduced by Johnny Carson as "the greatest revolutionary of all time . . . greater and more dangerous than the late lamented Malcolm X." Attired in a "boss dashiki" and sunglasses, the estimable Jomo Mamadou Zero the Third acknowledged Carson's greeting by glaring at the cameras and spitting across the footlights at the studio audience. "I wished all of you pale-faced pigs a bad damn evening, you swinish cannibalistic motherfuckas!," he growled. "And after them few kind words of salutation, I'm going to say some mean things to you." The theatre exploded with applause, Johnny shouting over the din, "Isn't it truly tremendous? Give him a big hand, fellow Americans . . . Isn't he wonderful, ladies and gentlemen!"[149] Having failed to internalize blackness, to join rage and reason, Super Blacks like Zero were little more than whitey's nightmare court jesters. They could say "Boo" and frighten Middle America for a terrifying, guilt-riden moment or two. But, after whites regained their composure, the laughter began, growing louder and louder with each ludicrous blast of militant bombast. Unwittingly co-opted by the media, Super Blacks became white American cultural oddities, fit more for entertaining than for leading the revolution.

Fortunately, the annals of blackness contained many stories documenting a far more thoroughgoing psychological transformation. As conceptualized by black writers, culture played an integral role in the development and realization of true black consciousness. Their novels, short stories, and plays revealed how the black culture-maker could become a nonviolent "creator of/change" by making curl-free, processed Negroes uncomfortable with their "imitationwhite" existence. Without ocean liner or jet they would conduct theatrical excursions to the land of their ancestors, showing the "conked-head Negro" that "his forefathers were once kings and queens and the builders of great civilizations." Through dagger-worded poetry and mind-defogging music they would lead the unconverted "out of the wilderness of self-hatred into the Promised Land of self-esteem." Here, violent anti-white words and deeds were optional. After all, the central focus of the Negro-to-Black conversion process was not on evaluating white people, but on encouraging black people to reevaluate themselves.[150]

Success in this endeavor could be judged by the culturally expressive behavior of recent converts. As they became conscious of their new mental state, the characters created by Black Power-era writers said they "felt like singing." As was the case with Muffin in Sharon Bell Mathis' novel *Listen for the Fig Tree*, they literally were "bursting with some kind of magnificent-feeling Black thing."[151] They grew naturals, violated mainstream dress codes, flavored their speech with "street-words," worshipped a black God, celebrated Kwanzaa, and listened to Miles Davis records.[152] By their actions, those who employed cultural aids to complete and authenticate their psychological metamorphosis were helping to win others to the cause. One day they would remember how they had strutted—not skulked, stumbled, or bludgeoned their way—"home to blk/ness."[153]

Through cultural expression, Afro-American writers provided their generation with a series of easy-to-follow thematic road maps to both personal and group empowerment. As their stories and plays revealed, even the most obdurate member of the black bourgeoisie could be liberated if they followed directional signs carefully and adhered to the rules of the road. Moreover, it was the authors' contention that although minor backsliding might occur after an individual had completed the Negro-to-Black conversion process, wholesale recanting was extremely rare. In most cases, when internalized, blackness was indelible.[154] This suggested that the movement toward psychological liberation was irreversible, its effects cumulative in a transgenerational, group context. If so, while Black Power's political base might erode over time, future generations still would be able to experience and appreciate tangible benefits stemming from the activist writers' efforts to escape mental and cultural domination.

Conclusion: Whatever Happened to Black Power?

Everybody talkin bout
What happened to the Revolution
And the 'mean-bad-militant-children-of-the
   Sixties'

. . . .

Did I dream them times?

Jo-Ann Kelly, 1972

Clutching coat collars against a bitterly cold Chicago wind, the faithful began queuing up some three hours before the scheduled 11:00 A.M. service. Three days earlier, on 25 February 1975 Allah's Last Messenger, Elijah Muhammad, had succumbed to congestive heart failure at age 77. Now, they were assembling in long, winding double lines outside Holy Temple of Islam No. 2 to pay their last respects.

Following the ceremony, a five hundred-car procession slowly made its way to Mount Glenwood Cemetery. There, flanked by blue-uniformed Fruit of Islam guards, brothers Elijah Jr., Akbar, Emmanuel, Nathaniel, Wallace, and Herbert gently scattered dirt on top of their father's coffin and said their own goodbyes to the tiny china doll-fragile man with the high thin voice who had led the Nation of Islam for more than four decades. As Rev. Jesse Jackson noted, the Messenger's physical presence belied his formative influence. "He was the father of black consciousness," said the up and coming head of Operation PUSH. "During our colored and Negro days, he was black." And now he, like his wayward spiritual son Malcolm X, was gone.[1]

Elijah Muhammad with wife and daughters at the Chicago Temple.

In the days to come, Muslim ministers assured their flocks that there was no need for remorse, no cause for dissention or disunity. The Messenger's spirit lived on in the Nation's new leader, Wallace Muhammad. But it was impossible to exorcise the feeling that some great change was imminent. The Black Power torch ignited at the time of Malcolm X's assassination seemed to be flickering as Elijah breathed his last. Subsequent events did little to ease this disquietude.

After being hoisted aloft on the shoulders of cheering disciples assembled at Chicago's International Amphitheater for the annual Our Savior's Day observance, Wallace Muhammad set his course on reform. Before long, members could salute the American flag, serve as members of the U.S. Armed Forces, and engage in electoral politics. Evidencing his desire to close the theological gap between the Nation and orthodox Islam, Wallace pronounced the Koran—not his father's doctrines—as the group's supreme authority. The original Arabian Muhammad, not the Honorable Elijah, now was considered the last of God's prophets. Even bolder directives scrapped the goal of a separate black state and opened places of worship to the faithful of all races.[2] Within the twinkling of an eye, it seemed, formerly quarantined Caucasian devils were set loose to run amok in the temple. Whither Black Power?

By 1975 the Black Power movement stood in danger of vanishing from the public consciousness. Guided by the familiar adage "out of sight, out of mind," most Americans—both black and white—expended far fewer brain cells contemplating the "radicals" than they had five years earlier. Who could blame them? As the nation experienced a welcome hiatus from urban rioting and as the most vocal of the activists either were "rehabilitated," exiled, or permanently silenced, both the press and the public lost interest in Black Power. Without a regular regimen of angry militants waving lists of non-negotiable demands at reporters, the average American couch potato slipped easily into a post-Vietnam-era stupor. To many, the words "Black Power" came to connote scarcely more than the slogan of a short-lived political fringe movement. Like hippies, yippies, and other segments of the interracial brotherhood of "the great unwashed," black militants no longer were news. Once part of a major sixties "phenomenon," they now were mere period-piece oddities slated for paragraph-length treatment in future history texts.[3] Continuing to the present day, this narrow, intellectually limiting conceptualization of Black Power's scope and character has contributed to the belief that the movement made little difference to its generation or to ours. Such a view is misleading and incorrect. But it *is* plausible if one defines Black Power outside the sphere of culture or overlooks the realm of the psyche—if its impact is measured only in terms of quantifiable "political" gains. After all, how many 'fro-headed, bandolier-bedecked radicals won seats in Congress or joined the boards of major corporations between 1965 and 1975? How many independent nation-states were carved out of the Deep South—or out of Newark, for that matter? Where, outside of fiction, are the accounts of guerrilla army triumphs?

Several interrelated factors hindered movement participants from making greater inroads in politics and economics. The same factors have served to limit our understanding of Black Power's impact on other areas. First, from the beginning, Black Power was beset by a formidable contingent of disbelievers and nay-sayers. Perhaps never before or since has such an unlikely assortment of negativist nabobs combined forces to discredit activist ideals. Second, as other sixties radicals discovered, idealism—even of the revolutionary variety—was no match for ingrained prejudices, entrenched bureaucracies, and societal inertia. In terms of materially transforming the lives of poor folk, the Age of Aquarius was a bust. Saffron robes and love beads could not disguise the fact that poverty flourished within—and beyond—the Great Society. Third, even before 1975, internal dissension and a number of well-publicized "defections" made it seem as if movement leaders were "mellowing out" and following their generational cadre into the graying buppiedom of middle age.

During the Black Power years, all manner of publications carried spirited critiques of the movement. From the pages of the *Crisis* and *Liberator, Ms.* and the *National Review,* critics made it appear that *none* of the activists' programmatic approaches to empowerment were viable. Black Studies programs were "conceived in error, born in haste, fostered by guilt," and doomed to failure. Black English speakers talked in a "provincial patois" which greatly limited their opportunities in the world at large. Independent black factory-workers' unions were mere "pawns" in management's union-busting game of divide-and-conquer. The "segregation-inspired black-jacking of funds" promoted by James Forman's Manifesto demeaned the integrity of Afro-American church-goers. It, like most other Black Power initiatives amounted to little more than "bombast combined with . . . delusions of grandeur." Failing to meet their opponents' high standards of acceptability, the militants were consigned to the oblivion reserved for those deemed incapable of advancing beyond "woolly" conceptualization and "sloppy analysis."[4] Each ideological tack was said to have its own specific set of irredeemable flaws.

Pluralism / Community control.—Critics warned that decentralization of institutional power would "mark a reversion to tribalism" in metropolitan areas. If key urban institutions were "resegregated," outside capital would shun the black-controlled sectors. As a result, job opportunities for Afro-Americans would remain limited and the ghetto economy underdeveloped. As for the political sphere, it was predicted that the community control enthusiasm would cause inner-city residents to divide into factions, fighting one another for meaningless perquisites. Instead of promoting the general welfare of all, elected representatives would become consumed with parochial concerns. In the end, said the skeptics, black control of central city institutions might change the skin color of a few administrators, but it was unlikely to improve the quality of life for most urban residents. In their estimation, community control was a "blind-alley approach" which would bring negligible or even negative returns.[5]

Separatism / territorial nationalism.—Separatism, said the critics, was an escapist fantasy, a coward's way out of the black American predicament. Promoters of this ideology were thought to be seeking a cocoon of refuge from reality. Proof of the extent to which the whites' "racist disease" had affected its victims, the separatists' tough talk was interpreted as a wail of defeat; their exclusionist organizations a sign of personal insecurity. To nonbelievers, "cockeyed" ideas about sundering ties with "responsible" Negro leaders and "decent" working class whites in order to campaign for a separate state seemed a plot from a third-rate farce. Only a few years earlier, they asserted, such notions would have been "laughed into oblivion." Then, as now, the basic task confronting black Americans was coalition-building, not disengagement and flight.[6]

Retaliatory violence / revolutionary nationalism.—Because they were held both to encourage and to provide a rationale for the spread of anti-black sentiment, calls for violent confrontations with White Power were considered foolhardy. If implemented, said critics, such a plan would be suicidal. Outnumbered ten to one, black folk hoping to overthrow the oppressor by force would find themselves trapped in a descending spiral of destruction and death. The well armed, wealthy, white majority—aided by its fanatical right wing—would triumph over rag-tag rebel forces quickly and easily. Black American history, asserted the skeptics, proves that violent rebellion is doomed from the start—a truly "Impossible Revolution." One only had to look at Watts to see that, at best, precipitous acts of this nature produce only a small additional dose of antipoverty palliatives and a few more water sprinklers to cool overheated ghettos.[7]

Black arts / cultural nationalism.—This variant of the nationalist enthusiasm was likened to a sugary treat that provided momentary satisfaction, but no lasting strength for the fight. Indeed, neo-African rituals and ceremonies were thought to be a drain on the common storehouse of revolutionary energy. Cultural nationalists were said to engage in endless sloganeering and meaningless, if shrill and sometimes quite splendid, posturing. Instead of physically confronting the enemy, they preferred "flying around the country in . . . dashiki[s]" to promote a "goon squad aesthetic." It was predicted that their highly touted Black Arts movement would constitute no more than a minor chapter in the history of black letters. Allegedly, this failure was the tragic result of allowing aesthetic judgements to be dictated by political agendas. By reducing artistic expression to "black chauvinist" propaganda, cultural nationalists had succeeded only in "vulgarizing" their own skills, thereby making it unlikely that they would leave anything of value to posterity. Surely, said the critics, a poem for the ages should be something more than a "piece of writing with choppy non-sentences, perverted word order and four-letter words set in stanzaic form."[8]

In addition to being subjected to these attacks on their core beliefs, the men of the movement found themselves encumbered with the additional burden of defending their integrity against the charges of black feminists. With the formation of groups such as the National Black Feminist Organization (1972) and the Combahee River Collective (1976) more and more Afro-American women began to revise their perceptions both of the formerly white-dominated women's liberation movement and of black macho. Before long, it was clear that there were those within the Black Power movement who no longer would tolerate gender-based discrimination or remain silent when militant artists portrayed women as bitches, bimbos, or babymakers for the revolution. That many male activists richly deserved to be picking verbal barbs out of their sexist posteriors in no way lessened the possibility that the new black feminist critique could have deleterious affects on Black Power's image and attractive power.

For centuries, black Muslims schooled young women in the domestic arts, taught submission to male authority, and discouraged the use of cosmetics and fancy dress.[9] For generations, the bluesman countered white stereotypes of black "boys" by describing himself as a "Man and a Half" who would tolerate "no back talk" from a female as long as he was "paying the cost to be the boss."[10] For decades, black men of letters had portrayed women as "gloriously stupid," wide-hipped, big-breasted "chicks" who always seemed "ready to give up some drawers" the minute they "smelled a drink or saw a dollar bill."[11] For years, Stokely Carmichael's joking remark about the proper position of women in the movement ("prone") had been greeted with raucous, juvenile male laughter whenever it was retold.[12] In all cases, the black man's attempts at self-definition presumed the right to define Afro-American women as well. But no more. Fully developed in the years after 1975, the black feminist critique considered such talk narcissistic, chauvinistic, and counterrevolutionary.

Forwarding a gender-specific variation of the gospel of "me" power, female activists accused their male counterparts of "acting like white-sexist bastards." To them, it made no sense for men of the Black Power generation to reject white mores in most areas while taking instruction in male-female relations from the pages of the Ladies' Home Journal and Good Housekeeping. The bourgeois model had to go, they said, not only because of its effect on the feminine self-image, but also because the relegation of women to domestic support duties surely would weaken the revolution. No sweet, submissive keeper of the house, kids, and incense burner could hope to transcend her role as "slave of a slave." Chained to an ironing board, no black woman could become a Harriet Tubman. The fight against sex discrimination surely could be postponed no longer.

Black women's liberation had to be considered an integral part of the movement for the liberation of all black people.[13]

In taking this determined stand against "revolutionary servitude," Afro-American women made clear their understanding of the insidious connection between white capitalist oppression and black macho. They said that men had no reason to feel weakened by this new assertion of personhood or by any woman's claim to a "political" leadership role. Theirs was no castrating, matriarchal ploy to cripple black manhood.[14] Nevertheless, for seasoned practitioners of black macho, feisty assertions that women no longer would "take unending shit off Black men" or "fuck for the revolution" could be disconcerting.[15] Along with the more ideological and programmatic critiques of the movement, this debate over male chauvinism encouraged infighting within the Black Power camp and contributed to the negativist notion that Black Power was a fractured, ineffective enthusiasm.

In the years after 1975, those wishing to cast aspersions on Black Power as a reform ethic had little need to engage in gender analysis. All one had to do was take a day trip to the nearest inner-city welfare office and watch the depressing parade. While there, it was likely that you would be able to spot a "poverty researcher" counting heads and calculating AFDC benefits among the queues. Throughout the 1980s, social scientists who had spent the preceding years trying to fathom the "tangle of pathology" affecting urban black Americans kept head down in the steamy urban jungle, surfacing occasionally to shock and astound middle-class folk with their quantified studies of teenage pregnancies, single-parent families, random homicides, and substance abuse. By decade's end, there seemed to be more than enough quantitative data to show that no Black Power wand had transformed *these* mean streets into gold.

According to the social scientists, poverty both increased and deepened during the eighties, culminating in what one study termed a crisis "as bad as any since the 1930s."[16] How bad was it?

—One of three Afro-Americans and more than 40 percent of all black children lived in households with incomes below official poverty standards. Blacks' median income was scarcely more than half that of whites. Thirty percent of blacks had incomes under $10,000; 14 percent under $5,000.[17]

—Although African-Americans constituted 12 percent of the U.S. population, black-owned businesses accounted for only one-third of 1 percent of the nation's total sales receipts.[18]

—Nationwide, black children were twice as likely as white children to die before attaining their first birthday. In Chicago, Detroit, and Washington, D.C., the black infant mortality rate was three times higher than the national rate for whites.[19]

—Between 1984 and 1986, life expectancy for the white population rose from 75.3 to 75.4 years; for blacks it declined from 69.7 to 69.4 years.[20]

—Afro-Americans were about twice as likely to be victims of robbery, vehicle theft, and aggravated assault as whites. They were six to seven times as likely to be victims of homicide, the leading cause of death among young black males.[21]

Constituting over 60 percent of all persons arrested for robbery, nearly half of those arrested for murder and non-negligent manslaughter, and almost 40 percent of those arrested for aggravated assault, blacks were imprisoned at a rate more than six times greater than whites. The number of young Afro-American men either in jail, on probation, or on parole exceeded the total number enrolled in the nation's colleges by more than 170,000.[22]

As one report concluded, millions of black people continued to live in a "desolate world where physical survival is a triumph, where fear and hopelessness reign, and where the future holds no promises and few opportunities."[23]

Why was this permitted to happen? As the century's last decade began, how could it be that black folk still were considered a "powerless minority" facing a "bleak future?"[24] Explanations, postulations, and lamentations issued forth from think tanks and advocacy institutions only to be greeted by gasps, yawns, finger-pointing, and a further furrowing of brows. The new urban reality or, more correctly, the old urban reality updated with fresh vocabulary words such as "re-" and "hyper-" segregation, was said to be the product of (a) faltering economic growth, rising inflation, and a string of recessions; (b) declining employment opportunities in urban manufacturing plants; (c) the post-Vietnam majority's disinclination to expend energy or resources on the poor and minorities; (d) a racial polarization in presidential politics which greatly inhibited civil rights enforcement and affirmative action initiatives; (e) all of the above. Whatever reason or combination of reasons an individual prognosticator accepted as central to the urban equation, most seemed to agree that the black American situation of the eighties presented "a palpable contradiction to the idea of an egalitarian society."[25] This, of course, was the same conclusion reached by Gunnar Myrdal in 1944 and by the Kerner Commission in 1968. Socioeconomic impediments to black progress continued to have a chilling effect both on group advancement and on any view of Black Power that credited the movement with making positive, lasting contributions to Afro-American life.

During the seventies and eighties, journalists burdened with the unenviable task of preparing readable popular accounts of the poverty researchers' findings occasionally took a break from their labors to pen "whatever happened to . . . " profiles of major Black Power-era personalities. Produced in the midst of a progressively thorough Black Power news blackout, these irregular reports of the militants', ex-militants', and pseudo-militants' comings and goings more often focused on tribulations than triumphs. Ideological change was celebrated, continuity largely ignored. "Gone are the saber-rattlers of the 1960s, the street demonstrators, the instant prophets, the revolutionaries—Afro-coifed, clench-fisted, chic in their daishikis, black leather jackets and Malcolm X tee-shirts," trumpeted one such account. Any who lingered, "stubbornly clutching the shreds of a seemingly unrealizable dream," were thought certain to be "crushed by the brutality of the establishment."[26] From these stories, movement supporters learned that the Black Power ship had gone down with virtually none of its frontline officers on deck.

What, exactly, was the Black Power elite doing while they were "out of sight, out of mind"? Some reportedly experienced such dramatic lifestyle shifts that former allies wouldn't even be able to recognize them. The inner circle of the Black Panther Party, for example, seemed utterly transformed. Instead of policing the police and screaming "off the pigs!" they now appeared to be looking out for number one and living high on the hog.

As early as 1970, Huey Newton was reported to be living in a luxurious $650-a-month lakeshore apartment in Oakland. Eventually, he was forced to defend himself against (among other) charges that he and an associate had diverted for their own use some $60,000 in state Department of Education funds that had been earmarked for support of their Oakland Community Learning Center.[27]

Bobby Seale exchanged black leather and bullets for ballots and barbecue sauce. After receiving over 43,000 votes in an unsuccessful 1973 bid for the office of mayor of Oakland, he left the Party, moved his family to a comfortable two-story home in a Denver suburb, and devoted himself to honing skills first developed as a youngster at his uncle's Barbecue Pit in Liberty, Texas. The result: a tribute to "soulful, down-home righteous good cooking," *Barbeque'n with Bobby.*[28]

Eldridge Cleaver surrendered first to God and then to the authorities. After returning from overseas in 1975 to face assault charges, he negotiated a probation/community service sentence and began a new career as a spokesperson for evangelical Christianity, anti-communism, and mainline American patriotism. His "brand new friends, brothers and sisters in Christ" included Watergate conspirator-turned-prison evangelist Charles Colson, television evangelist Jerry Falwell, and members of CARP, the politically conservative campus-based affiliate of Rev. Sun Myung Moon's Unification Church.[29]

Cultural nationalists also converted to new faiths. In 1974, Amiri Baraka and his Congress of African Peoples (CAP) publicly embraced Marxism-Leninism–Maoism as the socialist "solution" that would free black and other oppressed peoples from the "yoke of capitalism." Repulsed by the growth and consolidation of Newark's black bureaucratic elite and petty bourgeoisie, Baraka changed the name of his CAP newspaper from *Black New Ark* to *Unity and Struggle,* and its motto from "Black People must unify" to "Unite the many to defeat the few." Before long, posters announcing his plays included the phrase "poor whites are welcome." Some performances were double-billed with an Eisenstein film. "Not so ironically," he wrote in 1977, "it was much easier for work of mine screaming 'Hate Whitey' to get published than work which states unequivocally, 'MARXIST-LENNINISTS UNITE. . .'"[30]

After what he termed "a vigorous and multidimensional-ideological struggle," US leader Maulana Karenga joined Baraka in turning his back on "narrow-mindedness and exclusiveness." Upon his emergence from a four-year stay at California Men's Colony in San Luis Obispo (where he had served five times the minimum sentence for assault with intent to do great bodily harm), Karenga sought to convince others of the need for an expansion and enrichment of Kawaida theory. This was to be done through the melding of nationalist form and socialist content. Blacks, he said, needed to conceptualize themselves both as an independent and interdependent social force in order to succeed in breaking the chains of racial and class oppression.[31]

What were the loyal constituents of Black Power to think of these unanticipated changes? How was one supposed to respond to reports that Betty Shabazz, Malcolm X's widow, had accepted a Bicentennial Committee appointment from President Gerald Ford; or that the SNCC's H. Rap Brown, who once had talked about "liberating" Fort Knox, had been caught robbing black crapshooters in a Manhattan bar; or that filmmaker/playwright Melvin Van Peebles had become a Wall Street floor trader and author of a guidebook on "How to Get Rich in the Options Market."[32] Had they all been co-opted by the siren song of white culture? Or were they driven to radical lifestyle changes by white police power? As more and more federal records were made public under the provisions of the 1966 Freedom of Information Act, the latter explanation in particular seemed increasingly plausible.

In the hope of preventing "the rise of a messiah who could unify and electrify the militant nationalist movement," the FBI, assisted by other law enforcement agencies, conducted an extensive covert action campaign against so-called "Black Nationalist Hate Groups." Between 1967 and 1971, J. Edgar Hoover's COINTELPRO program sought to limit the growth of black militant organizations, to discourage cooperation between them, and to discredit their leaders. In pursuit of these goals, U.S. counterintelligence operatives engaged in a truly incredible array of repressive tactics, many of which apparently were being tested for use in other Nixon-era "dirty tricks" initiatives. Detailed "Rabble Rouser" and "Agitator" indices, a Racial Calendar, and a Black Nationalist Photograph Album were compiled and circulated. Insurgent groups were subjected to numerous harassment arrests and to increased tax surveillance by the IRS. A veritably army of informants and "snitch jackets" infiltrated Black Power groups, spreading rumors about the "disloyalty" of bona fide members and supplying authorities with inside information useful in conducting police raids. Existing tensions between members of US and the Black Panthers were purposely inflamed, sometimes with deadly results. The press and electronic media were manipulated shamelessly. There even were attempts made to prevent militants from keeping speaking engagements, to get them in trouble with their landlords, and to break up marriages.[33]

COINTELPRO created what one seasoned activist later characterized as "beaucoup dissention and disunity" within the movement.[34] Determined efforts to suppress Afro-American militancy placed increased financial burdens on targeted groups, made recruitment increasingly difficult, and fostered a siege mentality. Paranoia spread as the number of those either killed, jailed, driven underground or into foreign exile grew throughout the late sixties and early seventies. Reasoning that clusters of supporters would invite additional confrontations with the police and/or the Panthers, Maulana Karenga effected a *dabuka* ("splitting apart") within US. It was said that to be on the safe side he also placed a machine gun on a tripod in his living room facing the front door.[35] The same caution was observed at Republic of New Africa headquarters in the Berkeley ghetto, where a note scribbled on brown paper informed members that "This office is bugged. The phone is bugged. Don't say anything you don't want the boy to know."[36] Indeed, how could any militant organization know which of its seemingly loyal followers actually were part of Hoover's 7,000-person "Ghetto Listening Post" corps of "racial informants"?

Black Panther leader Elaine Brown recalled the mental state of veteran militants under siege: "I saw my friends' brains splattered on the sidewalk by police bullets. I saw their faces in caskets. Things got so bad that funeral attire became a regular part of our wardrobe. I became paranoid; I learned to look over my shoulder." Gone were the days of Panther marches and "Free Huey" songs sung to the tune of "Wade in the Water." Gone were the big Panther buttons and colorful flags; the black berets and leather jackets. Because of police harassment, members had been ordered not to wear their uniforms, except on special occasions.[37]

Even before mid-decade, it appeared that the Black Power "threat" had subsided. Police bullets, "dirty tricks," and nationalist infighting seemed to have drained the capacity of the militants to sustain insurgency. Mainstream Americans could return to business as usual. Henceforward, they would take cognizance of the revolutionaries only for a brief time whenever one returned from Cuba or Algeria to confess and receive punishment for their wrongdoing. With memories of the more overt aspects of the campaign to quash black radicalism still fresh in the collective consciousness—and with a sufficient number of recanting militants to serve as case studies in ideological reclamation—it is understandable that declining activity in this area would be taken as a sign of Black Power's near total eradication (i.e., there *must* be no continuing Black Power thrust or it too would be targeted and destroyed.)

Frustrated and discouraged by external persecution and internal dissention, surviving militants contributed to the belief that the movement—if it survived at all after the early seventies—had suffered the loss of its "revolutionary initiative." There was said to be a "lull" in the drive for liberation. As Amiri Baraka noted in 1978, Black Power had "reached a valley as opposed to its 1960s peaks."[38] In a sense, this was true. Deeply shaken by recent events, movement stalwarts entered into a period of introspection and self-criticism. Whether attempting to shore up and rehabilitate old beliefs, defend new ones, or castigate those of their ideological adversaries, bruised and battered Black Power advocates tended to accentuate the negative.

Many commentaries bordered on self-flagellation. It was said that the sixties activists had been "novice[s] in search of blackness," young people just out of adolescence who exhibited a marked tendency toward hero worship and the flexing of muscles. They fell victim to "ego masturbation" and "cultism," dissipated their energies in endless internecine strife, and failed to translate sexy slogans into substantive programs. Better known for disrupting meetings than for controlling constituencies, the militants either became slaves to "secondhand Marxism" or thought themselves so black and bad that *everything* was considered some kind of conspiracy or "jiveass racist shuck." As a result, said the self-critics, the revolution became ensnared in a web of illusion.[39]

This uninspiring view of the movement, as well as the related notion that white American police power had succeeded in destroying it, served to promote both an overly narrow definition of the empowerment concept and an underestimation of its tenacity. In truth, Black Power was bigger than any single individual or targeted "hate" group—bigger even than black nationalism. It was generated and sustained by something far more substantial than political rhetoric. Indeed, fixation on the "political" hinders appreciation of the movement's cultural manifestations and unnecessarily obscures black culture's role in promoting the psychological well-being of the Afro-American people. As even Black Power's most severe critics recognized, the movement raised both individual and group expectations, made black folk feel good about themselves, and steered them away from "cultural homicide."[40] Although dulled by the setbacks of the late sixties and early seventies, this energizing spirit was not deadened. As they had done so many times in the past, black Americans responded to oppression with their traditional ace in the hole, their soulful group culture.

Considerably less threatening to whites than the average well-armed guerrilla warrior, black culture nevertheless promoted resistance and survival during slavery, offered spiritual sustenance throughout the Segregation era, and provided a foundation and reference point for the early civil rights movement. Through various forms of cultural expression, the socially and economically disenfranchised of the Black Power years learned that they could define themselves without paying obeisance to whitey. Whether represented by subversive slave folktales or celebratory soul serenades, Afro-American culture was the central, irreducible, irreplaceable element in the ongoing struggle for psychological liberation and empowerment.

To their credit, a good number of those charged with evaluating the nature of the "lull" in the contemporary movement recognized that strength and staying power were inherent in black culture. They also understood that there was more to the militant ethic than fuzzy thinking and factionalism. It had a life span far longer than five or six years. Black Power, they said, was part of a determined revolt against white domination that had been in progress since 1619. Advancing in "greater and lesser circles" over time, the black freedom movement was an ongoing concern. The primary task given each new generation was to maintain hope and vision—to advance the collective to the next stage of the struggle.[41]

The odds seemed overwhelming and the revolutionary road was known to contain many twists and turns, but historical checks were not to be considered checkmates. Even during periods of "somber reassessment" there could be growth: rhetorical revisions, modifications of style, the testing of fresh ideas, and the tapping of new energy sources. Certainly, part of the larger black freedom movement's time-honored genius was that it couldn't be kept within predictable bounds.[42]

In this context, could the Black Panthers' increased commitment to getting out the vote and feeding the hungry be considered any less worthy than its mid-sixties approach to serving the needs of its constituents—or any less noble than "pluralist" community control efforts? Didn't Stokely Carmichael still perceive himself to be in the vanguard of a Black Power revolt after he set up shop in Guinea, changed his name to Kwame Ture and formed the All-African People's Revolutionary Party? Wasn't Amiri Baraka still talking about unity and self-definition following his ideological "conversion"? Might not some of the major players of the sixties simply be exchanging uniforms as they engaged new ideas or adapted to the altered circumstances of a new era? Certainly, unless one was wedded to a thoroughly inflexible conceptualization of Black Power thought, such changes conceivably could be considered signs of advancing maturity and proof that the activist camp still contained a few agile minds. As Bobby Rush, a one-time Panther deputy defense minister and newly elected Chicago alderman noted in 1983, "militancy is an important part of the maturation process." Rush would not disavow his radical past, but neither did he any longer feel it necessary to "stand in front of a crowd and incite people." His values hadn't changed, he said, just his methodology.[43]

While rightfully regretting tactical errors, squandered opportunities, and the loss of old comrades, true freedom fighters—those who had joined for the long haul—had many positive memories of what Bobby Seale called those "gallant times" spent in the quest for Black Power.[44] But what were the fruits of their endeavors? Did black activists advance the freedom struggle to a new plateau? Was theirs more a holding action against oppression? Or did the Black Power threat stimulate so much white backlash that it actually impeded racial progress?

While one may not wish to claim as much for the movement as did those sixties idealists who talked about the revolution as if it already were reality, neither should statements that Black Power produced only a "legacy of bitterness and dissension" be accepted without considerable skepticism.[45] The movement had tangible political and psychological effects and left a distinctive cachet on the American cultural landscape.

As sociologist Herbert H. Haines' study of the relationship between black radicals and the civil rights mainstream has demonstrated, the militants created a "positive radical flank effect" in '60s political affairs. Black Power generated a crisis in American institutions which made the legislative agenda of "polite, 'realistic,' and businesslike" mainstream organizations more attractive to societal decision-makers. Instead of hindering the cause of civil rights, these more strident voices enhanced the moderates' bargaining position.[46]

Black Power energized and educated black Americans, introducing many to the concept of political pluralism. It spurred new interest in African liberation struggles and the plight of the powerless worldwide. Newly sensitized to the political nature of oppression, Black Power converts set out to remedy the situation by forming numerous political-action caucuses and grass roots community associations. These, in turn, served as often-utilized models for the various ethnic, gender, and class consciousness movements of the seventies and eighties.

While the Black Power movement didn't solve all—or even most—of Afro-America's "political" problems, it did provide a useful mechanism for dealing with those of a psychological nature. Movement leaders never were as successful in winning power for the people as they were in convincing people that they had sufficient power within themselves to escape "the prison of self-deprecation."[47] As they abandoned processed hair and white folks' ways, the Black Power generation accepted racial difference and rejoiced in it. By decolonizing their minds, cultivating feelings of racial solidarity, and contrasting their world with that of the oppressor, black Americans came to understand themselves better. In developing a greater pride in blackness than had any generation before them, the sixties activists discovered a deep well of untapped energy which enabled ordinary people to do extraordinary things.

The process of self-discovery that took place during the Black Power era remained a special part of the activists' lives in later years. As several recent studies have shown, the notion of a generational "sell-out" is wildly overblown.[48] Vital increments of racial consciousness and identity won in epic battles with whitey were not readily abandoned or exchanged for the confining mental structures of an earlier day. In fact, this empowering gift of psychological freedom was passed on to the next generation. As one of the respondents in Bob Blauner's longitudinal oral history of U.S. race relations noted in 1986, the movement's emphasis on black pride has had a lasting effect: "I don't think it's 'Black is beautiful' [anymore]. It's 'I am beautiful and I'm black,'" he said. "It's not the symbolic thing, the afro, power sign. . . . That phase is over and it succeeded. My children feel better about theirselves and they know that they're black."[49] The Black Power movement brought irrevocable changes in the Afro-Americans' attitudes both about themselves and about the legitimacy of the white world order.

Black Power also raised substantive issues in aesthetics, revised prevailing notions about the "function" of art, and stimulated creativity by giving artists and writers a central role in the revolution. Black Arts movement participants exposed codified (as well as unwritten) conventions, myths, and stereotypes. They rejected white definitions of acsthetic beauty, crafting alternative formulations that were far more relevant to black people. As creative artists developed new characterizations and themes, their fictional works became agencies of spiritual renewal—metaphors for actual lifestyle transformations. Black Power cultural expression convinced many of the need to reform the nation's value system. It encouraged black unity and forever consigned both black invisibility and Little Black Sambo to oblivion.

A primary conduit of the militants' message during Black Power years, cultural expression continues to provide essential education for those who seek to take the black freedom struggle to its next stage. Even if certain of its achievements are, today, either ignored or taken for granted, Black Power's unconquerable spirit and its message of self-definition are visible to all who take the time to familiarize themselves with contemporary Afro-American culture. However "modern" in appearance, much of black cultural expression remains grounded in traditional folkways and resonates with themes introduced by movement writers. From the pan-Afrocentric studies of Ivan Van Sertima and Molefi Asante to the increasingly widespread celebration of Kwanzaa;[50] from black versions of Trivial Pursuit to Captain Africa comics;[51] from the Cosby Kids and other pluralistic "cultural mulattoes" of the "New Black Aesthetic" movement to the world-heavy social realism and rage of hardcore hip-hopping rappers, contemporary black culture continues to reveal its sixties roots.[52]

While indelibly stamping their own identity on the material—and thereby engaging in a bit of spunky generational rebellion—today's writers and performers recognize that they owe a great deal to Black

Power's explosion of cultural orthodoxy. They also know, as did their parents, that the mainstream will go to almost any length to synthesize or appropriate what Afro-America generates spontaneously within the racial soul. This can be seen in the labored musical copy-catting of the Beastie Boys, Vanilla Ice, and New Kids on the Block;[53] in Republican National Committee chairman Lee Atwater's attempt to add some ooh-poo-pah-doo to George Bush's 1989 inaugural week celebration with a three-and-a-half hour rhythm and blues/photo opportunity raveup;[54] and in pop vocalist Madonna Ciccone's wide-eyed assertion that "if being black is synonymous with having soul, then, yes, I feel that I am."[55]

As a movement in and of culture, Black Power was itself an art form. In the words of Lerone Bennett, Jr., it "made everything political and everything cultural."[56] Influencing the lives and aspirations of everyday people in ways unrevealed by membership rosters and public opinion polls, Black Power motivated Afro-Americans of the sixties and early seventies to redefine themselves. In the process, it forced a reappraisal of American social and cultural values. Those dismayed that the activists' efforts to reshape the world have not been more visibly translated into economic and political gains need not, however, rest content with the progress that has been made. Drawing upon the Black Power generation's vast catalogue of experiences, they can restate its foundational principles, update its operational agenda, and attempt to resurrect something of its idealism and commitment. They can try to learn from its mistakes. Then, armed with the culture-borne wisdom of the ages, they too can set out to expand the boundaries of black freedom. If black empowerment truly does advance in stages, they will be able to say—with increasing confidence—that black America's redemption is "in the wind." Remembering Malcolm X's description of his father quoting from Marcus Garvey, they will tell others "it is coming." One day, "like a storm," it will be here.

Notes

Introduction

1. "Death of a Desperado," *Newsweek*, 8 March 1965, 24.

2. *The End of White World Supremacy: Four Speeches by Malcolm X*, ed. Imam Benjamin Karim (New York: Seaver, 1971), 131–32.

3. Malcolm X, "Malcolm X at Yale," in *When the Word is Given . . .* , ed. Louis E. Lomax (New York: New American Library, 1964), 162–63.

4. H. Rap Brown, *Die Nigger Die!* (New York: Dial, 1969), 85.

5. Rolland Snellings, "Malcolm X: as International Statesman," *Liberator* 6 (February 1966): 6–7.

6. Huey P. Newton, *Revolutionary Suicide* (New York: Ballantine, 1974), 125; Lee Lockwood, *Conversation with Eldridge Cleaver: Algiers* (New York: McGraw-Hill, 1970), 86.

7. *Eldridge Cleaver: Post-Prison Writings and Speeches*, ed. Robert Scheer (New York: Random House, 1969), 38.

8. James Baldwin, *No Name in the Street* (New York: Dial, 1972), 119–20; Len Holt, "Malcolm X: The Mirror," *Liberator* 6 (February 1966): 4.

9. Peter Goldman, "Malcolm X: Witness for the Prosecution," in *Black Leaders of the Twentieth Century*, ed. John Hope Franklin and August Meier (Urbana: University of Illinois Press, 1982), 321.

10. *The Autobiography of Malcolm X* (New York: Grove, 1966), 339.

11. *Malcolm X on Afro-American History* (New York: Pathfinder, 1970), 44; Malcolm X, *White World Supremacy*, 133–34.

12. *Malcolm X Speaks: Selected Speeches and Statements*, ed. George Breitman (New York: Grove, 1966), 5–6, 38–40.

13. Stokely Carmichael, "Pan-Africanism—Land and Power," *Black Scholar* 1 (November 1969): 40.

14. George Breitman, ed. *By Any Means Necessary: Speeches, Interviews and a Letter by Malcolm X* (New York: Pathfinder, 1970), 53–56.

15. Ibid., 98, 117, 146; Malcolm X, *Afro-American History*, 16; Lawrence P.

Neal, "Malcolm and the Conscience of Black America," *Liberator* 6 (February 1966): 11.

16. Baldwin, *No Name*, 99. The screenplay was published as *One Day, When I Was Lost* (New York: Dial, 1973).

17. Malcolm X, *Autobiography*, 99.

18. N. R. Davidson, Jr., *El Hajj Malik*, in *New Plays from the Black Theatre*, ed. Ed Bullins (New York: Bantam, 1969), 202–03; LeRoi Jones, *The Death of Malcolm X*, in Bullins, *New Plays*, 13; William Wellington Mackey, *Requiem for Brother X*, in *Black Drama Anthology*, ed. Woodie King and Ron Milner (New York: New American Library, 1972), 336.

19. Poems quoted here were written by Etheridge Knight, Margaret Burroughs, Christine C. Johnson, Robert Hayden, Don L. Lee, Ted Joans, and Bobb Hamilton and collected in *For Malcolm: Poems on the Life and the Death of Malcolm X*, ed. Dudley Randall and Margaret Burroughs (Detroit: Broadside, 1969).

20. Breitman, *By Any Means*, 159–60; Malcolm X, *Two Speeches by Malcolm X* (New York: Pathfinder, 1965), 26.

21. The most comprehensive treatments of Malcolm X's legacy are Peter Goldman, *The Death and Life of Malcolm X* (Urbana: University of Illinois Press, 1979) and Bruce Perry, *Malcolm: The Life of a Man Who Changed Black America* (Barrytown, New York: Station Hill, 1991).

Chapter One

1. " 'Black Power' Must Be Defined," *Life*, 22 July 1966, 4; "At the Breaking Point," *Time*, 15 July 1966, 16; "The New Racism," *Time*, 1 July 1966, 11; Frank S. Meyer, "The Negro Revolution—A New Phase," *National Review*, 4 October 1966, 998; " 'Black Power': Politics of Frustration," *Newsweek*, 11 July 1966, 26; "Black Power: Road to Disaster?," *Newsweek*, 22 August 1966, 36.

2. "New Racism," 11.

3. Bobby Seale, "Free Huey," in *Rhetoric of Black Revolution*, ed. Arthur L. Smith (Boston: Allyn and Bacon, 1969), 177–78.

4. Arnold Hano, "The Black Rebel Who 'Whitelists' the Olympics," *New York Times Magazine*, 12 May 1968, 50; H. Rap Brown, *Die Nigger Die!* (New York: Dial, 1969), 120–21, 136–37; Fred C. Shapiro, "The Successor to Floyd McKissick May Not Be So Reasonable," *New York Times Magazine*, 1 October 1967, 103.

5. *The Autobiography of Malcolm X* (New York: Grove, 1966), 243.

6. *Report of the National Advisory Commission on Civil Disorders* (Washington, D.C.: U.S. Government Printing Office, 1968), 208.

7. For a more detailed critique of mainstream media coverage, see Carolyn Martindale, *The White Press and Black America* (Westport: Greenwood, 1986).

8. Peter Goldman, "Malcolm X: Witness for the Prosecution," in *Black Leaders of the Twentieth Century*, ed. John Hope Franklin and August Meier (Urbana: University of Illinois Press, 1982), 317.

9. Roger Beardwood, "A Fortune Study of the New Negro Mood," *Fortune* 77 (January 1968): 148; *The Harris Survey Yearbook of Public Opinion, 1970* (New York: Louis Harris and Associates, 1971), 256; "New Findings—Negro Attitudes on Racial Issues," *U.S. News & World Report*, 5 August 1968, 10.

10. Daniel U. Levine, Norman S. Fiddmont, Robert S. Stephenson, and Charles Wilkinson, "Differences Between Black Youth Who Support the Black Panthers and the NAACP," *Journal of Negro Education* 42 (Winter 1973): 22; Peter Goldman, *Report from Black America* (New York: Simon and Schuster, 1971), 100; "The Black Mood: More Militant, More Hopeful, More Determined," *Time*, 6 April 1970, 28; *Harris Survey, 1970*, 222; Joel D. Aberbach and Jack L. Walker, "The Meanings of Black Power: A Comparison of White and Black Interpretations of a Political Slogan," *American Political Science Review* 64 (June 1970): 383; Gary T. Marx, *Protest and Prejudice: A Study of Belief in the Black Community* (New York: Harper & Row, 1969), 217–18; William Brink and Louis Harris, *Black and White: A Study of U.S. Racial Attitudes Today* (New York: Simon and Schuster, 1967), 252, 254.

11. William McCord, John Howard, Bernard Friedberg, and Edwin Harwood, *Life Styles in the Black Ghetto* (New York: W. W. Norton, 1969), 102–03, 275, 283; Russell Sackett, "Plotting a War on 'Whitey'," *Life*, 10 June 1966, 106–07.

12. Angus Campbell and Howard Schuman, *Racial Attitudes in Fifteen American Cities* (Ann Arbor: Survey Research Center, Institute for Social Research, University of Michigan, 1968), 20; *Report of the National Advisory Commission*, 333; *Harris Survey, 1970*, 262.

13. "Black Mood," 28.

14. Goldman, *Report*, 156, 205, 263; Marx, *Protest and Prejudice*, 228.

15. Goldman, *Report*, 261, 264; Jan E. Dizard, "Black Identity, Social Class, and Black Power," *Psychiatry* 33 (May 1970): 199–200; Campbell and Schuman, *Racial Attitudes*, 19.

16. For more detailed discussions of the problems involved with conducting survey research on urban black respondents, see Kenneth B. Clark, *Dark Ghetto: Dilemmas of Social Power* (New York: Harper & Row, 1967), xiii–xxv; Robert Blauner and David Wellman, "Toward the Decolonization of Social Research," in *The Death of White Sociology*, ed. Joyce A. Ladner (New York: Vintage, 1973), 310–30; Ethel Sawyer, "Methodological Problems in Studying So-Called 'Deviant' Communities," in Ladner, *Death*, 361–79; Carl O. Word, "Crosscultural Methods for Survey Research in Black Urban Areas," *Journal of Black Psychology* 3 (February 1977): 72–87.

17. For a sampling of the studies employing these testing instruments, see Brian D. Stenfors and John J. Woodmansee, "A Scale of Black Power Sentiment," *Psychological Reports* 22 (June 1968): 802; John J. Woodmansee and Richard D. Tucker, "A Scale of Black Separatism," *Psychological Reports* 27 (December 1970): 855–58; Howard Schuman and Shirley Hatchett, *Black Racial Attitudes: Trends and Complexities* (Ann Arbor: Survey Research Center, Institute for Social Research, University of Michigan, 1974); Henry A. Banks, "Black Consciousness: A Student Survey," *Black Scholar* 2 (September 1970): 46–49; Elise E. Lessing and Susan W. Zagorin, "Black Power Ideology and College Students' Attitudes Toward Their Own and Other Racial Groups," *Journal of Personality and Social Psychology* 21 (January 1972): 61–73; Murray Gruber, "Four Types of Black Protest: A Study," *Social Work* 18 (January 1973): 42–51.

18. Aberbach and Walker, "Meanings of Black Power," 370–73, 387.

19. Stokely Carmichael, *Stokely Speaks: Black Power Back to Pan-*

Africanism (New York: Vintage, 1971), 190; "Black Power: The Widening Dialogue," *New South* 21 (Summer 1966): 69.

20. Stokely Carmichael and Charles V. Hamilton, *Black Power: The Politics of Liberation in America* (New York: Random House, 1967), 52; Nathan Hare, "How White Power Whitewashes Black Power," in *The Black Power Revolt*, ed. Floyd B. Barbour (Boston: Porter Sargent, 1968); John O. Killens et al., "Black Power: Its Meaning and Measure," *Negro Digest* 16 (November 1966): 34. Robert L. Scott, "Justifying Violence: The Rhetoric of Militant Black Power," in *The Rhetoric of Black Power*, ed. Robert L. Scott and Wayne Brockriede (New York: Harper & Row, 1969), 134–40.

21. Stokely Carmichael, "What We Want," *New York Review of Books*, 22 September 1966, 6, 8; "In Defense of Self Defense: An Exclusive Interview with Minister of Defense, Huey P. Newton," in *Black Nationalism in America*, ed. John H. Bracey, Jr., August Meier, Elliott Rudwick (Indianapolis: Bobbs-Merrill, 1970), 536.

22. C. E. Wilson, "Black Power and the Myth of Black Racism," *Liberation* 11 (September 1966): 27.

23. Seale, "Free Huey," 180–81.

24. Carmichael and Hamilton, *Black Power*, 47, 167; Bobby Seale, *Seize the Time: The Story of the Black Panther Party and Huey P. Newton* (New York: Random House, 1970), 71, 218; George L. Jackson, *Blood in My Eye* (New York: Random House, 1972), 111; Brown, *Die Nigger*, 121, 124.

25. *Eldridge Cleaver: Post-Prison Writings and Speeches*, ed. Robert Scheer (New York: Random House, 1969), 142.

26. Carmichael, *Stokely Speaks*, 204.

27. Julius Lester, *Look Out, Whitey! Black Power's Gon' Get Your Mama!* (New York: Grove, 1969), 97.

28. Carmichael, "What We Want," 5; Killens, "Meaning and Measure," 92; Carmichael, *Stokely Speaks*, 57; Donald Jackson, "Unite or Perish," *Liberator* 7 (February 1967): 17; Hare, "Whitewashes," 183.

29. Aberbach and Walker, "Meanings of Black Power," 372, 387.

30. Franklin Florence, "The Meaning of Black Power," in Smith, *Rhetoric*, 164.

31. Huey P. Newton, *To Die for the People: The Writings of Huey P. Newton* (New York: Vintage, 1972), 101.

32. For additional commentary on all three ideologies as they relate to black protest thought of the late '60s, see especially Solomon P. Gethers, "Black Power: Three Years Later," *Negro Digest* 19 (December 1969): 4–10, 69–81; Solomon P. Gethers, "Black Nationalism and Human Liberation," *Black Scholar* 1 (May 1970): 43–50.

33. Representative encapsulations of these concepts may be found in Carmichael and Hamilton *Black Power*, 44–47; Richard C. Tolbert, "A New Brand of Black Nationalism," *Negro Digest* 16 (August 1967): 20–23.

34. Ronald Walters, "African-American Nationalism: A Unifying Ideology," *Black World* 22 (October 1973): 26.

35. Joyce Ladner, "What 'Black Power' Means to Negroes in Mississippi," *Trans-Action* 5 (November 1967): 9–10; Carmichael and Hamilton, *Black Power*, 37–38; Cleaver, *Post-Prison Writings*, 54–56; Lester, *Look Out*, 100;

Robert S. Browne, "The Case for Two Americas—One Black, One White," *New York Times Magazine*, 11 August 1968, 50.

36. "Huey Newton Talks to the Movement About the Black Panther Party, Cultural Nationalism, SNCC, Liberals and White Revolutionaries," in *The Black Panthers Speak*, ed. Philip S. Foner (Philadelphia: J. B. Lippincott, 1970), 61.

37. Vincent Harding, "Black Radicalism: The Road from Montgomery," in *Dissent: Explorations in the History of American Radicalism*," ed. Alfred F. Young (DeKalb: Northern Illinois University Press, 1968), 342.

38. Stokely Carmichael, "Toward Black Liberation," *Massachusetts Review* 7 (Autumn 1966): 639.

39. For representative statements affirming the need for black cultural self-definition, see James Turner, "The Sociology of Black Nationalism," *Black Scholar* 1 (December 1969): 18–27; Carmichael and Hamilton, *Black Power*, 34–39; Killens, "Meaning and Measure," 33; Calvin C. Hernton, *Coming Together: Black Power, White Hatred and Sexual Hang-Ups* (New York: Random House, 1971), 33–37; Alvin F. Poussaint, "A Psychiatrist Looks at Black Power," *Ebony* 24 (March 1969): 142.

Chapter Two

1. John A. Williams, *Flashbacks: A Twenty-Year Diary of Article Writing*, (Garden City, New York: Anchor/Doubleday, 1973), 34–36.

2. John A. Williams, *This Is My Country Too* (New York: New American Library, 1966), 26, 35, 37, 39, 57, 98.

3. Ibid., 48–49, 59, 63, 66–67, 96–97, 114, 132.

4. Ibid., 31, 56, 80, 129, 153.

5. Ibid., 41, 75, 156–57.

6. Cleveland Sellers, *The River of No Return: The Autobiography of a Black Militant and the Life and Death of SNCC* (New York: William Morrow, 1973), 166–67.

7. Paul Good, "A White Look at Black Power," *Nation*, 8 August 1966, 113; Paul Good, "The Meredith March," *New South* 21 (Summer 1966): 5.

8. James H. Meredith, "Big Changes are Coming," *Saturday Evening Post*, 13 August 1966, 24.

9. Stephen B. Oates, *Let the Trumpet Sound: The Life of Martin Luther King, Jr.* (New York: New American Library, 1985), 386–387; Sellers, *River*, 168; Joyce Ladner, "What 'Black Power' Means to Negroes in Mississippi," *Trans-action* 5 (November 1967): 8; Martin Luther King, Jr., *Where Do We Go From Here: Chaos or Community?* (New York: Bantam, 1968), 34–35.

10. Good, "Meredith," 15; Clayborne Carson, *In Struggle: SNCC and the Black Awakening of the 1960s* (Cambridge: Harvard University Press, 1981), 210–11; Oates, *King*, 390.

11. Robert L. Scott and Wayne Brockriede, "Hubert Humphrey Faces the 'Black Power' Issue," *Speaker and Gavel* 4 (November 1966): 11; Robert H. Brisbane, *Black Activism: Racial Revolution in the United States, 1954–1970* (Valley Forge, Pennsylvania: Judson, 1974), 139–40; Adam Clayton Powell, "Can There Any Good Thing Come Out of Nazareth?" in *Rhetoric of Black Revolution*, ed. Arthur L. Smith (Boston: Allyn and Bacon, 1969), 154–60; Milton

Viorst, *Fire in the Streets: America in the 1960s* (New York: Simon and Schuster, 1979), 373–74; James Forman, *The Making of Black Revolutionaries* (New York: Macmillan, 1972), 456; King, *Where Do We Go*, 36.

12. Richard Wright, *Black Power: A Record of Reactions in a Land of Pathos* (New York: Harper & Brothers, 1954); Lerone Bennett, Jr., "Black Power," *Ebony* 21 (November 1965): 28–29, 32, 34–36, 38; Carl T. Rowan, "Has Paul Robeson Betrayed the Negro?" *Ebony* 12 (October 1957): 41.

13. *By Any Means Necessary: Speeches, Interviews and a Letter by Malcolm X*, ed. George Breitman (New York: Pathfinder, 1970), 64; *Malcolm X Speaks: Selected Speeches and Statements*, ed. George Breitman (New York: Grove, 1966), 150.

14. Louis E. Lomax, *The Negro Revolt* (New York: Harper & Row, 1971), 325–26.

15. William Hamilton, *Address to the Fourth Annual Convention of the Free People of Color of the United States* (New York: S. W. Benedict, 1834), 4; Howard H. Bell, "Expressions of Negro Militancy in the North, 1840–1860," *Journal of Negro History* 45 (January 1960): 11; Thomas S. Sidney, "William Whipper's Letters: No. II," *Colored American*, 20 February 1841, 1; Thomas S. Sidney, "William Whipper's Letters: No. III," *Colored American*, 6 March 1841, 1.

16. See, for example, R. B. Lewis, *Light and Truth; Collected from the Bible and Ancient and Modern History, Containing the Universal History of the Colored and the Indian Race, From the Creation of the World to the Present Time* (Boston: Benjamin F. Roberts, 1844); Hosea Easton, *A Treatise on the Intellectual Character, and Civil and Political Condition of the Colored People of the U. States; and the Prejudice Exercised Towards Them* (Boston: Isaac Knapp, 1837).

17. Henry Highland Garnet, "The Past and the Present Condition and the Destiny of the Colored Race, Troy, 1848," in Earl Ofari, *"Let Your Motto Be Resistance": The Life and Thought of Henry Highland Garnet* (Boston: Beacon, 1972), 166.

18. On pre-Civil War pan-Africanism, see Floyd J. Miller, *The Search for a Black Nationality: Black Emigration and Colonization, 1787–1863* (Urbana: University of Illinois Press, 1975); Cyril E. Griffith, *The African Dream: Martin R. Delany and the Emergence of Pan-African Thought* (University Park: Pennsylvania State University Press, 1975); Joel Schor, *Henry Highland Garnet: A Voice of Black Radicalism in the Nineteenth Century* (Westport, Connecticut: Greenwood, 1977); On Turner, see Edwin S. Redkey, *Black Exodus: Black Nationalist Movements, 1890–1910* (New Haven: Yale University Press, 1969); On Garvey, see E. David Cronon, *Black Moses: The Story of Marcus Garvey and the Universal Negro Improvement Association* (Madison: University of Wisconsin Press, 1955); Tony Martin, *Race First: The Ideological and Organizational Struggles of Marcus Garvey and the Universal Negro Improvement Association* (Westport, Connecticut: Greenwood, 1976); Judith Stein, *The World of Marcus Garvey: Race and Class in Modern Society* (Baton Rouge: Louisiana State University Press, 1986).

19. On slaves "flying" to Africa, see Work Projects Administration, Savannah Unit, Georgia Writers' Project, *Drums and Shadows: Survival Studies Among the Georgia Coastal Negroes* (Garden City, New York: Doubleday, 1972), 16, 26,

74, 101–02, 143; John Bennett, *The Doctor to the Dead: Grotesque Legends & Folk Tales of Old Charleston* (New York: Rinehart, 1946), 139–42. On the variants of twentieth-century pan-Africanism, see Robert G. Weisbord, *Ebony Kinship: Africa, Africans, and the Afro-American* (Westport, Connecticut: Greenwood, 1973); On Malcolm X's pan-Africanist heritage, see *The Autobiography of Malcolm X* (New York: Grove, 1966), 1–7.

20. Booker T. Washington, "Boley, A Negro Town in the West," *Outlook*, 4 January 1908, 31. On Afro-American emigration to the Plains States, see Nell Irvin Painter, *Exodusters: Black Migration to Kansas after Reconstruction* (New York: Alfred A. Knopf, 1976); Robert G. Athearn, *In Search of Canaan: Black Migration to Kansas, 1879–80* (Lawrence: Regents Press of Kansas, 1978); Norman L. Crockett, *The Black Towns* (Lawrence: Regents Press of Kansas, 1979).

21. On Briggs and the pan-Africanist-oriented ABB, see "Racial and Radical: Cyril V. Briggs, the *Crusader* Magazine, and the African Blood Brotherhood, 1918–1922," in *The Crusader*, ed. Robert A. Hill (New York: Garland, 1987), 1: v–lxvi; "Cyril V. Briggs," in *The Marcus Garvey and Universal Negro Improvement Association Papers*, ed. Robert A. Hill (Berkeley: University of California Press, 1983), 1: 521–27; Theodore G. Vincent, *Black Power and the Garvey Movement* (Berkeley: Ramparts Press, 1972), 74–85. On the National Movement for the Establishment of a Forty-Ninth State, see Raymond L. Hall, *Black Separatism in the United States* (Hanover, New Hampshire: University Press of New England, 1978), 86. On the Communists and black self-determination, see James S. Allen, *The Negro Question in the United States* (New York: International Publishers, 1936); Wilson Record, *The Negro and the Communist Party* (Chapel Hill: University of North Carolina Press, 1951), 54–119; Theodore Draper, *American Communism and Soviet Russia: The Formative Period* (New York: Viking, 1960), 342–56; Harvey Klehr and William Tompson, "Self-Determination in the Black Belt: Origins of a Communist Policy," *Labor History* 30 (Summer 1989): 354–66; John W. Van Zanten, "Communist Theory and the Negro Question," *Review of Politics* 29 (October 1967): 435–56.

22. "Declaration of Sentiments of the Colored Citizens of Boston on the Fugitive Slave Bill," *Liberator*, 11 October 1850, 162; Henry Highland Garnet, *An Address to the Slaves of the United States of America* (New York: Arno Press and the New York Times, 1969), 96; Hollis R. Lynch, *Edward Wilmot Blyden: Pan-Negro Patriot, 1832–1912* (London: Oxford University Press, 1967), 12; David Walker, *Walker's Appeal in Four Articles* (New York: Arno Press and the New York Times, 1969), 37; Bell, "Negro Militancy," 14–15; *Proceedings of the National Convention of Colored People* (Troy, New York: J. C. Kneeland, 1847), 17.

23. Garnet, *Address*, 95–96; Frederick Douglass, "The Heroic Slave," *Frederick Douglass' Paper*, 4–25 March 1853; Benjamin Quarles, ed., *Blacks on John Brown* (Urbana: University of Illinois Press, 1972), 11–44.

24. "Fugitive Slave Convention," *National Anti-Slavery Standard*, 5 September 1850, 58.

25. Roy Reed, "The Deacons, Too, Ride by Night," *New York Times Magazine*, 15 August 1965, 20. For background on these black self-defense initiatives, see Robert F. Williams, *Negroes With Guns* (New York: Marzani & Munsell,

1962); Robert Carl Cohen, *Black Crusader: A Biography of Robert Franklin Williams* (Secaucus, New Jersey: Lyle Stuart, 1972); "The Deacons," *Newsweek*, 2 August 1965, 28–29; "The Deacons Go North," *Newsweek*, 2 May 1966, 20–21; "The Deacons—and Their Impact," *National Guardian*, 4 September 1965, 4–5; Howell Raines, *My Soul is Rested: Movement Days in the Deep South Remembered* (New York: Penguin, 1983), 416–23.

26. Lerone Bennett, Jr., "What's in a Name?: Negro vs. Afro-American vs. Black," *Ebony* 23 (November 1967): 48; "The Boston Massacre, March 5, 1770: Commemorative Festival in Faneuil Hall," *Liberator*, 12 March 1858, 42.

27. Martin Robison Delany, *The Condition, Elevation, Emigration, and Destiny of the Colored People of the United States* (New York: Arno Press and the New York Times, 1969), 8, 10; Joseph C. Holly, "Injustice—not Law," in *Freedom's Offering, A Collection of Poems* (Rochester: Charles H. McDonnell, 1853), 27; Frances Ellen Watkins, "Bible Defense of Slavery," in *Poems on Miscellaneous Subjects* (Philadelphia: Merrihew & Thompson, 1857), 9; Watkins, "Eliza Harris," in *Poems*, 11; James M. Whitfield, "America," in *Early Black American Poets*, ed. William H. Robinson, Jr. (Dubuque: Wm. C. Brown, 1969), 40.

28. W. E. B. DuBois, "The National Emancipation Exposition," *Crisis* 7 (November 1913): 339–41.

29. Langston Hughes, *Don't You Want To Be Free?*, in *Black Theater, U.S.A.: Forty-Five Plays by Black Americans, 1847–1974*, ed. James V. Hatch and Ted Shine (New York: Free Press, 1974), 263.

30. On the Harlem Renaissance, see Alain Locke, ed., *The New Negro* (New York: Albert & Charles Boni, 1925); Nathan Irvin Huggins, *Harlem Renaissance* (New York: Oxford University Press, 1971); Margaret Perry, *Silence to the Drums: A Survey of the Literature of the Harlem Renaissance* (Westport, Connecticut: Greenwood, 1976); David Levering Lewis, *When Harlem Was In Vogue* (New York: Alfred A. Knopf, 1981).

31. Alain Locke, "Self-Criticism: The Third Dimension in Culture," *Phylon* 11 (December 1950): 391; W. E. Burghardt DuBois, *The Souls of Black Folk: Essays and Sketches* (Greenwich, Connecticut: Fawcett, 1961), 16–17; Langston Hughes, "The Negro Artist and the Racial Mountain," *Nation*, 23 June 1926, 692; James Weldon Johnson, "The Dilemma of the Negro Author," *American Mercury* 15 (December 1928): 481.

32. DuBois, *Souls*, 17.

33. On the depression-era "Don't-Buy-Where-You-Can't-Work" campaigns, see Claude McKay, *Harlem: Negro Metropolis* (New York: Harcourt, Brace, Jovanovich, 1968), 185–205; August Meier and Elliott Rudwick, "The Origins of Nonviolent Direct Action in Afro-American Protest: A Note on Historical Discontinuities," in *Along the Color Line: Explorations in the Black Experience*, ed. August Meier and Elliott Rudwick (Urbana: University of Illinois Press, 1976), 314–32; William Muraskin, "The Harlem Boycott of 1934: Black Nationalism and the Rise of Labor-Union Consciousness," *Labor History* 13 (Summer 1972): 361–73.

34. On MOWM, see Herbert Garfinkel, *When Negroes March: The March on Washington Movement in the Organizational Politics for FEPC* (Glencoe, Illi-

nois: Free Press, 1959); Jervis Anderson, *A. Philip Randolph: A Biographical Portrait* (New York: Harcourt, Brace, Jovanovich, 1973), 241–67.

35. On the early political movements, see Hanes Walton, Jr., *Black Political Parties: An Historical and Political Analysis* (New York: Free Press, 1972).

36. A. Philip Randolph, "Why Should We March?" *Survey Graphic* 31 (November 1942): 489.

37. Raymond Wolters, *The New Negro on Campus: Black College Rebellions of the 1920s* (Princeton: Princeton University Press, 1975), 340–48.

38. For an overview and critique of competing sociological theories seeking to explain the emergence of social movements, see Doug McAdam, *Political Process and the Development of Black Insurgency, 1930–1970* (Chicago: University of Chicago Press, 1982), 5–64.

39. John Hope Franklin, *From Slavery to Freedom: A History of Negro Americans* (New York: Alfred A. Knopf, 1980), 481, 484–85, 487; August Meier and Elliott Rudwick, *From Plantation to Ghetto*, (New York: Hill and Wang, 1976), 287, 294–95, 298, 300, 304–05, 308; Benjamin Quarles, *The Negro in the Making of America* (New York: Macmillan, 1987), 273; Mary Frances Berry and John W. Blassingame, *Long Memory: The Black Experience in America* (New York: Oxford University Press, 1982), 384–85, 387, 418.

40. On the Younge murder, see James Forman, *Sammy Younge, Jr.: The First Black College Student to Die in the Black Liberation Movement* (New York: Grove, 1968), Robert J. Norrell, *Reaping the Whirlwind. The Civil Rights Movement in Tuskegee* (New York: Alfred A. Knopf, 1985), 179–84.

41. On the MFDP, see Carson, *In Struggle*, 108–9, 123–28; Len Holt, *The Summer That Didn't End* (London: William Heinemann, 1966), 149–83; Forman, *Black Revolutionaries*, 386–96; Jean Smith, "I Learned to Feel Black," in *The Black Power Revolt*, ed. Floyd B. Barbour (Boston: Porter Sargent, 1968), 210–14.

42. On the Selma demonstrations, see David J. Garrow, *Protest at Selma: Martin Luther King, Jr., and the Voting Rights Act of 1965* (New Haven: Yale University Press, 1978); Charles E. Fager, *Selma, 1965* (New York: Charles Scribner's Sons, 1974).

43. Steven F. Lawson, *Black Ballots: Voting Rights in the South, 1944–1969* (New York: Columbia University Press, 1976), 330; Steven F. Lawson, *In Pursuit of Power: Southern Blacks and Electoral Politics, 1965–1982* (New York: Columbia University Press, 1985), 19, 21.

44. Lawson, *Black Ballots*, 333–36; Lawson, *In Pursuit*, 20–21; Pat Watters and Reese Cleghorn, *Climbing Jacob's Ladder: The Arrival of Negroes in Southern Politics* (New York: Harcourt, Brace & World, 1967), 262.

45. Garrow, *Protest at Selma*, 190, 192; Watters and Cleghorn, *Jacob's Ladder*, 263–64; Lawson, *In Pursuit*, 100.

46. James Boggs and Grace Boggs, "The City is the Black Man's Land," *Monthly Review* 17 (April 1966): 41; C. E. Wilson, "Can the Civil Rights Movement Overcome Defeat?" *Negro Digest* 16 (January 1967): 15; Stokely Carmichael, "Toward Black Liberation," *Massachusetts Review* 7 (Autumn 1966): 646, 649; Stokely Carmichael and Charles V. Hamilton, *Black Power: The Politics of Liberation in America* (New York: Random House, 1967), 50–51;

Larry Neal, "New Space/The Growth of Black Consciousness in the Sixties," in *The Black Seventies*, ed. Floyd B. Barbour (Boston: Porter Sargent, 1970), 10.

47. Carmichael and Hamilton, *Black Power*, 40–41, 53–55; Eldridge Cleaver, "The Land Question," *Ramparts* 6 (May 1968): 51; Charles V. Hamilton, "The Nationalist vs. the Integrationist," *New York Times Magazine*, 1 October 1972, 46.

48. Robert S. Browne, "The Case for Two Americas—One Black, One White," *New York Times Magazine*, 11 August 1968, 51, 56; Addison Gayle, Jr., "Existential Politics," *Liberator* 9 (January 1969): 5.

49. Wilson, "Civil Rights Movement," 23; Elijah Muhammad, *Message to the Blackman in America* (Chicago: Muhammad's Temple No. 2, 1965), 236; Meredith, "Big Changes," 26; Ossie Sykes, "The Dream World of Rev. King: A Critical Analysis, Part 2," *Liberator* 5 (March 1965): 12; John Oliver Killens, *Black Man's Burden* (New York: Trident, 1965), 112.

50. Julius Lester, *Look Out, Whitey! Black Power's Gon' Get Your Mama!* (New York: Grove, 1969), 105; Stokely Carmichael, *Stokely Speaks: Black Power Back to Pan-Africanism* (New York: Vintage, 1971), 56; Addison Gayle, Jr., "Nat Turner vs. Black Nationalists," *Liberator* 8 (February 1968), 6; Killens, *Black Man's Burden*, 108; Donald W. Jackson, "Violence is Necessary," *Liberator* 6 (March 1966): 7; Ossie Sykes, "The Dream World of Rev. King: A Critical Analysis, Part 1," *Liberator* 5 (February 1965), 13; LeRoi Jones, *Home: Social Essays* (New York: William Morrow, 1966), 144–154.

51. Jones, *Home*, 138–41; Malcolm X, *Malcolm X Speaks*, 134; Wilson, "Civil Rights Movement," 22.

52. Lester, *Look Out*, 98; "A Visit From the FBI," in *Malcolm X: The Man and His Times*, ed. John Henrik Clarke (New York: Collier, 1969), 201; Louis E. Lomax, *To Kill a Black Man* (Los Angeles: Holloway House, 1968), 79; Louis E. Lomax, *When the Word is Given. . .* (New York: New American Library, 1964), 74, 174; Muhammad, *Message*, 318; Buford Thompson, "Twilight of the God," *Liberator* 5 (May 1965): 4–6; Sykes, "Dream World, Part 2," 12–13.

53. Neal, "New Space," 20–21.

54. James Baldwin, Nathan Glazer, Sidney Hook, Gunnar Myrdal, "Liberalism and the Negro: A Round-Table Discussion," *Commentary* 37 (March 1964): 37; George Henderson, "The White Liberal: A Shadow of the Man," *Negro Digest* 15 (October 1966): 36–37; Lerone Bennett, Jr., *The Negro Mood* (New York: Ballantine Books, 1965), 120–21, 140, 147; Carmichael, *Stokely Speaks*, 171; Killens, *Black Man's Burden*, 19–20; John O. Killens, James Wechsler, Lorraine Hansberry, "The Black Revolution and the White Backlash," in *Black Protest*, ed. Joanne Grant (Greenwich, Conn.: Fawcett, 1974), 443; James Farmer, "Are White Liberals Obsolete in the Black Struggle?" *Progressive* 32 (January 1968): 15; Carmichael and Hamilton, *Black Power*, 62, 83; Lester, *Look Out*, 103, 105.

55. Stokely Carmichael, "Stokely Carmichael Explains Black Power to a Black Audience in Detroit," in *The Rhetoric of Black Power*, ed. Robert L. Scott and Wayne Brockriede (New York: Harper & Row, 1969), 91–92; Clayton Riley, "Black Nationalists and the Hippies," *Liberator* 7 (December 1967), 4–7; Nicholas von Hoffman, *We Are the People Our Parents Warned Us Against* (Chicago: Quadrangle, 1968), 124–125.

56. Askia Muhammad Toure, "Jihad!" *Negro Digest* 18 (July 1969): 11; Harold Cruse, *The Crisis of the Negro Intellectual* (New York: William Morrow, 1967), 92, 226, 263; Stokely Carmichael, "Pan-Africanism—Land and Power," *Black Scholar* 1 (November 1969): 39; Carmichael, *Stokely Speaks*, 121–22; Wanyandey Songha, "Marxism and the Black Revolution," *Liberator* 9 (September 1969): 16–17; Carlos Moore, *Were Marx and Engels White Racists?: The Prolet-Aryan Outlook of Marx and Engels* (Chicago: Institute of Positive Education, 1972), 7, 41–42; Haki R. Madhubuti, "The Latest Purge: The Attack on Black Nationalism and Pan-Afrikanism by the New Left, the Sons and Daughters of the Old Left," *Black Scholar* 6 (September 1974): 49–53; Ronald Walters, "A Response to Haki Madhubuti," *Black Scholar* 6 (October 1974): 47, 49.

57. Forman, *Black Revolutionaries*, 372.

58. Elizabeth Sutherland, ed. *Letters from Mississippi* (New York: New American Library, 1966), 18–19, 22–23; Tracy Sugarman, *Stranger at the Gates: A Summer in Mississippi*, (New York: Hill and Wang, 1966), 29–31; Sally Belfrage, *Freedom Summer* (Greenwich, Connecticut: Fawcett, 1966), 23–25, 48–49.

59. Holt, *Summer*, 37–38, 281–85; Sellers, *River*, 89.

60. Carson, *In Struggle*, 122; Holt, *Summer*, 207–10; Sutherland, *Letters*, 117.

61. Allen J. Matusow, "From Civil Rights to Black Power: The Case of SNCC, 1960–66," in *Twentieth-Century America: Recent Interpretations*, ed. Barton J. Bernstein and Allen J. Matusow (New York: Harcourt, Brace & World, 1969), 544; Carson, *In Struggle*, 110, 144.

62. Alvin F. Poussaint, "How the 'White Problem' Spawned 'Black Power,'" *Ebony* 22 (August 1967): 89–90, 92, 94; Carson, *In Struggle*, 151.

63. Holt, *Summer*, 322, 335; Howard Zinn, *SNCC: The New Abolitionists* (Boston: Beacon, 1965), 248–49.

64. Holt, *Summer*, 83, 111, 322; Mary Aickin Rothschild, *A Case of Black and White: Northern Volunteers and the Southern Freedom Summers, 1964–1965* (Westport, Connecticut: Greenwood, 1982), 102; Anne Moody, *Coming of Age in Mississippi* (New York: Dell, 1970), 372–73; Carson, *In Struggle*, 113, 120.

65. Roderick W. Pugh, "Psychological Aspects of the Black Revolution," in *Black Psychology*, ed. Reginald L. Jones (New York: Harper & Row, 1972), 345, 355; Charles W. Thomas, "On Being a Black Man," in *Boys No More: A Black Psychologist's View of Community*, ed. Charles W. Thomas (Beverly Hills: Glencoe, 1971), 117; William H. Grier and Price M. Cobbs, *The Jesus Bag* (New York: McGraw-Hill, 1971), 115; Charles W. Thomas, "Boys No More: Some Social-Psychological Aspects of the New Black Ethic," in Thomas, *Boys*, 20; Doris P. Mosby, "Toward a Theory of the Unique Personality of Blacks—a Psychocultural Assessment," in Jones, *Black Psychology*, 132.

66. Charles V. Hamilton, "How Black is Black?" in *The Black Revolution: An Ebony Special Issue* (Chicago: Johnson Publishing Company, 1970), 23–24; Thomas, "Black Man," 121; Charles W. Thomas and Shirley W. Thomas, "Something Borrowed, Something Black," in *Boys*, 110, 114.

67. James Turner, "The Sociology of Black Nationalism," *Black Scholar* 1 (December 1969): 18, 20, 22–23; Calvin C. Hernton, *Coming Together: Black*

Power, White Hatred and Sexual Hang-Ups (New York: Random House, 1971),
35; Sellers, *River,* 156–57.

68. Thomas and Thomas, "Something Borrowed," 102–3, 114; Nathan Hare,
"The Plasma of Thinking Black," *Negro Digest* 18 (January 1969): 13, 18;
Malcolm X, *Malcolm X Speaks,* 39–40.

69. The description of the "conversion experience" provided here is a com-
posite of the conceptualizations described in the following: William E. Cross, Jr.,
"The Negro-to-Black Conversion Experience: Toward a Psychology of Black
Liberation," *Black World* 20 (July 1971): 13–27; William S. Hall, William E.
Cross, Jr., and Roy Freedle, "Stages in the Development of Black Awareness: An
Exploratory Investigation," in Jones, *Black Psychology,* 156–65; Thomas and
Thomas, "Something Borrowed," 113–14; JoAnn E. Gardner and Charles W.
Thomas, "Different Strokes for Different Folks," *Psychology Today* 4 (Septem-
ber 1970): 78; William E. Cross, Jr., "The Thomas and Cross Models of Psycho-
logical Nigrescence: A Review," *Journal of Black Psychology* 5 (August 1978):
13–31.

70. The "blacker than thou" syndrome is discussed in Hamilton, "How
Black," 24–26; Grier and Cobbs, *Jesus Bag,* 116–25; Alvin F. Poussaint, *Why
Blacks Kill Blacks* (New York: Emerson Hall, 1972), 64–65; Hare, "Plasma," 18.

71. Carmichael, *Stokely Speaks,* 149–52.

72. For surveys of this literature, see Charles A. Valentine, *Culture and Poverty: Critique and Counter-Proposals* (Chicago: University of Chicago Press,
1968); John D. McCarthy and William L. Yancey, "Uncle Tom and Mr. Charlie:
Metaphysical Pathos in the Study of Racism and Personal Disorganization,"
American Journal of Sociology 76 (January 1971): 648–72.

73. Nathan Glazer and Daniel Patrick Moynihan, *Beyond the Melting Pot:
The Negroes, Puerto Ricans, Jews, Italians, and Irish of New York City* (Cam-
bridge: M.I.T. Press, 1964), 53; Gunnar Myrdal, *An American Dilemma: The
Negro Problem and Modern Democracy* (New York: Harper & Brothers, 1944),
928–30; Kenneth B. Clark, *Dark Ghetto: Dilemmas of Social Power* (New York:
Harper & Row, 1967), 219; Elliot Liebow, *Tally's Corner: A Study of Negro
Streetcorner Men* (Boston: Little, Brown, 1967), 220–23.

74. Daniel P. Moynihan, *The Negro Family: The Case for National Action*
(Washington, D.C.: U.S. Government Printing Office, 1965), 29–30, 47, 65;
Abram Kardiner and Lionel Ovesey, *The Mark of Oppression: Explorations in
the Personality of the American Negro* (Cleveland: World, 1962), 38–41, 44, 47,
81, 283, 297, 310, 352, 365, 384, 387; Clark, *Dark Ghetto,* 63, 65, 81; Alvin F.
Poussaint, "The Negro American: His Self-Image and Integration," in Barbour,
Black Power Revolt, 95–96.

75. Alexander Thomas and Samuel Sillen, *Racism and Psychiatry* (New
York: Brunner/Mazel, 1972), 46–47, 59, 68, 72, 76, 81–82; Alvin F. Poussaint,
"Black Alienation and Black Consciousness," in *Alienation: Concept, Term,
and Meanings,* ed. Frank Johnson (New York: Seminar, 1973), 361; Robert
Blauner, "Black Culture: Myth or Reality?" in *Afro-American Anthropology:
Contemporary Perspectives,* ed. Norman E. Whitten, Jr. and John F. Szwed (New
York: Free Press, 1970), 364; E. Earl Baughman, *Black Americans: A Psychologi-
cal Analysis* (New York: Academic, 1971), 37–42; Ross A. Evans, "The 'Rele-
vance' of Academic Psychology to the Black Experience," in *Topics in Afro-*

American Studies, ed. Henry J. Richards (Buffalo: Black Academy, 1971), 31; William Ryan, *Blaming the Victim* (New York: Pantheon, 1971).

76. Jesse J. Johnson, "The Black Psychologist: Pawn or Professional?" in Jones, *Black Psychology*, 362; Baughman, *Black Americans*, 58–59; Alvin F. Poussaint, "A Negro Psychiatrist Explains the Negro Psyche," *New York Times Magazine*, 20 August 1967, 73, 75–76, 78; William H. Grier and Price M. Cobbs, *Black Rage* (New York: Bantam, 1969), 1–2, 31, 93–95, 176–77; Poussaint, *Why Blacks Kill*, 25–27, 70; Frances Cress Welsing, "The Cress Theory of Color-Confrontation," *Black Scholar* 5 (May 1974): 32–40.

77. On Fanon, see Emmanuel Hansen, *Frantz Fanon: Social and Political Thought* (Columbus: Ohio State University Press, 1977).

78. Frantz Fanon, *The Wretched of the Earth* (New York: Grove, 1968), 53, 94, 210, 218, 236–37; Frantz Fanon, *Black Skin, White Masks* (New York: Grove, 1968), 192.

79. Fanon, *Wretched*, 43, 224, 232–33, 240, 244–47.

80. Wade W. Nobles, "Extended Self: Rethinking the So-Called Negro Self-Concept," *Journal of Black Psychology* 2 (February 1976): 15–17; Robert Williams, "A History of the Association of Black Psychologists: Early Formation and Development," *Journal of Black Psychology* 1 (August 1974): 24; Joseph White, "Guidelines for Black Psychologists," in *Contemporary Black Thought*, ed. Robert Chrisman and Nathan Hare (Indianapolis: Bobbs-Merrill, 1973), 115; Gardner and Thomas, "Different Strokes," 52, 78.

81. Wade W. Nobles, "African Philosophy: Foundations for Black Psychology," in Jones, *Black Psychology*, 18, 28.

82. Cedric X (Clark), D. Phillip McGee, Wade Nobles, and Luther X (Weems), "Voodoo or IQ: An Introduction to African Psychology," *Journal of Black Psychology* 1 (February 1975): 22–23, 26–27; Nobles, "Extended Self," 18–21; Ivory L. Toldson and Alfred B. Pasteur, "Therapeutic Dimensions of the Black Aesthetic," *Journal of Non-White Concerns in Personnel and Guidance* 4 (April 1976): 107–8.

83. Clark, McGee, Nobles, and Weems, "Voodoo," 9, 28; Gerald Jackson, "The Origin and Development of Black Psychology: Implications for Black Studies and Human Behavior," *Studia Africana* 1 (Fall 1979): 276.

84. Lee Lockwood, *Conversation with Eldridge Cleaver: Algiers* (New York: McGraw-Hill, 1970), 90; *Eldridge Cleaver: Post-Prison Writings and Speeches*, ed. Robert Scheer (New York: Random House, 1969), 18, 20; Bobby Seale, *Seize the Time: The Story of the Black Panther Party and Huey P. Newton* (New York: Random House, 1970), 25, 34; Forman, *Black Revolutionaries*, 451; Richard David Ralston, "Fanon and His Critics: The New Battle of Algiers," *Cultures et developpement* 8 (No. 3, 1976): 491; Ted Stewart, "Fanon: New Messiah of Black Militants," *Sepia* 20 (December 1971): 30.

85. Brisbane, *Black Activism*, 279; Aristide Zolberg and Vera Zolberg, "The Americanization of Frantz Fanon," *Public Interest* 9 (Fall 1967): 50.

Chapter Three

1. Nathan Hare, "Algiers 1969: A Report on the Pan-African Cultural Festival," in *Pan-Africanism*, ed. Robert Chrisman and Nathan Hare (Indianapolis: Bobbs-Merrill, 1974), 46.

2. Luther P. Gerlach and Virginia H. Hine, "The Social Organization of a Movement of Revolutionary Change: Case Study, Black Power," in *Afro-American Anthropology: Contemporary Perspectives*, ed. Norman E. Whitten, Jr. and John F. Szwed (New York: Free Press, 1970), 397–400.

3. William H. Orrick, Jr., *Shut It Down! A College in Crisis: San Francisco State College, October, 1968–April, 1969.* A Report to the National Commission on the Causes and Prevention of Violence (Washington, D.C.: U.S. Government Printing Office, 1969), 37–41; Dikran Karagueuzian, *Blow It Up! The Black Student Revolt at San Francisco State College and the Emergence of Dr. Hayakawa* (Boston: Gambit, 1971), 121.

4. "Ole Miss Enters the '60s," *Newsweek*, 30 March 1970, 83.

5. Calvin Trillin, "U.S. Journal: Oshkosh," *New Yorker*, 4 January 1969, 62–66.

6. "The Agony of Cornell," *Time*, 2 May 1969, 37–38; Harry Edwards, *Black Students* (New York: Free Press, 1970), 163, 168–70.

7. Lerone Bennett, Jr., "Confrontation on the Campus," *Ebony* 23 (May 1968): 30; Edwards, *Black Students*, 201.

8. "Campus Unrest: Now Force Meets Force," *U.S. News & World Report*, 24 February 1969, 8, 10; "A New Group at Vassar," *Newsweek*, 10 November 1969, 69.

9. Richard Flacks, "The Liberated Generation: An Exploration of the Roots of Student Protest," *Journal of Social Issues* 23 (July 1967): 52, 56–58.

10. William H. Exum, *Paradoxes of Protest: Black Student Activism in a White University* (Philadelphia: Temple University Press, 1985), 3; "Student Strikes: 1968–69," *Black Scholar* 1 (January–February 1970): 65–75.

11. Exum, *Paradoxes*, 7–8; Allen B. Ballard, *The Education of Black Folk: The Afro-American Struggle for Knowledge in White America* (New York: Harper & Row, 1974), 65; Edwards, *Black Students*, 61.

12. James Turner, "Black Nationalism," in *Topics in Afro-American Studies*, ed. Henry J. Richards (Buffalo: Black Academy Press, 1971), 70–71.

13. Ione D. Vargus, *Revival of Ideology: The Afro-American Society Movement* (San Francisco: R & E Research Associates, 1977), 91.

14. Allan Kornberg and Joel Smith, " 'It Ain't Over Yet': Activism in a Southern University," in *Black Power and Student Rebellion*, ed. James McEvoy and Abraham Miller (Belmont, California: Wadsworth, 1969), 107, 120.

15. Bennett, "Confrontation," 32.

16. James Turner, "Black Students: A Changing Perspective," in *The Black Revolution: An Ebony Special Issue* (Chicago: Johnson Publishing Company, 1970), 171.

17. S. E. Anderson, "Toward Racial Relevancy: Militancy and Black Students," *Negro Digest* 16 (September 1967): 13, 16; Nathan Hare, "The Struggle of Black Students," *Journal of Afro-American Issues* 1 (Fall 1972): 123; Preston Wilcox, "Black Studies as an Academic Discipline," *Negro Digest* 19 (March 1970): 85.

18. Max Stanford, "Revolutionary Nationalism and the Afroamerican Student," *Liberator* 5 (January 1965): 13.

19. Nathan Hare, "Behind the Black College Student Revolt," *Ebony* 22 (August 1967): 60.

20. Hare, "Struggle," 114; Bennett, "Confrontation," 27.

21. Michele Russell, "Erased, Debased, and Encased: The Dynamics of African Educational Colonization in America," *College English* 31 (April 1970): 673–74; Bennett, "Confrontation," 29–30.

22. Bennett, "Confrontation," 32.

23. Edwards, *Black Students*, 98.

24. "Black is Beautiful—and Belligerent," *Time*, 24 January 1969, 43.

25. Earl Anthony, *The Time of the Furnaces: A Case Study of Black Student Revolt* (New York: Dial, 1971), 82.

26. Bennett, "Confrontation," 28.

27. H. Rap Brown, *Die Nigger Die!* (New York: Dial, 1969), 67–68; Eldridge Cleaver, "Education and Revolution," *Black Scholar* 1 (November 1969): 49–51; Max Stanford, "Black Nationalism and the Afro-American Student," *Black Scholar* 2 (June 1971): 30–31.

28. Vincent Harding, "Black Students and the Impossible Revolution," *Journal of Black Studies* 1 (September 1970): 81.

29. Andrew Billingsley, "The Black Presence in American Higher Education," in *What Black Educators are Saying*, ed. Nathan Wright, Jr. (New York: Hawthorn, 1970), 126, 146; Mike Thelwell, "Black Studies: A Political Perspective," *Massachusetts Review* 10 (Autumn 1969): 707–08; Turner, "Black Nationalism," 69–75.

30. Nathan Hare, "The Case for Separatism: 'Black Perspective,'" *Newsweek*, 10 February 1969, 56.

31. Theodore Draper, *The Rediscovery of Black Nationalism* (New York: Viking, 1970), 153.

32. John W. Blassingame, "Black Studies: An Intellectual Crisis," *American Scholar* 38 (Autumn 1969): 553.

33. Billingsley, "Black Presence," 141; Orlando L. Taylor, "New Directions for American Education: A Black Perspective," *Journal of Black Studies* 1 (September 1970): 105, 110.

34. Boniface I. Obichere, "The Significance and Challenge of Afro-American Studies," *Journal of Black Studies* 1 (December 1970): 167; Sterling Stuckey, "Twilight of Our Past: Reflections on the Origins of Black History," in *Amistad 2*, ed. John A. Williams and Charles F. Harris (New York: Vintage, 1971), 291; Nathan Hare, "A Radical Perspective on Social Science Curricula," in *Black Studies in the University: A Symposium*, ed. Armstead L. Robinson, Craig C. Foster, Donald H. Ogilvie (New York: Bantam, 1969), 110; Edwards, *Black Students*, 104.

35. Billingsley, "Black Presence," 146; Hare, "Case for Separatism," 56.

36. Stephen Lythcott, "The Case for Black Studies," *Antioch Review* 29 (Summer 1969), 151; Edwards, *Black Students*, 102; Catharine R. Stimpson, "Black Culture/White Teacher," *Change* 2 (May–June 1970): 36.

37. Nathan Hare, "What Should Be the Role of Afro-American Education in the Undergraduate Curriculum?," *Liberal Education* 55 (March 1969): 42, 49; Harold Cruse, "The Integrationist Ethic as a Basis for Scholarly Endeavors," in Robinson, *Black Studies*, 10; Maulana Ron Karenga, "The Black Community and the University: A Community Organizer's Perspective," in Robinson, *Black Studies*, 38–39; Thelwell, "Political Perspective," 709.

38. Arnold Hano, "The Black Rebel Who 'Whitelists' the Olympics," *New York Times Magazine*, 12 May 1968, 39.

39. Blassingame, "Intellectual Crisis," 551.

40. Ronald Davis, "The Black University: In Peril Before Birth," *Negro Digest* 19 (March 1970): 63.

41. James P. Pitts, "The Politicalization of Black Students: Northwestern University," *Journal of Black Studies* 5 (March 1975): 307–8; Anthony, *Time of the Furnaces*, 131; Vargus, *Revival of Ideology*, 37–38.

42. James R. Lawson, Benjamin E. Mays, Samuel D. Proctor, Benjamin F. Payton, "The Black University Concept: Educators Respond," *Negro Digest* 18 (March 1969): 73, 77; John O. Killens, "The Artist and the Black University," *Black Scholar* 1 (November 1969): 64–65; Darwin T. Turner, "The Black University: A Practical Approach," *Negro Digest* 17 (March 1968): 37; Keith Lowe, "Towards a Black University," *Liberator* 8 (September 1968): 9.

43. Robert S. Browne, "Financing the Black University," in Wright, *Black Educators*, 88–92; Gerald A. McWorter, "Struggle, Ideology and the Black University," *Negro Digest* 18 (March 1969): 20.

44. Preston Wilcox, "On the Black University: Movement or Institution?," *Negro Digest* 19 (December 1969): 22; Lowe, "Black University," 8; Killens, "Artist," 64.

45. *Black Power Conference Reports: Philadelphia Aug. 30–Sept. 1, 1968; Bermuda July 13, 1969* (New York: Afram Associates, 1970), 21.

46. "The Communiversity: An Alternative Independent System," *Negro Digest* 19 (March 1970): 24–29, 72–74; Killens, "Artist," 62.

47. Edgar F. Beckham, "Problems of 'Place,' Personnel, and Practicality," *Negro Digest* 18 (March 1969): 23; Nathan Wright, Jr., *Black Power and Urban Unrest: Creative Possibilities* (New York: Hawthorn, 1967), 32–38.

48. "Monument to Blackness," *Newsweek*, 2 August 1971, 46–47; Charles G. Hurst, Jr. "Malcolm X: A Community College With a New Perspective," *Negro Digest* 19 (March 1970): 33, 36; Charles G. Hurst, Jr., *Passport to Freedom: Education, Humanism & Malcolm X* (Hamden, Conn.: Linnet, 1972), 213–23.

49. Chuck Hopkins, "Malcolm X Liberation University," *Negro Digest* 19 (March 1970); 41–42.

50. John Egerton, "Success Comes to Nairobi College," *Change* 4 (May 1972): 26–27; Orde Coombs, "Nairobi College: The Necessity of Excellence," *Change* 5 (April 1973): 40, 42–43; Alphonso Pinkney, *Red, Black, and Green: Black Nationalism in the United States* (Cambridge: Cambridge University Press, 1978), 192–93.

51. Charles G. Hurst, "'. . . the entire institution is encouraged to become involved in helping the student develop his skills,'" *Christian Science Monitor*, 7 May 1971, 9.

52. Hopkins, "Malcolm X," 46.

53. "Black (Studies) Vatican," *Newsweek*, 11 August 1969, 38.

54. Vincent Harding, "New Creation or Familiar Death?," *Negro Digest* 18 (March 1969): 14.

55. "The Institute of the Black World . . . Statement of Purpose and Program, Fall, 1969," *Massachusetts Review* 10 (Autumn 1969): 713–17; "Institute of the Black World," *Negro Digest* 19 (March 1970): 19–23; *IBW and Education for*

Liberation (Chicago: Third World Press, 1973), iii–8; Alex Poinsett, "Think Tank for Black Scholars," *Ebony* 25 (February 1970): 46–48, 50, 52, 54.

56. Wilcox, "Black University," 21.

57. Edgar F. Beckham, "What We Mean by 'the Black University,'" *College Board Review* (Spring 1969): 14. For an account of the demonstrations at Howard in support of the Black University concept, see Alex Poinsett, "The Metamorphosis of Howard University," *Ebony* 27 (December 1971): 110–22.

58. Stanford, "Black Nationalism," 28–31; Cleaver, "Education and Revolution," 50–51.

59. Dick Schaap, "The Revolt of the Black Athletes," *Look*, 6 August 1968, 74.

60. Harry Edwards, *The Revolt of the Black Athlete* (New York: Free Press, 1969), 11; "The Olympic Jolt: 'Hell no, don't go!'" *Life*, 15 March 1968, 22–27.

61. Jack Olsen, "The Black Athlete—A Shameful Story: The Cruel Deception," *Sports Illustrated*, 1 July 1968, 15–16.

62. Mal Whitfield, "Let's Boycott the Olympics," *Ebony* 19 (March 1964): 95.

63. Thomas A. Johnson, "Boycott of Sports by Negroes Asked," *New York Times*, 24 July 1967, 1, 16.

64. Edwards, *Revolt*, 40; Schaap, "Revolt," 72; Jack Scott and Harry Edwards, "After the Olympics: Buying Off Protest," *Ramparts* 8 (November 1969): 16.

65. Hano, "Black Rebel," 41.

66. "The Black Boycott," *Time*, 23 February 1968, 61; Harry Edwards, *The Struggle That Must Be: An Autobiography* (New York: Macmillan, 1980), 184.

67. Johnathan Rodgers, "A Step to an Olympic Boycott," *Sports Illustrated*, 4 December 1967, 30–31; "Olympic Boycott," *Newsweek*, 4 December 1967, 59; Hano, "Black Rebel," 42.

68. Harry Edwards, "Why Negroes Should Boycott Whitey's Olympics," *Saturday Evening Post*, 9 March 1968, 6; Hano, "Black Rebel," 42.

69. "Black Boycott," 61.

70. Jack Scott, "The White Olympics," *Ramparts* 6 (May 1968): 59; Edwards, "Whitey's Olympics," 6.

71. "Should Negroes Boycott the Olympics?" *Ebony* 23 (March 1968): 112.

72. Edwards, *Revolt*, 59; Edwards, *Struggle*, 182; Stokely Carmichael, *Stokely Speaks: Black Power Back to Pan-Africanism* (New York: Vintage, 1971), 123.

73. In 1968, ex-Olympic great Owens was 57 years old and a partner in a Chicago public relations firm. "Should Negroes Boycott," 112; Scott, "White Olympics," 56.

74. Scott, "White Olympics," 56–57.

75. Edwards, *Struggle*, 179–80.

76. Scott, "White Olympics," 60.

77. Scott and Edwards, "After the Olympics," 16.

78. Edwards, *Revolt*, 98–99, 104; Edwards, *Struggle*, 195; "Olympic Trials: Black Athletes Prepare for Mexico City," *Ebony* 23 (October 1968): 186.

79. "'Black Power' at the Olympics," *U.S. News & World Report*, 28 October 1968, 10; Edwards, *Revolt*, 104.

80. "Black Complaint," *Time*, 25 October 1968, 62–63; Edwards, *Revolt*, 103–5; Jeremy Larner and David Wolf, "Amid Gold Medals, Raised Black Fists," *Life*, 1 November 1968, 64.

81. Edwards, "Whitey's Olympics," 6; Hano, "Black Rebel," 32; Edwards,

Struggle, 217; Harry Edwards, "The Olympic Project for Human Rights: An Assessment Ten Years Later," *Black Scholar* 10 (March–April 1979): 2.

82. Scott, "White Olympics," 61.

83. Charles Denby, "Black Caucuses in the Unions," *New Politics* 7, no. 3 (1968): 12; Philip S. Foner, *Organized Labor and the Black Worker, 1619–1973* (New York: Praeger, 1974), 412.

84. Thomas R. Brooks, "Black Upsurge in the Unions," *Dissent* 17 (March–April 1970): 130–31.

85. Herbert Hill, "Black Dissent in Organized Labor," in *Seasons of Rebellion: Protest and Radicalism in Recent America*, ed. Joseph Boskin and Robert A. Rosenstone (New York: Holt, Rinehart and Winston, 1972), 73–75; Ozell Bonds, Jr., "The Case for Independent Black Trade Unions," *Ebony* 25 (August 1970): 143.

86. "Constitution of the Dodge Revolutionary Union Movement," in *Black Nationalism in America*, ed. John H. Bracey, Jr., August Meier, Elliott Rudwick (Indianapolis: Bobbs-Merrill, 1970), 552.

87. James A. Geschwender, "The League of Revolutionary Black Workers: Problems Confronting Black Marxist-Leninist Organizations," *Journal of Ethnic Studies* 2 (Fall 1974): 5.

88. Thomas R. Brooks, "DRUMbeats in Detroit," *Dissent* 17 (January–February 1970): 16; "'A Plague on Both Your Houses!'" *Business Week*, 24 May 1969, 56.

89. Brooks, "DRUMbeats," 22–23.

90. Ibid., 23; Geschwender, "League," 4, 6; James A. Geschwender, *Class, Race, and Worker Insurgency: The League of Revolutionary Black Workers* (Cambridge: Cambridge University Press, 1977), 93–94; "Constitution," 554.

91. Jim Jacobs and David Wellman, "Fight on to Victory: An Interview with Ken Cockrel and Mike Hamlin of The League for Revolutionary Workers," *Leviathan* 2 (June 1970): 6; James A. Geschwender, "Black Marxist-Leninist Worker Movements: Class or National Consciousness?" in *Black Separatism and Social Reality: Rhetoric and Reason*, ed. Raymond L. Hall (New York: Pergamon, 1977), 119.

92. Geschwender, "League," 12; Foner, *Organized Labor*, 417–18.

93. Geschwender, "Worker Movements," 116, 119, 122.

94. Brooks, "DRUMbeats," 23.

95. John Oliver Killens, "Black Labor and the Black Liberation Movement," in *Contemporary Black Thought*, ed. Robert Chrisman and Nathan Hare (Indianapolis: Bobbs-Merrill, 1973), 289; Geschwender, "Worker Movements, 119, 121.

96. Geschwender, "Worker Movements," 123; Geschwender, *Worker Insurgency*, 153.

97. Brooks, "DRUMbeats," 20; "Plague," 56; Foner, *Organized Labor*, 421.

98. Jacobs and Wellman, "Fight," 9.

99. United Black Workers, "What We are Fighting For," in *Black Protest*, ed. Joanne Grant (Greenwich, Conn.: Fawcett, 1974), 552.

100. A total institution is defined as "a place of residence and work where a large number of like-situated individuals, cut off from the wider society for an appreciable period of time, together lead an enclosed, formally administered

round of life." Erving Goffman, *Asylums: Essays on the Social Situation of Mental Patients and Other Inmates* (Garden City, New York: Anchor/Doubleday, 1969), xiii.

101. Stanley M. Elkins, *Slavery: A Problem in American Institutional and Intellectual Life* (New York: Grosset & Dunlop, 1963), 81–139; 225.

102. A sampling of this commentary can be found in *The Debate Over Slavery: Stanley Elkins and His Critics*, ed. Ann J. Lane (Urbana: University of Illinois Press, 1971). See also John W. Blassingame, *The Slave Community: Plantation Life in the Antebellum South* (New York: Oxford University Press, 1972), 189–90, 217–26; Mina Davis Caulfield, "Slavery and the Origins of Black Culture: Elkins Revisited," in *Americans from Africa: Slavery and Its Aftermath*, ed. Peter I. Rose (New York: Atherton, 1970), 171–93; Thomas L. Webber, *Deep Like the Rivers: Education in the Slave Quarter Community, 1831–1865* (New York: W. W. Norton, 1978), 251–62.

103. Peter Goldman, *Report from Black America* (New York: Simon and Schuster, 1971), 45, 230.

104. J. Carleton Hayden, "The Congress of African Peoples (Atlanta, Georgia, September 3–7, 1970)," *Black Academy Review* 1 (Winter 1970): 61.

105. Eldridge Cleaver, "To My Black Brothers in Viet Nam," in *Off The Pigs!: The History and Literature of the Black Panther Party*, ed. G. Louis Heath (Metuchen, New Jersey: Scarecrow, 1976), 259.

106. Nathan Hare, "It's Time to Turn the Guns the Other Way," in *Vietnam and Black America: An Anthology of Protest and Resistance*, ed. Clyde Taylor (Garden City, New York: Anchor/Doubleday, 1973), 288.

107. Robert Carl Cohen, *Black Crusader: A Biography of Robert Franklin Williams* (Secaucus, New Jersey: Lyle Stuart, 1972), 332–33; Rolland Snellings, "Vietnam; Whitey: I Will Not Serve!" *Liberator* 6 (March 1966): 9.

108. Brown, *Die*, 136; Samuel F. Yette, *The Choice: The Issue of Black Survival in America* (New York: Berkley, 1972), 79; Eldridge Cleaver, *Soul on Ice* (New York: Dell, 1968), 127.

109. Student Nonviolent Coordinating Committee, "Statement on Vietnam, January 6, 1966," in Grant, *Black Protest*, 416–18; Hare, "Turn the Guns," 285. See also Robert W. Mullen, "An Analysis of the Issues Developed by Select Black Americans on the War in Vietnam" (Ph.D. diss., Ohio State University, 1971).

110. Jack D. Foner, *Blacks and the Military in American History: A New Perspective* (New York: Praeger, 1974), 202–3.

111. Richard Halloran, "Air Force Racism Charged in Study," *New York Times*, 31 August, 1971, 1; Foner, *Blacks and the Military*, 213, 217–18.

112. During the entire wartime period (1961–72), blacks suffered 13 percent of the combat deaths. This figure is slightly above the percentage of blacks in the relevant age group and almost exactly the same percentage as that of blacks in the army's enlisted ranks. Martin Binkin and Mark J. Eitelberg, *Blacks and the Military* (Washington, D.C.: Brookings Institution, 1982), 76–77.

113. "Letters to the Editor," *Ebony* 23 (August 1968): 15, 17.

114. Foner, *Blacks and the Military*, 211.

115. Wallace Terry II, "Bringing the War Home," *Black Scholar* 2 (November 1970): 10.

116. Ibid., 13–14; Jack White, "The Angry Black Soldiers," *Progressive* 34

(March 1970): 25; Milton White, "Self-Determination for Black Soldiers," *Black Scholar* 2 (November 1970), 45–46; William Stuart Gould, "Racial Conflict in the U.S. Army," *Race* 15 (July 1973): 15.

117. Fred Halstead, *GIs Speak Out Against the War: The Case of the Ft. Jackson 8* (New York: Pathfinder, 1970), 37.

118. "Black Power in Viet Nam," *Time*, 19 September 1969, 23.

119. Ibid., 22; Terry, "War," 13–14; Bernard C. Nalty, *Strength for the Fight: A History of Black Americans in the Military* (New York: Free Press, 1986), 307; Alvin J. Schexnider, "The Development of Racial Solidarity in the Armed Forces," *Journal of Black Studies* 5 (June 1975): 426.

120. Terry, "War," 14.

121. *Malcolm X Speaks: Selected Speeches and Statements*, ed. George Breitman (New York: Grove, 1966), 144.

122. Halstead, *Speak Out*, 55; Milton White, "Malcolm X in the Military," *Black Scholar* 1 (May 1970): 33–34.

123. Terry, "War," 11, 13; Nalty, *Strength*, 321.

124. Terry, "War," 6, 9–11, 17–18; "Black Power in Viet Nam," 23.

125. White, "Black Soldiers," 23; Sol Stern, "When the Black G.I. Comes Back from Vietnam," *New York Times Magazine*, 24 March 1968, 37, 40; White, "Malcolm X," 35.

126. *The Autobiography of Malcolm X* (New York: Grove, 1966), 150–90.

127. At the midpoint of the 1965–75 period, Afro-Americans composed about 40 percent of the total number of inmates in federal and state correctional institutions. Only 8 percent of all correctional employees were black. None were institution administrators in the adult correctional system. National Advisory Commission on Criminal Justice Standards and Goals, *Report on Corrections* (Washington, D.C.: U.S. Government Printing Office, 1973), 474.

128. *Eldridge Cleaver: Post-Prison Writings and Speeches*, ed. Robert Scheer (New York: Random House, 1969), 183.

129. George Jackson, *Soledad Brother: The Prison Letters of George Jackson* (New York: Bantam, 1970), 24–25, 28, 161–62, 168, 218–19.

130. Ibid., 31; George L. Jackson, *Blood in My Eye* (New York: Random House, 1972), 106–7; Angela Y. Davis, "Political Prisoners, Prisons and Black Liberation," in *If They Come in the Morning: Voices of Resistance*, ed. Angela Y. Davis and Bettina Aptheker (New York: New American Library, 1971), 32–33, 37; Huey P. Newton, *Revolutionary Suicide* (New York: Ballantine, 1974), 291.

131. "The Folsom Prisoners Manifesto of Demands and Anti-Oppression Platform," in Davis and Aptheker, *Morning*, 68–74.

132. Huey P. Newton: *To Die for the People: The Writings of Huey P. Newton* (New York: Vintage, 1972), 226; Newton, *Suicide*, 288.

133. Jackson, *Soledad*, 21, 30; "October 1966 Black Panther Party Platform and Program," in *The Black Panthers Speak*, ed. Philip S. Foner (Philadelphia: J. B. Lippincott, 1970), 3.

134. Newton, *To Die*, 218–20; Newton, *Suicide*, 5–6, 292, 294–95.

135. Donald Bogle, "Black and Proud Behind Bars," in *Black Revolution*, 56–61.

136. Etheridge Knight, *Poems from Prison* (Detroit: Broadside Press, 1968), 11, 26–28; Juno Bakali Tshombe, "Beware of the Flowers of Despair," "The

White Thorn in the Black Flesh of Your Mind," "The Struggle," "Psychological Warfare at Norfolk Prison Camp;" James Shields, "Time Was Spent;" James A. Lang, "For My Ex-Wife;" Sayif, "revolution is," in Norfolk Prison Brothers, *Who Took the Weight?: Black Voices from Norfolk Prison* (Boston: Little, Brown and Company, 1972), 17, 23, 37, 55, 59, 85, 92–93; Ericka Huggins, "for connie a rollingstone," in Davis and Aptheker, *Morning*, 118.

137. Etheridge Knight, "The Day the Young Blacks Came," in *Black Voices from Prison*, ed. Etheridge Knight (New York: Pathfinder, 1970), 164.

138. Ibid., 165.

139. Roberta Ann Johnson, "The Prison Birth of Black Power," *Journal of Black Studies* 5 (June 1975): 396; Cleaver, *Soul*, 58, 134; Newton, *Suicide*, 294.

Chapter Four

1. *Malcolm X Speaks: Selected Speeches and Statements*, ed. George Breitman (New York: Grove, 1966), 9, 38–39; *By Any Means Necessary: Speeches, Interviews and a Letter by Malcolm X*, ed. George Breitman (New York: Pathfinder, 1970), 43–56.

2. Raymond S. Franklin, "The Political Economy of Black Power," *Social Problems* 16 (Winter 1969): 292; Edward C. Smith, "The Coming of the Black Ghetto-State," *Yale Review* 61 (December 1971): 171.

3. Grace Boggs and James Boggs, "The City is the Black Man's Land," *Monthly Review* 17 (April 1966): 41; Herb Ottley, "Nation Time or Integration Time?" *Black World* 20 (July 1971): 70; James Turner, "Blacks in the Cities: Land and Self-Determination," *Black Scholar* 1 (April 1970): 11; Nathan Wright, Jr., "The Social Arena of Black Political Action," in *What Black Politicians are Saying*, ed. Nathan Wright, Jr. (New York: Hawthorn, 1972), 184–86.

4. Ralph H. Metcalf, Jr., "Chicago Model Cities and Neocolonization," *Black Scholar* 1 (April 1970): 24, 26, 30.

5. Peter Goldman, *Report from Black America* (New York: Simon and Schuster, 1971), 179–81; Howard Schuman and Shirley Hatchett, *Black Racial Attitudes: Trends and Complexities* (Ann Arbor: Survey Research Center, Institute for Social Research, University of Michigan, 1974), 7.

6. James Boggs, "The Revolutionary Struggle for Black Power," in *The Black Seventies*, ed. Floyd B. Barbour (Boston: Porter Sargent, 1970), 44–45; Douglas Glasgow, "Black Power Through Community Control," *Social Work* 17 (May 1972): 62.

7. Mel King, *Chain of Change: Struggles for Black Community Development* (Boston: South End, 1981), 292, 297.

8. Richard F. America, Jr., " 'What Do You People Want?' " *Review of Black Political Economy* 1 (Spring–Summer 1970): 47; Robert S. Browne, "Black Economic Autonomy," *Black Scholar* 3 (October 1971): 26–27; Glasgow, "Community Control," 60, 62; James R. Cleaveland, "Planning vs. Participation," *New Generation* 51 (Summer 1969): 29–30.

9. Alan A. Altshuler, *Community Control: The Black Demand for Participation in Large American Cities* (Indianapolis: Pegasus, 1970), 60–61; Whitney M. Young, Jr., "Minorities and Community Control of the Schools," *Journal of Negro Education* 38 (Summer 1969): 285–90.

10. Stokely Carmichael and Charles V. Hamilton, *Black Power: The Politics*

of Liberation in America (New York: Random House, 1967), 171–73; America, "People," 47–57; Chuck Stone, "The National Conference on Black Power," in *The Black Power Revolt,* ed. Floyd B. Barbour (Boston: Porter Sargent, 1968), 196–97; *Black Power Conference Reports: Philadelphia Aug. 30–Sept. 1, 1968: Bermuda July 13, 1969* (New York: Afram Associates, 1970), 23–26; Altshuler, *Community Control,* 14.

11. Peter Bailey, "N.E.G.R.O. Charts New Path to Freedom," *Ebony* 23 (April 1968): 49, 53; "New Meaning for 'Black Power,'" *U.S. News & World Report,* 22 July 1968, 33.

12. "New Meaning," 33.

13. Ibid., Bailey, "N.E.G.R.O.," 53.

14. Arthur I. Blaustein and Geoffrey Faux, *The Star-Spangled Hustle* (Garden City, New York: Doubleday, 1972), 12–29; Joe McGinniss, *The Selling of the President 1968* (New York: Trident, 1969), 244–45, 248–49; "Nixon on Racial Accommodation," *Time,* 3 May 1968, 21; Thomas L. Blair, *Retreat to the Ghetto: The End of a Dream?* (New York: Hill and Wang, 1977), 165.

15. Andrew F. Brimmer, "Economic Integration and the Progress of the Negro Community," *Ebony* 25 (August 1970): 118–21; Andrew F. Brimmer, "Profit Versus Pride: The Trouble with Black Capitalism," *Nation's Business* 57 (May 1969): 78–79; Dunbar S. McLaurin, "'Short-Range Separatism,'" *Ebony* 25 (August 1970): 124.

16. Robert E. Wright, "'Black Capitalism': Toward Controlled Development of Black America," *Negro Digest* 19 (December 1969): 28–29; Talmadge Anderson, "Black Economic Liberation Under Capitalism," *Black Scholar* 2 (October 1970): 14; McLaurin, "Separatism," 124–25.

17. Earl Ofari, *The Myth of Black Capitalism* (New York: Monthly Review, 1970), 122–23; James Boggs, "The Myth and Irrationality of Black Capitalism," *Review of Black Political Economy* 1 (Spring–Summer 1970); 31, 35.

18. *Black Power Conference,* 17; Lonetta Gaines, "Methodology of the Pan-African Pre-School," *Black World* 24 (August 1975): 19; Carmichael and Hamilton, *Black Power,* 167; Milton R. Coleman, "A Cultural Approach to Education," *Negro Digest* 18 (March 1969): 33, 35–36, 38.

19. Coleman, "Cultural Approach," 34, 36, 37; Preston R. Wilcox, "The Community-Centered School," in *The Schoolhouse in the City,* ed. Alvin Toffler (New York: Frederick A. Praeger, 1968), 100; David Selden, "The Future of Community Participation in Educational Policy Making," in *Community Participation in Education,* ed. Carl A. Grant (Boston: Allyn and Bacon, 1979), 72; Mario D. Fantini and Richard Magat, "Decentralizing Urban School Systems," in Toffler, *Schoolhouse,* 112.

20. Carmichael and Hamilton, *Black Power,* 167, 171; Allan C. Ornstein, *Race and Politics in School/Community Organizations* (Pacific Palisades, California: Goodyear, 1974), 12–13.

21. Kenneth W. Haskins, "A Black Perspective on Community Control," *Inequality in Education* 15 (November 1973): 28–29.

22. Ornstein, *Race and Politics,* 3–4; "The Communiversity: An Alternative Independent System," *Negro Digest* 19 (March 1970): 29, 72–73; Roy Innis and Victor Solomon, "Harlem Must Control Its Schools," *New Generation* 49 (Fall 1967): 4; *Black Power Conference,* 11–12; M. Lee Montgomery, "Community

Building and Learning Centers," in *What Black Educators are Saying*, ed. Nathan Wright, Jr. (New York: Hawthorn, 1970), 278–82.

23. Barbara A. Sizemore, "Is There a Case for Separate Schools?" *Phi Delta Kappan* 53 (January 1972): 281; Haskins, "Black Perspective," 27; Doreen H. Wilkinson, *Community Schools: Education for Change* (Boston: National Association of Independent Schools, 1973), 12, 14.

24. Jacqueline S. Mithun, "Black Power and Community Change: An Assessment," *Journal of Black Studies* 7 (March 1977): 270; Gaines, "Methodology," 19–25; Haskins, "Black Perspective," 26.

25. H. Rap Brown, *Die Nigger Die!* (New York: Dial, 1969), 130.

26. Carmichael and Hamilton, *Black Power*, 39.

27. Julian Bond, "A Black Southern Strategy," in Wright, *Black Politicians*, 137–38.

28. "National Black Political Agenda: The Gary Conference Report," *Black World* 21 (October 1972): 29.

29. United States Commission on Civil Rights, *Report on Political Participation* (Washington, D.C.: U.S. Government Printing Office, 1968), 21, 41, 58; Steven F. Lawson, *In Pursuit of Power: Southern Blacks and Electoral Politics, 1965–1982* (New York: Columbia University Press, 1985), 204, 217–18, 232–33.

30. Ronald Walters, "Strategy for 1976: A Black Political Party," *Black Scholar* 7 (October 1975): 9; M. Margaret Conway, *Political Participation in the United States* (Washington, D.C.: CQ Press, 1985), 25.

31. Adam C. Powell, "My Black Position Paper," in Barbour, *Black Power Revolt*, 258.

32. Carmichael and Hamilton, *Black Power*, 47; "New Politics for Black People: A Statement of Principles, Goals, Guidelines, Definitions and Direction for the National Black Political Assembly," *Black World* 24 (October 1975): 63; Dick Gregory, "From Poverty to President," in Wright, *Black Politicians*, 71; "Gary Conference," 31; Bill Strickland, "The Gary Convention and the Crisis of American Politics," *Black World* 21 (October 1972): 23, 25–26.

33. "The Black Caucus and Nixon," *Black Politician* 3 (July 1971): 4–12; Louis Stokes, "The Caucus: Progress Through Legislation," *Focus* 1 (September 1973): 3; Hanes Walton, Jr., *Black Political Parties: An Historical and Political Analysis* (New York: Free Press, 1972), 259–60; Blair, *Retreat*, 204–5.

34. John Dean, "Black Political Assembly: Birth of a New Force," *Focus* 2 (November 1973): 4; "New Politics," 63–64.

35. Stokes, "Caucus," 3.

36. Harry Holloway, "Negro Political Strategy: Coalition or Independent Power Politics?" *Social Science Quarterly* 49 (December 1968): 544–47; "New Politics," 62–63; Carmichael and Hamilton, *Black Power*, 77–81.

37. Walters, "Strategy," 14–17; Chuck Stone, "Black Politics: Third Force, Third Party or Third-Class Influence?" in *Contemporary Black Thought*, ed. Robert Chrisman and Nathan Hare (Indianapolis: Bobbs-Merrill, 1973), 271–78.

38. Hardy T. Frye, *Black Parties and Political Power: A Case Study* (Boston: G. K. Hall, 1980), 70; Clayborne Carson, *In Struggle: SNCC and the Black Awakening of the 1960s* (Cambridge: Harvard University Press, 1981), 165; Lawson, *In Pursuit*, 108.

39. Chuck Stone, *Black Political Power in America* (New York: Dell, 1970), 212; Blair, *Retreat*, 193, 195; Hanes Walton, Jr., "Blacks and the 1968 Third Parties," *Negro Educational Review* 21 (January 1970): 22; Ronald Walters, "The Black Politician," *Current History* 67 (November 1974): 233; Carmichael and Hamilton, *Black Power*, 46–47.

40. For commentary on these proposals, see Matthew Holden, Jr., *The White Man's Burden* (New York: Chandler, 1973), 245–52; Smith, "Ghetto-State," 176–78.

41. For a discussion of the Freedom Library Day School's educational philosophy, see John E. Churchville, "On Correct Black Education," in Wright, *Black Educators*, 177–82.

42. Theodore Draper, *The Rediscovery of Black Nationalism* (New York: Viking, 1970), 147.

43. Milton D. Morris, *The Politics of Black America* (New York: Harper & Row, 1975), 300–1; Robert S. Browne, "Black Economic Autonomy," *Black Scholar* 3 (October 1971): 31; Robert E. Wright, " 'Black Capitalism': Toward Controlled Development of Black America," *Negro Digest* 19 (December 1969): 29; Max Stanford, "Black Nationalism and the Afro-American Student," *Black Scholar* 2 (June 1971): 28.

44. Robert S. Browne, "The Case for Black Separation," *Ramparts* 6 (December 1967): 46–7; 51; Browne, "Economic Autonomy," 27–31, Harold Cruse, "Black and White: Outlines of the Next Stage, Chapter One," *Black World* 20 (January 1971): 24.

45. Goldman, *Report*, 29; James Boggs, "The Revolutionary Struggle for Black Power," in Barbour, *Black Seventies*, 39; James Turner, "Black Nationalism: The Inevitable Response," *Black World* 20 (January 1971): 6–13; Solomon P. Gethers, "Black Power: Three Years Later," *Negro Digest* 19 (December 1969): 71–72; Charles V. Hamilton, "The Nationalist vs. the Integrationist," *New York Times Magazine*, 1 October 1972, 51; Ronald Walters, "African-American Nationalism: A Unifying Ideology," *Black World* 22 (October 1973): 25–6, 84.

46. A 1968 survey of blacks in fifteen cities showed community control to be three times more popular than territorial nationalism. In a 1969 *Newsweek* poll, however, 12 percent of the black respondents thought that someday there would be a separate black nation formed within the U.S. Fully 21 percent thought that such a state *should* be created. This was a dramatic increase from surveys conducted in 1963 and 1966, when only four percent of the respondents favored the separate nation concept. In a separate survey item, only 13 percent of the respondents favored community control over integration as a way to "get ahead" in American society. At the same time, the three *Newsweek* surveys revealed a constant low level of support for the Nation of Islam and seemed to show that the Congress of Racial Equality was declining in popularity the more firmly it became attached to nationalism. "New Findings—Negro Attitudes on Racial Issues," *U.S. News & World Report*, 5 August 1968, 10; Goldman, *Report*, 233, 240–41, 265–66, 270.

47. August Meier and Elliott Rudwick, *CORE: A Study in the Civil Rights Movement, 1942–1968* (Urbana: University of Illinois Press, 1975), 316–17, 360–63, 367–68; Hamilton Bims, "CORE: Wild Child of Civil Rights," *Ebony*

20 (October 1965): 35, James Farmer, *Freedom—When?* (New York: Random House, 1965), 73–76, 104–105.

48. Farmer, *Freedom*, 74, 88; Meier and Rudwick, *CORE*, 383, 403.

49. Meier and Rudwick, *CORE*, 379–80.

50. Charlie L. Russell, "CORE's Floyd McKissick: The Man for the Job," *Negro Digest* 16 (May 1967): 19, 21; Fred C. Shapiro, "The Successor to Floyd McKissick May Not Be So Reasonable," *New York Times Magazine*, 1 October 1967, 98; Meier and Rudwick, *CORE*, 409–10.

51. Shapiro, "McKissick," 103–4.

52. Ibid., 101–2; Meier and Rudwick, *CORE*, 414, 417; "Black Power for Whom?" *Christian Century*, 20 July 1966, 904.

53. Floyd B. McKissick, "Black Business Development with Social Commitment to Black Communities," in *Black Nationalism in America*, ed. John H. Bracey, Jr, August Meier, and Elliott Rudwick (Indianapolis: Bobbs-Merrill, 1970), 494–95, 497, 500, 503.

54. Geoffrey Gould, "Soul City," *New Republic*, 3 July 1971, 9–10.

55. Ibid., Kalamu ya Salaam, "Floyd McKissick, Architect of Soul City: A Bold New Experiment in Living," *Black Collegian* 4 (March–April 1974): 33, 48.

56. Floyd McKissick, *Three-Fifths of a Man* (New York: Macmillan, 1969), 152, 155–59, 163–64.

57. Meier and Rudwick, *CORE*, 424; Roy Innis and Victor Solomon, "Harlem Must Control Its Schools," *New Generation* 49 (Fall 1967): 4–5; "Dialogue: Which Way for Better Schools?" *New Generation* 49 (Fall 1967): 7.

58. "Talking Up Racism," *New Republic*, 20 July 1968, 9.

59. William K. Tabb, *The Political Economy of the Black Ghetto* (New York: W. W. Norton, 1970), 51–52; Alex Poinsett, "Roy Innis: Nation-Builder," *Ebony* 24 (October 1969): 176, Roy Innis and Norman Hill, "Black Self-Determination: A Debate," *New Generation* 51 (Summer 1969): 22.

60. Roy Innis, "Separatist Economics: A New Social Contract," in *Black Economic Development*, ed. William Haddad and C. Douglas Pugh (Englewood Cliffs, New Jersey: Prentice-Hall, 1969), 58; "Roy Innis: Black Nationalist," *Penthouse* 1 (January 1970): 30; Innis and Hill, "Self-Determination," 21.

61. Poinsett, "Innis," 176; Innis and Hill, "Self-Determination," 20; "Dialogue," 6; Innis, "Separatist Economics," 52–55.

62. Poinsett, "Innis," 176; "Black Nationalist," 29; "Dialogue," 10; Innis, "Separatist Economics," 50–51; Robert L. Allen, *Black Awakening in Capitalist America: An Analytic History* (Garden City, New York: Doubleday, 1970), 183–188.

63. Innis and Solomon, "Harlem," 4–5.

64. Allen, *Black Awakening*, 187.

65. E. U. Essien-Udom, *Black Nationalism: A Search for an Identity in America* (Chicago: University of Chicago Press, 1962), 6, 130–31, 259; Elijah Muhammad, "What Do the Muslims Want?" in Bracey, Meier, and Rudwick, *Black Nationalism*, 404; Elijah Muhammad, *Message to the Blackman in America* (Chicago: Muhammad's Temple No. 2, 1965), 37–38, 56, 204, 223–24; C. Eric Lincoln, "Extremist Attitudes in the Black Muslim Movement," *New South* 18 (January 1963): 6.

66. Morroe Berger, "The Black Muslims," *Horizon* 6 (Winter 1964): 58; Muhammad, "Muslims," 404; Muhammad, *Message*, 222, 226, 233–34, 317.

67. C. Eric Lincoln, *The Black Muslims in America* (Boston: Beacon, 1961), 95–97, Muhammad, *Message*, 223, 227–28; Essien-Udom, *Black Nationalism*, 260, 263.

68. Muhammad, *Message*, 170–71; Essien-Udom, *Black Nationalism*, 262.

69. Muhammad, *Message*, 163; "The Black Supremacists," *Time*, 10 August 1959, 25; *The Autobiography of Malcolm X* (New York: Grove, 1966), 238; Peter Goldman, *The Death and Life of Malcolm X* (Urbana: University of Illinois Press, 1979), 77.

70. *The End of White World Supremacy: Four Speeches by Malcolm X*, ed. Imam Benjamin Karim (New York: Seaver, 1971), 147; William McCord, John Howard, Bernard Friedberg, and Edwin Harwood, *Life Styles in the Black Ghetto* (New York: W. W. Norton, 1969), 248; John Howard, "The Making of a Black Muslim," in *Black Experience: Soul*, ed. Lee Rainwater (Chicago: Aldine, 1970): 84.

71. Ernest Dunbar, "The Making of a Militant," *Saturday Review*, 16 December 1972, 29.

72. Ibid., 29–30; Brother Imari, *War in America: The Malcolm X Doctrine* (Detroit: Malcolm X Society, 1968), 1–64.

73. "The Republic of New Africa," in *The Black Experience in American Politics*, ed. Charles V. Hamilton (New York: G. P. Putnam's Sons, 1973), 60; Imari Abubakari Obadele, "The Republic of New Africa—An Independent Black Nation," *Black World* 20 (May 1971): 81–82; Robert Sherrill, "We Want Georgia, South Carolina, Louisiana, Mississippi and Alabama—Right Now . . . We Also Want Four Hundred Billion Dollars Back Pay," *Esquire* 71 (January 1969): 72, 75.

74. Milton R. Henry. "An Independent Black Republic in North America," in *Black Separatism and Social Reality: Rhetoric and Reason*, ed. Raymond L. Hall (New York: Pergamon, 1977), 39; Imari Abubakari Obadele, "The Struggle is for Land," *Black Scholar* 3 (February 1972): 24, 32; Sherrill, "Back Pay," 73. In March 1971, members of the RNA dedicated land for El Malik in Hinds County, Mississippi. They then began to organize support for a plebiscite which would declare the "Kush District"—twenty-five counties along the Mississippi River from Memphis to the Louisiana border—independent by popular vote. The predictable entanglements with local landholders and law enforcement officials are detailed in Dunbar, "Militant," 31–32; "The Repression of the RNA," *Black Scholar* 3 (October 1971): 57; Imari Abubakari Obadele, "The Struggle of the Republic of New Africa," *Black Scholar* 5 (June 1974): 32–41; Imari Abubakari Obadele, "National Black Elections Held by Republic of New Africa," *Black Scholar* 7 (October 1975): 27–38.

75. Obadele, "Black Nation," 84; Obadele, "Land," 33.

76. Obadele, "Black Nation," 88; Obadele, "Land," 34–35.

77. Garry Wills, *The Second Civil War: Arming for Armageddon* (New York: New American Library, 1968), 130–31; Sherrill, "Back Pay," 75; Obadele, "Land," 34.

78. Henry, "Black Republic," 37; Sherrill, "Back Pay," 74–75, 147–148.

79. Obadele, "Black Nation," 89; Henry, "Black Republic," 36; Sherrill, "Back Pay," 74, 147–48.

80. Sherrill, "Back Pay," 148; Obadele, "Land," 31; Obadele, "Black Nation," 82.

81. Ronald Walters, "The Re-Africanization of the Black American," in *Topics in Afro-American Studies*, ed. Henry J. Richards (Buffalo: Black Academy Press, 1971), 114; Sherrill "Back Pay," 147; Henry, "Black Republic," 36–37.

82. Malcolm X, *Autobiography*, 347; Breitman, *Malcolm X Speaks*, 63, 168–69, 172.

83. Malcolm X, *Autobiography*, 351; Ruby M. Essien-Udom and E. U. Essien-Udom, "Malcolm X: An International Man," in *Malcolm X: The Man and His Times*, ed. John Henrik Clarke (New York: Collier, 1969), 246–50.

84. Stokely Carmichael, "Pan-Africanism—Land and Power," *Black Scholar* 1 (November 1969): 39–40; Stokely Carmichael, *Stokely Speaks: Black Power Back to Pan-Africanism* (New York: Vintage, 1971), 203; Stokely Carmichael, "'We Are All Africans,'" *Black Scholar* 1 (May 1970): 16; Herb Ottley, "Nation Time or Integration Time?" *Black World* 20 (July 1971): 41, 69–75; John Oliver Killens, *Black Man's Burden* (New York: Trident, 1965), 161–67; Calvin H. Sinnette, "Repatriation—Dead Issue or Resurrected Alternative," *Freedomways* 8 (Winter 1968): 60–62; Breitman, *Malcolm X Speaks*, 210–11.

85. Era Bell Thompson, "Are Black Americans Welcome in Africa?" *Ebony* 24 (January 1969): 50; Tom Mboya, *The Challenge of Nationhood* (New York: Praeger, 1970), 226–29; "Mboya's Rebuttal," *Ebony* 24 (August 1969): 90–91, 94. Taban lo Liyong, *The Last Word: Cultural Synthesism* (Nairobi: East African Publishing House, 1969), 83–92; David Jenkins, *Black Zion: Africa, Imagined and Real, as Seen by Today's Blacks* (New York: Harcourt Brace Jovanovich, 1975), 153.

86. David Graham DuBois, "Afro-American Militants in Africa: Problems and Responsibilities," *Black World* 21 (February 1972): 4–11 Bill Sutherland, "Tanzania," in *The Black Expatriates: A Study of American Negroes in Exile*, ed. Ernest Dunbar (New York: E. P. Dutton, 1968), 107–8.

87. Priscilla Stevens Kruize, "Ghana," in Dunbar, *Black Expatriates*, 64; Leslie Alexander Lacy, *The Rise and Fall of a Proper Negro* (New York: Macmillan, 1970), 239.

88. Mboya, *Challenge*, 224; John Nagenda, "Pride or Prejudice? Relationships Between Africans and American Negroes," *Race* 9 (October 1967): 159–60.

89. Carmichael, *Stokely Speaks*, 202, 224–25; Robert G. Weisbord, *Ebony Kinship: Africa, Africans, and the Afro-American* (Westport, Connecticut: Greenwood, 1974), 129–35, 149; Boniface I. Obichere, "Afro-Americans in Africa: Recent Experiences," in *Black Homeland/Black Diaspora: Cross-Currents of the African Relationship*, ed. Jacob Drachler (Port Washington, New York: Kennikat, 1975), 26–30.

90. S. E. Anderson, "Revolutionary Black Nationalism and the Pan-African Idea," in Barbour, *Black Seventies*, 108–10, 112, 120–22; Carmichael, *Stokely Speaks*, 206, 221, 224–27; Muhammad Ahmad, "Toward Pan African Liberation," *Black Scholar* 5 (April 1974): 24.

91. Muhammad Ahmed, "The Roots of Pan-African Revolution," *Black Scholar* 3 (May 1972): 52–53.

92. Brown, *Die*, 135.

93. E. Mkalimoto, "Basic Tenets of Revolutionary Black Nationalism," in

Barbour, *Black Seventies*, 309–10; Amiri Baraka, "The Congress of Afrikan People: A Position Paper," *Black Scholar* 6 (January—February, 1975): 7–9; Maulana Ron Karenga, "Which Road: Nationalism, Pan-Africanism, Socialism?" *Black Scholar* 6 (October 1974): 25; Ahmad, "Pan African Liberation," 24, 28–31; Lawrence P. Neal, "Black Power in the International Context," in Barbour, *Black Power Revolt*, 136, 141; Anderson, "Pan-African Idea," 113, 118–19; Robert L. Allen, "Black Liberation and World Revolution," in *Contemporary Black Thought*, ed. Robert Chrisman and Nathan Hare (Indianapolis: Bobbs-Merrill, 1973), 265–69; Ronald W. Walters, "Marxism-Leninism and the Black Revolution: A Critical Essay," in Hall, *Black Separatism*, 131–32.

94. Anderson, "Pan-African Idea," 112, 117–18; Karenga, "Which Road," 30.

95. Baraka, "Position Paper," 9; Max Stanford, "Black Guerrilla Warfare: Strategy and Tactics," *Black Scholar* 2 (November 1970): 30–31; Allen, "Black Liberation," 248; Ahmad, "Pan African Liberation," 25, 27–28.

96. Carmichael, *Stokely Speaks*, 159–160.

97. H. Rap Brown, "A Letter from H. Rap Brown," in Barbour, *Black Seventies*, 312; Julius Lester, *Revolutionary Notes* (New York: Richard W. Baron, 1969), 41–43, 129; Julius Lester, *Look Out, Whitey! Black Power's Gon' Get Your Mama!* (New York: Grove, 1969), 138; Carmichael, *Stokely Speaks*, 157, 217–18, 220; Acklyn Lynch and Alma Mathieu Lynch, "Images of the 21st Century . . . Blackness," in Barbour, *Black Seventies*, 222–23; George L. Jackson, *Blood in My Eye* (New York: Random House, 1972), 42; Brown, *Die*, pp. 85, 144–45.

98. *Off the Pigs!: The History and Literature of the Black Panther Party*, ed. G. Louis Heath (Metuchen, New Jersey: Scarecrow, 1976), 117.

99. Earl Anthony, *Picking Up the Gun: A Report on the Black Panthers* (New York: Dial, 1970), 88. In a 1970 *Time*-Louis Harris poll of 1,255 blacks nationwide, one in four respondents agreed with the statement, "The Black Panthers represent my own personal views." This figure rose to 43 percent among those under 21. Other surveys showed a consistent concentration of support for the Party in the 21-and-under age group. There was more general cross-generational agreement with the view that the Panthers gave all blacks a sense of pride by "standing up for the rights of black people and by saying things about white people that ought to be said." "The Black Mood: More Militant, More Hopeful, More Determined," *Time*, 6 April 1970, 29; *The Harris Survey Yearbook of Public Opinion, 1970* (New York: Louis Harris and Associates, 1971), 259; *The Harris Survey Yearbook of Public Opinion, 1971* (New York: Louis Harris and Associates, 1975), 334; Daniel U. Levine, Norman S. Fiddmont, Robert S. Stephenson, and Charles Wilkinson, "Differences Between Black Youth Who Support the Black Panthers and the NAACP," *Journal of Negro Education* 42 (Winter 1973): 19–32; Goldman, *Report*, 239.

100. *Eldridge Cleaver: Post-Prison Writings and Speeches*, ed. Robert Scheer (New York: Random House, 1969), 38, 189; Reginald Major, *A Panther is a Black Cat* (New York: William Morrow, 1971), 58; David Hilliard, "Interview with CBS News, December 28, 1969," in *The Black Panthers Speak*, ed. Philip S. Foner (Philadelphia: J. B. Lippincott, 1970), 133.

101. Bobby Seale, *Seize the Time: The Story of the Black Panther Party and Huey P. Newton* (New York: Random House, 1970), 30–31; Carolyn R. Calloway,

"Group Cohesiveness in the Black Panther Party," *Journal of Black Studies* 8 (September 1977): 55–73; Huey P. Newton, *To Die for the People: The Writings of Huey P. Newton* (New York: Vintage: 1972), 48–49; Gene Marine, *The Black Panthers* (New York: New American Library, 1969), 40–41, 73. In July 1967, the California legislature prohibited the carrying of loaded firearms on one's person, in a vehicle, or on any public street.

102. Anthony, *Gun*, 95; Heath, *Off the Pigs!*, 63–64; Seale, *Seize the Time*, 368–69; Marine, *Black Panthers*, 41.

103. Seale, *Seize the Time*, 71, 375, 391; Newton, *To Die*, 175–76; Huey P. Newton, *Revolutionary Suicide* (New York: Ballantine, 1974), 2–4, 126. The Panthers dropped the "Self-Defense" designation in 1967 because "people seemed to misinterpret the definition of what self defense was all about." Their political orientation was obscured by the paramilitary "body guard" image. "In Defense of Self Defense: An Exclusive Interview with Minister of Defense, Huey P. Newton," in Bracey, Meier, and Rudwick, *Black Nationalism*, 535.

104. Eldridge Cleaver, *Soul on Ice* (New York: Dell, 1968), 129, 134, 137; "Huey Must be Set Free!" *Black Panther*, 23 November 1967, 1; Bobby Seale, "Free Huey," in *Rhetoric of Black Revolution*, ed. Arthur L. Smith (Boston: Allyn and Bacon, 1969), 184–85.

105. Seale, "Free Huey," 184; Newton, *Revolutionary Suicide*, 134–35, 176–77; Seale, *Seize the Time*, 404, 420–21; In April 1971, a Panther-sponsored referendum calling for the establishment of three separate police departments in Berkeley was defeated by a margin of almost two to one. If implemented, the decentralization plan would have created separate departments to serve the black community, the white community, and the student/"hippie" area near the University of California campus.

106. "Huey Newton Talks to the Movement About the Black Panther Party, Cultural Nationalism, SNCC, Liberals and White Revolutionaries," in Foner, *Panthers Speak*, 60; Seale, *Seize the Time*, 79–85.

107. Marine, *Black Panthers*, 67–72; Seale, "Free Huey," 178; Newton, *Revolutionary Suicide*, 369; *Harris Survey, 1970*, 231, *Harris Survey, 1971*, 332.

108. Seale, *Seize the Time*, 412–13, 418; Newton, *To Die*, 52–53, 104.

109. Art Goldberg, "The Panthers After the Trial," *Ramparts* 10 (March 1972): 25.

110. Ibid., 25–27; "Liberation Means Freedom," *Black Panther*, 5 July 1969, 3.

111. Seale, *Seize the Time*, 415; Marine, *Black Panthers*, 73–74; Newton, *To Die*, 21.

112. Newton, *To Die*, 31–37, 39–42, 207–210; Huey P. Newton, "Intercommunalism," in *In Search of Common Ground: Conversations with Erik H. Erikson and Huey P. Newton* (New York: W. W. Norton, 1973), 27–32, 41–42.

113. Lee Lockwood, *Conversation with Eldridge Cleaver: Algiers* (New York: McGraw-Hill, 1970), 51, 63, 67–73; "Speech by Field Marshall D.C. at Fillmore Auditorium, S.F., *"Black Panther*, 20 April 1969, 16; "George Murray Press Conference," *Black Panther*, 12 October 1968, 14.

114. Newton, *To Die*, 28; Heath, *Off the Pigs!*, 151; Fred Hampton, "Complete Satisfaction!" in Heath, *Off the Pigs!*, 244.

115. Newton, *To Die*, 97–99; Huey P. Newton, "The Black Panthers," in *The*

Black Revolution: An Ebony Special Issue (Chicago: Johnson Publishing Company, 1970), 129–30; Lockwood, *Conversation*, 106–7.

116. "We Must Develop a United Front Against Fascism," in Foner, *Panthers Speak*, 222.

117. Ronald Steel, "Letter from Oakland: The Panthers," *New York Review of Books*, 11 September 1969, 19; Seale, *Seize the Time*, 217; Sol Stern, "The Call of the Black Panthers," *New York Times Magazine*, 6 August 1967, 68. Commentary on the troubled Panther-SNCC alliance may be found in James Forman, *The Making of Black Revolutionaries* (New York: Macmillan, 1972), 522–43; Eldridge Cleaver, "Political Struggle in America," in Smith, *Rhetoric*, 166–74; Lester, *Revolutionary Notes*, 144–49.

118. "Huey Newton Talks," 55–57.

119. Kathleen Cleaver, "Black Power, Black Lawyers, and White Courts," *Black Panther*, 18 May 1968, 5, 13; Senate Committee on Governmental Operations, *Riots, Civil and Criminal Disorders: Hearings Before the Permanent Subcommittee on Investigations of the Committee on Government Operations*. U.S. Senate, 91st Cong., 1st Sess., June 26, 30, 1969, Part 20: 4436; Steel, "Letter," 22; Cleaver, *Post-Prison Writings*, 188; Eldridge Cleaver, "The Fire Now: Field Nigger Power Takes Over the Black Movement," *Commonweal*, 14 June 1968, 377; Heath, *Off the Pigs!*, 95–96; "Masi Speaks at the Revolutionary Labor Conference," *Black Panther*, 4 May 1969, 13.

120. *Criminal Disorders*, 4437.

121. "'Guerrilla Warfare in the U.S.'—FBI Report," *U.S. News & World Report*, 9 November 1970, 53–55.

122. Cleaver, *Post-Prison Writings*, 165; Malcolm X *Autobiography*, 417; Newton, *To Die*, 14; Lockwood, *Conversation*, 52.

123. Newton, *To Die*, 16–17, 44–45.

124. Ibid., 16, 45; Breitman, *Malcolm X Speaks*, 36–38.

125. *Black Power Conference*, 7; "Equality Defined," *Newsweek*, 3 July 1967, 30; Robert Daley, *Target Blue: An Insider's View of the N.Y.P.D.* (New York: Delacorte, 1973), 77; "Max Stanford Calls for Independent Black Nation," in Bracey, Meier, and Rudwick, *Black Nationalism*, 515.

126. Stanford, "Guerrilla Warfare," 30–38; Russell Sackett, "Plotting a War on 'Whitey,'" *Life*, 10 June 1966, 106.

127. John Howard Griffin, "Is There Really a Black Guerrilla Army?" *Sepia* 22 (September 1973): 22.

128. Sol Stern, "America's Black Guerrillas," *Ramparts* 6 (September 1967): 27.

129. Homer Bigart, "4 Held in Plot to Blast Statue of Liberty, Liberty Bell and Washington Monument," *New York Times*, 17 February 1965, 1, 34; "Detective Tells of Shrines Plot," *New York Times*, 19 May 1965, 53; "Vietnamese Tied to Bombing Plot," *New York Times*, 20 May 1965, 46; "Plans for Bombings Heard by Plot Jury," *New York Times*, 25 May 1965, 13.

130. "Mass Poison Plot Laid to Negroes," *New York Times*, 28 September 1967, 33; Emanuel Perlmutter, "16 Negroes Seized; Plot to Kill Wilkins and Young Charged," *New York Times*, 22 June 1967, 1, 25; "3 Names Added as Plot Targets," *New York Times*, 23 June 1967, 16; "Witness Links Ferguson to Assassination Talk," *New York Times*, 5 June 1968, 41; "Busting RAM," *Time*, 30

June 1967, 20; "Equality Defined," 30; "Hoover Links Carmichael to Negro Leftist Group," *New York Times*, 17 May 1967, 30.

131. Newton, *Revolutionary Suicide*, 336–338; "Open Letter to Weatherman Underground From Panther 21," *Liberated Guardian*, 25 February 1971, 16–17; "Enemies of the People," *Black Panther*, 13 February 1971, 12–13.

132. "De Mau Mau," *Time*, 30 October 1972, 28; "De Mau Mau," *Newsweek*, 30 October 1972, 48; Martin Weston, "De Mau Mau: Fast Eddie's Last Draw," *Ramparts* 11 (February 1973): 11–12.

133. Louis H. Masotti and Jerome R. Corsi, *Shoot-Out in Cleveland: Black Militants and the Police: July 23, 1968* (New York: Frederick A. Praeger, 1969), 26–27; Don A. Schanche, *The Panther Paradox: A Liberal's Dilemma* (New York: David McKay, 1970), 92.

134. Buckett, "Plotting a War," 100A; Griffin, "Black Guerrilla Army," 17, 20; "The Cop Killers," *Newsweek*, 12 February 1973, 29, 32.

135. Newton, *To Die*, 92; Seale, *Seize the Time*, 34; Brown, *Die*, 143.

136. Imamu Amiri Baraka, *Raise, Race, Rays, Raze: Essays Since 1965* (New York: Vintage, 1972) 130–131.

137. Askia Muhammad Touré, "The Crisis in Black Culture," *Journal of Black Poetry* 1(Spring 1968): 3; Imamu Amiri Baraka, ed., *African Congress: A Documentary of the First Modern Pan-African Congress* (New York: William Morrow, 1972), 95, 99; Harold Cruse, *Rebellion or Revolution?* (New York: William Morrow, 1968), 49, 52–53.

138. Baraka, *Raze*, 112; Baraka, *African Congress*, 95, 119.

139. For an etymology of the concept of cultural revolution, see Cruse, "Black and White," 30–31.

140. Maulana Karenga, *Kwanzaa: Origin, Concepts, Practice* (Los Angeles: Kawaida, 1977), 53–54.

141. "Interview: Dr. Malauna Karenga," *African Commentary* 1 (October 1989): 61.

142. Clyde Halisi, ed., *The Quotable Karenga* (Los Angeles: US Organization, 1967), 8, 12–14.

143. Halisi, *Karenga*, 13; Karenga, *Kwanzaa*, 40.

144. Karenga, *Kwanzaa*, 12, 15, 20, 37–39, 47–48.

145. Halisi, *Karenga*, 22; Karenga, *Kwanzaa*, 40.

146. Karenga, *Kwanzaa*, 18, 40–41; Halisi, *Karenga*. 8, 12–14; Ron Karenga, "Black Nationalist Cultural Organisation," *Présence Africaine* (No. 2, 1968): 197, "BBB Interviews Maulana Ron Karenga," *Black Books Bulletin* 4 (Summer 1976): 34.

147. Earl Anthony, *The Time of the Furnaces: A Case Study of Black Student Revolt*, (New York: Dial, 1971). 24; Halisi, *Karenga*, 6.

148. Baraka, *African Congress*, viii; Ron Karenga, "Overturning Ourselves: From Mystification to Meaningful Struggle," *Black Scholar* 4 (October 1972): 8, 10; Earl Caldwell, "Two Police Inspectors from Here Among the Newark Delegates," *New York Times*, 22 July 1967, 11.

149. Halisi, *Karenga*, 9, 23–24.

150. Anthony, *Gun*, 75.

151. Halisi, *Karenga*, 12.

152. Seale, *Seize the Time*, 271; Costas Axios and Nikos Syvriotis, *Papa Doc*

Baraka: Fascism in Newark (New York: National Caucus of Labor Committees, 1973), 12. For popular accounts of the US-Black Panther confrontations, see Marine, *Black Panthers*, 208–211; Gail Sheehy, *Panthermania: The Clash of Black Against Black in One American City* (New York: Harper & Row, 1971), 16–21.

153. Seale, *Seize the Time*, 72; Brown, *Die*, 104; Jackson, *Blood*, 31–32.

154. Brown, *Die*, 141; Seale, *Seize the Time*, 247; Ernie Mkalimoto, "Revolutionary Black Culture: The Cultural Arm of Revolutionary Nationalism," *Negro Digest* 19 (December 1969): 13–17; Eldridge Cleaver, "Culture and Revolution: Their Synthesis in Africa," *Black Scholar* 3 (October 1971): 34–35; Muhammad Ahmed, "The Roots of the Pan-African Revolution," *Black Scholar* 3 (May 1972): 51; Linda Harrison, "On Cultural Nationalism," in Foner, *Panthers Speak*, 151; Newton, "Black Panthers," 130.

155. Newton, *To Die*, 69, 93.

156. Seale, *Seize the Time*, 256.

157. Newton, *Revolutionary Suicide*, vii; Brown, *Die*, 115, 117; Forman, *Black Revolutionaries*, 510–512; Daley, *Target Blue*, 173.

158. "Militant Negro Leader: Ron Ndabezitha Everett-Karenga," *New York Times*, 2 September 1968, 13.

159. Carmichael, *Stokely Speaks*, 101, 109.

160. "Roy Innis: Black Nationalist," *Penthouse* 1 (January 1970): 28.

161. Essien-Udom, *Black Nationalism*, 188; Malcolm X, *Autobiography*, 250.

162. Baraka, *Raze*, 146.

163. *The Autobiography of LeRoi Jones/Amiri Baraka* (New York: Freundlich, 1984), 252–255.

164. LeRoi Jones, *Home: Social Essays* (New York: William Morrow, 1966), 193.

165. Ibid., 244, 246; LeRoi Jones, "The Need for a Cultural Base to Civil Rites & Bpower Mooments," in Barbour, *Black Power Revolt*, 123–126.

166. Werner Sollors, *Amiri Baraka/LeRoi Jones: The Quest for a "Populist Modernism"* (New York: Columbia University Press, 1978), 177.

167. Baraka, *Raze*, 99–100.

168. Baraka, *Autobiography*, 202–205; Theodore R. Hudson, *From LeRoi Jones to Amiri Baraka: The Literary Works* (Durham: Duke University Press, 1973), 21.

169. Baraka, *Autobiography*, 236; Imamu Amiri Baraka and Fundi, *In Our Terribleness: Some Elements and Meaning in Black Style* (Indianapolis: Bobbs-Merrill, 1970), 70; Baraka, *Raze*, 125, 127; Mel Gussow, "Baraka Discusses Politics as an Art," *New York Times*, 13 March 1973, 30; *Black Power Conference*, 39; Jones, "Cultural Base," 123.

170. Baraka, *Raze*, 112.

171. Baraka, *African Congress*, 118, 120; Baraka, *Raze*, 160; Baraka, *Autobiography*, 274.

172. *Black Power Conference*, 40; Baraka and Fundi, *Terribleness*, 133.

173. Baraka, *Raze*, 65, 79–80; Baraka, *Autobiography*, 302; Imamu Amiri Baraka, "Toward the Creation of Political Institutions for All African Peoples," *Black World* 21 (October 1972): 78; Imamu Amiri Baraka, "The Pan-African

Party and the Black Nation," *Black Scholar* 2 (March 1971): 24–25; Baraka, *African Congress*, 92–94, 115–122; Imamu Amiri Baraka, "Strategies & Tactics of an Afro-American Party," *Black Politician* 3 (October 1971), 40–43.

174. Baraka, *Raze*, 160; Baraka, "Strategies," 40.

175. Baraka, *African Congress*, 101.

176. Baraka, *Autobiography*, 283–284.

177. Ibid., 224–225.

178. LeRoi Jones, "Black People!" in *Black Magic: Collected Poetry, 1961–1967* (Indianapolis: Bobbs-Merrill, 1969), 225.

179. Baraka, *Autobiography*, 258–272; Stephen Schneck, "LeRoi Jones or, Poetics & Policemen or, Trying Heart, Bleeding Heart," *Ramparts* 6 (13 July 1968): 14–19, "Poetic Justice," *Newsweek*, 15 January 1968, 24; Hudson, *Baraka*, 27–31.

180. Baraka, *Autobiography*, 221.

181. Charles T. Davis, *Black is the Color of the Cosmos: Essays on Afro-American Literature and Culture, 1942–1981*, (New York: Garland, 1982), 33.

182. Larry Neal, "The Black Arts Movement," *Drama Review* 12 (Summer 1968): 29–30; Larry Neal, "Black Art and Black Liberation," in *Black Revolution*, 39; Eugene Perkins, "The Black Arts Movement: Its Challenge and Responsibility," in Barbour, *Black Seventies*, 88, 96.

183. "The Task of the Negro Writer as Artist: A Symposium," *Negro Digest* 14 (April 1965): 69, 72.

184. *Black Power Conference*, 39; Eugene B. Redmond, *Drum Voices: The Mission of Afro-American Poetry* (Garden City, New York: Anchor Press/Doubleday, 1976), 306–7, 351–52; C. Eric Lincoln, "The Excellence of Soul," in *New Black Voices*, ed. Abraham Chapman (New York: New American Library, 1972), 583.

185. Abby Arthur Johnson and Ronald Maberry Johnson, *Propaganda and Aesthetics: The Literary Politics of Afro-American Magazines in the Twentieth Century* (Amherst: University of Massachusetts Press, 1979), 166–169; Hoyt Fuller, "Black Images and White Critics," *Negro Digest* 19 (November 1969): 50; Willard T. Pinn, Jr., "Towards a Black Communication System," *Soulbook* 3 (Fall–Winter 1970): 42–44; Don L. Lee, "Black Poetry: Which Direction?" *Negro Digest* 17 (September–October 1968): 31; Don L. Lee, "Toward a Definition: Black Poetry of the Sixties (After LeRoi Jones)," in *The Black Aesthetic*, ed. Addison Gayle, Jr. (Garden City, New York: Doubleday, 1972), 232.

186. Addison Gayle, Jr., "Introduction," in Gayle, *Black Aesthetic*, xxii.

187. Julian Mayfield, "You Touch My Black Aesthetic and I'll Touch Yours," in Gayle, *Black Aesthetic*, 26; Adam David Miller, "Some Observations on a Black Aesthetic," in Gayle, *Black Aesthetic*, 380; Baraka and Fundi, *In Our Terribleness*, 60; Larry Neal, "And Shine Swam On," in *Black Fire*, ed. LeRoi Jones and Larry Neal (New York: William Morrow, 1968), 655; Ishmael Reed, ed., *19 Necromancers from Now* (Garden City, New York: Doubleday, 1970) xviii; Francis Ward and Val Gray Ward, "The Black Artist—His Role in the Struggle," *Black Scholar* 2 (January 1971): 29; Ameer Baraka, "The Black Aesthetic," *Negro Digest* 18 (September 1969): 6.

188. "Task of the Negro Writer," 60, 79; Mercer Cook and Stephen E. Henderson,

The Militant Black Writer in Africa and the United States (Madison: University of Wisconsin Press, 1969), 72; Ronald Milner, "Black Magic: Black Art," *Negro Digest* 16 (April 1967): 11; Baraka, *Raze*, 128.

189. Carole A. Parks, "Self-Determination and the Black Aesthetic: An Interview With Max Roach," *Black World* 23 (November 1973): 69.

190. Robert Chrisman, "The Formation of a Revolutionary Black Culture," *Black Scholar* 1 (June 1970): 5, Neal, "Black Art," 33; Halisi, *Karenga*, 30.

191. Jones, *Home*, 173–178, 232; Baraka, *Raze*, 80.

192. Johari Amini, "Re-definition: Concept as Being." *Black World* 21 (May 1972): 11; John Oliver Killens, *Black Man's Burden* (New York: Trident, 1965), 29; Ward and Ward, "Black Artist," 27–28; Don L. Lee, "The Black Writer and the Black Community," *Black World* 21 (May, 1972): 85.

193. Cruse, *Rebellion*, 56–57; Don L. Lee, "Black Writing: this is u, thisisu," *Negro Digest* 18 (March 1969): 78; Halisi, *Karenga*, 29–31; Carolyn Rodgers, "The Literature of Black," *Black World* 19 (June 1970): 7.

194. Ron Karenga, "Black Cultural Nationalism," in Gayle, *Black Aesthetic*, 31–37.

195. LeRoi Jones, "Black Art" in *Black Magic*, 116.

196. John O'Neal, "Black Arts: Notebook," in Gayle, *Black Aesthetic*, 46–47, 56; Hoyt W. Fuller, "Toward a Black Aesthetic," *Critic* 26 (April–May 1968): 72–73; Cruse, "Black and White," 35–36; Martin Kilson and Addison Gayle, "The Black Aesthetic," *Black World* 24 (December 1974): 36–37; "Artist in an Age of Revolution: A Symposium," *Arts in Society* 5 (No. 2, 1968): 220.

197. "Age of Revolution," 229; Hoyt W. Fuller, "The New Black Literature: Protest or Affirmation," in Gayle, *Black Aesthetic*, 338; "Task of the Negro Writer," 64, 78; Jervis Anderson, "Black Writing: The Other Side," *Dissent* 15 (May–June 1968): 236; Larry Neal, "New Space/The Growth of Black Consciousness in the Sixties, in Barbour, *Black Seventies*, 29; Neal, "Shine," 647–648.

198. Lance Jeffers, "The Death of the Defensive Posture: Toward Grandeur in Afro-American Letters," in Barbour, *Black Seventies*, 263.

199. Halisi, *Karenga*, 29; Melvin Dixon, "Black Theater: The Aesthetics," *Negro Digest* 18 (July 1969): 43.

200. Sherry Turner, "An Overview of The New Black Arts," *Freedomways* 9 (Spring 1969): 159.

201. Ronald Milner, "Black Theater—Go Home!" in Gayle, *Black Aesthetic*, 293–294; Dixon, "Black Theater," 43–44.

202. Turner, "Overview," 156.

203. Larry Neal, "Don't Say Goodbye to the Porkpie Hat," in *Hoodoo Hollerin' Bebop Ghosts* (Washington, D.C.: Howard University Press, 1974), 23–24.

204. Don L. Lee, "Move Un-noticed to be Noticed: An Nationhood Poem," in *We Walk the Way of the New World* (Detroit: Broadside Press, 1970), 69.

205. Rodgers, "Literature of Black," 9.

206. Stephen Henderson, *Understanding the New Black Poetry: Black Speech and Black Music as Poetic References* (New York: William Morrow, 1973), 28–61; Geneva Smitherman, "The Power of the Rap: The Black Idiom and the New Black Poetry," *Twentieth Century Literature* 19 (October 1973): 263–

272; Carolyn Rodgers, "Black Poetry—Where It's At," *Negro Digest* 18 (September 1969): 7–16.

207. Rodgers, "Literature of Black," 10; John Oliver Killens, *The Cotillion; or, One Good Bull is Half the Herd* (New York: Trident, 1971), 6.

208. Sherley Anne Williams, *Give Birth to Brightness: A Thematic Study in Neo-Black Literature* (New York: Dial, 1972), 234; "Ishmael Reed," in *Interviews with Black Writers*, ed. John O'Brien (New York: Liveright, 1973), 181.

209. Sonia Sanchez, "Queens of the Universe," *Black Scholar* 1 (January–February, 1970): 33.

210. Carmichael, "Pan-Africanism," 42; Walters, "Re-Africanization," 101; Baraka, "Pan-African Party," 26; Robert Chrisman and Nathan Hare, eds., *Pan-Africanism* (Indianapolis: Bobbs Merrill, 1974): 1.

211. Brown, *Die*, 130; James Turner, "Black Nationalism: The Inevitable Response," *Black World* 20 (January 1971): 12; Lawrence P. Neal, "Black Power in the International Context," in Barbour, *Black Power Revolt*, 140; Lester, *Revolutionary Notes* 165, 191; Mkalimoto, "Revolutionary Black Culture," 12, 14, 17.

212. Neal, "Black Art," 40, 46, 49; Baraka, *Raze*, 98, 126; Williams, *Brightness*, 240; Ronald Walters, "African-American Nationalism: A Unifying Ideology," *Black World* 22 (October 1973): 27; Chrisman, "Revolutionary Black Culture," 6; Lester, *Revolutionary Notes*, 190.

Chapter Five

1. See, for example, Leonard Broom and Norval D. Glenn, "Negro-White Difference in Reported Attitudes and Behavior," *Sociology and Social Research* 50 (January 1966): 187–200; Angus Campbell and Howard Schuman, *Racial Attitudes in Fifteen American Cities* (Ann Arbor: Survey Research Center, Institute for Social Research, 1968), 39–59; Ralph W. Conant, Sheldon Levy, and Ralph Lewis, "Mass Polarization: Negro and White Attitudes on the Pace of Integration," *American Behavioral Scientist* 13 (November–December 1969): 247–63.

2. Joseph Scott, "Black Science and Nation-Building," in *The Death of White Sociology*, ed. Joyce A. Ladner (New York: Vintage, 1973), 291.

3. More than half of the black respondents in a 1969 *Newsweek* poll agreed that most Afro-Americans possess "a spiritual quality . . . a special soul" that sets them apart from whites. Only 22 percent disagreed. "Soul," *Newsweek*, 30 June 1969, 22.

4. C. Eric Lincoln, "The Excellence of Soul," in *New Black Voices*, ed. Abraham Chapman (New York: New American Library, 1972), 585; W. A. Jeanpierre, "African Negritude—Black American Soul," *Africa Today* 14 (December 1967): 10–11; Herman S. Hughes, "Soul," *America*, 2 August 1969, 62–63; Mercer Cook and Stephen E. Henderson, *The Militant Black Writer in Africa and the United States* (Madison: University of Wisconsin Press, 1969), 124; Al Calloway and Claude Brown, "An Introduction to Soul," *Esquire* 69 (April 1968): 80. For studies of "la négritude" as developed by French-speaking black intellectuals responding to the colonialism and cultural chauvinism of the 1930s and 1940s, see Lilyan Kesteloot. *Black Writers in French: A Literary History of Negritude* (Philadelphia: Temple University Press, 1974); Edward A. Jones, "Afro-French

Writers of the 1930's and Creation of the *Négritude* School," *CLA Journal* 14 (September 1970): 18–34; Irving Leonard Markovitz, *Léopold Sédar Senghor and the Politics of Negritude* (London: Heinemann, 1969); A. James Arnold, *Modernism and Negritude: The Poetry and Poetics of Aimé Césaire* (Cambridge: Harvard University Press, 1981).

5. David A. Schulz, *Coming Up Black: Patterns of Ghetto Socialization* (Englewood Cliffs, New Jersey: Prentice-Hall, 1969), 78–87; Edith A. Folb, *Runnin' Down Some Lines: The Language and Culture of Black Teenagers* (Cambridge: Harvard University Press, 1980), 127; Calloway and Brown, "Soul," 79, 86; Paul Carter Harrison, *The Drama of Nommo* (New York: Grove, 1972), 73.

6. Calloway and Brown, "Soul," 79.

7. Kenneth R. Johnson, "Black Kinesics—Some Non-Verbal Communication Patterns in the Black Culture," in *Perspectives on Black English*, ed. J. Dillard (The Hague, The Netherlands: Mouton, 1975), 33–42, 61, 304–5; Malachi Andrews and Paul T. Owens, *Black Language* (Los Angeles: Seymour-Smith, 1973), 71; John Horton, "Time and Cool People," *Trans-action* 4 (April 1967): 11.

8. Clarence Brown, "Wayout Look is Said on the Way Out," *Jet*, 7 March 1974, 20; Robert G. Weisbord, *Ebony Kinship: Africa, Africans, and the Afro-American* (Westport, Connecticut: Greenwood, 1973), 193.

9. Bil Howard, "New Look by New Breed," *Sepia* 17 (September 1968): 38, 40.

10. Advertisement for Flori Roberts pantyhose, *Essence* 3 (December 1972): 30.

11. Larry Neal, "Black Art and Black Liberation," in *The Black Revolution: An Ebony Special Issue* (Chicago: Johnson Publishing Company, 1970), 49; Phyl Garland, "The Natural Look," *Ebony* 21 (June 1966): 143–44, Willie Morrow, *400 Years Without a Comb* (San Diego: Black Publishers of San Diego, 1973), 17; Stokely Carmichael, "Stokely Carmichael on Black Power," in *The Afro-Americans: Selected Documents*, ed. John H. Bracey, Jr., August Meier, and Elliott Rudwick (Boston: Allyn and Bacon, 1972), 741.

12. A quantitative study of advertisements appearing in *Ebony* between January 1949 and December 1972 revealed a rapid and continuous decline in the number of ads for hair straighteners after 1967. The first ad for hair care products featuring a model wearing a natural appeared in December 1967. The incidence of such ads increased markedly in each succeeding year. J. Spencer Condie and James W. Christiansen, "An Indirect Technique for the Measurement of Changes in Black Identity," *Phylon* 38 (Spring 1977): 46–54.

13. Hank Ballard & The Dapps, "How You Gonna Get Respect (When You Haven't Cut Your Process Yet)," King 6196, 1968; Willie L. Morrow, *Curly Hair* (San Diego: Black Publishers of San Diego, 1973), 6, 13; Phyl Garland, "Is the Afro on Its Way Out?" *Ebony* 28 (February 1973): 136, Valerie M. Thomas, *Accent African: Traditional and Contemporary Hair Styles for The Black Woman* (New York: Col-Bob Associates, 1973), 2, 5, 6, 8, 28.

14. "Headliners," *Essence* 5 (February 1975): 42; "Your Best Wraps, Naturally," *Essence* 3 (February 1973): 58–59.

15. David Llorens, "Natural Hair: New Symbol of Race Pride," *Ebony* 23 (December 1967): 140–41.

16. Craig Claiborne, "Cooking With Soul" *New York Times Magazine*, 3 November 1968, 107.

17. Verta Mae Smart Grosvenor, "Soul Food," *McCall's* 97 (September 1970): 72, 75; Verta Mae, *Vibration Cooking or The Travel Notes of a Geechee Girl* (New York: Doubleday, 1970), xiii.

18. Freda DeKnight, *The Ebony Cookbook: A Date With a Dish* (Chicago: Johnson Publishing Company, 1973), vii.

19. Mary Jackson and Lelia Wishart, *The Integrated Cookbook or The Soul of Good Cooking* (Chicago: Johnson Publishing Company, 1971), 1–2. For an opposing view, see Gene Baro, "Soul Food," *Vogue* 155 (March 1970): 80, 92.

20. Jackson and Wishart, *Integrated Cookbook*, 1; Helen Mendes, *The African Heritage Cookbook* (New York: Macmillan, 1971), 11–12, 34–37, 64, 76, 78–79.

21. Jackson and Wishart, *Integrated Cookbook*, 3, 17, 22; Verta Mae, *Vibration*, xiii, 147.

22. King Curtis, "Memphis Soul Stew," Atco 6511, 1967; 100 Proof Aged in Soul, "Too Many Cooks (Spoil the Soup)," Hot Wax 6904, 1969, Soul Runners, "Chittlin' Salad," MoSoul 5104, 1967; Johnny "Guitar" Watson, "Soul Food," Okeh 7290, 1967.

23. Marvin L. Sims, "Talkin' About Soul" Revue 11024, 1968; Willie Mitchell, "Soul Serenade," Hi 2140, 1968; Booker T. & the MG's, "Soul-Limbo," Stax 0001, 1968; 5th Dimension, "Stoned Soul Picnic," Soul City 766, 1968; James Brown, "Soul Power," King 6368, 1971, Capitols, "Soul Brother, Soul Sister," Karen 1543, 1969; James Brown, "Soul Pride," King 6222, 1969; Gladys Knight & the Pips, "The Nitty Gritty," Soul 35063, 1969; Shan Miles, "Soul People" Shout 222, 1967.

24. Phyl Garland, *The Sound of Soul* (Chicago: Henry Regnery, 1969), i; Robert Tyler "The Musical Culture of Afro-America," *Black Scholar* 3 (Summer 1972): 27; Olly Wilson, "The Significance of the Relationship Between Afro-American Music and West African Music," *Black Perspective in Music* 2 (Spring 1974): 3, 6, 19–20; Ron Wellburn, "The Black Aesthetic Imperative," in *The Black Aesthetic*, ed. Addison Gayle, Jr. (Garden City, New York: Doubleday, 1972), 126–27, 142; William H. McClendon, "Black Music: Sound and Feeling for Black Liberation," *Black Scholar* 7 (January–February 1976): 23–24; A.X. Nicholas, *The Poetry of Soul* (New York: Bantam, 1971), xiii; Max Roach, "What 'Jazz' Means to Me," *Black Scholar* 3 (Summer 1972): 6.

25. Eldridge Cleaver, *Soul on Ice* (New York: McGraw-Hill, 1968), 192–93; Nicholas, *Poetry*, xiii.

26. Errol Green, "Black Music," *Liberator* 8 (April 1968): 13; Hubert Walters, "Black Music and the Black University," *Black Scholar* 3 (Summer 1972): 20; Askia Muhammad Touré, "The Crises in Black Culture," *Journal of Black Poetry* 1 (Spring 1968): 3–5; Nat Hentoff, "The New Jazz—Black, Angry, and Hard to Understand," *New York Times Magazine*, 25 December 1966, 10.

27. LeRoi Jones, *Black Music* (New York: William Morrow, 1968), 205–6; Ortiz M. Walton, "A Comparative Analysis of the African and the Western Aesthetics," in Gayle, *Black Aesthetic*, 155–161.

28. Ortiz Walton, *Music: Black, White & Blue—A Sociological Survey of the Use and Misuse of Afro-American Music* (New York: William Morrow, 1972), 121, 142; Wellburn, "Aesthetic Imperative," 140–41.

29. Roach, "Jazz," 6; Jones, *Black Music*, 206.

30. Walton, *Music*, 115; Tyler, "Musical Culture," 27; Garland, *Soul*, 12; Donald Byrd, "The Meaning of Black Music," *Black Scholar* 3 (Summer 1972): 31.

31. Roger D. Abrahams, *Positively Black* (Englewood Cliffs, New Jersey: Prentice-Hall, 1970), 137.

32. Ray Charles, "Eleanor Rigby," ABC 11090, 1968; Vontastics, "Day Tripper," St. Lawrence 1014, 1966; Aretha Franklin, "Bridge Over Troubled Water," Atlantic 2796, 1971; Aretha Franklin, "Son of a Preacher Man," Atlantic 2706, 1970.

33. Michael Haralambos, *Right On: From Blues to Soul in Black America* (New York: Drake, 1975).

34. James Brown, "Let Yourself Go," King 6100, 1967.

35. Sam & Dave, "I Thank You," Stax 242, 1968.

36. Rolland Snellings, "Keep on Pushin': Rhythm & Blues as a Weapon," *Liberator* 5 (October 1965): 8.

37. Hues Corporation, "Go to the Poet," *Freedom For The Stallion*, RCA Victor 0323, 1974.

38. Jervis Anderson, "Black Writing: The Other Side," *Dissent* 15 (May–June 1968): 237.

39. Mel Watkins, "The Lyrics of James Brown: Ain't it Funky Now, or Money Won't Change Your Licking Stick," in *Amistad 2*, ed. John A. Williams and Charles F. Harris (New York: Vintage, 1971), 22.

40. Gerri Hirshey, *Nowhere to Run: The Story of Soul Music* (New York: Times Books, 1984), 319.

41. Charles Keil, *Urban Blues* (Chicago: University of Chicago Press, 1966), 166.

42. Haralambos, *Right On*, 146; *Wattstax II: The Living Word*, Stax 3018, 1973.

43. Tony Clarke, "Ghetto Man," Chicory 409, 1969.

44. Staple Singers, "Be What You Are," Stax 0164, 1973; Aretha Franklin, "A Natural Woman," Atlantic 2441, 1967; Detroit Emeralds "(I'm An Ordinary Man) Take Me the Way I Am," Ric Tic, 141, 1968; Temptations. "Message From a Black Man," *Puzzle People*, Gordy 949, 1970.

45. Carole A. Parks, "Self-Determination and the Black Aesthetic: An Interview With Max Roach," *Black World* 23 (November 1973): 69–70.

46. Haralambos, *Right On*, 123–24.

47. Nina Simone, "Revolution," RCA Victor 9730, 1969.

48. James Carr, "Freedom Train," Goldwax 338, 1968. For a selection of the songs of the Civil Rights movement, see Pete Seeger and Bob Reiser, *Everybody Says Freedom* (New York: W. W. Norton, 1989).

49. Impressions, "Keep on Pushing," ABC Paramount 10554, 1964; Chi-Lites, "(For God's Sake) Give More Power to the People," Brunswick 55450, 1971; Willie Hightower, "Time Has Brought About a Change," Fame 1474, 1970; Simone, "Revolution."

50. Sam Cooke, "Chain Gang," RCA Victor 7783, 1960.

51. Edwin Starr, "Ain't it Hell Up in Harlem," *Hell Up in Harlem*, Motown 802, 1974; Syl Johnson, "Concrete Reservation," Twinight 129, 1970.

52. Syl Johnson, "Is It Because I'm Black," Twinight 125, 1969.

53. Temptations, "Message."

54. Gil Scott-Heron, "The Revolution Will Not Be Televised" *The Revolution Will Not Be Televised*, Flying Dutchman, 3818, 1974.

55. Last Poets, "Run, Nigger," *The Last Poets*, Douglas 3, 1970.

56. Impressions, "It's All Right," ABC Paramount 10487, 1963; Impressions, "We're a Winner," ABC, 11022, 1967; Impressions, "Keep On Pushing."

57. Charles Wood and John Cacavas, "Black Is Beautiful," (New York: Chappell, 1968).

58. Nina Simone, "To Be Young, Gifted and Black," RCA Victor 0269, 1969.

59. Dyke and the Blazers, "We Got More Soul," Original Sound 86, 1969.

60. Johnnie Taylor, "I Am Somebody," Stax 078, 1970.

61. James Brown, "Say It Loud—I'm Black and I'm Proud," King 6187, 1968.

62. Vernon Gibbs, "The Entertainers: The Last Poets," *Essence* 3 (May 1972): 15; Sherry Turner, "An Overview of the New Black Arts," *Freedomways* 9 (Spring 1969): 156; Last Poets, "Mean Machine," *This is Madness*, Douglas 7, 1971; Last Poets, "Wake Up, Niggers," *Last Poets*.

63. Last Poets, "Niggers Are Scared of Revolution," *Last Poets*.

64. Last Poets, "Time," "Black People What Y'All Gon' Do," "Opposites," *This Is Madness*; Last Poets, "Niggers Are Scared," "When the Revolution Comes," *Last Poets*. See also The Watts Prophets, *Rappin' Black in a White World*, ALA 1971, 1971.

65. Jimmy Stewart, "Introduction to Black Aesthetics in Music," in Gayle, *Black Aesthetic*, 90.

66. Frank Kofsky, *Black Nationalism and the Revolution in Music* (New York: Pathfinder, 1970), 65–66. George Breitman, ed., *By Any Means Necessary: Speeches, Interviews and a Letter by Malcolm X* (New York: Pathfinder, 1970), 63–64.

67. Advertisement for Eve cigarettes, *Essence* 3 (September 1972): 25; Advertisement for L & M cigarettes, *Essence* 3 (May 1972): 26; Advertisement for Johnnie Walker Scotch whiskey, *Ebony* 29 (July 1974): 16; Advertisement for Oriental Wig Imports, *Essence* 3 (January 1973): 13.

68. Advertisement for Chevrolet Vega, *Essence* 3 (May 1972): 29; Advertisement for Kraft barbecue sauce, *Ebony* 29 (July 1974): 35; Advertisement for Nice'n Easy haircolor, *Essence* 3 (July 1972): 9; Advertisement for Bonne Bell Ten-O-Six Lotion, *Essence* 3 (July 1972): 22; Advertisement for U.S. Navy, *Essence* 3 (January 1973): 27.

69. Huey P. Newton, *Revolutionary Suicide* (New York: Ballantine, 1974), 183–85; Claude Brown, "The Language of Soul," *Esquire* 69 (April 1968): 88.

70. Preston Wilcox, "Black Studies as an Academic Discipline, "*Negro Digest* 19 (March 1970): 83; Ron Karenga, "Black Cultural Nationalism," in Gayle, *Black Aesthetic*, 35; Maulana Ron Karenga, "The Black Community and the University: A Community Organizer's Perspective," in *Black Studies in the University: A Symposium*, ed. Armstead L. Robinson, Craig C. Foster, and Donald H. Ogilvie (New York: Bantam, 1969), 44–45; Roach, "Jazz," 3.

71. Brown, "Language," 88, 160.

72. Ken Johnson, "The Vocabulary of Race," in *Rappin' and Stylin' Out:*

Communication in Urban Black America, ed. Thomas Kochman (Urbana: University of Illinois Press, 1972), 142–46; Folb, *Language and Culture,* 60.

73. Johnson, "Vocabulary," 10; David Hilliard, "Interview with CBS News, December 28, 1969," in *The Black Panthers Speak,* ed. Philip S. Foner (Philadelphia: J.B. Lippincott, 1970), 133.

74. Sylvia Wallace Holton, *Down Home and Uptown: The Representation of Black Speech in American Fiction* (Rutherford: Fairleigh Dickinson University Press, 1984), 182–85; Imari Abubakari Obadele, "National Black Elections Held by Republic of New Africa," *Black Scholar* 7 (October 1975): 27; *The Autobiography of LeRoi Jones/Amiri Baraka* (New York: Freundlich, 1984), 292.

75. *Eldridge Cleaver: Post-Prison Writings and Speeches,* ed. Robert Scheer (New York: Random House, 1969), 54–56.

76. Andrews and Owens, *Black Language,* 4.

77. Jim Haskins and Hugh F. Butts, *The Psychology of Black Language* (New York: Barnes & Noble, 1973), 3; Franz Fanon, *Black Skin, White Masks* (New York: Grove, 1968), 17–18.

78. Edward Sagarin and James Moneymaker, "Language and Nationalist, Separatist, and Secessionist Movements," in *Ethnic Autonomy—Comparative Dynamics: The Americas, Europe and the Developing World,* ed. Raymond L. Hall (New York: Pergamon, 1979), 25–26, 35; Fanon, *Black Skin,* 25.

79. June Jordan, "White English: The Politics of Language," *Black World* 22 (August 1973): 6.

80. Martin Luther King, Jr., *Where Do We Go From Here: Chaos or Community?* (New York: Harper & Row, 1967), 41, Ossie Davis, "The English Language is My Enemy!": *Negro History Bulletin* 30 (April 1967): 18.

81. David R. Burgest, "The Racist Use of the English Language," *Black Scholar* 5 (September 1973): 40.

82. Stokely Carmichael, *Stokely Speaks: Black Power Back to Pan-Africanism* (New York: Vintage, 1971), 149–50.

83. David Walker, *Walker's Appeal in Four Articles* (New York: Arno Press and The New York Times, 1969), 65; Sterling Stuckey, *Slave Culture: Nationalist Theory and the Foundations of Black America* (New York: Oxford University Press, 1987), 193–244; Donald L. Grant and Mildred Bricker Grant, "Some Notes on the Capital 'N'," *Phylon* 36 (December 1975): 435–43.

84. Malcolm X, "Some Reflections on 'Negro History Week' and the Role of the Black People in History," in *Malcolm X: The Man and His Times,* ed. John Henrik Clarke (New York: Collier, 1969), 322–23; George Breitman, *The Last Year of Malcolm X: The Evolution of a Revolutionary* (New York: Schocken, 1967), 120–21.

85. Don L. Lee, *We Walk the Way of the New World* (Detroit: Broadside Press, 1970), 11. In a 1968 *Jet* readers' poll, 37 percent of the respondents said that they preferred to be called "Afro-American," 22 percent favored "black," 18 percent elected to use "Negro," and 6 percent chose "colored." "What's In a Name?" *Senior Scholastic,* 14 February 1969, 11.

86. Thomas A. Johnson, "Black Nationalist Leader Stirs Watts Teen-Agers," *New York Times,* 27 May 1966, 30; Lerone Bennett, Jr., "What's In a Name?: Negro vs. Afro-American vs. Black," *Ebony* 23 (November 1967): 52.

87. Beverly Coleman, "Relevancy in Teaching and Learning Swahili," *Black*

World 19 (October 1970): 11–24; Adhama Oluwa Kijembe, "Swahili and Black Americans," *Negro Digest* 18 (July 1969): 4–8.

88. Imamu Amiri Baraka, *Raise, Race, Rays, Raze: Essays Since 1965* (New York: Vintage, 1972), 46–47; Andrews and Owens, *Black Language* 139; Jordan, "White English," 5, 9.

89. Geneva Smitherman, "Grammar and Goodness," *English Journal* 62 (May 1973): 778; idem, "Soul 'n Style," *English Journal* 63 (February 1974): 17; Sheila Walker, "Black English: Expression of the Afro-American Experience," *Black World* 20 (June 1971): 6, 8.

90. J. L. Dillard, *Black English: Its History and Usage in the United States* (New York: Vintage, 1973), 270; Kenneth R. Johnson, "Teacher's Attitude Toward the Nonstandard Negro Dialect—Let's Change It," in *Language, Society, and Education: A Profile of Black English,* ed. Johanna S. DeStefano (Worthington, Ohio: Charles A. Jones, 1973), 179, 185–87.

91. Gloria Toliver-Weddington, "The Scope of Black English," *Journal of Black Studies* 4 (December 1973): 111; William Labov, *Language in the Inner City: Studies in the Black English Vernacular* (Philadelphia: University of Pennsylvania Press, 1972), 201, 237; Ralph W. Fasold and Walt Wolfram, "Some Linguistic Features of Negro Dialect," in *Black American English: Its Background and Its Usage in the Schools and in Literature,* ed. Paul Stoller (New York: Dell, 1975), 49–50.

92. Dillard, *Black English,* 229.

93. Robert L. Williams, ed., *Ebonics: The True Language of Black Folks* (St. Louis: Institute of Black Studies, 1975), xii; Grace Holt, "Black English: Surviving the Bastardization Process," in Williams, *Ebonics,* 65–66; Haskins and Butts, *Black Language,* 44.

94. See, for example, Clarence Major, *Dictionary of Afro-American Slang* (New York: International Publishers, 1970); David Claerbaut, *Black Jargon in White America* (Grand Rapids: William B. Eerdmans, 1972); Hermese E. Roberts, *The Third Ear: A Black Glossary* (Chicago: English-Language Institute of America, 1971).

95. For a review of this literature, see Walter M. Brasch, *Black English and the Mass Media* (Amherst: University of Massachusetts Press, 1981), 256–88.

96. See, for example, June Jordan, *Dry Victories* (New York: Holt, Rinehart & Winston, 1972); June Jordan, *His Own Where* (New York: Thomas Crowell, 1971); Shane Stevens, *Go Down Dead* (New York: William Morrow, 1966); Robert L. Williams, "The BITCH-100: A Culture-Specific Test," *Journal of Afro-American Issues* 3 (Winter 1975): 103–16; Adrian Dove, "Chitling Test of Intelligence," in *The Race Bomb: Skin Color, Prejudice, and Intelligence,* by Paul R. Ehrlich and S. Shirley Feldman (New York: Quadrangle/New York Times, 1977), 72–73; Samuel D. Crawford and Robert H. Bentley, "An Inner-City 'IQ' Test," in *Black Language Reader,* ed. Robert H. Bentley and Samuel D. Crawford (Glenview, Illinois; Scott Foresman, 1973), 80–83.

97. Robert D. Twiggs, *Pan-African Language in the Western Hemisphere* (North Quincy, Massachusetts: Christopher, 1973).

98. Williams, *Ebonics,* 100–101.

99. Andrews and Owens, *Black Language,* 30.

100. Ibid., 18.

101. Twiggs, *Pan-African*, 39.

102. Robert L. Williams, "Scientific Racism and IQ: The Silent Mugging of the Black Community," *Psychology Today* 7 (May 1974): 101.

103. Toliver-Weddington, "Black English," 112.

104. Grace Holt, "Metaphor, Black Discourse Style, and Cultural Reality," in Williams, *Ebonics*, 86–95; Andrews and Owens, *Black Language*, 21, 26.

105. Thomas Kochman, *Black and White Styles in Conflict* (Chicago: University of Chicago Press, 1981), 29–30, 130; Geneva Smitherman, *Talking and Testifyin: The Language of Black America* (Boston: Houghton Mifflin, 1977), 79–85; Folb, *Language and Culture*, 90–91; Roger D. Abrahams, *Deep Down in the Jungle . . . : Negro Narrative Folklore from the Streets of Philadelphia* (Chicago: Aldine, 1970), 39, 42, 58.

106. For studies of the folk heroic tradition of Afro-Americans, see John W. Roberts, *From Trickster to Badman: The Black Folk Hero in Slavery and Freedom* (Philadelphia: University of Pennsylvania Press, 1989); Lawrence W. Levine, *Black Culture and Black Consciousness: Afro-American Folk Thought from Slavery to Freedom* (New York: Oxford University Press, 1977), 81–135, 367–440.

107. Dennis Wepman, Ronald B. Newman, and Murray B. Binderman, *The Life: The Lore and Folk Poetry of the Black Hustler* (Philadelphia: University of Pennsylvania Press, 1976), 36.

108. Bruce Jackson, *"Get Your Ass in the Water and Swim Like Me": Narrative Poetry from Black Oral Tradition* (Cambridge: Harvard University Press 1974), 207.

109. Ibid; Daryl Cumber Dance, *Shuckin' and Jivin': Folklore from Contemporary Black Americans* (Bloomington: Indiana University Press, 1978), 192–193.

110. Dance, *Shuckin'*, 115, 230–31; Jackson, *Narrative Poetry*, 151–52; Wepman, Newman, Binderman, *Life*, 148.

111. Dance, *Shuckin',* 217; Jackson, *Narrative Poetry*, 191–92, 195.

112. Dance, *Shuckin'*, 230–31.

113. Jackson, *Narrative Poetry*, 168; Wepman, Newman, Binderman, *Life*, 58, 64, 156–57.

114. Nancy Levi Arnez and Clara B. Anthony, "Contemporary Negro Humor as Social Satire," *Phylon* 29 (Winter 1968): 340, 345–46; Donald Bogle, "Black Humor—Full Circle from Slave Quarters to Richard Pryor," *Ebony* 30 (August 1975): 126, 128; Jim Haskins, *Jokes from Black Folks* (Garden City, New York: Doubleday, 1973), 72, 74.

115. Cartoon by Pollard, *Black World* 22 (May 1973): 15; Cartoon by Morrie, *Ebony* 28 (September 1973): 102; Cartoon by Roberts, *Negro Digest* 18 (July 1969): 9.

116. Norine Dresser, "The Metamorphosis of the Humor of the Black Man," *New York Folklore Quarterly* 26 (September 1970): 227.

117. Cartoon by Mack Leslie, *Ebony* 30 (January 1974): 107.

118. Cartoon by Chuck, *Ebony* 30 (December 1974): 72; Cartoon by Morrie, *Negro Digest* 16 (December 1966): 25; Henry D. Spalding, ed. *Encyclopedia of Black Folklore and Humor* (Middle Village, New York: Jonathan David, 1972), 451.

119. Murry N. DePillars, *The People of the Sun*, 1972, reproduced in Samella Lewis, *Art: African American* (New York: Harcourt Brace Jovanovich, 1978), 203; Betye Saar, *The Liberation of Aunt Jemima*, 1972, reproduced in Lewis, *Art*, 173.

120. Elsa Honig Fine, *The Afro-American Artist: A Search for Identity* (New York: Holt, Rinehart and Winston, 1973), 209.

121. "The Black Artist in America: A Symposium," *Metropolitan Museum of Art Bulletin* 27 (January 1969): 251.

122. For city-by-city coverage of the wall murals, see Alan W. Barnett, *Community Murals: The People's Art* (Philadelphia: Art Alliance Press, 1984).

123. Samella S. Lewis and Ruth G. Waddy, *Black Artists on Art* (Los Angeles: Contemporary Crafts, 1976), 1:iv–v; Fine, *Identity*, 8, 203; Jeff Donaldson, "The Role We Want for Black Art," *College Board Review* 71 (Spring 1969): 18.

124. *Tradition and Conflict: Images of a Turbulent Decade, 1963–1973* (New York: Studio Museum in Harlem, 1985), 58.

125. Samella S. Lewis and Ruth G. Waddy, *Black Artists on Art* (Los Angeles: Contemporary Crafts, 1971), 2:8; Thomas Albright, " 'Life in a Visual Image,' " *Art Gallery* 13 (April 1970): 42.

126. Frederick Campbell, *Burn, Baby, Burn*, circa 1965, reproduced in *Negro Digest* 16 (August 1967): 92; William Curtis, *Riot: USA*, 1968, reproduced in Lewis and Waddy, *Black Artists*, 1:92; Vincent Smith, *Molotov Cocktail*, 1967, reproduced in *Afro-American Artists: New York and Boston* (Boston: Museum of the National Center of Afro-American Artists, Museum of Fine Arts, School of the Museum of Fine Arts, 1970), 38.

127. Dana C. Chandler, Jr., *LeRoi Jones—House Arrest*, 1969, reproduced in Lewis and Waddy, *Black Artists*, 1: 41; Dana C. Chandler, Jr., "Fred Hampton's Door," 1970, reproduced in Fine, *Identity*, 203; Emory Douglas, *Free Huey Newton*, 1969, reproduced in *Black Collectibles Sold in America*, by P. J. Gibbs (Paducah, Kentucky: Collector, 1987), 81; Emory Douglas, "The Lumpen," 1969, reproduced in Gibbs, *Collectibles*, 82.

128. Nelson Stevens, "Our Nation Calls," 1971, reproduced in Lewis and Waddy, *Black Artists*, 2: 34; Barbara Jones-Hogu, "Black Men We Need You," 1971, reproduced in *Tradition and Conflict*, 57; Barbara J. Jones, "Your Brother's Keeper," 1968, reproduced in *Black Dimensions in Contemporary American Art*, ed. J. Edward Atkinson (New York: New American Library, 1971), 73.

129. Laurence P. Neal, "The Black Revolution in Art: A Conversation with Joe Overstreet," *Liberator* 5 (October 1965): 10; Elizabeth Catlett, "The Role of the Black Artist, *Black Scholar* 6 (June 1975): 13.

130. William H. Johnson, *Jesus and the Three Marys*, 1935, reproduced in *Harlem Renaissance: Art of Black America*, The Studio Museum in Harlem (New York: Harry N. Abrams, 1987), 48.

131. W. E. B. DuBois, *Darkwater: Voices from Within the Veil* (New York: Harcourt, Brace and Howe, 1920), 27, 105–8; W. E. Burghardt DuBois, *Dark Princess: A Romance* (New York: Harcourt, Brace, 1928), 145, 153–54; Countee Cullen, "Heritage," in *Color* (New York: Harper & Brothers, 1925), 40.

132. Alex Poinsett, "The Quest for a Black Christ," *Ebony* 24 (March 1969): 171; "Artists Portray a Black Christ," *Ebony* 26 (April 1971): 177–78, 180; "An Artist Challenges the Bible," *Sepia* 19 (March 1970): 44.

133. Albert B. Cleage, Jr., *The Black Messiah* (New York: Sheed and Ward, 1968), 277.

134. Ibid., 3–4, 42–44, 61–62, 84; Albert B. Cleage, Jr., *Black Christian Nationalism: New Directions for the Black Church* (New York: William Morrow, 1972), xiii, 3–4; Albert B. Cleage, Jr., "The Black Messiah and the Black Revolution," in *Quest for a Black Theology*, ed. James J. Gardiner and J. Deotis Roberts, Sr., (Philadelphia: Pilgrim Press, 1971), 14–16.

135. Cleage, *Black Messiah*, 4, 39–40, 44, 89–90, 92, 106, 111; James Haskins, *Profiles in Black Power* (Garden City, New York: Doubleday, 1972), 65. For other manifestations of this belief in the "blackness" of the ancient Hebrews, see Howard Brotz. *The Black Jews of Harlem: Negro Nationalism and the Dilemmas of Negro Leadership* (New York: Schocken, 1970); Clarke Jenkins, *The Black Hebrews of the Seed of Abraham, Isaac, and Jacob, of the Tribe of Judah, Benjamin, and Levi, After 430 Years in America* (Detroit: The Author, 1969); Raymond Julius Jones, *A Comparative Study of Religious Cult Behavior Among Negroes* (Washington, D.C.: Graduate School, Howard University, 1939); Arthur Huff Fauset, *Black Gods of the Metropolis: Negro Religious Cults of the Urban North* (Philadelphia: University of Pennsylvania Press, 1971), 31–40.

136. Cleage, *Black Messiah*, 7, 20, 24, 112–13.

137. Ibid., 37.

138. J. Deotis Roberts, *A Black Political Theology* (Philadelphia: Westminster, 1974), 33; J. Deotis Roberts, *Liberation and Reconciliation: A Black Theology* (Philadelphia: Westminster, 1971), 130, 134, 137; James H. Cone, *God of the Oppressed* (New York: Seabury, 1975), 134–37; James H. Cone, *A Black Theology of Liberation* (Philadelphia: J. B. Lippincott, 1970), 11, 24.

139. Sister Mary Roger Thibodeaux, *A Black Nun Looks at Black Power* (New York: Sheed & Ward, 1972), 5, 96, 107; James H. Cone, *Black Theology and Black Power* (New York: Seabury, 1969), 123–27; Cone, *Oppressed*, 223–24; Cone, *Liberation*, 20–21, 33, 39; Joseph A. Johnson, Jr., "Jesus, the Liberator," in Gardiner and Roberts, *Quest*, 110; Vincent Harding, "Black Power and the American Christ," *Christian Century*, 4 January 1967, 13; Roberts, *Political Theology*, 73, 204.

140. Cone, *Black Power*, 1, 37–38; Cone, *Liberation*, 130–32, 143, 220; Roberts, *Political Theology*, 114–16; Joseph R. Washington, Jr., *Black and White Power Subreption* (Boston: Beacon, 1969), 127.

141. National Committee of Negro Churchmen, "Black Power Anti-Dote: Freedom, Love, Justice and Truth," *Negro Digest* 16 (December 1966): 16–19; Cone, *Oppressed*, 219; Cone, *Black Power*, 38; Vincent Harding, "The Religion of Black Power," *The Religious Situation: 1968*, ed. Donald R. Cutler (Boston: Beacon, 1968), 5, 8, 11, 31.

142. Cone, *Oppressed*, 47, 50, 96–97; James H. Cone, "Failure of the Black Church," *Liberator* 9 (May 1969): 22: Cone, *Black Power*, 80; Johnson, "Liberator," 103.

143. Cone, "Failure," 22; National Committee of Negro Churchmen, "Black Power," 21; Cleage, *Christian Nationalism*, 16–17, 33; Charles V. Hamilton, *The Black Preacher in America* (New York: William Morrow, 1972), 168–69.

144. Cleage, *Christian Nationalism*, 75–76, 259.

145. Cone, *Liberation*, 196; Cone, *Black Power*, 52–53, 137, 149.

146. For a sampling of the literature calling for the white church to confront "Christian racism," see C. Freeman Sleeper, *Black Power and Christian Responsibility: Some Biblical Foundations for Social Ethics* (Nashville: Abingdon, 1969); Joseph R. Barndt, *Why Black Power?* (New York: Friendship, 1968); Joseph C. Hough, Jr., *Black Power and White Protestants: A Christian Response to the New Negro Pluralism* (New York: Oxford University Press, 1968); Columbus Salley and Ronald Behm, *Your God is Too White* (Downers Grove, Illinois; Inter-Varsity, 1970).

147. On early black messianism, see Wilson Jeremiah Moses, *Black Messiahs and Uncle Toms: Social and Literary Manipulations of a Religious Myth* (University Park; Pennsylvania State University Press, 1982).

148. Henry M. Turner, "God is a Negro," *Voice of Missions*, 1 February 1898, reprinted in *Black Nationalism in America*, ed. John H. Bracey, Jr., August Meier, and Elliott Rudwick (Indianapolis: Bobbs-Merrill, 1970), 154–55; Edwin S. Redkey, "Bishop Turner's African Dream," *Journal of American History* 54 (September 1967): 275.

149. Fauset, *Black Gods*, 41–51; Clifton E. Marsh, *From Black Muslims to Muslims: The Transition from Separatism to Islam, 1930–1980* (Metuchen, New Jersey; Scarecrow, 1984), 41–49.

150. Hans A. Baer, *The Black Spiritual Movement: A Religious Response to Racism* (Knoxville: University of Tennessee Press, 1984), 94, 96, 105, 107–8.

151. Sara Harris, *Father Divine* (New York: Collier, 1971), 185–86.

152. Robert Weisbrot, *Father Divine* (Boston: Beacon, 1984), 6, 7, 109, 135, 145, 147, 158, 171.

153. Amy Jacques Garvey, *Garvey and Garveyism* (London: Collier, 1970), 201–2; Randall K. Burkett, *Garveyism as a Religious Movement: The Institutionalization of a Black Civil Religion* (Metuchen, New Jersey: Scarecrow Press and the American Theological Library Association, 1978), 18–24, 29–32, 65, 82–88; Tony Martin, *Race First: The Ideological and Organizational Struggles of Marcus Garvey and the Universal Negro Improvement Association* (Westport, Connecticut: Greenwood, 1976), 69–70.

154. Martin, *Race First*, 77.

155. *Philosophy and Opinions of Marcus Garvey*, ed. Amy Jacques-Garvey (New York: Atheneum, 1974), 2:238–39.

156. Elijah Muhammad, *Message to the Blackman in America* (Chicago Muhammad's Temple No. 2, 1965), 53, 306; Malcolm X, "Malcolm X's 'University Speech,'" in *When the Word is Given . . .*, ed. Louis E. Lomax (New York: New American Library, 1964), 138–40; *The End of White World Supremacy: Four Speeches by Malcolm X*, ed. Imam Benjamin Karim (New York: Seaver, 1971), 148.

157. Rolland Snellings, "Malcolm X: as International Statesman," *Liberator* 6 (February 1966): 6–7; George Norman, "To Malcolm X," in *For Malcolm: Poems on the Life and the Death of Malcolm X*, ed. Dudley Randall and Margaret Burroughs (Detroit: Broadside, 1969), 23; Edward S. Spriggs, "Berkeley's Blue Black," in Randall and Burroughs, *For Malcolm*, 74.

158. Preston N. Williams, "The Ethics of Black Power," in Gardiner and

Roberts, *Quest*, 91; Imamu Amiri Baraka, ed., *African Congress: A Documentary of the First Modern Pan-African Congress* (New York: William Morrow, 1972), 262.

159. Washington, *Power*, 160–66; Black Methodists for Church Renewal, "The Black Paper, 1968," in *Black Theology: A Documentary History, 1966–1979*, ed. Gayraud S. Wilmore and James H. Cone (Maryknoll, New York: Orbis, 1979), 268–74.

160. "The Black Manifesto," in *Black Manifesto: Religion, Racism, and Reparations*, ed. Robert S. Lecky and H. Elliott Wright (New York: Sheed and Ward, 1969), 119, 123; James Forman, "Control, Conflict and Change: The Underlying Concepts of the Black Manifesto," in Lecky and Wright, *Black Manifesto*, 50–51; Jerry K. Frye, "The 'Black Manifesto' and the Tactic of Objectification," *Journal of Black Studies* 5 (September 1974): 65–68.

161. Hamilton, *Black Preacher*, 125–26; National Committee of Black Churchmen, "The Black Declaration of Independence, July 4, 1970," in Wilmore and Cone, *Documentary History*, 109.

162. Sister M. Martin de Porres Grey, "The Church, Revolution and Black Catholics," *Black Scholar* 2 (December 1970): 23; Paul Holmer, "About Black Theology," *Lutheran Quarterly* 28 (August 1976): 233.

Chapter Six

1. Barbara Ann Teer, "Needed: A New Image", in *The Black Power Revolt*, ed. Floyd B. Barbour (Boston: Porter Sargent, 1968), 222.

2. Studies of early black portraiture include: Joseph Boskin, *Sambo: The Rise & Demise of an American Jester* (New York: Oxford University Press, 1986); Sam Dennison, *Scandalize My Name: Black Imagery in American Popular Music* (New York: Garland, 1982); Catherine Juanita Starke, *Black Portraiture in American Fiction: Stock Characters, Archetypes, and Individuals* (New York: Basic, 1971); Robert C. Toll, *Blacking Up: The Minstrel Show in Nineteenth-Century America* (New York: Oxford University Press, 1974); Jean Fagan Yellin, *The Intricate Knot: Black Figures in American Literature, 1776–1863* (New York: New York University Press, 1972); William L. Van Deburg, *Slavery & Race in American Popular Culture* (Madison: University of Wisconsin Press, 1984).

3. Marilyn Diane Fife, "Black Image in American TV: The First Two Decades", *Black Scholar* 6 (November 1974): 11.

4. Martin Maloney, "Black is the Color of Our New TV," *TV Guide*, 16 November 1968, 10; Bart Andrews and Ahrgus Juilliard, *Holy Mackerel!: The Amos 'n' Andy Story* (New York: E. P. Dutton, 1986), 122; Richard Lemon, "Black is the Color of TV's Newest Stars," *Saturday Evening Post*, 30 November 1968, 42.

5. John F. Seggar and Penny Wheeler, "World of Work on TV: Ethnic and Sex Representation in TV Drama," *Journal of Broadcasting* 17 (Spring 1973): 201–14. See also John F. Seggar, "Television's Portrayal of Minorities and Women, 1971–75," *Journal of Broadcasting* 21 (Fall 1977): 435–46. United States Commission on Civil Rights, *Window Dressing on the Set: Women and Minorities in Television* (Washington, D.C.: U.S. Government Printing Office, 1977).

6. James L. Hinton, John F. Seggar, Herbert C. Northcott, Brian F. Fontes, "To-

kenism and Improving Imagery of Blacks in TV Drama and Comedy: 1973." *Journal of Broadcasting* 18 (Fall 1974): 423. On *Between Time and Timbuktu*, see John R. Cooley, *Savages and Naturals: Black Portraits by White Writers in Modern American Literature* (Newark: University of Delaware Press, 1982), 161–73, 194–95. On *Jane Pittman*, see Alvin Ramsey, "Through a Glass Whitely: The Televised Rape of *Miss Jane Pittman*," *Black World* 23 (August 1974): 31–36.

7. "The Negro Stereotype", *Newsweek*, 3 April 1967, 59; Jean Carey Bond, "The Media Image of Black Women", *Freedomways* 15 (no. 1, 1975): 34.

8. Knolly Moses, "The Black Image on Television: Who Controls It?" *Black Enterprise* 10 (September 1979): 36.

9. Ellen Holly, "The Role of Media in the Programming of an Underclass," *Black Scholar* 10 (January–February, 1979): 33; Henry Louis Gates Jr., "Portraits in Black From *Amos 'n' Andy* to *Coonskin*," *Harper's* 252 (June 1976): 24.

10. Herbert C. Northcott, John F. Seggar, and James L. Hinton, "Trends in TV Portrayal of Blacks and Women," *Journalism Quarterly* 52 (Winter 1975): 741–44.

11. Cedric C. Clark, "Television and Social Controls: Some Observations on the Portrayals of Ethnic Minorities," *Television Quarterly* 8 (Spring 1969): 20–21.

12. Stokely Carmichael, *Stokely Speaks: Black Power Back to Pan-Africanism* (New York: Vintage, 1971), 160.

13. Robert Lewis Shayon, "Changes," *Saturday Review*, 18 April 1970, 46; "Julia," *Ebony* 24 (November 1968): 57; Eugenia Collier, "TV Still Evades the Nitty-Gritty Truth!" *TV Guide*, 12 January 1974, 7.

14. George Jackson, *Soledad Brother: The Prison Letters of George Jackson* (New York: Bantam, 1970), 177.

15. Ben Stein, *The View from Sunset Boulevard* (New York: Basic, 1979), 105–116; Benjamin Stein, "Welcome to the Land of Shiny Cars, Fake Waterfalls and Happy Endings," *TV Guide*, 20 January 1979, 5–6, 8, 10.

16. Fife, "Black Image," 14.

17. James Baldwin, "The Price May Be Too High," *New York Times*, 2 February 1969, 9.

18. Alfred E. Opubur and Adebayo Ogunbi, "Ooga Booga: The African Image in American Films," in *Other Voices, Other Views: An International Collection of Essays from the Bicentennial*, ed. Robin W. Winks (Westport: Greenwood, 1978) 370–73; "Black Power: The Widening Dialogue," *New South* 21 (Summer 1966): 73.

19. Edward D.C. Campbell, Jr., "'Burn, Mandingo, Burn': The Plantation South in Film, 1958–1978," *Southern Quarterly* 19 (Spring–Summer 1981): 110–16.

20. Allen Woll, *Black Musical Theatre: From Coontown to Dreamgirls* (Baton Rouge: Louisiana State University Press, 1989), 226–27. For commentary on the stage adaptation of *Mandingo*, see John McCarten, "The Laddie's Not for Boiling," *New Yorker*, 3 June 1961, 90; *The Best Plays of 1960–1961*, ed. Louis Kronenberger (New York: Dodd, Mead, 1961), 12, 341.

21. "Stage, Screen and Black Hegemony: Black World Interviews Woodie King Jr.," *Black World* 24 (April 1975): 12–13; Adam David Miller, "It's a Long Way to

St. Louis: Notes on the Audience for Black Drama," *Drama Review* 12 (Summer 1968): 149.

22. John Lohr, "Black Theatre: The American Tragic Voice," *Evergreen Review* 13 (August 1969): 60; Ronald Milner, "Black Theater—Go Home!," in *The Black Aesthetic*, ed. Addison Gayle, Jr. (Garden City, New York: Doubleday, 1972), 293; LeRoi Jones, "The Revolutionary Theatre," *Liberator* 5 (July 1965): 5; Larry Neal, "The Black Arts Movement," *Drama Review* 12 (Summer 1968): 33; Woodie King, Jr., "Black Theatre: Present Condition," *Drama Review* 12 (Summer 1968): 117–18; Douglas Turner Ward, "American Theater: For Whites Only?" *New York Times*, 14 August 1966, 1, 3.

23. Nancy Larrick, "The All-White World of Children's Books," *Saturday Review*, 11 September 1965, 64; Jeanne S. Chall, Eugene Radwin, Valarie W. French, and Cynthia R. Hall, "Blacks in the World of Children's Books," *Reading Teacher* 32 (February 1979): 529.

24. Barbara Glasser, *Leroy, OOPS* (Chicago: Cowles, 1971); Betty Horvath, *Hooray for Jasper* (New York: Franklin Watts, 1966); Lisl Weil, *Fat Ernest* (New York: Parents Magazine Press, 1973); Jean Merill, *The Toothpaste Millionaire* (Boston: Houghton Mifflin, 1972).

25. For studies of black portraiture in children's fiction, see Dorothy M. Broderick, *Image of the Black in Children's Fiction* (New York: R. R. Bowker, 1973), Rudine Sims, *Shadow and Substance: Afro-American Experience in Contemporary Children's Fiction* (Urbana: National Council of Teachers of English, 1982).

26. Julius Lester and George A. Woods, "Black and White: An Exchange", *New York Times Book Review*, 24 May 1970, 38.

27. Julian Mayfield, "You Touch My Black Aesthetic and I'll Touch Yours," in Gayle, *Black Aesthetic*, 23.

28. Eugenia Collier, "A House of Twisted Mirrors: The Black Reflection in the Media," *Current History* 67 (November 1974): 230.

29. Charles H. Rowell, "Poetry, History and Humanism: An Interview with Margaret Walker," *Black World* 25 (December 1975): 11; Lerone Bennett, Jr., "Nat's Last White Man," in *William Styron's Nat Turner: Ten Black Writers Respond*, ed. John Henrik Clarke (Boston: Beacon, 1968), 4; Ernest Kaiser, "The Failure of William Styron," in Clark, *Ten Black Writers*, 57, 65; Darwin T. Turner, review of *The Confessions of Nat Turner*, in *Journal of Negro History* 53 (April 1968): 185–86.

30. William Styron, *The Confessions of Nat Turner* (New York: Random House, 1967), 70, 232, 322, 410; Herbert Aptheker and William Styron, "Truth and Nat Turner: An Exchange," *Nation*, 22 April 1968, 546; Rowell, "Margaret Walker," 10.

31. For additional commentary on the filmmaker-audience interface, see Randall M. Miller, "On Ethnic Television: Seeing and Responding to Ethnic and Racial Images in Prime-Time Programming," *Ethnic Forum* 5 (Fall 1985): 52–65; Thomas M. Leitch, "The Case for Studying Popular Culture," *South Atlantic Quarterly* 84 (Spring 1985): 115–26; Martin Laba, "Making Sense: Expressiveness, Stylization and the Popular Culture Process," *Journal of Popular Culture* 19 (Spring 1986): 107–17.

32. For observations on the psychological comfort black cultural stereotypes

offer to whites, see Nathan Irvin Huggins, *Harlem Renaissance* (New York: Oxford University Press, 1971), 244–301; Stuart M. Kaminsky and Jeffrey H. Mahan, *American Television Genres* (Chicago: Nelson-Hall, 1985), 177–78; Michael Steward Blayney, "*Roots* and the Noble Savage," *Tennessee Historical Quarterly* 45 (Spring 1986): 56–73.

33. Gil Scott-Heron, "the ones who . . . ," in *Small Talk at 125th and Lenox* (New York: World, 1970), 10; Joseph Bevans Bush, "Nittygritty," in *We Speak as Liberators: Young Black Poets*, ed. Orde Coombs (New York: Dodd, Mead, 1970), 5.

34. Ben Caldwell, *Mission Accomplished, Drama Review* 12 (Summer 1968): 50–52; Julian Moreau, *The Black Commandos* (Atlanta: Cultural Institute Press, 1967), 185.

35. LeRoi Jones, "I Am Speaking of Future Good-ness and Social Philosophy," in *Black Magic: Collected Poetry, 1961–1967* (Indianapolis: Bobbs-Merrill, 1969), 99; Ted Joans, "Wild West Savages," in Ted Joans, *Afrodisia* (New York: Hill & Wang, 1970), 22; Carol Freeman, "I Saw Them Lynch," in *Black Fire*, ed. LeRoi Jones and Larry Neal (New York: William Morrow, 1968), 330; Ted Joans, "For the Viet Congo," in *Black Pow-Wow* (New York: Hill and Wang, 1969), 13; Askia Muhammad Touré, "Dago Red (A Harlem Snow Song)", in *Black Spirits*, ed. Woodie King (New York: Vintage, 1972), 223–27; Moreau, *Black Commandos*, 137; LeRoi Joncs, *Madheart (A Morality Play)*, in *Four Black Revolutionary Plays* (Indianapolis: Bobbs-Merrill, 1969), 70–71; Ted Joans, "The Sink", in Joans *Afrodisia*, 81; Sonia Sanchez, "To All Sisters," in *Home Coming* (Detroit: Broadside, 1969), 27.

36. LeRoi Jones, "The Black Man is making new Gods," in Jones, *Black Magic*, 206; Nikki Giovanni, "A Revolutionary Tale," in *Black Short Story Anthology*, ed. Woodie King (New York: Columbia University Press, 1972), 28; Joans, "Wild West Savages," 22; Ted Joans, "Advice Alphabeticamerica," in Joans, *Afrodisia*, 108–113; Calvin C. Hernton, "Wasn't It Sad When the Great Titanic Went Down," in *The New Black Poetry*, ed. Clarence Major (New York: International, 1969), 66.

37. Melvin Van Peebles, *Aint Supposed to Die a Natural Death* (New York: Bantam, 1973), 13, 43–45; Joseph A. Walker, *Ododo*, in *Black Drama Anthology*, ed. Woodie King and Ron Milner (New York: New American Library, 1971), 383; Ted Joans, "The White Ban," in Joans, *Pow-Wow*, 67.

38. On black fears of genocide, see Samuel F. Yette, *The Choice: The Issue of Black Survival in America* (New York: Berkley, 1971); Robert G. Weisbord, *Genocide? Birth Control and the Black American* (Westport: Greenwood, 1975); Bobby Wright, *The Psychopathic Racial Personality* (Chicago: Institute of Positive Education, 1975), 3–11.

39. Floyd McKissick, "Diary of a Black Man," in *Three-Fifths of a Man* (New York: Macmillan, 1969), 160–63.

40. Ben Caldwell, *Top Secret or a Few Million After B.C., Drama Review* 12 (Summer 1968): 47–50.

41. John A. Williams, *The Man Who Cried I Am* (Boston: Little, Brown, 1967), 371–76; Rob Bennett, "It is Time for Action," in Jones and Neal, *Black Fire*, 421; Mari Evans, "The Third Stop in Caraway Park," *Black World* 22 (March 1975): 54–62; Julia Wright Herve, "The Forget-For-Peace-Program," *Black World* 22

(May 1973): 57–64; Raymond Washington, "Moon Bound," in *New Black Voices*, ed. Abraham Chapman (New York: New American Library, 1972), 389–90.

42. Larry Neal, "A Jive Eschatology," in *Hoodoo Hollerin' Bebop Ghosts* (Washington, D.C.: Howard University Press, 1974), 77; Nikki Giovanni, "Ugly Honkies, or The Election Game and How to Win It," in *Black Feeling, Black Talk-Black Judgement* (New York: William Morrow, 1970), 84.

43. Haki R. Madhubuti, "Positive Movement Will Be Difficult but Necessary," in *Book of Life* (Detroit: Broadside, 1973), 18; Ed Bullins, *The Gentleman Caller*, in *A Black Quartet* (New York: New American Library, 1970), 117, 133.

44. Neal "Jive," 78; Imamu Amiri Baraka, *Jello* (Chicago: Third World, 1970), 9; Arthur Pfister, "The Funny Company (or, why ain't him and his girls on t.v.?), in King, *Black Spirits*, 161; Touré, "Dago Red," 227; Amiri Baraka, *The Motion of History*, in *The Motion of History and Other Plays* (New York: William Morrow, 1978), 91; Ted Joans, "Top Creep," in Joans, *Pow-Wow*, 89; Ted Joans, "Santa Claws," in Joans, *Pow-Wow*, 54.

45. LeRoi Jones, *Experimental Death Unit #1*, in Jones, *Revolutionary Plays*, 1–15; Barry Beckham, *Runner Mack* (Washington, D.C.: Howard University Press, 1983), 205.

46. Ed Bullins, *Goin'a Buffalo*, in *New Black Playwrights*, ed. William Couch, Jr. (New York: Avon, 1970), 155–216; Herbert Stokes, "The Man Who Trusted the Devil Twice," in *New Plays from the Black Theatre*, ed. Ed Bullins (New York: Bantam, 1969), 119–28; LeRoi Jones, "Madness," in Jones, *Black Magic*, 162–65.

47. Sam Greenlee, *The Spook Who Sat by the Door* (New York: Bantam, 1970), 32.

48. Nikki Giovanni, "Of Liberation," in Giovanni, *Black Feeling*, 47.

49. Gil Scott-Heron, "comment #1," in Scott-Heron, *Small Talk*, 15; Richard Wesley, *Black Terror: A Revolutionary Adventure Story*, in *The New Lafayette Theatre Presents*, ed. Ed Bullins (Garden City, New York: Anchor/ Doubleday, 1974), 240–41; Ted Jones, "Yeah I Dig," in Joans, *Pow-Wow*, 45.

50. Douglas Turner Ward, *Brotherhood*, in King and Milner, *Black Drama*, 229–41.

51. Chuck Stone, *King Strut* (Indianapolis: Bobbs-Merrill, 1970), 40.

52. Moreau, *Black Commandos*, 106–7; John Oliver Killens, *'Sippi* (New York: Thunder's Mouth, 1988), 358, 407–10; Kalamu Ya Salaam, *The Destruction of the American Stage*, *Black World* 21 (April 1972): 68–69.

53. Walker, *Ododo*, 385.

54. Mari Evans, "Speak the Truth to the People," in *I Am A Black Woman* (New York: William Morrow, 1970), 91–92.

55. Baraka, *Jello*, 26.

56. LeRoi Jones, *The Death of Malcolm X*, in Bullins, *New Plays*, 2–3; Stokes, *Devil*, 121, 125; Killens, *'Sippi*, 421–22; Salaam, *Destruction*, 59.

57. Amiri Baraka, *Slave Ship*, in Baraka, *Motion*, 138–39; Baraka, *Motion*, 64–65, 67; Clifford Mason, *Gabriel: The Story of a Slave Rebellion*, in King and Milner, *Black Drama*, 172.

58. Ronald L. Fair, *Hog Butcher* (New York: Harcourt, Brace & World, 1966), 73–74.

59. Kingsley B. Bass, Jr., *We Righteous Bombers*, in Bullins, *New Plays*, 35; Haki R. Madhubuti, "Spirit Flight into the Coming," in Madhubuti, *Book*, 30; Woodie King, Jr., "The Game", *Liberator* 5 (August 1965): 24; Sonia Sanchez, "Memorial," in Sanchez, *Home Coming*, 29; Don L. Lee, "On Seeing Diana go Maddddddddd," in *We Walk the Way of the New World* (Detroit: Broadside, 1970), 38.

60. Baraka, *Motion*, 99; James Danner, "My Brother," in Jones and Neal, *Black Fire*, 271; LeRoi Jones, "Election Day (Newark, New Jersey)," in Jones and Neal, *Black Fire*, 296–98.

61. Ted Joans, "He Spy," in Joans, *Pow-Wow*, 51; LeRoi Jones, *Police*, *Drama Review* 12 (Summer 1968): 114; Bobb Hamilton, "Poem to a Nigger Cop," in Jones and Neal, *Black Fire*, 452.

62. Blyden Jackson, *Operation Burning Candle* (New York: Pyramid, 1974), 146–49; James Baldwin, *Tell Me How Long the Train's Been Gone* (New York: Dell, 1969), 367; John A. Williams, *Sons of Darkness, Sons of Light* (New York: Pocket, 1970), 8, 202.

63. Joseph White, *The Leader*, in Jones and Neal, *Black Fire*, 605–30.

64. Evan K. Walker, "Harlem Transfer," *Black World* 19 (May 1970): 66–76; Jones, *Malcolm X*, 8.

65. Ed Bullins, *Clara's Ole Man*, *Drama Review* 12 (Summer 1968): 161; Ed Bullins, *The Electronic Nigger*, in *Five Plays by Ed Bullins* (Indianapolis: Bobbs-Merrill, 1969), 220–21.

66. John Oliver Killens, *The Cotillion; or One Good Bull is Half the Herd* (New York: Trident, 1971), 53, 77; Alice Childress, *Wedding Band*, in *9 Plays by Black Women*, ed. Margaret B. Wilkerson (New York: New American Library, 1986), 81; Don L. Lee, "Wake-Up Niggers (you ain't part Indian), in *Think Black!* (Detroit: Broadside, 1969), 15.

67. Don L. Lee, "DON'T CRY, SCREAM," in *Don't Cry, Scream* (Detroit: Broadside, 1969), 30.

68. James Alan McPherson, "Private Domain," in *Hue and Cry* (Greenwich, Connecticut: Fawcett, 1970), 146, 155.

69. Killens, *Cotillion*, 142.

70. Greenlee, *Spook*, 56.

71. Henry Van Dyke, *Dead Piano* (New York: Farrar, Strauss & Giroux, 1971), 46; Madhubuti, "Spirit Flight," 29; Edgar White, *The Life and Times of J. Walter Smintheus*, in *The Crucificado* (New York: William Morrow, 1973), 34.

72. Salimu, *Growin' Into Blackness*, in Bullins, *New Plays*, 196; Salaam, *Destruction*, 62; Killens, *Cotillion*, 179.

73. Van Dyke, *Dead Piano*, 15.

74. Killens, *Cotillion*, 138; Charles Oyamo Gordon, *The Breakout*, in King and Milner, *Black Drama*, 407–28; Ed Bullins, *Night of the Beast: A Screenplay*, in *Four Dynamite Plays* (New York: William Morrow, 1972), 121–79; Jones, *Malcolm X*, 2–20; LeRoi Jones, *Great Goodness of Life: A Coon Show*, in Jones, *Revolutionary Plays*, 45–63.

75. Stokes, *Devil*, 121; Killens, *Cotillion*, 152–53; Don L. Lee, "Re-Act for Action," in Lee, *Think Black!*, 16.

76. Ed Bullins, *Death List*, in Bullins, *Dynamite*, 35; Van Dyke, *Dead Piano*, 73; Jimmy Garrett, *And We Own the Night*, *Drama Review* 12 (Summer 1968):

68–69; Nikki Giovanni, "Concerning One Responsible Negro with Too Much Power," in Giovanni, *Black Feeling*, 52–53; Ted Joans, "How Do You Want Yours?," in Joans, *Pow-Wow*, 7.

77. Bullins, *Death List*, 34; Raymond R. Patterson, "What We Know," in *26 Ways of Looking At a Black Man* (New York: Award, 1969), 41; Jackson, *Burning Candle*, 25; Marvin X, *The Black Bird*, in Bullins, *New Plays*, 110–18.

78. Toni Cade Bambara, *Gorilla, My Love* (New York: Random House, 1972), 6, 10; Carolyn M. Rodgers, "Jesus Was Crucified, or It Must Be Deep," in *how i got ovah* (Garden City, New York: Anchor Press/Doubleday, 1976), 61; Fareedah Allah, "The Generation Gap," in *Black Sister: Poetry by Black American Women, 1746–1980*, ed. Erlene Stetson (Bloomington: Indiana University Press, 1981), 174–75.

79. Alice Walker, "Women," in *Revolutionary Petunias & Other Poems* (New York: Harcourt Brace Jovanovich, 1973), 5; Carolyn M. Rodgers, "For Our Fathers," in Rodgers, *ovah*, 61; LeRoi Jones, "Leroy," in Jones, *Black Magic*, 217; Killens, *Cotillion*, 199.

80. Moreau, *Black Commandos*, 173–79; Greenlee, *Spook*, 207–9; Douglas Turner Ward, *Day of Absence*, in *Black Theater, U.S.A.*, ed. James V. Hatch and Ted Shine (New York: Free Press, 1974), 696–710.

81. Ed Bullins, *How Do You Do*, in Jones and Neal, *Black Fire*, 595–604.

82. James Thompson, "And There Are Those," in King, *Black Spirits*, 213.

83. Jon Eckels, "Hell, Mary," in *A Broadside Treasury*, ed. Gwendolyn Brooks (Detroit: Broadside, 1971), 43.

84. Gil Scott-Heron, "enough," in Scott-Heron, *Small Talk*, 54–55; Baraka, *Motion*, 57–58; Val Ferdinand, *Blk Love Song #1*, in Hatch and Shine, *Black Theater*, 867.

85. Calvin C. Hernton, "Jitterbugging in the Streets," in Jones and Neal, *Black Fire*, 205–9; N. R. Davidson, Jr., *El Hajj Malik*, in Bullins, *New Plays*, 203–4; Ronald L. Fair, *Many Thousand Gone* (New York: Bantam, 1971), 81–82.

86. Killens, *'Sippi*, 262–63.

87. LeRoi Jones, *Home: Social Essays* (New York: William Morrow, 1966), 211, 213.

88. Herschell Johnson, "We Are Not Mantan," in Coombs, *Liberators*, 79–80; LeRoi Jones, "Black Art" in Jones, *Black Magic*, 117.

89. Jackie Earley, "The Gospel Truth," in King, *Black Spirits*, 62–64; Lance Jeffers, "Black Soul of the Land," in Jones and Neal, *Black Fire*, 275.

90. Walker, *Ododo*, 349–350, 357; Ferdinand, *Love Song*, 868; Sharon Bourke, "People of Gleaming Cities, and of the Lion's and the Leopard's Brood," in Stephen Henderson, *Understanding the New Black Poetry: Black Speech and Black Music as Poetic References* (New York: William Morrow, 1973), 374; Etheridge Knight, "The Idea of Ancestry," in *Poems from Prison* (Detroit: Broadside Press, 1968), 17; Askia Muhammad Touré, "Tauhid," in *Natural Process: An Anthology of New Black Poetry*, ed. Ted Wilentz and Tom Weatherly (New York: Hill and Wang, 1971), 140.

91. Wesley, *Black Terror*, 221–25; Robert Macbeth, *A Black Ritual*, Drama Review 13 (Summer 1969): 129–30; Akbar Balagoon Ahmed, "Harlem Farewell," *Liberator* 10 (February 1970): 14.

92. LeRoi Jones, "Ka 'Ba" in Jones, *Black Magic*, 146.

93. Jayne Cortez, "How Long Has Trane Been Gone," in *Pisstained Stairs and the Monkey Man's Wares* (New York: Phrase Text, 1969), 42.

94. Paul Carter Harrison, *The Great MacDaddy*, in *Kuntu Drama: Plays of the African Continuum*, ed. Paul Carter Harrison (New York: Grove, 1974), 270–73, 323–26; Etheridge Knight, "Dark Prophesy: I Sing of Shine," in Henderson, *Understanding*, 330–31; Ishmael Reed, "Railroad Bill, A Conjure Man," in *Chattanooga* (New York: Random House, 1973), 9–15.

95. Mason, *Gabriel*, 193; Baraka, *Motion*, 62–72.

96. John O. Killens, *Slaves* (New York: Pyramid, 1969), 24.

97. Walker, *Ododo*, 371.

98. Alice S. Cobb, "Angela Davis," in Stetson, *Black Sister*, 147; Melvin Newton, "We Call Him the General," in Huey P. Newton, *Revolutionary Suicide* (New York: Ballantine, 1974), 348; Sonia Sanchez, "Memorial 2, bobby hutton," in Sanchez, *Home Coming*, 30; Killens, *'Sippi*, 240, 414.

99. Etheridge Knight, "To Gwendolyn Brooks," in Knight, *Poems*, 30; Etheridge Knight, "For Langston Hughes" in Knight, *Poems*, 29; Larry Neal, "Don't Say Goodbye to the Porkpic Hat," in Neal, *Hoodoo*, 20–21; Quincy Troupe, "Ode to John Coltrane," in King, *Black Spirits*, 230–37; LeRoi Jones, "Note to America," in Jones, *Black Magic*, 178. Michael S. Harper, "Ode to Tenochtitlan," in Wilentz and Weatherly, *Natural Process*, 33–35.

100. Don L. Lee, "Knocking Donkey Fleas off a Poet from the Southside of Chi," in Lee, *Walk*, 47; Ted Joans, "Never," in Joans, *Pow-Wow*, 86; H. Rap Brown, *Die Nigger Die!* (New York: Dial, 1969), 28.

101. Charles H. Fuller, Jr., *The Rise*, in Bullins, *New Plays*, 285.

102. Ibid., 272; Askia Muhammad Touré, "Extension," in Henderson, *Understanding*, 304–5.

103. Loften Mitchell, *Tell Pharaoh*, in *The Black Teacher and the Dramatic Arts*, ed. William R. Reardon and Thomas D. Pawley (Westport, Connecticut: Negro Universities Press, 1970), 263; Doughtry Long, "Where My Grandmother Lived," in Long, *Black Love Black Hope* (Detroit: Broadside, 1971), 8; Nikki Giovanni, "Nikki-Rosa," in Giovanni, *Black Feeling*, 59.

104. Ed Bullins, *In the Wine Time*, in Bullins, *Five Plays*; Bullins, *Ole Man*. On Bullins' theatre of "experience," see Geneviève Fabre, *Drumbeats, Masks, and Metaphor: Contemporary Afro-American Theatre* (Cambridge: Harvard University Press, 1983), 106–215.

105. Melvin Van Peebles, *Aint Supposed to Die a Natural Death* (New York: Bantam, 1973), 3; "The Electronic Nigger Meets the Gold Dust Twins: Cifford Mason Talks with Robert Macbeth and Ed Bullins," *Black Theatre* 1 (No. 1, 1968); 29; Clyde Sumpter, "Militating for Change: The Black Revolutionary Theatre Movement in the United States," (Ph.D. diss., University of Kansas, 1970), 247.

106. Van Peebles, *Natural Death*, 12, 41.

107. Larry Thompson, "Black Is Best," in *Black Out Loud: An Anthology of Modern Poems by Black Americans*, ed. Arnold Adoff (New York: Macmillan, 1970), 2; Bobb Hamilton, " 'Brother Harlem Bedford Watts Tells Mr. Charlie Where Its At'," in Jones and Neal, *Black Fire*, 449; Don L. Lee, "Move Un-

noticed to be Noticed: A Nationhood Poem," in Lee, *Walk*, 67; LeRoi Jones, *Tales* (New York: Grove, 1968), 96, 127–32; Chuck Stone, *King Strut* (Indianapolis: Bobbs-Merrill, 1970), 194–96.

108. Stone, *King Strut*, 195; "The National Black Theatre," *Essence* 2 (March 1971): 50; Paul Carter Harrison, "Black Theater and the African Continuum," *Black World* 21 (August 1972): 43.

109. Killens, *'Sippi*, 418; John McCluskey, *Look What They Done to My Song* (New York: Random House, 1974), 234–35, 245–46, 251.

110. Ted Joans, "Afrodisia," in Jones, *Afrodisia*, 71; Val Ferdinand, "The Blues (in two parts)," *The Blues Merchant* (New Orleans, Nkombo, 1969), 10.

111. Walker, *Ododo*, 383–84; Sonia Sanchez, "To Anita," in *It's a New Day* (Detroit: Broadside, 1971), 8; Stephen Wilmore, "The Committee," *Negro Digest* 19 (December 1969): 56–61.

112. Haki R. Madhubuti, "Book of Life," in Madhubuti, *Book*, 63.

113. Salaam, *Destruction*, 67–68.

114. Stone, *King Strut*, 167–73; Williams, *Sons*, 140–42; Van Dyke, *Dead Piano*, 59; Ann Allen Shockley, "The President," *Freedomways* 10 (No. 4, 1970): 344–48; Mitchell, *Tell Pharaoh*, 264.

115. Moreau, *Black Commandos*, 186–94.

116. Wesley, *Black Terror*, 245–46.

117. Baraka, *Motion*, 75, 118–19, 121–22.

118. Beckham, *Runner Mack*, 199–203, 212.

119. Bullins, *Beast*, 135; Sonia Sanchez, "so this is our revolution," in Wilentz and Weatherly, *Natural Process*, 127; Don L. Lee, "Two Poems," in Henderson, *New Black Poetry*, 332.

120. Greenlee, *Spook*, 129, 168, 187; Charles Patterson, *Black-Ice*, in Jones and Neal, *Black Fire*, 564–65; Chester Himes, *Black on Black* (Garden City, New York: Doubleday, 1973), 285–86; Clarence Farmer, *Soul On Fire* (New York: Belmont, 1969), 172.

121. Nikki Giovanni, "The True Import of Present Dialogue, Black vs. Negro," in Giovanni, *Black Feeling*, 19–20.

122. Giovanni, "Ugly Honkies," 83.

123. Bass, *Righteous Bombers* 75–76; Wesley, *Black Terror*, 236–37; S. E. Anderson, "A New Dance," in Major, *New Black Poetry*, 23; Giovanni, "True Import," 20; Kuwasi Balagon, "Untitle," in Jones and Neal, *Black Fire*, 446; Julius Lester, "On the Birth of My Son, Malcolm Coltrane," in *Soulscript*, ed. June Jordan (Garden City, New York: Doubleday, 1970), 24.

124. Sonia Sanchez, *The Bronx is Next*, *Drama Review* 12 (Summer 1968): 78–83.

125. Jackson, *Burning Candle*, 110, 115, 201–5, 232–33.

126. Ed Bullins, *A Short Play for a Small Theater*, *Black World* 20 (April 1971): 39.

127. Jackson, *Burning Candle*, 201.

128. Sylvia Young, "Three Thoughts," in *Black Poets Write On!: An Anthology of Black Philadelphia Poets* (Philadelphia: Black History Museum Committee, 1970), 24; Madhubuti, "Book," 39.

129. Williams, *Man Who Cried*, 48–49; Greenlee, *Spook*, 123–24; Raymond Washington, "Freedom Hair," in Chapman, *New Black Voices*, 388–89.

130. Bullins, *Beast*, 145; Ted Joans, "Southern Landscapers," in Joans, *Pow-Wow*, 106; Don L. Lee, "The Wall," in *Black Pride* (Detroit: Broadside, 1968), 26.

131. Alice Walker, *In Love & Trouble: Stories of Black Women* (New York: Harcourt Brace Jovanovich, 1973), 70–72; Larry Neal, "Sinner Man Where You Gonna Run To?", in Jones and Neal, *Black Fire*, 511; Hal Bennett, *Insanity Runs in Our Family* (Garden City, New York: Doubleday, 1977), 60–67.

132. Henry Dumas, "Will the Circle be Unbroken?" *Negro Digest* 16 (November 1966): 76–80; Sonia Sanchez, "to blk/record/buyers," in Sanchez, *Home Coming*, 26.

133. Ted Joans, "Two Words," in Joans, *Pow-Wow*, 20.

134. Williams, *Man Who Cried*, 51; Al Young, "A Dance for Militant Dilettantes," in *The Poetry of Black America*, ed. Arnold Adoff (New York: Harper & Row, 1973), 362.

135. Ben Caldwell, *The King of Soul or the Devil and Otis Redding*, in Bullins, *New Plays*, 176–87; Oyamo, *His First Step*, in Bullins, *New Lafayette*, 151–60.

136. Stokes, *Devil*, 125; Ben Caldwell, *All White Caste (After the Separation)*, in King and Milner, *Black Drama*, 395–96.

137. Greenlee, *Spook*, 229–30; Williams, *Sons*, 184–86; Jackson *Burning Candle*, 173–76; Bullins, *Beast*, 142–43; Bass, *Bombers*, 23–25, 77, 94–95.

138. Moreau, *Black Commandos*, 209; Quentin Hill, "Time Poem," in Major, *New Black Poetry*, 68–69; Don L. Lee, "For Black People," in Lee, *Walk*, 58–60; Arnold Kemp, "The End of the World" in Coombs, *Liberators*, 88–90; Mari Evans, "Vive Noir!", in *I Am a Black Woman* (New York: William Morrow, 1970), 72–73.

139. Ben Caldwell, *Riot Sale or Dollar Psyche Fake Out*, Drama Review 12 (Summer 1968): 41–42; Beckham, *Runner Mack*, 211–12; Caldwell, *White Caste*, 389–97.

140. Baldwin, *Tell Me*, 56; Ben Caldwell, *Prayer Meeting or, the First Militant Minister*, in *A Black Quartet: Four New Black Plays*, by Ben Caldwell, Ronald Milner, Ed. Bullins and LeRoi Jones (New York: New American Library, 1970), 29–36; Giovanni, "Revolutionary Tale," 19–34.

141. Raymond R. Patterson, "Black Power," in Patterson, *26 Ways*, 29. Rolland Snellings, "Sunrise!!," in Jones and Neal, *Black Fire*, 322; Marvin X, "Three Parables," *Black World* 19 (June 1970): 85–86; Askia Muhammad Touré, "Extension," in Henderson, *New Black Poetry*, 304–6; Don L. Lee, "a poem to complement other poems," in Lee, *Don't Cry*, 36–38; Giovanni, "Of Liberation," 49; Rockie Taylor, "Black Henry," in *Drum Song* (Milwaukee, published by the author, 1969), 16–17.

142. *Three the Hard Way* (Allied Artists, 1974); *Coffy* (American International, 1973); *Friday Foster* (American International, 1975); *Foxy Brown* (American International, 1974).

143. Jones, *Home*, 198; *Superfly* (Warner Brothers, 1972); *Trouble Man* (Twentieth Century-Fox, 1972); Thomas Cripps, *Black Film as Genre* (Bloomington: Indiana University Press, 1978).

144. Mae Jackson, "I Remember Omar," *Negro Digest* 18 (June 1969): 85; Edward S. Spriggs, "For the TRUTH (because it is necessary)," in Jones and Neal, *Black Fire*, 340; Gordon, *Breakout*, 419–20.

145. Madhubuti, "Book," 39; Don L. Lee, "But He Was Cool or: he even stopped for green lights," in Lee *Don't Cry*, 24.

146. Jackson, "Omar," 83–85.

147. Van Dyke, *Dead Piano*, 58, 76.

148. Ann Allen Shockley, "Is She Relevant?," *Black World* 20 (January 1971): 58–65; B. B. Johnson, *Black is Beautiful* (New York: Paperback Library, 1970), 21.

149. Killens, *Cotillion*, 175–76.

150. Jewel C. Latimore, "Identity," in *Images in Black* (Chicago: Third World, 1969), 2–3; Killens, *'Sippi*, 412–14; "Mecca for Blackness," *Ebony* 25 (May 1970): 96; N. R. Davidson, Jr., *El Hajj Malik*, in Bullins, *New Plays*, 238.

151. Sharon Bell Mathis, *Listen for the Fig Tree* (New York: Avon, 1975), 72.

152. Killens, *Cotillion*, 243–56; William Melvin Kelley, *Dunfords Travels Everywheres* (Garden City, New York: Doubleday, 1970), 46–47; Ray McIver, *God Is a (Guess What?)*, St. Marks Playhouse, New York City, 17 December 1968; Mathis, *Listen*, 135–41; Greenlee, *Spook*, 110–11.

153. Sonia Sanchez, *Sister Son/ji*, in Bullins, *New Plays*, 102.

154. Mathis, *Listen*, 122; Killens, *'Sippi*, 421–22; Loyle Hairston, "Harlem on the Rocks," *Freedomways* 9 (Spring 1969): 139–43; Ann Allen Shockley, "The Faculty Party," *Black World* 21 (November 1971): 60–61.

Conclusion

1. "The Nation of Islam Mourns Elijah Muhammad," *Ebony* 30 (May 1975): 74–81; "7,000 Mourn Muhammad," *Chicago Tribune*, 1 March 1975, 4; Peter Goldman, "The Founding Father," *Newsweek*, 10 March 1975, 21.

2. Kalamu ya Salaam, "Which Way Are They Going," *Black Collegian* 6 (March–April, 1976): 38, 40, 90–91; Kenneth L. Woodward, "Second Resurrection," *Newsweek*, 22 August 1977, 67; C. Eric Lincoln, "The American Muslim Mission in the Context of American Social History," in *The Muslim Community in North America*, ed. Earle H. Waugh, Baha Abu-Laban, and Regula B. Qureshi (Edmonton: University of Alberta Press, 1983), 224–31; Clifton E. Marsh, *From Black Muslims to Muslims: The Transition from Separatism to Islam, 1930–1980* (Metuchen, New Jersey: Scarecrow, 1984), 92–101; Martha F. Lee, *The Nation of Islam: An American Millenarian Movement* (Lewiston, New York: Edwin Mellen, 1988), 77–101.

3. Typically, American history survey texts produced for both secondary school and college audiences during the 1980s devote between two and four paragraphs, or less than one page of a 500- to 900-page book, to "Black Power." Often, this brief commentary appears in tandem with accounts and pictures of the sixties riots. See, for example, John A. Garraty, *American History* (Chicago: Harcourt Brace Jovanovich, 1986), 894; Daniel J. Boorstin and Brooks Mather Kelley, *A History of the United States* (Lexington, Massachusetts: Ginn, 1981), 669–70; Maldwyn A. Jones, *The Limits of Liberty: American History 1607–1980* (New York: Oxford University Press, 1983), 553–54.

4. Ernest Van Den Haag, "Black Cop-Out," *National Review*, 30 August 1974, 970–74; Martin Kilson, "Anatomy of the Black Studies Movement," *Massachusetts Review* 10 (Autumn 1969): 718–25; "Black Nonsense," *Crisis* 78 (April–May 1971): 78. Bayard Rustin, "The Failure of Black Separatism," *Harper's Magazine* 240 (January 1970): 29, 31; Roy Wilkins, "Integration," *Ebony* 25

(August 1970): 58; Paul Feldman, "The Pathos of 'Black Power'," *Dissent* 14 (January–February 1967): 70; Christopher Lasch, *The Agony of the American Left* (New York: Alfred A. Knopf, 1969), 143.

5. Dan W. Dodson, "Separate Can't Be Equal," *New Generation* 49 (Fall 1967): 3; James R. Cleaveland, "Planning vs. Participation," *New Generation* 51 (Summer 1969): 28; Roy Innis and Norman Hill, "Black Self-Determination: A Debate," *New Generation* 51 (Summer 1969): 22–23; Kenneth B. Clark, "Thoughts on Black Power," *Dissent* 15 (March–April 1968): 98, 192.

6. Whitney M. Young, Jr., "Separatism? 'We ARE Separated—and That's the Cause of All Our Woes,'" *Ebony* 25 (August 1970): 90, 94; "The Black Neo-Segregationists," *Crisis* 74 (November 1967): 439–40; Roy Wilkins, "Whither 'Black Power'?" *Crisis* 73 (August–September 1966): 354; Clark, "Thoughts," 192; *New Program of the Communist Party, U.S.A.* (New York: New Outlook, 1970), 61; Robert Sherrill, "Whitey's Reaction," *Esquire* 71 (January 1969): 76; Lionel Lokos, *The New Racism: Reverse Discrimination in America* (New Rochelle, New York: Arlington House, 1971), 73; Rustin, "Failure," 34.

7. Bayard Rustin, "'Black Power' and Coalition Politics," *Commentary* 42 (September 1966): 35–36; Lewis M. Killian, *The Impossible Revolution?: Black Power and the American Dream* (New York: Random House, 1968), 156–57, 173–76; Martin Luther King, Jr., *Where Do We Go From Here: Chaos or Community?* (New York: Harper & Row, 1967), 54, 59, 61–63.

8. Joseph R. Washington, Jr., "Black Nationalism: Potentially Anti-Folk and Anti-Intellectual," *Black World* 22 (July 1973): 32–39; John V. Hagopian, "Mau-Mauing the Literary Establishment," *Studies in the Novel* 3 (Summer 1971): 135–46; Charles T. Davis, *Black is the Color of the Cosmos: Essays on Afro-American Literature and Culture, 1942–1981* (New York: Garland, 1982), 29–46; Kathryn Jackson, "LeRoi Jones and the New Black Writers of the Sixties," *Freedomways* 9 (Summer 1969): 232–46; Saunders Redding, "The Black Arts Movement in Negro Poetry," *American Scholar* 42 (Spring 1973): 330–35; "When State Magicians Fail: An Interview with Ishmael Reed," *Journal of Black Poetry* 1 (Summer–Fall 1969): 73–75; Sherely Anne Williams, *Give Birth to Brightness: A Thematic Study in Neo-Black Literature* (New York: Dial, 1972), 240.

9. On the Nation of Islam's view of women's "place," see E.U. Essien-Udom, *Black Nationalism: A Search for an Identity in America* (Chicago: University of Chicago Press, 1962), 157–59; Elijah Muhammad, *Message to the Blackman in America* (Chicago: Muhammad's Temple No. 2, 1965), 58–61.

10. Wilson Pickett, "A Man and a Half," Atlantic 2575, 1968; B.B. King, "Paying the Cost to Be the Boss," Bluesway 61015, 1968.

11. Hal Bennett, *Insanity Runs in Our Family* (Garden City, New York: Doubleday, 1977), 134; Ted Joans, "Little Brown Bitch Blues (or; I've Got the Sun in My Soul)," in *Black Pow-Wow* (New York: Hill and Wang, 1969), 127.

12. Sara Evans, *Personal Politics: The Roots of Women's Liberation in the Civil Rights Movement and the New Left* (New York: Vintage, 1980), 87.

13. Jo Ann E. Gardner and Charles W. Thomas, "Different Strokes for Different Folks," *Psychology Today* 4 (September 1970): 49; Frances Beale, "Double Jeopardy: To Be Black and Female," in *The Black Woman: An Anthology*, ed. Toni Cade (New York: New American Library, 1970), 92–94; Frances M. Beal,

"Slave of a Slave No More: Black Women in Struggle," *Black Scholar* 6 (March 1975): 3; "Black Feminism: A New Mandate," *Ms.* 2 (May 1974): 99; Linda La Rue, "The Black Movement and Women's Liberation," *Black Scholar* 1 (May 1970): 41; Pamela Newman, "Take a Good Look at Our Problems," *Militant*, 30 October 1970, 6; Pauli Murray, "The Liberation of Black Women," in *Voices of the New Feminism*, ed. Mary Lou Thompson (Boston: Beacon, 1970), 101–2.

14. Gwendolyn Evans, "The Panthers' Elaine Brown, Does She Say What She Means, Does She Mean What She Says?" *Ms.* 4 (March 1976): 106; "*Black Scholar* Interviews Kathleen Cleaver," *Black Scholar* 3 (December 1971): 59; "Panther Sisters on Women's Liberation," in *Off The Pigs!: The History and Literature of the Black Panther Party*, ed. G. Louis Heath (Metuchen, New Jersey: Scarecrow, 1976), 339–45; Evelyn Rodgers, "Sisters—Stop Castrating the Black Man!" *Liberator* 6 (May 1966): 21; Pearl Lomax, "Black Women's Lib?" *Essence* 3 (August 1972): 68.

15. Michele Wallace, "A Black Feminist's Search for Sisterhood," in *All the Women Are White, All the Blacks are Men, But Some of Us Are Brave: Black Women's Studies*, ed. Gloria T. Hull, Patricia Bell Scott, and Barbara Smith (Old Westbury, New York: Feminist Press, 1982), 6–7; Sonia Sanchez, "Memorial 3. rev pimps," in *Home Coming* (Detroit: Broadside, 1969), 31; Louise Moore, "Black Men vs. Black Women," *Liberator* 6 (August 1966): 16–17.

16. 1988 Commission on the Cities, "Race and Poverty in the United States— and What Should be Done," in *Quiet Riots: Race and Poverty in the United States*, ed. Fred R. Harris and Roger W. Wilkins (New York: Pantheon: 1988), 173–75.

17. Gerald David Jaynes and Robin M. Williams, Jr., eds., *A Common Destiny: Blacks and American Society* (Washington D.C.: National Academy Press, 1989), 3, 8; *The State of Black America 1989* (New York: National Urban League, 1989), 95.

18. Jaynes and Williams, *Common Destiny*, 181.

19. Reynolds Farley and Walter R. Allen. *The Color Line and the Quality of Life in America* (New York: Oxford University Press 1989), 47; Jaynes and Williams, *Common Destiny*, 50.

20. *State of Black America*, 41.

21. Jaynes and Williams, *Common Destiny*, 22–23, 464.

22. William Julius Wilson, *The Truly Disadvantaged: The Inner City, the Underclass, and Public Policy* (Chicago: University of Chicago Press, 1987), 22; Frederick H. Lowe, "Doing Time Instead of Doing Good," *North Star* 2 (April 1990): 1–2.

23. *State of Black America*, 63.

24. Alphonso Pinkney, *The Myth of Black Progress* (Cambridge: Cambridge University Press, 1984), 178; Robert Staples, *The Urban Plantation: Racism & Colonialism in the Post Civil Rights Era* (Oakland: Black Scholar, 1987), 191–221.

25. Farley and Allen, *Color Line*, 2.

26. Alex Poinsett, "Where Are the Revolutionaries?" *Ebony* 31 (February 1976): 84.

27. Walt Thompson, "What's Left of the Black Left?" *Ramparts* 10 (June

1972): 52; Peter Collier and David Horowitz, *Destructive Generation: Second Thoughts About the '60s* (New York: Summit, 1990), 141–65.

28. Mel Assagi, "Black Panthers Today: Pussycats? Or Stalking Cats?" *Sepia* 26 (September 1977): 23–24, 26–29; Bobby Seale, *Barbeque'n With Bobby* (Berkeley: Ten Speed, 1988).

29. Eldridge Cleaver, *Soul on Fire* (Waco, Texas: Word, 1978), 224. See also John A. Oliver, *Eldridge Cleaver: Reborn* (Plainfield, New Jersey: Logos International, 1977); George Otis, *Eldridge Cleaver: Ice and Fire!* (Van Nuys, California: Bible Voice, 1977).

30. Amiri Baraka, "Black Nationalism and Socialist Revolution," *Black World* 24 (July 1975): 30–42; Amiri Baraka, "The Congress of Afrikan People: A Position Paper." *Black Scholar* 6 (January–February 1975): 2–15; Werner Sollors, *Amiri Bakara/LeRoi Jones: The Quest for a "Populist Modernism"* (New York: Columbia University Press, 1978), 224–37; Amiri Baraka, *The Motion of History and Other Plays* (New York: William Morrow, 1978), 16.

31. Maulana Ron Karenga, "Which Road: Nationalism, Pan-Africanism, Socialism?" *Black Scholar* 6 (October 1974): 21–30; "Whatever Happened to Ron Karenga?" *Ebony* 30 (September 1975): 170; M. Ron Karenga, "Kawaida and Its Critics: A Sociohistorical Analysis," *Journal of Black Studies* 8 (December 1977): 136–47.

32. Manning Marable, *Blackwater: Historical Studies in Race, Class Consciousness, and Revolution* (Dayton, Ohio: Black Praxis, 1981), 118; Walt Thompson, "What's Left of the Black Left, Part II," *Ramparts* 11 (August 1972): 57; Melvin Van Peebles, *Bold Money: How to Get Rich in the Options Market* (New York: Warner, 1987).

33. On COINTELPRO, see Kenneth O'Reilly, *"Racial Matters": The FBI's Secret File on Black America, 1960–1972* (New York: Free Press, 1989), 261–353; Ward Churchill and Jim Vander Wall, *Agents of Repression: The FBI's Secret Wars Against the Black Panther Party and the American Indian Movement* (Boston: South End, 1988), 37–99; Congress, Senate, Select Committee to Study Governmental Operations with Respect to Intelligence Activities, *Final Report—Book III, Supplementary Detailed Staff Reports on Intelligence Activities and the Rights of Americans*, 94th Cong., 2d sess., 1976, Senate Report 94-755, 187–223.

34. Assata Shakur, *Assata: An Autobiography* (Westport, Connecticut: Lawrence Hill, 1987), 230.

35. Karenga, "Kawaida," 131–32; *The Autobiography of LeRoi Jones/Amiri Baraka* (New York: Freundlich, 1984), 280.

36. Thompson, "Black Left," 47.

37. Evans, "Elaine Brown," 106; Shakur, *Assata,* 231.

38. Nathan Hare, "What Happened to the Black Movement," *Black World* 25 (January 1976): 32; Oba T'Shaka, "Assessing the Lull in the Black Liberation Struggle," *Black Books Bulletin* 6 (Spring 1978): 26–29; Amiri Baraka, *Daggers and Javelins: Essays, 1974–1979* (New York: Quill, 1984), 276.

39. Baraka, *Autobiography,* 323, 326; Carolyn M. Rodgers, "Uh Nat'chal Thang—The Whole Truth—Us" *Black World* 20 (September 1971): 9; Hare, "Black Movement," 20, 30–31; Ron Karenga, "Overturning Ourselves: From

Mystification to Meaningful Struggle," *Black Scholar* 4 (October 1972): 7, 12–13; Julius Lester, "The Current State of Black America," *New Politics* 10 (Spring 1973): 10.

40. Samuel DuBois Cook, "The Tragic Myth of Black Power," *New South* 21 (Summer 1966): 63; King, *Where Do We Go*, 38–44.

41. Rodgers, "Nat'chal Thang," 5–6; Carolyn M. Rodgers, "The Revolution is Resting," *how i got ovah* (Garden City, New York: Anchor/Doubleday, 1976), 2–3. For commentary on the notion that most social movements have a limited time frame or "window of opportunity" in which to make their impact felt, see Frances Fox Piven and Richard A. Cloward, *Poor People's Movements: Why They Succeed, How They Fail* (New York: Pantheon, 1977), 14–34; Robert Korstad and Nelson Lichtenstein, "Opportunities Found and Lost: Labor, Radicals, and the Early Civil Rights Movement," *Journal of American History* 75 (December 1988): 811.

42. Karenga, "Kawaida," 137–38; Vincent Harding, "The Black Wedge in America: Struggle, Crisis and Hope, 1955–1975," *Black Scholar* 7 (December 1975): 35.

43. "Former Black Panther Takes Aldermanic Post," *Wisconsin State Journal*, 29 April 1983, 15.

44. Gordon Parks, "What Became of the Prophets of Rage?" *Life* 11 (Spring 1988): 32.

45. Barbara D. Lyles, "POWER: Rhetoric, Rap, or Reality?" *Crisis* 80 (November 1973): 297.

46. Herbert H. Haines, *Black Radicals and the Civil Rights Mainstream, 1954–1970* (Knoxville, University of Tennessee Press, 1988), 2–4, 184–85, See also Abby Arthur Johnson and Ronald Maberry Johnson, *Propaganda and Aesthetics: The Literary Politics of Afro-American Magazines in the Twentieth Century* (Amherst: University of Massachusetts Press, 1979), 200.

47. Baraka, *Autobiography*, 322.

48. Doug McAdam, *Freedom Summer* (New York: Oxford University Press, 1988), 212–19; Richard A. Braungart and Margaret M. Braungart, "Political Career Patterns of Radical Activists in the 1960s and 1970s: Some Historical Comparisons," *Sociological Focus* 13 (August 1980): 237–54; George Lipsitz, *A Life in the Struggle: Ivory Perry and the Culture of Opposition* (Philadelphia: Temple University Press, 1988).

49. Bob Blauner, *Black Lives, White Lives: Three Decades of Race Relations in America* (Berkeley: University of California Press, 1989), 234.

50. Ivan Van Sertima, *They Came Before Columbus* (New York: Random House, 1976); Molefi K. Asante, *Afrocentricity: The Theory of Social Change* (Buffalo: Amulefi, 1980); Molefi Kete Asante, *The Afrocentric Idea* (Philadelphia: Temple University Press, 1987). By the mid-eighties it was estimated that more than thirteen million Americans were observing Kwanzaa. Cedric McClester, *Kwanzaa: Everything You Always Wanted to Know But Didn't Know Where to Ask* (New York: Gumbs & Thomas, 1985), 111.

51. "Toying With Pride," *North Star* 1 (November 1989): 13; James Brooke, "Goodby to Tarzan, Meet Captain Africa," *New York Times*, 27 September 1988, C22.

52. Charles Johnson, *Being & Race: Black Writing Since 1970* (Bloomington:

Indiana University Press, 1988), 83, 120; Trey Ellis, "The New Black Aesthetic," *Callaloo* 12 (Winter 1989): 233–43; Public Enemy, *Fear of a Black Planet*, Def Jam 45413, 1990.

53. Beastie Boys, *Paul's Boutique*, Capitol 91743, 1989; Vanilla Ice, *To the Extreme*, SBK 95325, 1990; New Kids on the Block, *Step by Step*, Columbia 45129, 1990.

54. Gerri Hirshey. "Attaché Case Full of Blues," *Rolling Stone*, 9 March 1989, 19–20.

55. Bill Zehme, "Madonna: The Rolling Stone Interview," *Rolling Stone*, 23 March 1989, 58.

56. *Tradition and Conflict: Images of a Turbulent Decade, 1963–1973* (New York: Studio Museum in Harlem, 1985), 10.

Index